Dictionary of the
FUTURE

FAITH POPCORN and **ADAM HANFT**

Dictionary of the FUTURE

The words, terms and trends that define
the way we'll live, work and talk

HYPERION NEW YORK

Library of Congress Cataloging-in-Publication Data

Popcorn, Faith.
    Dictionary of the future : the words, terms and trends that define the way
we'll live, work and talk / Faith Popcorn and Adam Hanft.— 1st ed.
        p. cm.
    ISBN: 0-7868-6657-8
    1. Twenty-first century—Forecasts—Dictionaries.   2. United States—
Civilization—21st century—Forecasting—Dictionaries.   3. English
language—Terms and phrases.   I. Hanft, Adam.   II. Title.
CB161 .P66   2001
303.4973'01'4—dc21   2001022282

FIRST EDITION
10 9 8 7 6 5 4 3 2 1

For Mary Kay Adams Moment,
with respect and love,
for all her help
in capturing the
DNA of *DOF.*

Faith

For Flora, Simon and Lucas,
you are the words
in my life.

Adam

contents

ABCDEFGHIJKLMN

ACKNOWLEDGMENTS

Ralph Waldo Emerson wrote that "every new relation is a new word." More than a hundred years later, the Czech author Daniela Fischerova reciprocally observed, "Every new word is a new reality." If we have, through this book, helped enlarge that reality, it is due—in no small measure—to the help and support of many. Thus, we need to thank all the trend-spotters at Brain-Reserve, Faith's company, including—of course—Mary Kay Adams Moment, who was her usually spectacular and elaborately dedicated self. She organized, she read, she sharpened, she cajoled (and was known, on occasion, to threaten).

The talented people at Adam's company, Hanft Byrne Raboy & Partners, were invaluable during the process, and we thank them for their minds, antennae and encouragement. A special thank you goes to Silvia Frascaroli, whose flawless gift for design was responsible for the cover and inside pages of this book. Tricia Civello and Tonya Genchur were always there with high commitment and high spirits, and they helped preserve our sanity through the hair-pulling editing process.

Our deep appreciation goes to all at Hyperion who believe in the power and radiance of words, especially Bob Miller, President, and Leslie Wells, our editor, who championed this book from the first moment she heard about it. We also want to thank Ellen Archer, Publisher, Katie Long, Publicity Director, and Phil Rose, Creative Director, for helping make this book a reality. Our indefatigable agent Jan Miller—who said a big yes to the idea based just on embryonic ramblings—was the animating angel of the process. Marion Jacobson, Regan Good and Ash DeLorenzo were relentless, culture-scouring researchers. Flora, Adam's wife, was dedicated to *DOF* from the outset—she read, she listened, she invented, and these significant researching and coining contributions go well beyond the specific credits she has in the book.

We must also thank all those who visited our Web site and deposited their own words and phrases for our inspection.

And now, it is necessary to depart from the authorial we to reside, briefly, in the first-person pronoun.

From Faith: As always, a million thanks to the BrainReserve family (immediate and extended), who continually support and contribute, in the end making all things possible. To Kathleen McLaughlin Cantwell, my trusted assistant, for making my multiple lives seamless. To Robin McIver, Creative Director, and Pam Palk and Alissa Stakgold, Senior Consultants, who brilliantly connect the cultural dots that make our clients' best futures possible. To Milly Massey, strategist extraordinaire, to Billie Brouse, Managing Associate, for her style, panache and ability to always move things forward. To Johanna Busch Skier, Director of Creative Design and Licensing, whose visual sense of the world adds clarity to all that we do. To Eileen Daily Pejanovic, TalentBank Director, and Lauren Rothman, Trend Analyst, for keeping us connected, on Trend and in the future. To Michele Rodriguez-Cruz, Controller, whose intelligence and continued dedication over the years keeps the business efficient and smart. To Tara Lynch, Administrative Associate, for her everyday help and warmth. To Kim Brown, Assistant Controller, for her patience and stick-to-itiveness, and Carl Einbeck, Finance Associate, a thoughtful contributor to all. Also, special appreciation to Dan Klores for his insight and strategic vision, to Ruth Sarfaty for her grace and acumen, and to Bruce Bobbins for his patience and persistence. And to Lys Marigold, trusted counselor, a heartfelt thanks for your guidance and support.

To my little g.g., who, as I am discovering the future through words, is discovering the first joy and wonder of words. She is my special inspiration.

From Adam: This is a book about words that was made possible by people. My partners Dick Byrne and Doug Raboy kept things fully caffeinated while I was out prowling for syllables. I am indebted to both; Dick, whose honesty and business imagination serve us and our clients impeccably well, and Doug, brilliant writer and fearless groundbreaker. I don't know what I would have done without Ali Demos, John Prendergast and Marty Rowe, whose dedication is boundless. Allan Cohen's many years of loyalty and pluck have also meant, and mean, a lot to me. Thanks to all of our clients, past, present and future, who entrust us with their businesses and are our partners in all manner of marketing adventures. A word of gratitude as well to our many friends who encouraged me during this long and often digressive mission. As for my wife Flora and my sons Simon and Lucas, the word "acknowledgments" struggles gamely to rise to the occasion but staggers back, exhausted. They had to sacrifice much, and endure long periods where words were my only world. Through it all, though, their oceanic patience, witty indulgence, emotional armature and scouting skills ("Hey Dad, I have a word for you") led me to a daily rediscovery of the one word that will always defeat definition, and that word is love.

A DICTIONARY OF WHAT?

There is, for those of us who might need one, a dictionary of embroidery stitches and a dictionary of farm animal behavior. There is a dictionary of science fiction places and of Russian obscenities. There is a dictionary of funghi. There is a dictionary of conflict resolution and a dictionary of diplomacy—and should those helpful reference works fail, there is always the dictionary of military terms to fall back on—something that is probably enormously comforting to readers of the Cynics' Dictionary.

These are all listed on Amazon.com, along with around 22,000 other dictionaries. But there is not one dictionary of the future to be found. That's quite astonishing, considering that the future is something we talk, fret, argue and speculate about somewhat more often than funghi or neurotic chickens. Thus it seemed to us that such a dictionary needed to be written, a dictionary of the future that would let its readers imagine and contemplate—word by word, thought by thought, shock by shock—the shape, sense, texture and experience of life tomorrow. A speak preview, if you will.

Why has no one gotten around to this until now? It seems to us that the reason the dictionary of the future remained unwritten is that dictionary makers, lexicographers, are trained to do precisely the opposite of what we did. They have one job, and that is to track the ebb and flow of language, guarding the gates of dictionary entry and only adding those words that are on the tip of enough tongues to warrant inclusion. The Merriam-Webster Web site couldn't be clearer: "To be included in a Merriam-Webster dictionary, a word must be used in a substantial number of citations that come from a wide range of publications over a considerable period of time."

Merriam-Webster is articulating a long tradition. Most dictionary makers have seen themselves as "linguistic law givers," Jonathon Green's apt description from his history of dictionaries called *Chasing the Sun*. (Green uses the phrase to describe the eighteenth-century lexicographer Ephraim Chambers, whom Dr. Johnson—the greatest of all dictionary makers—credited as his primary literary influence.) By contrast, we are linguistic prospectors and anticipators. While the process of dictionary creation generally requires great quantities of patience, this is one dictionary that can't wait, because it is a collection of the "not yet" and the "almost there." Led by our reading, listening, researching, asking and thinking, we have herded together those words and phrases that are just beginning their long march to acceptance by traditional dictionaries (and Scrabble players). So our debates were the opposite of the quarrels at Merriam-Webster and American Heritage. They worry over whether a word is too new; we anguished over whether it was too old.

We are also different than conventional dictionaries in terms of where we stand in the sequence of word-hunting. Dictionaries tend to be final destinations—you open one, check the spelling or a definition (usually to prove yourself right or someone else wrong) and you move on. By contrast, we've written the *Dictionary of the Future* to be a beginning, not an end, since so many of our entries are small portions of emerging subjects that are ripe for further investigation; many could be books in and of themselves. And probably will.

The *Dictionary of the Future* brings together words and terms that are so new they are barely cracking out of their chrysalis, as well as others that are poking tentatively out of their cocoons before zooming into the language of everyday life. We have, as well, occasionally opted to let some words slip in that are relatively well-circulated, but little understood—like "charter schools"—because we thought the need for clarification should prevail.

We recognize that some of our terms might be familiar to specialists. But most of the *Dictionary of the Future* should ring new to almost all of our readers. And the newest of all are those words listed under the rubric of the "Dictionary of the Future Predicts." These are terms we manufactured. We got into the manufacturing business when we found voids in the language that needed to be filled, and these neologisms are our best shot at expressing a future reality in a newly nuanced package.

As reckless as this mission of language creation might appear, there is some historical precedent for it, and it is comforting to us—as it would be to you—not to be hanging out there on an historical limb. The idea of including neologisms in a dictionary dates back to 1531, when Sir Thomas Elyot compiled a "dictionary of new and useful words in English for the benefits of [his] countrymen." These benefits included many words of his own invention. Elyot was convinced that the English vocabulary was starved for originality and scope in comparison to its European counterparts, so he did the only logical thing: he expanded it. His contributions include: "involve," "exactly," "articulate," "clemency," "democracy," "education," "loyalty," "society" and "mediocrity." (His innovations that didn't make it to any crossword puzzle clue list include "decerpt," "falcate" and "ostent.") And there is also Shakespeare—who was an unrepentant serial coiner—responsible for thousands of words including "critic," "majestic," "laughable," "courtship," "negotiate," "leapfrog" and "lonely." The familiar always starts life as the friendless radical.

A word about organization. We thought a thematic structure would be more helpful than alphabetical order. It allows our definitions to breathe and grow in meaning—as well as in their ability to provoke thought—through the juxtapositions of conceptually linked ideas in the same section. Our hope is that this structure, in which the new and the invented appear together, will yield a pointillist panorama of the future. And it is through this muralistic presentation that a noisy mix of multiple and (sometimes) competing realities can emerge.

You will also find that the entries reside both on the macro and micro levels. There are ideas that are big and small, mighty and tiny, global and resolutely intimate listed side-by-side. The criteria were whether the word, and the idea lodged inside it, would become a significant part of our national conversation in some way—whether it represented a future controversy or serious issue that could not be ignored. We have tried, in each case, to define the term, place it in a broader context (cultural, scientific, aesthetic) and offer some follow-up information—Web sites for example—for those who want to look further.

But our goal is not just to define, but to provoke. So on occasion, our definitions include an element of "the way things should be." This polemical tendency is something we tried (somewhat) to suppress, but there were times when a future development seemed like such a really good idea that it needed to be supported. Other times, we were quite pleased that something or someone that had long been ignored would get its moment in the sun, and we expressed our delight accordingly. We make no representations that this dictionary is complete, or completely objective in any way. It does not attempt to rise to the level of Dr. Johnson's "inventory of the language." But as vetted as the *Dictionary of the Future* is it is by definition (*sic*) a subjective task, which means we are sure we have gone astray in places, and some of these words won't stick. (And we are alert to the chance that some critics might call this a "fictionary of the future.")

One question inevitably came up during our work on *Dictionary of the Future*: where do you get the words, people would ask us, relieved that it wasn't their responsibility. The process is much like what lexicographers go through when editing conventional dictionaries—which is what goes on at BrainReserve every day: you read everything, watch everything, listen to everything, ignore nothing. All of our decisions were guided by our work as futurists, trend-dissectors, cultural assessors and what our TalentBank—BrainReserve's extended family of experts, seers and *agents provocateurs*—has reported. (And we thank them all for their time and generosity of spirit and language.) Once word of our *Dictionary of the Future* project got out, there began a stream of helpful emails, faxes and phone call alerts from word-trackers everywhere.

As you might imagine, doing our research was a joyride through the culture, the media, scientific journals, the latest and the greatest in just about every zip code of American life. Having completed the process of placing ourselves into the future, we can report that while we found much to be distressed about, the fullness of our prospects—especially in medicine and health—are a potent rejoinder to arguments of despair.

Of course, a dictionary has to be as alert to what it excludes as to what it incorporates. We have tried to avoid slang and jargon unless there was a compelling reason to include a word or phrase. The former is studied by etymologists and folklore scholars; the latter is collected on the Internet, almost obsessively, by those in jargon-rich fields like technology. We were not interested in obscurities that are fated to remain so; if we believed that a technical term had the potential to waft out into the popular ether—like DSL has done—we have included it. We have also tried to discipline ourselves about two categories of words: "smart" this, and "e-" that. One could probably fill this entire volume with just those coinages. We only included those examples that we thought were particularly instructive and would endure.

By now you might be wondering—and we have asked this question of ourselves—how should *Dictionary of the Future* be read? Traditional dictionaries are not read at all, other than by prisoners, idiot savants and the ferociously autodidactic. But we have written this book to be read straight through, if you are so inclined, although there is also no reason why it cannot be read in a nonlinear sort of fashion; the perfect brain-jolt for our disjointed time.

It seems to us that if ever there was a need for a dictionary that anticipates the life to come, it is now. Change, not only in the areas that are obvious accelerants, like technology, is clipping along at a faster rate than ever before. The Internet is not just the initiator of change, but a distributor of it. The rapid recalibration of our demographics is shocking us into a new notion of what America is, and will be. Language is our most obvious (and meaningful) monitor of this cultural and technological flux, a way to help us "approach the Future as a friend" in Auden's words. *Dictionary of the Future* seeks to help our readers make that approach less scary, or abstract, so that we can become sharper observers, more engaged participants—and perhaps even predictors—of the many shapes and corners of the world we will come to inhabit. Should we accomplish that, we will be fortunate enough to have created even more than the editor of *The Ortus* sought to achieve in 1502 with his "garden of words." We will have cultivated a garden of ideas.

There was a time when getting old was a slow period of detachment from the mainstream of the culture. Today, we are redefining our concept of what it means to get old. Not only thanks to medicine, but thanks to the baby boomers—the largest demographic group ever to control the dials of American culture—who are certainly not about to reproduce the aging patterns of their parents.

Consider the statistics: the number of Americans over 65 will nearly triple by 2030. There will also be nine million people over 85. What do we know about them? That they will be more focused on their "biological age" than their chronological age; that they will consider new options like "phased retirement"—and that when they finally pack it in, they will either "age in place" or look to move to "yogurt cities" where there is an active culture—again, not the sedentary retirement patches to which their parents fled.

It's not going to be a time without conflict, as young Americans will not be happy about the medical resources (and money) being spent on what they will call "over-stayers." But you can be certain that our population realities will continue to create an emerging vocabulary that articulates a torrent of new ideas and thinking about retirement, leisure, vacationing, healthcare, and relationships. It's a new kind of aging, and a fresh young vocabulary is capturing it.

Active Aging — a catchall term to describe a combination of physical and psychological efforts that convert the aging process from a slow decline into a period of vigorous commitment and growth. It includes elements of preventive and alternative medicine, volunteerism and mentoring, entrepreneurship and consulting. Magazines, Web sites, seminars, TV programs, the medical community and consumer marketers will rally around—and capitalize on—this attempt to "rebrand" aging. If it succeeds, it will be the ultimate triumph of marketing over inevitability.

ADLs — you don't know how important ADLs are until you aren't capable of doing them anymore. The term stands for Activities of Daily Living, and included among them are dressing, bathing and eating. It's language that the bureaucrats in the health care industry have adopted as criteria to determine when someone can remain at home, versus moving into an assisted living facility or something more dramatic. As the population ages, ADLs will become a sadly familiar acronym.

Aging in Place — the trend which finds retirees staying put rather than packing up. Unlike previous generations, baby boomers appear to be remaining in their nests; a survey conducted by the American Association of Retired Persons found that 89 percent of those 55 and over planned to age in place, and only 4.9 percent of Americans over 65 moved during 1999, a 20 percent decline over the mobility of older Americans a decade ago. The implications of aging in place are substantial—potential housing shortages in areas where older homeowners have traditionally given way to younger ones, economic benefits to regions that have lots of retirees (they pay tons of taxes), and new kinds of housing developments. Example: Del Web, builder of retirement communities in Sun Belt areas, is launching their first community in the Wind Belt, outside Chicago. *DOF* also expects an explosion in home repair and maintenance services; it's not that easy to get up on the roof and clean the leaders and gutters when you're 66.

Biologic Age — an indicator which is calculated by measuring and assessing one's physiological age through various tests, including DNA degradation, oxidative stress, hormone levels, bone density, etc. Innovations in medicine as well as our new national pastime—slowing or reversing the aging process— mean that our biologic age will become increasingly more important than our chronological age. ("I'm 103, but who's counting?") A new home test, available without a prescription, has been developed for use in North America based on a similar test available in Japan. A group called Lexcore (http:// worldhealth.net/journal/aain/lexcore.html) is establishing an ongoing panel and database to study the progression of biologic age, much as the legendary Framingham Study provided invaluable insight into epidemiological trends several generations ago.

We foresee that entirely new industries dedicated to helping consumers measure and lower their biologic age will emerge. And it won't be long now before personal ads will say: DWF, biologic age 35.

Cluster Care — as aging baby boomers do whatever they can to avoid the dreaded nursing home, they will increasingly have the option of cluster care. Chronically ill men and women who live near each other—in convenient clusters— will be served by a battery of home health care providers who can move quickly from residence to residence to meet ongoing and acute needs.

Cochlear Implants — these chip-based implants, tucked gently into the inner ear, process sound waves and send the information straight to the brain. They improve hearing, and have actually restored it in some cases. Experts anticipate that years of rock music, leaf blowers, and noise pollution in general will result in millions of baby boomers needing this kind of aural assist. According to a recent study by the National Institutes of Health, there has been a stunning 26 percent increase in those suffering permanent hearing loss between the ages of 35 and 60, compared to 15 years earlier.

Combat Hapkido — a defensive-only martial arts technique that is gaining in popularity because it can be learned by those who are older, disabled, or out of shape (www.ichf.com/cbhk. htm). As the *Wall Street Journal* put it, combat hapkido "gives the weaker and creakier members of society a fighting chance." There is nothing polite or elegant about combat hapkido; as the *Journal* describes the teachings of John Pellegrini, the "guru" of the movement, "He encourages eye-gouging and hair-pulling, always done with one hand while the other is used to inflict pain or gain control of another part of an attacker's anatomy." With the aging population, and the low crime rate poised for an uptick, expect combat hapkido to continue to attract adherents. Also expect other martial arts to develop age-appropriate twists on their basic approach.

Compression of Morbidity — the focus of much geriatric research; how to live not just long, but well, and to "compress" the act (and art) of dying into as short a period of time as possible. See also *futile care theory*.

Death Extension — when we are living longer, but those years are really more about delaying death than prolonging a robust life, we have entered into death extension. So says Dr. Ron Klatz, of the American Academy of Anti-Aging Medicine. The challenge of tomorrow's medicine—with its ability to keep the mechanical part of us functioning—will be to make sure that we are expanding the richness of life, rather than merely creating a longer prelude to death. Not just longevity, in other words, but *lifegevity*.

Elderweds — a whole new nuptial nomenclature: couples who are getting married in their sixties, seventies and beyond. It's a logical by-product (if not bio-product) of all the age-denial trends we're seeing. Of course, these new marriages create a cascade of financial and familial problems for children and grandchildren. Elderweds also put a renewed focus on the sexual implications of these later marriages. In the early part of the last century Freud shocked us with his insights into infant sexuality; today, we are being shocked by geriatric sexuality, which in many ways is the last taboo. See also *elderotica.*

Gentle Tech — describes a number of initiatives that will use technology and the Internet to help those with memory problems remain alert and in their homes. *Scientific American* writes of a unique video screen being tested at the Georgia Institute of Technology that uses "a running montage of snapshots that can remind people what they were doing before they were interrupted." The *Financial Times* notes that the house of the future may "remind elderly inhabitants of tasks such as taking pills by flashing little red lights near objects or by alerting them with a digital voice." And *Wired* magazine writes of Memory Glasses, "Video-cam equipped eyeglasses attached to a wearable computer programmed to recognize certain faces and objects and tell the user (such as Alzheimer's sufferers) what they're seeing." This goes beyond the smart home and creates something closer to an *aware* home.

Geriborg — baby boomers growing old in the digital age will have a lot of technology available to ease their way. One of the biggest aids will be the geriborg—from the Greek "geri" for old, and "borg" for trusty old cyborg—a robot built with technology that assists the physically disabled. Geriborgs will be there to do the laundry, carry heavy loads, make fresh coffee and even take out the trash. A company called Rehab Robots has built a robot that helps people eat, drink, shave, brush their teeth and put on makeup. In a way, the depersonalization of robot care reduces the indignities that are part of the process of aging; and—unexpectedly—their tangle of microprocessors can even provide a kind of companionship—not unlike Aibo, Sony's electronic dog.

Hip Bumpers — small, oval devices that will be worn by seniors to protect their hips in the event of a fall. Finnish researchers who studied these plastic hip guards found that they protected just about all those who wore them from broken bones. (Broken hip bones are often fatal; as many as 30 percent of seniors who break their hips die within a year.) *Time* writes that these "crash helmets for hips are recommended for people with osteoporosis, especially those who suffer dizzy spells or are otherwise tumble prone." *DOF* predicts that hip bumpers will be made in cool colors and shapes, and will become protective fashion accessories, just like elbow and knee pads for inline skaters and helmets for bicyclists. See also *disability chic*.

Phased Retirement — rather than the bright line between the commute and the gold watch, a new, incremental approach to retirement is finding its way into the workplace. As the consulting firm Watson Wyatt puts it: "Traditionally, retirement has been viewed as a one-time act that signifies the end of one's working life. In many organizations today, however, retirement is evolving from an abrupt act into a gradual process of easing out of a full-time work schedule." Those organizations include Monsanto, PepsiCo, Lockheed Martin and many universities (where phased retirement helps to gently dispose of tenured professors). The concept fits neatly into the trends—many older Americans who had productive careers aren't ready for traditional retirement—but raises all sorts of issues. How do you handle pension fund distributions? Is this a back-door way for employers to encourage early retirement and reduce their benefit obligations? What happens to the younger workers who now find their upward mobility stalled? *DOF* believes that phased retirement will become a defining aspect of the economy as baby boomers age, and its implications will be felt in housing (see also *aging in place*), pension and health care policy and fashion.

Sarcopenia — the loss of muscle mass in elderly people. It's a little-known condition that we will be hearing a great deal about, as this under-researched problem becomes the subject of a great deal of attention. Baby boomers, who have spent a lifetime working out, will not gently yield to turning weak and quivery. Recent research suggests that a failure in myosin, a critical protein, is at fault. We expect an outpouring of books about the condition, as well as all kinds of innovative anti-sarcopenia products.

Volunteer Vacationing — a new trend in which retirees, seeking more meaning in their lives, combine vacations with public service work, ranging from conservation, wildlife censuses, planting and restoring parks. Picking up where Jimmy Carter's Habitat for Humanity leaves off, the phrase was coined by Theodore Roszak, who invented the term "Counter Culture" way back in 1968. He knows his neologisms.

Dictionary of the Future Predicts

Age Rage — as baby boomers, who are used to controlling the planet and having everything their own way, get older, they will find that being the most privileged generation cannot inoculate them from the depredations of age. This will result in outbursts of Age Rage, expressed in the ill-treatment of caregivers and in surprising acts of violence. Adding more boil to the cauldron of Age Rage: the fact that without major breakthroughs, some 14 million baby boomers are on track to develop Alzheimher's.

Driving Miss Daisy Syndrome — also known as the Killer Grandpa problem. This looming crisis on the roads is a result of incapable senior citizens behind the wheel; experts predict that the number of people killed in crashes involving elderly motorists is likely to exceed the number killed by drunk drivers. Laws are pending in several states that would compel those 75 and over to take written, vision and driving tests to renew their licenses. One such law—dubbed the Brandi Jo bill after 15-year-old Brandi Jo Mitock, who was killed by a 96-year-old driver with dementia (see *memorial statutes*)—has been pending in the California legislature. While AARP adamantly opposes these restrictions, popular sentiment seems to be moving in this direction. As we live longer—by 2018 the number of drivers past 70 will be 30 million—this will become a high visibility public health issue and will create new marketing opportunities; see also *chauffeurs-to-go*.

Ear Electronics — old-fashioned hearing aids are one of the most stereotypical signals of aging, which is why so many senior citizens would rather go through life saying "Can you talk a little louder?" than wear one. Ear Electronics will allow users to avoid this stigma; far from being a cause of embarrassment, they will be in demand as a new kind of hot techno-toy—part hearing aid, part cell phone earbud, part tiny MP3 player. Rather than looking like dreary, hospital-supply prescriptions, they will be award-winning examples of industrial design—like the iMac. No one will be able to tell if you're sporting a hearing aid, or if you're listening to a downloaded song from Radiohead's latest CD. See also *disability chic.*

Elderotica — erotica for senior citizens. See also *elderweds.*

Geriatmosphere — describes an environment that is dominated by older Americans, and as such, ironically, is unappealing to them. Florida, Sun Valley, restaurants serving dinner at 5 P.M. and assisted-living facilities all have a geriatmosphere. It also describes a place we all end up, whether we like it or not: at a certain age, you are launched into the geriatmosphere. We see the senior citizens of tomorrow as falling into two categories: those who feel comfortable and secure in these environments, and others who avoid them at all costs and seek to hang out with younger people. See also *reurbanize, yogurt cities.*

ODOs — the fast-growing group of Americans who are 100 years old or older; the acronym is short for "odometer," as when a car's odometer passes 100,000 miles and it moves into another land of measurement.

Over-Stayers — also called left-olders. A derogatory term that will be used by young people to describe oldsters whose lives have been extended into the aging stratosphere, thanks to advanced medical technologies. Younger Americans will resent these baby boomers—who are hanging on by their cloned fingertips—because of the health care funds and biomedical attention they will be demanding.

Returnment — when bored baby boomers—what *DOF* also calls Boom Backers—recognize that they miss the action, and yes, even the stress of work and decide to reverse their retirement and head back to the office. Younger workers—those in their twenties and early thirties—will welcome the wisdom they bring and will connect with them (in the same way that grandparents and grandchildren can develop a special relationship). Because they are working for the challenge and not the money, these Boom Backers will not be politically motivated and will pull no punches about what needs to be done. The most threatened will be workers in the middle—those in their mid-thirties to late forties—who could feel under siege and turn resentful. See also *phased retirement.*

Reurbanize — when suburban-dwellers return to the city, either because their children have grown, they have recently separated or divorced, or perhaps have mowed one lawn too many. We expect to see millions of reurbanizers head for neighborhoods where they don't roll up the sidewalks at nine. These reurbanizers are accustomed to certain levels of convenience and comfort, and as a result developers are designing new buildings (or renovating old ones) to satisfy them—including spas, concierge services, valet parking, plus rooms and services for children and grandchildren. Ironically, these buildings are often in gritty, emerging neighborhoods, so reurbanizers can feel really cool while they're really coddled. This will have substantial implications for cities (as well as the suburbs themselves). Younger people will find themselves priced out of neighborhoods that were once exclusively for them by older folks. In other words: "Hey mom, what are you doing on *my* block." See also *aging in place.*

Twilight Agony — as new medications forestall the onset of Alzheimer's disease, the unintended consequence will be a prolonged period when the sufferer is aware of what is slowly but inexorably happening. This Twilight Agony will create all sorts of ethical and moral dilemmas; some family members will decide to withhold the latest drugs, believing that a more rapid descent into unknowingness is preferable to the misery of powerless awareness. See also *beta secretase.*

Spa Finale — the carefully planned ending of your life at one of many luxurious resorts that will be dedicated to providing venues for voluntary termination of existence as we know it. These destinations—which were pre-figured in the film *Soylent Green*—will be staffed with four-star chefs, the hottest acts in entertainment, and facilities for life-ending celebrations for family and friends. No low-fat meals will be served.

Sputtering — will be used to describe the slow and agonizing process of dying as a result of Alzheimer's. As Marcelle-Morrison Bogorad, neuroscience chief at the National Institute of Aging, puts it: "How do you want to go out? With a sputter? Nothing sputters longer than Alzheimer's. It lasts eight to 10 years on average, but can linger for up to 20."

Voice Modulation Surgery — one of the most telltale signs of aging is when your voice gets thinner and shakier. There are physiological reasons for this, but soon they will be reversible. *DOF* predicts that—driven by baby boomers who want to sound robust and resonant until the end—researchers will develop a simple, outpatient voice modulation surgery technique that eliminates the problem and returns the patient's voice to what it used to be.

Yogurt Cities — places to live that have active cultures: vital museums, symphonies, independent bookstores, downtown neighborhoods with throbbing street life. Retiring baby boomers will insist on moving to Yogurt Cities rather than the "retirement communities" their parents gravitated to. "Tennis anyone?" will be replaced by "Tennyson anyone?" See also *geriatmosphere, reurbanize.*

ARCHITECTURE, THE ARTS AND DESIGN

There are no great demands being put on language today as it relates to the creative arts. In previous eras, language was busy, racing from movement to movement to find (and pin) new definitions on the grand, sweeping alterations in architecture, painting and the way creative individuals engaged with, and comprehended the universe. Today, the inventive energy that caffeinates new artistic directions—and spurs their antagonists—seems to be directed elsewhere in the culture. Perhaps our ability to be staggered or outraged is limited to religious affronts; other than that, watching artists struggle to force us into new ways of contemplating the world is a bit like watching a little boy try to open a large steel door.

For those reasons, our entries in this category are less about cohering themes; artists—in the broadest sense of the term—seem to be waging a series of mini-assaults on politeness and complacency. We see skirmishes rather than a world war. One exception might be the term "Ecstatic Architecture," which describes the sensual, pleasure-extending (and enveloping) work of Frank Gehry and Rem Koolhas, and should become part of our artistic vernacular.

Aesthetic Aging — a design philosophy which can be seen in the translucent, elastomeric rubber casings that are used on smart phones, PDAs and other products. Because the material conforms to your hand, the more you use it the more like you it becomes, and thus the more personal value it acquires over time. Here, technology, once viewed as cold, rigid and impersonal, becomes as warm as a comfortable pair of jeans.

Archityranny — the control exerted over us (and our environment) by over-bearing, over-designed buildings that are either structurally flawed (the windows leak, there's no natural light, the air makes us sick) or are functionally useless. It happens when architects fall so much in love with architecture that they forget that buildings have to work for the people who work in them. The perpetrators of this: archityrants.

Art Cars — the practice of transforming cars into moving works of art, while long practiced by a few (www.artcars.com) will become far more widespread in the years to come. Art cars are ornamented with everything from hundreds of plastic dollars, bones, and skulls to stuffed animal heads. Their appeal? Let us quote the words of one Nancy Josephson, whose vehicle *"La Baroness"* is a blue sequinned and bead-encrusted creation: "The media and advertising are continually telling you what to do, what to be; it's nonstop. People are so fed up of being manipulated, so Art Cars are a very guerrilla way of subverting how we relate to people." See also *culture jamming*.

Blobject — coined by the eruditely imaginative designer Karim Rashid to describe rounded, fluidly designed objects such as the Apple iMAC or the Gillette Mach 3 razor. Blobjects defy rigid geometry and invite the touch of the human hand. As *Artbyte* magazine puts it, "The humpy-perky, retro-moderne New Beetle . . . the laser-guided Microsoft Explorer mouse—gliding under one's sweaty palm with a slick red glare like a molten hockey puck. There are thousands of examples of the new Blobjectivity." For a fascinating tour of the social narrative behind blobjects, go to www.artbyte.com/shared/articles/ blobjects/blobject.html.

Dictator Chic — collectors will pounce upon the propaganda artifacts of communist and totalitarian countries, and create a new collecting mania. (There is already a serious market for Soviet Realism of the pre–World War II period.) The Sotheby's-Amazon Internet venture frequently auctions off a range of material created during the Mao years, including posters, plates, vases and other objects that served both functional and mind-control purposes. Our favorite from one auction was a statuette of the cherished leader in casual clothes, which was described drolly as "Dress Down Friday for Chairman Mao." Also part of this phenomenon will be the conversion of former dictator residences to luxury tourist destinations; already the guesthouse of Romanian bully Ceausescu has been turned into a hotel.

Digital Artworks — as you would expect, this term covers a range of activities—"from interactive Web sites to screensavers to multimedia narratives that can be read online" (as *The New York Times* describes it)—that eschew canvas and clay for bits and bytes. Though expectedly controversial, the category went a long way to legitimacy when the 2000 Whitney Biennial included Internet art—its first new category since video was let through the door in 1975 (www.whitney.org/exhibition/ 2kb/internet.html). James Buckhouse, a San Francisco artist, has curated an exhibit of free, downloadable screensavers; he says the screensaver has moved beyond its utilitarian function and has become a medium for public art, much like the murals on abandoned buildings and subway cars. Art moves forward, and Internet art will become the darling collectible of the digital generation—which will have enormous implications for the way art is distributed and displayed; static, wall-based art will give way to new viewing modes.

Docomomo — short for its massively elongated full name "Documentation and Conservation of Buildings, Sites and Neighborhoods of the Modern Movement," Docomomo is an

Aa

international movement with chapters in 40 countries. Its objective is to study the principles of the post-war modernist movement in architecture—and to preserve the many examples of it that are falling into disrepair. This is a controversial period; many scholars see the late forties, fifties and sixties as an undistinguished architectural period. Challenging that orthodoxy, Docomomo brings together preservationists and devotees of modernism in a unique moment of solidarity, as the architecture critic Hubert Muschamp has written. It's not surprising that given the rediscovery of 1950s furniture—including the work of Ray and Charles Eames—that the architecture of the period will similarly find a new generation of admirers. *DOF* predicts that residential architecture will also rediscover the fifties, and that the ubiquitous ranch house and split-level will be re-expressed for today's sensibility while maintaining the spirit of optimism and modified Mission traditions that shaped the original designs.

Ecstatic Architecture — from the book by Charles A. Jencks, this term describes the global architectural movement that includes key figures like Frank Gehry, Shin Takamatsu and Rem Koolhas. The style is simultaneously powerful, sensual (almost hedonistic), joyful and richly tactile. As Jencks notes, even though Ecstatic Architecture refers to contemporary structures, it also looks back: "The term encompasses buildings widely distant in function and time, from cave art to the new cinema center in Dresden, from explicitly erotic architecture to buildings which have a spiritual role." While drawing from many sources, the pluralism of Ecstatic Architecture is disciplined, unlike the disjointed and exaggerated effects of post-modernism. Ecstatic Architecture's iconic moment: Gehry's Guggenheim at Bilbao.

Façadism — the preservation process which maintains the architectural façade of a structure, but demolishes everything else in preparation for a new building. While conservationists argue that at least it preserves an element of the original building, others argue that it both destroys the integrity of the original, and gives developers an excuse for over-building—

creating massive new structures that aesthetically intimidate the neighboring buildings. Sydney, Australia, is cited by *National Geographic* as an example of façadism where new skyscrapers menace a neighborhood of charming Victorian houses. There is something revealing about a society that maintains a façade but destroys everything behind it. Either way, façadism will become even more of an architectural reality, as preservationists continue to arm wrestle with developers.

Fashion-Tech — the trend that has technology products, from iMac to humble Sharp microwave ovens, coming to market in anything but basic beige. Nokia, for example, has introduced a line of phones with interchangeable shells in 37 colors, according to *Brand Marketing*. Game Boy also has snap-on faceplates that keep the technology looking fresh. It's a reflection of the fact that technology has become both a given and a form of personal expression, so marketers no longer have to impress us with how "serious" their products look. *DOF* expects the fashion-tech trend to spread to products that have been drab for decades: tires, air conditioners, radiators.

Hypersurface Architecture — suddenly, the "skin" or epidermis of a building can take on a whole new utility and function, which is the idea beyond hypersurface architecture. New electronic and digital technologies can transform an outside wall into a communication platform—it can project images (short movies and films); it can send back a video image of what's on the street; it can deliver (needless to say) advertising; it can connect the people *inside* the building with the people outside, in ways not contemplated (or possible) before. Hypersurface architecture takes a building and turns it into a giant TV or computer screen that broadcasts from and to the city in which it resides. Suddenly, a building—fixed, static, local—becomes a dynamic global medium.

Industrial Cool — raw and rough industrial design and architecture is becoming a fashion statement. The magnetic allure of this trend is its naked authenticity. Unlike a number of

Aa

twentieth-century artistic movements—including the Bauhaus, and painters as diverse as Leger and Sheeler—industrial cool is less interested in the abstract and functional elegance of industry, and more drawn by the gritty and funky reality. It's not that we're sacrificing comfort, but that we're less infatuated with splendor and polish. *The Austin Chronicle* put it this way in an article about a gentrifying neighborhood: "the Seaholm Power Plant is cutting-edge urban industrial cool . . . it's a 1950s art deco structure whose glowing red 'City of Austin Power Plant' sign still illuminates the skyline." Leading-edge hotels and interior designers have embraced industrial cool, but *DOF* expects it to extend to more public spaces: malls, airport, entertainment venues.

Mass Adoption — *DOF*'s term for the trend that finds museums using mass marketing strategies to raise money by letting consumers "adopt" paintings for small amounts of money. The Brooklyn Museum, for example, is inviting mini-philanthropists to adopt a painting for as little as $500 for one person or $250 each if the public service spirit is split between two people. For that donation you get your name on a plaque next to the painting, just like big-deal billionaire givers. It's the subject of debate in museum circles, and the argument returns to the old class vs. mass divide: making the museum more populist and democratic (and the institutions need the money, besides) as opposed to over-commercializing the museum experience with every item, from a painting to a men's room sign (potentially) "branded" with a giver's name.

MEG — Museum Exhibition Guide, introduced at Paul Allen's Experience Music Project in Seattle. This handheld device relegates the old museum headphones to a museum themselves. As reported in the *MIT Technology Review*, "You point the infrared remote unit at specially marked exhibits and it downloads relevant text and audio for immediate playback, bookmarking your selections for later retrieval in the Experience Music Project's computer lab or Web site." Museums—which have become entertainment destinations as opposed to sanctuaries where we experience art on a personal level—will pick up on the technology. And it won't be long before sponsor messages insinuate themselves into the experience: "If you liked Andy Warhol's Campbell Soup cans, stop by Kroger—just two blocks away—for a special price on our cream of mushroom . . ."

Michael Anastassiades — an innovative industrial designer whom *DOF* believes we will be hearing more from. He sees his work as a "combination of product, furniture and environmental design . . . which establishes a psychological dimension between objects and users." For example, his message cup does more than hold coffee—it is also a tape recorder and playback device; everyone in the house gets one, and family members leave messages through this exchange mechanism. He also has created a bedside table that vibrates when it's time to get up, and interactive lighting that includes an "antisocial light" that goes on in the absence of conversation, and a "social light" that illuminates when you speak to it. "It needs to be talked to, to glow" says Michael. "It's very therapeutic."

New Edge Design — a generational step beyond aerodynamics. Rather than one fluid curve flowing into another—think of car body design, for example—the shape is surprisingly interrupted by sharp creases. Ford is a leader in this aesthetic; Jack Telnack, vice president of Corporate Design, described their 2000 New Edge Mercury MC2 as having "smooth, sculpted surfaces and clean, crisp intersections." We're also seeing New Edge Design appear in computers, stereos and other appliances. Is there a cultural subtext to this design aesthetic? The original aerodynamic design—also called streamlining—which was pioneered in the machine age of the 1930s, was a reflection of a belief in the power of progress. Perhaps New Edge Design is a reflection of our ambivalence: fluidity for progress, sharp creases for the limitations that we face.

Piggyback Art — the practice of taking existing paintings—such as thrift-store art—and adding to them to create a new aesthetic. Eddie Breen is one of the practitioners, and here is what he says about himself: "Eddie Breen is my 'brush-name.' Taking flea-market and yard-sale paintings that I consider 'incomplete,' I spiff 'em up by adding elements which will invigorate the works. Unwilling to show in public due to past criticisms of my work as 'parasitic,' I toil away in utter obscurity—yet I am perhaps one of the most prolific painters today in the genre known by the names of 'piggyback art', 'improved art' or 'congloms.' " Piggyback art is an expression of a larger trend toward pastiche, overlay and stylistic hybridizing that we're seeing in music, dance and literature.

Pragmatist Architecture — a contemporary architectural movement that is marked by its freedom from specific forms and philosophies. It is neither modernist nor post-modernist, but is focused on what seems to work best in the moment, given the realities at hand. This tracks with the theories of the philosopher William James, who helped create the pragmatist movement, and who coined the phrase "things in the making." In other words, celebrate the process of problem solving, don't be slavish to any received theory. As *The New York Times* described it, pragmatist architecture is willing to "roll with the punches." For example, buildings in Taiwan are forced to incorporate a large Buddha or dragon on their façade; some might find this restrictive, but to pragmatist architects, these restrictions are spurs to creativity. Columbia and Princeton have already held seminars on Pragmatist Architecture; only time will tell whether it will become a coherent theory or merely a method of coping with the challenges that every creative person must face.

Quibco — an award-winning concept house designed by architect Stefan Lindfors; this single-occupant home can be erected within a week. It's bright red and full of personality—the residential equivalent of a small, fun-to-drive car. We see Quibco, and houses like it, gaining in popularity as low-cost, fashionable housing alternatives—you can put one on your own property (a grown-up tent, if you will) or on land in the country. It can also be used for housing by governments, the military, and educational institutions—as well as for cheerful and affordable low-income housing.

Softroom — an innovative, future-tilted architectural and design firm that will emerge as one of the leading forces in the field. For example, they have created an innovative structure for parks—called the Belvedere—where walkers can take shelter and still be in a close relationship with the environment (check it out at www.softroom.com). Conceptual projects include "a foldaway home ('Maison Canif') in the form of a large Swiss Army knife, a tow-away floating retreat (complete with its own inflatable beach), a treehouse, a flexible hotel suite based upon a child's sliding block puzzle." They have also been hired by *Vogue* and *Time* to "visualize the unbuilt future" because of their digital imaging capabilities.

StARTups — *DOF*'s term for new ventures that combine technology and entrepreneurship. That's unusual in the rarefied art world, a precinct that is usually focused more on the aesthetics than the economics of a market. As an example of a corporate-funded StARTup, Absolut vodka is investing in two art- and technology-driven business plans a year, to the tune of $50,000 each. Their objective is to help artists survive and prosper in the digital world. Winners have included Art Angels.org and Rhizome.org, two nonprofits: the former raises donations for the arts, the latter is dedicated to the preservation and propagation of Internet art. As technology continues to extend the way that art can enter and influence our lives, we can expect many more StARTups, funded by museums, publishing companies and artists' collectives.

Trash Art — art meets environmentalism, with artists who use recycled materials in their craft. (Also called eco-artware.) It includes jewelry made from old typewriter keys and rugs created from tossed-out rags. Zulu basket-makers take it one step further: because the grasses they use for their woven *imbenge* baskets have been depleted, they now use colorful, PVC-

A|**a**

coated telephone wire. Check out www.eco-artware.com for some terrific examples. And remember, today's Dumpster can be turned into tomorrow's Degas.

Vertical Writing — when a narrative form—either a novel, short story, film or play—tells a story from several simultaneous viewpoints rather than using a linear thread. Traditional linear storytelling, by contrast, is horizontal writing. While vertical writing isn't new—William Faulkner was famous for it, and the classic Japanese film *Rashomon* used the technique to tell the story of a crime from differing perspectives—the style is very likely to gain popularity in the years to come, since the Internet and contemporary technology are training us to receive "multiple presents" at the same time. The playwright Yasmina Reza, author of the hit *Art,* said in a *New York Times* interview, "I wanted to avoid classical horizontal writing . . . the character enters the room, a series of events occurs, and he leaves. Mine is vertical writing. The character enters again, goes 10 feet, then enters again, slightly differently . . . it's like digging a hole and studying the geological layers."

Visible Storage — a new exhibition approach that is being adopted by museums to give the public access to a larger portion of their collections. In contrast to blockbuster exhibitions which use a great deal of space to showcase—worshipfully—a few items, visible storage elbows as many items into a small exhibition space as possible: decorative objects are massed in display cases, paintings are hung cheek-by-jowl. An Associated Press story calls it a "radical new breed of gallery" and describes the Henry Luce III Center for the Study of American Culture—a recent convert to visible storage—as "very transparent . . . with its hundreds of glass-enclosed cases and shelves, it resembles a library you can see through." The museum no longer pays $500,000 a year to store 10,000 items, but displays them in just 21,000 square feet. *DOF* believes that an increasing number of museums will adopt some form of visible storage, not only as a way to make their total collections come alive, but as a strategy for continuing to attract contributions: it's tough to say "give us your painting and we'll keep it in the attic."

Dictionary of the Future Predicts

Artiture — photographer Helmut Newton's book *Sumo* was sold with its own specially designed coffee table—designed by Philippe Starck—for $1,500. (Only 10,000 copies were produced.) *DOF* sees this as the start of a trend linking writers, artists and famous architects/furniture designers. Expect to see volumes of poetry sold with aromatherapy candles; photographs sold with architect-created frames; limited-edition autographed novels sold with writer-designed easels for display purposes. (A personal example: Faith Popcorn's Home Office Cocoon comes complete with a copy of *EVEolution*.)

Art Lease Programs — most museums are too small to exhibit the vast majority of their collections; thus, many art objects are stored away in climate-controlled warehouses, doing no good to anybody—including the benefactors whose largesse made their acquisition possible. Art Lease Programs (also called Rent-a-Renoir) will appear on the scene to solve this dilemma. Museums, who have art but no walls, will lease their archives to wealthy individuals who have walls but no art. They will pay a monthly fee (insurance included) for the privilege and status of living with works of art from America's finest museums. Museums can generate significant revenue, and gain additional exposure as well. And here's a way to help offset the costs of leasing a Picasso: just charge your guests $10 for an audio guide. See also *visible storage.*

Connectionism — a new art movement in the tradition of impressionism, expressionism and abstract expressionism, but which will be a break from them at the same time. Connectionism is a kind of sculpture and painting that links expression to technology in ways not possible before. As an example, an artist executes a portrait—just as it has been done for hundreds of years. But the portrait has been done on an Internet-enabled flat screen, so you can study the subject of the painting and then instantly link it to an image or to digital information specially assembled by the artist as part of the experience. You will be able to connect to the subject's accomplishments, to actual footage of the subject (as a child or an adult), to objects and moments that are especially important to the subject (or artist). Connectionism is a way of bringing the past and the present together to add layers of meaning and response to a work of art.

Creative Futures — struggling creative people will use the Internet to attract investors who will "own" a portion of their future earnings. If you like someone's paintings, music, writing or fashion design, you can help support them now—for a percentage of what might come later. It's a form of creative indentured servitude, for sure, but it could mean the difference between a life of art and a life of burger-flipping. See also *indentured studenthood.*

Designer Departures — wanting to be remembered with the same style in which they lived, baby boomers will be changing the look of the cemetery. Expect to see designer headstones (Philippe Starck, for example) and celebrity architect–built mausoleums (Michael Graves, I. M. Pei). It does have a kind of historical logic, though—the pyramids were designed by the Frank Gehrys of their time, and the Greeks used their finest sculptors for memorial architecture. See also *spa finale.*

Galleries-to-Go — recognizing that they are missing out on the vast wealth that resides in cities without vibrant gallery communities, the most prestigious dealers from New York, Chicago and San Francisco will take their exhibits on the road, much like the old-fashioned trunk shows. These exhibits, we believe, will be done in conjunction with local museums: they provide the space, and in return get a piece of the profits, plus increased local visibility. This is one aspect of the art market that the Internet cannot replace; there is no substitute for seeing the work in a dramatic setting, talking with the dealer—even the artist, perhaps—and rubbing elbows with fellow collectors. The cost of the travel and setup will be funded, in part, by local merchants, insurance companies, architects, banks and interior designers who want the chance to put their names in front of their communities' wealthiest individuals.

High Visibility Design — an architectural and design approach that "opens up" functional areas and treats them with aesthetic dignity. This style (and philosophy) celebrates—rather than hides—the way things work. High Visibility design has a long tradition—including the Bauhaus glass office building from 1925, and the Pompidou Center in Paris, with its heating and ventilation on the outside of the building. Today, High Visibility design can be found in restaurants and homes with open kitchens (including see-through refrigerators, as well as computers, consumer electronics and Swatch watches.) This Saran Wrapping of design will accelerate rapidly into areas like automobiles (particularly electric cars) with transparent hoods, airplanes—where you can see the pilot as opposed to being blocked by a polyester curtain—as well as humble, functional objects like mattresses. It's the design expression of our see-all, tell-all society.

Inflatism — a design trend which will take inflatables to the next generation. Driven by new technology and the increasing popularity of plastics, top designers will create must-have inflatable desks, tables (for small apartments that don't have a dining room), briefcases, lighting fixtures, even picture frames. It's a trend that also reflects the quick-change, ephemeral nature of life in the technological age.

Involved Frames — artists will look to frames as more than boundaries between the art and the wall, and as active components of their created experience. Using new materials, they will develop frames that change color, that react to heat and crowds, that display images through chips and tiny video cameras and that challenge our perception of where the art ends.

Museum Getting — museum going is what we do on weekends; museum getting is what cities around the world are starting to do every day, as they attempt to lure cultural institutions to their backyards. It all started with the Guggenheim Museum in Bilbao, Spain. Designed by Frank Gehry, this architectural marvel transformed a nondescript industrial town into a global destination, attracting millions of tourism dollars into the local economy. Thomas Krens, who runs the Guggenheim and is turning it into a global brand, is looking to expand into South America and other areas as well. Indeed, the Guggenheim is such a brand that Gehry uses the term unashamedly, saying about their next choice of a location: "We're in a situation where we really can't afford to have a failure. It would ruin the museum and the brand." Next up for the Guggenheim—and Russia's Hermitage (believe it or not) is Las Vegas. *DOF* predicts that other great museums, from Madrid's Prado to Florence's Uffizi to California's Getty will be looking to extend their brands globally, giving more cities around the world the chance to participate in the mad rush of museum getting.

BIOLOGY AND BIOTECHNOLOGY

There is a theory called "punctuated equilibrium" which argues that evolution doesn't occur on a continuing basis, but that there are long periods where little happens, punctuated by short but revolutionary moments. This is a useful way to think about the current intense and transformative developments in our ability to not just understand—but reshape—the fundamental chemistry of human life.

Not surprisingly, given the speed of these advances, new terms are jumping from the lab to the language in record time. Consider that stem cells, known to just a few researchers a handful of years ago, are now the subject of a grand national debate. Indeed, the term has achieved such instant ubiquity that we chose not to include it here, but rather have pursued the next contenders for tip-of-the-tongueness. In doing so we've tried to cover the gamut, and a thrilling gamut it is. Thus, this section includes existing language that will vault into prominence—like beta secretase, a brain enzyme that is the target for promising Alzheimer's drug development, as well as new language created to describe potentials that never existed before.

It will be especially interesting to monitor the migration of this new language beyond its technical meanings. When the science is revolutionary, metaphors erupt. Thus the word "antiseptic" has gone beyond its narrow definition of "germ killing" to have far more resonant implications—a work of art, a design approach can be antiseptic. In the same way we now use DNA to describe the essence of something, and we expect "stem cell" to become a metaphor for the ultimate beginning of just about anything: the Magna Carta as stem cell democracy. Science produces words that enter the vernacular, where we—the users and innovators of language—collaborate on making them even richer.

Bb

Abzyme — enzymes that have certain properties of antibodies. This unusual hybrid has the potential to attack and devour blood clots, as well as to reduce the presence of scar tissue. They also have industrial applications, and could help produce chemicals in a far more efficient manner.

AGE — compounds known as advanced glycation end products that are linked to the process of aging. The theory is that sugar consumption eventually leads to AGE deposits in human tissue—how perfect, AGE causes aging—where they bond with collagen and thicken arteries, stiffen joints and cause organ failure. This "sugar–cross linking" is observed in diabetics, where aging is accelerated. The trick to reversing the aging process, then, would be to break the sugar-protein bond with AGE breakers. Dr. Anthony Cerami, who has been pursuing the sugar/aging connection for 30 years, has developed an AGE breaker called ALT-711 that in tests among diabetic animals, as well as older dogs and monkeys, had stunning results. Cerami was quoted in *Scientific American* as saying that "the heart and major arteries, which were quite stiff, became more pliable and elastic. So the heart could pump more blood—similar to what you'd see in a young animal." ALT-711, which is in human trials, and could also be used to treat other conditions, like glaucoma, where a loss of tissue flexibility is the culprit, is about a decade away from approval, *Scientific American* says.

Amperkines — compounds that are the subject of intensive medical research, because they are believed to have the ability to augment nerve cell communication. By doing so, amperkines could improve memory, accelerate stroke recovery, boost sexual drive and treat schizophrenia. Existing antipsychotic medication interacts with the dopamine and serotonin pathways; amperkines affect the glutamate pathways which are more numerous and hence are believed to play a larger role in schizophrenia. (One day, people may be saying: "Did you Amp up today?") Cortex Pharmaceuticals, www.cortexphar. com, is involved in this research.

Anti-IgE — a new kind of asthma treatment which could revolutionize the management of the disease. (Astoundingly, while the death rate for many diseases has dropped, the rate for asthma has remained flat and its incidence is soaring.) IgE itself is an antibody that is responsible for many of the symptoms of asthma; when a foreign invader enters your body, it links to one of the tips of the IgE molecule. This, in turn, triggers the production of histamines, and the avalanche of symptoms. Anti-IgE shots use a substance that arrests its production. Still in early testing, Anti-IgE could change the way all allergies are treated.

Archaea — a recently-discovered early life form, found at the bottom of the sea, where they survive in water that is near the boiling point, independent of light and heat. They are neither bacteria nor eukaryotes but are a third form of life, a kind of living fossil. Scientists are studying them furiously because of the light that they shed on evolution, biodiversity and cellular functioning. The journal *Nature*, reviewing the book *The Surprising Archaea: Discovering Another Domain of Life* writes that "fuel scientists, chemical engineers and pharmacologists may well find that the Archea have already solved some of their problems for them."

Artificial Retinas — several teams of researchers are working on implants that incorporate silicon technology and other microelectronics to replace the photoreceptor cells—the rods and cones—that nature put there. If this works—and there is early evidence that it can—it would be the first and only total treatment for macular degeneration and RP (retinitis pigmentosa). Together, these scourges represent 25 percent of all cases of blindness around the world. Longer term, artificial vision systems—for those who don't have enough of a neural network remaining in the eye to allow retinal implants to function—would work by bypassing the eye and connecting directly to the visual cortex, where images are shipped directly to the brain for processing. See also *brain-machine interface, photodynamic therapy*.

Bb
27

Beta Secretase — a recently identified enzyme that is linked to the onset and progression of Alzheimer's. This enzyme now gives researchers an "identified target for drug development" according to Dr. Rudolph Tanzi, a professor of neurology at Harvard Medical School. You can expect that the inhibition and modification of beta secretase will become a great national crusade, with 14 million baby boomers predicted to develop Alzheimer's at some point in the future. The pharmaceutical company Elan is leading the way here with an Alzheimer's vaccine that entered clinical trials in the fall of 2001. See also *twilight agony*.

Bio-Bypass — the use of growth factors to stimulate angiogenesis—the production of blood vessels—which could eventually eliminate bypass operations for those who have heart disease. (Ironically, the same technology is being researched as a way to prevent cancer via anti-angiogenesis, since tumors need a supply of blood vessels to grow.) There's so much more going on than we could possibly tell you here, so we refer you to www.angio.org, the Web site of the Angiogenesis Foundation, for more information.

Biometrics — the science of identifying people by distinguishing characteristics, such as voice, real or optic fingerprints and, of course, DNA. Rather than passwords or other devices that can be forgotten, lost or stolen, biometric identification is inseparable from the individual. Corporations spend millions a year to keep their promises—and networks—secure, which is why it is estimated that the combined hardware and software biometric market will be nearly $600 million by 2003. Finger scanning (see also *thumbed*) will be the largest segment, at nearly 50 percent of the market. An innovative company called AuthenTec uses electrical impulses from living tissue to validate the user, at a cost that is projected to drop to just $15 a chip. The net net: no more borrowed keys, loaned passwords—or heaven forefend, fake IDs. See also *iris code*.

Bone Growth Factors — growth factors are proteins that tell our cells which tasks to perform. Bone growth factors tell our bones what to do next, and we are now at the point where these growth factors can be "manufactured" and introduced into the body, where they can pass along instructions for healing everything from broken hips to bones destroyed by cancers. One protein called BMP (bone morphogenic protein) has been shown to create bone formation in rodents, enhance spinal fusion in dogs, and most exciting—according to the American Academy of Orthopedic Surgeons—"in very early trials [in] humans it facilitates cartilage repair." Dr. Thomas Einhorn, chairman of orthopedics at Boston University School of Medicine, believes bone growth factors will "take the field of orthopedics into the 21st century, going beyond the replacement of tissue to the actual regeneration of entire parts of the skeleton." Suddenly, even the most sophisticated of today's orthopedic interventions seem astoundingly primitive.

Carnivora — a drug derived from the Venus's flytrap which those in the alternative medical community believe can raise the level of T cells, and thus be helpful in the fight against AIDS, as well as breast and prostate cancer. We make no recommendation one way or the other, but we do expect that Carnivora will be the focus of some media attention in the years to come.

Chimeraplasty — rather than replace defective genes by using disabled viruses to deliver replacements, chimeraplasty works by actually repairing them as a form of genetic therapy. It uses molecular messengers to, essentially, fix typos in the genetic alphabet. Scientists at Jefferson Medical College have been successful in using chimeraplasty to turn the hair of albino mice from white to dark, raising the hopes that one day the technique will be used on a variety of serious conditions.

Chimpanzee Genome Project — a next step after the Human Genome Project, and some scientists argue it's more important than the ongoing genome mapping of the mouse. Here's why: chimpanzees (who are genetically closer to humans than they are to monkeys) differ from us by only 1 to 1.5 percent—clearly, one of the differences is that they lack the gene for self-importance. Yet close as they are, chimps don't get AIDS or rheumatoid arthritis or Alzheimer's disease, never get blood cancers and have a very low incidence (five percent or so) of breast and prostate cancer. The Chimpanzee Genome Project—which is an example of the emerging field of Comparative Genetics—could be critically important to understanding why these diseases are so prevalent in human beings, and in identifying genetic pathways to prevent or treat them. See also *Plant Genome Project*.

Controlled Hibernation — scientists have discovered that the gene which allows squirrels to hibernate is also expressed in human beings. If that gene can be isolated and if medicines can be developed that target it, it could be possible to put our organs to "sleep," which would preserve them for later transplantation. Considering that roughly 70,000 desperate people are waiting for organs, controlled hibernation could be a revolutionary process. Details are available at www.d.umn.edu/biology/faculty/andrews.htm.

Corrositex — it doesn't exactly fall tripplingly off the tongue, but it's a major advance. For the first time, a federal panel of scientists has approved an artificial skin as a way of testing whether chemicals will burn or damage our skin and eyes. And you know what that means—no animal testing. *DOF* recommends that the folks at In Vitro International, who are selling the product, change the name and build a marketing campaign around it. (Maybe a set of fuzzy rabbit ears as the logo, since rabbits are often used to test these products.) Consumers would look for the logo and even pay more for products that spare animals.

Directed Evolution — a revolutionary process—also called molecular breeding—that uses biotechnology to emulate, and accelerate, evolution. The process works by triggering mutations in genes, inserting that gene into a bacteria, and then testing the resulting protein to see how effective it is at the prescribed task. If a mutated gene produces a superior protein, it can be mutated again and again, in an ongoing

Bb

process of self-improvement. In theory, directed evolution could create everything from superior medicines to industrial products to simply a better laundry detergent. So far, it is only the laundry detergent that has made it to market; a company called Genecor used directed evolution—according to *The New York Times*—to "achieve a fivefold improvement in the stain-removing ability of a bacterial enzyme in a year." Maxygen, a leader in the field, has shown that by using directed evolution it could improve the efficacy of interferon alpha—which is now used to treat hepatitis C and other diseases—by as much as a factor of 285,000. The possibilities are endless: faster development of better drugs; disease-resistant crops (without GMOs); viruses that can transport genes into the body to perform gene therapy; and the replacement of toxic chemical processes—including those that make petrochemical products—by environmentally safe biological manufacturing. We shall be hearing a lot about directed evolution in the future.

DNA Scanners — portable devices for instant DNA testing. The scanner contains probes that are coated with pre-identified DNA, which then match these samples to the target. The technology has applications for disease identification, food safety, environmental policing, forensics and more. A leading company in the field, Clinical Micro Sensors, recently entered into a strategic alliance with Motorola to commercialize the technology.

D-Serine — an unusual brain chemical that has recently been identified, and which holds forth the promise of being a novel and effective treatment for stroke and other neurological conditions. The full explanation is somewhat too technical for our purposes here. Suffice it to say that D-serine is a mirror image of its companion molecule L-serine (an amino acid). It is believed that D-serine could function as a regulator for glutamate, a neurotransmitter that goes haywire during strokes. (Over-production of glutamate is also implicated in Parkinson's and Alzheimer's.) Theoretically, by inhibiting D-serine, the glutamate receptors could be stabilized and stroke damage could be reduced. The patent is held by Johns Hopkins University, which is working with Guilford Pharmaceuticals on commercializing it (www.guilfordpharm.com).

Embryo Adoption — also called embryo donation. There are tens of thousands of fertilized human embryos that are in frozen repose at fertility labs across the country. They belong to couples who deposited these embryos as part of their insemination process, and have now had as many children as they want through successful insemination. Thus, they no longer need the embryos that were put into the deep freeze as back-up cellular potential. Some of these parents have started to donate their frozen embryos to those who cannot conceive on their own, with certain caveats. For example, some embryo donors insist on having access to the children as they are growing up. To complicate matters further, there are thousands of frozen embryos whose "parents" can no longer be tracked down, and thus aren't around to pay the yearly storage charge at fertility clinics—which can be as much as $2,000 a year. Will those frozen embryos be made available to parents who cannot conceive on their own, or will they end up in the controversial area of stem cell research? This promises to be another dramatic debate involving the definition of the family, ethics and the definition of when life starts. See also *pre-implantation genetic diagnosis.*

E2F Decoy — a natural substance that is being studied for its ability to block the genes that are responsible for the high percentage of graft failures in patients with coronary artery disease. The grafts—which eliminate the need for bypass surgery in some patients—fail because the new graft dutifully follows its genetic instructions and begins to develop its own atherosclerotic lesions. E2F decoy tricks the body into letting these grafts "take." One experimental protocol even showed promise in stimulating the body to repair vessels or grow new ones.

Expectancy Waves — neurologists are finding that brain action occurs as we are preparing to act, but haven't yet. These expectancy waves, which demonstrate neural activity prior to conscious thought or choice, are important because they can be used to gain insight into addiction and other behaviors. Some believe that those with more active expectancy waves are more creative and imaginative, and that by increasing our expectancy waves, we can liberate our minds. See also *lucid dreaming.*

Genetic Underclass — those who, as a result of gene testing, have been found to be more likely to develop certain illnesses, are not as intelligent, or suffer from other failings. These social risks of genetic testing are being hotly debated, and are explored in *Remaking Eden,* a book by Princeton biologist Lee Silver. He warns of a world where genetic testing and cloning have conspired to create a society divided into the "Naturals" and the "Gene-Enriched," who represent "a modern-day heredity class of genetic aristocrats." He also anticipates a time when there will be a division between GenRich—those whose parents could afford genetic engineering—and the less affluent "Naturals" who were conceived the old-fashioned way. GenRich, Silver believes, will come to view Naturals much as human beings now regard chimpanzees. See also *GENEology,* and *DNA'd.*

Getaway Genes — *DOF*'s description for what happens when modified genes that are never intended for human consumption end up in the food chain anyway. It happened with some errant StarLink corn, which landed in Taco Bell taco shells, but the sheer amount of gene-spliced agriculture, and the porous controls that exist, make getaway genes likely to be an increasing problem. *DOF* wonders, one, why is it okay for gene-spliced corn to be fed to animals, but not to humans— we are all part of the same giant food chain—and two, why the U.S. Department of Agriculture spent $100 million of its (our) money to buy the genetically engineered corn?

Good Gene Medicine — *DOF*'s terminology for the development of drugs that start with those people fortunate enough to have good genes. An example is ApoA-I Milano, a genetically engineered drug based on an observation made more

Bb

than 25 years ago: a small group of Italians had a genetic mutation that appeared to prevent them from getting heart disease. The drug—which is being developed by Esperion (www.esperion.com)—is a copy of the protein that appears to have the ability to raise HDL levels. Other individuals or groups that are similarly blessed—perhaps with the genes that protect them against cancer or arthritis—will be studied and their proteins will be cloned. See also *isopopulations*.

Kidney Belt — those parts of the Third World where poverty is such that organs are often sold (sometimes people are actually kidnapped and their organs are illegally "harvested"— there is a great deal of urban folklore about this). A new nonprofit called Organ Watch has been set up to monitor the situation, and according to *Time*, "tighten transplant laws and help poor donors get follow-up treatment after surgery." With 70,000 people waiting for organs—and thousands dying each year in the queue—there will be plenty of Kidney Belt commerce going on in the future. See also *controlled hibernation*.

Limpet — a mollusk that is the centerpiece of a cancer vaccine being developed at Memorial Sloan-Kettering Hospital in New York City. A protein derived from the limpet is spliced onto a protein fragment found only in cancer cells, along with different kinds of sugars; the resulting vaccine, according to *Time*, is then "mixed with Saponin, a soaplike derivative from a South American tree. This witch's brew serves to annoy the immune system, revving it up enough to attack cancer cells that are carryng the same sugars and protein fragment."

M-DNA — developed in the lab of Jeremy Lee at the University of Saskatchewan, M-DNA is DNA that is treated to allow it to conduct electricity. Previously, "DNA wires" that became conductive also lost their ability to bind to other molecules. M-DNA does both, which could enable it to have tons of valuable applications. For example, it could be used to create bio-sensors that could enable researchers to screen for genetic abnormalities, as well as identify toxins, drugs or proteins by using the conductivity of the bio-sensor as a signal.

Matrix Metaloproteinase Inhibitors — a new class of drugs that holds forth the promise of stopping or slowing the metastasis of cancer cells by inhibiting production of the enzyme that they use to destroy the cells of surrounding tissues by spreading into their structure and reproductive process.

Microdelivery — researchers at MIT have developed a microchip—about the size of a dime—that can hold drugs (and other substances) in tiny wells; *DOF* calls it microdelivery. The drugs can be in solid, liquid or gel form, and are released on a pre-programmed schedule. The applications are potentially vast, ranging from the perfectly timed delivery of chemotherapy drugs and painkillers to hormones to diagnostic tests. (It's a whole new generation of chipaceuticals, as we've also labeled it.) Moving beyond medicine, the technology can be used to deliver fragrance or aromatherapy throughout the day.

Missyplicity Project — a joint venture between the Bio Arts & Research Corporation and Texas A&M University that seeks to clone family pets; named after Missy, the 11-year-old dog whose anonymous millionaire owner funded over $2 million to launch the effort. A tissue bank will store cells from the mouth and skin of pets; when the cloning process is refined, these banked cells will be used to create a perfect genetic copy. Those seeking Perpetual Pets can log on to www. missyplicity.com; the kits are expected to cost under $1,000, and cell storage should run in the neighborhood of $50 to $100 per year. So far, no successful cloning has happened yet—it's taken longer than thought initially—but the science is there.

Molecular Farming — a technique that actually uses plants to "grow" drugs. Genetic material from a drug or a vaccine gets spliced into a plant; the plant grows, is harvested and the drug is extracted. Early stage work is being done on drugs for childhood diabetes and Crohn's disease. It's an ideal approach for drugs that are costly or exceedingly complicated to produce via traditional methods. And—irony of ironies—tobacco

Bb

plants are particularly hospitable to the process, which could mean economic salvation for tobacco farmers.

Nanoprobes — using nanotechnology, armadas of nano-probes will circulate in our bodies and perform a range of activities, from detecting illness and performing miraculous cell-by-cell surgery, to dispensing drugs and removing toxins, to Roto-Rootering our arteries and scooping up outlaw cancer cells. Science fiction? Not quite. As *Time* reports, "nanotech-nologists have built gears and motors far thinner than a human hair and tiny molecular 'motors' only 50 atoms long." It's one of the most exciting areas of medical research because it's both revolutionary and plausible.

Neuraminid Inhibitors — these drugs—which are the basis for a new influenza treatment—were developed through work done on the space shuttle mission (see *multitary use*). By block-ing an enzyme that is linked to the flu virus, these inhibitors can open a whole new treatment pathway against many strains of the bug. Protein crystals grown during space flights, which are larger and more defined than those grown on earth, enabled the molecular design of the drugs. When we consider the cost-benefit analysis of the space program, we have to take innovations like this into account. Thus far, no metric has been developed to assist in that calculation, but *DOF* suspects the pro–space exploration camp to pursue this analysis to help quantify the value of taxpayer investment.

Pharmacogenomics — the creation of pharmaceuticals that are customized to a patient's individualized genetics. As the *MIT Technology Review* puts it: "This is an era of transition in medicine: from the time of 'one size fits all,' to the emerging epoch of personalized medicines, in which the drugs are geared to the specific genetic makeup of groups or individu-als." We aren't there yet—actual development of these drugs is a decade away, and depends upon our ability to identify the genetic differences between individuals (see also *SNPS*) and then build drugs that are targeted to one's unique genetics.

Bb

Even more revolutionary, these pharmacogenomic drugs won't just treat, they will also prevent; if gene testing identifies a high risk patient, a "preventive" drug will be administered. The pharmacogenomic revolution will have profound implications for every link in our health care system—drug approval must change, for example, since there will be no such thing as "a drug" but thousands of minutely customized drugs. Ethical questions will also abound. As for the role of the doctor, according to Herbert Chase of the Yale Medical School, physicians will become "middlemen" mediating between the patient and the databases that will contain the genetically appropriate treatments. In other words, your doctor will no longer write the prescription, your doctor's computer will.

Photodynamic Therapy — the use of light-sensitive molecules, which are activated by lasers, to treat a variety of conditions from macular degeneration to cancer to blood vessel lesions. Here's how it works in the case of macular degeneration. The FDA has recently approved verteporfin for this condition—the drug is made by QLT PhotoTherapeutics (symbol QLTI for the investors among our readers). The physician injects the drug and the molecules travel to the damaged area in the eye. They are then zapped by a 90-second laser burst, which blocks the leaky blood vessels that cause macular degeneration. Conventional laser treatment is harsh and can actually cause blindness itself, while the gentle laser used with photodynamic therapy appears to be harmless. Other companies involved in the area: Dusa Pharmaceuticals and Pharmacyclics.

Plant Genome Project — the Human Genome Project is completed, the Chimpanzee Genome Project (see listing) is underway, and the study of proteomics (see listing) is also in the works. Less noted by the media, but as important in many ways, is the Plant Genome Project. The first to be successfully mapped was the *Arabidopsis thaliana*, which is a modest little plant with a relatively small genome. But the journal *Nature* writes that "the information it contains provides an unparalleled resource for understanding the evolution of flowering plants and the genetics of crop plants."

Of course, the entire area is fraught with controversy—genetically engineered "designer" crops can be disease-resistant (reducing the need for pesticides), drought-resistant and engineered to contain vitamins and minerals critical to healthy childhood development. But critics argue that the long-term effects are still unknown. Meanwhile, debates about ownership of the genetic material will continue; Paradigm Genetics has filed patents on more than 10,000 *Arabidopsis* genes, and "cereal scientists" in companies like DuPont and AstraZeneca are investing millions to sequence wheat, canola oil and maize. Just as the mapping of the human gene opens new vistas of opportunity, conflict and anxiety, so too does our rapidly growing knowledge of the plant genome.

Polyheal — an innovative company, whose wound-healing and tissue-regeneration technology has shown enormous promise in early testing. It uses synthetic microspheres made of natural material that accelerate the healing in ulcers, burns and other gaping wounds not responsive to traditional treatments. These microspheres, according to the company, have an electrical charge that enables links to be created between healthy cells and the cells in the wound area, thus triggering biochemical changes that promote healing and make skin grafts possible. In early tests, wounds healed twice as fast, with reduced pain. Polyheal expects the first products to reach the market in two years.

Pre-Implantation Genetic Diagnosis — also known as PGD, it describes genetic testing that is done *before* an egg that was fertilized in vitro is placed inside the womb. While in utero screening for genetic and other abnormalities is common via amniocentesis, what's different about this technique is that parents can have multiple eggs fertilized, perform PGD, and then implant the "clean" embryo. A Colorado couple (one of only 300 thus far who have used the technique) wanted to make sure that their new child would not only be free of a rare inherited bonemarrow disease, but that he or she would be a genetically compatible donor for another child of theirs who had that very problem (Fanconi anemia). The embryo proved clean, the baby was born and his cells were harvested and infused into his sister's bloodstream. While this seems ethically acceptable, we are on a slippery slope. As in vitro fertilization becomes even more routine, and genetic diagnosis improves, we can foresee a situation where multiple eggs are fertilized and tested, and only the high-IQ quarterback gets implanted, while the rest are destroyed. See also *embryo adoption, embryo menus, genetic underclass.*

Prion — the term is not new—it is an outlaw brain protein— but we have heard and will continue to hear a lot about it because it is the agent of infection in mad cow disease. Many are worried that the problem will jump the ocean and find a way to the United States; already, we have cases of sheep and elk suffering from a prion disorder that results in a wasting disease. Some wonder if those who eat venison are in jeopardy, because deer are closely related to elk. The latest findings suggest you may need a specific gene to make you vulnerable to mad cow—whose technical name is vCJ disease (variant Creutzfeld-Jacob disease)—which means a genetic test could identify those in danger.

Proteomics — now that the human genome has been mapped, the focus is on identifying and mapping every protein that the genome produces, and analyzing how these proteins interact with one another, the totality of which is called proteomics. The human "proteome" is larger and more complex than the genome, and understanding it will eventually give us insight into how each cell works and how disease begins on the most fundamental level. Proteomics, because it studies the way proteins are built and linked, will provide an enormous range of insights that will allow the success of the human genome project to be fully realized in new drugs and diagnostic techniques that recognize variances in protein "expression," as well as approaches for manipulating proteins on the cellular level. See also *bioinformatics.*

Bb

Quantum Dots — we'll be hearing more about these microscopic materials. They're tiny crystals—one ten-millionth of an inch—that dissolve in water, yet are actually semi-conductors. Originally intended for new electronic devices back in the ancient 1980s, quantum dots are re-emerging as a diagnostic tool in medicine. When injected into the body, they act as traveling monitors that latch onto molecules. Because they glow when exposed to light, they can be used to track antibodies, DNA or proteins. Currently, Quantum Dot Corp. (www.qdots.com) is working with the National Institutes of Health to use the technology in breast biopsies. One day, our doctors will inject us with dozens of quantum dot markers that will patrol our insides and illuminate (literally and figuratively) current and potential health problems.

Raman Spectroscopy — a technique that employs fiber optics and computer technology to beam light into breast tissue as a cancer diagnostic procedure. The noninvasive test, which is still in development as a mammogram replacement, could reduce the number of biopsies in the future.

Scaffolds — this term that conjures up images of buildings under renovation is being reborn as a phrase in the world of biotechnology. Skin cells are being farmed on scaffolding to be grafted in the future, and DNA wires provide a scaffold for the creation of conductive, bio-electrical probes.

SHH — the gene that controls the body's natural on-off cycles of hair growth. *Time* reports that when researchers inserted SHH into mouse hair follicles, the "dozing follicles woke up and performed." Of course, application in human beings is a long way off, so don't delete that Hair Club for Men number from your PalmPilot quite so fast.

SP-SAP — a promising new therapy for chronic pain, a debilitating condition that afflicts 50 million people who suffer from underlying conditions like sciatica, cancer and diabetes. This pain can be so intense that sufferers often resort to cutting nerves or removing parts of the brain. Researchers at the

University of Minnesota were able to relieve chronic pain in rats by fusing two substances: SP, which is absorbed by nerve cells as part of the pain transmission progress, and SAP, which is a nerve toxin. (The theory was that SP-SAP would be absorbed by the small number of nerve cells that send their deadly message to the brain, and would then be killed by the SAP.) The magazine *New Scientist* described it as sending nerve cells "a letter bomb." It worked. What's more, since only misprogrammed pain cells absorbed the toxin, no other cells were harmed and the rats were capable of feeling normal pain. Researchers now have to do toxicology studies in larger animals, and if those succeed they will seek approval to test SP-SAP in terminally ill patients. This is enormously encouraging research in the long-ignored area of pain management.

Sticky Switch — a biological defect believed to lead to manic depression. In normal individuals, the switch functions properly and either the left or the right hemisphere of the brain dominates. In those with manic depression, the switch "sticks." New categories of drugs will be developed to "free" the sticky switch.

Tandem Mass Spectrometry — a new screening technique that detects, with a high degree of accuracy, abnormal levels of fatty acids, amino acids and organic acids in the blood of newborns. Between 20 and 30 underlying conditions can be detected by this technique; many are curable, although they are rare. Currently, there is no national screening program; it varies on a state-by-state basis, which is why there is increasing debate about whether or not the screening should be mandated. As the testing parameter expands, new conditions will emerge as detectable—including many that can't be successfully treated. Thus, the ethical debate will grow—including issues of insurance coverage. It's another example of medicine's ability to diagnose beyond its ability to treat. Even so, expect parents to demand the testing, whether or not it is required in their locality. The next huge controversy: in utero testing.

Therapeutic Cloning — a telling example of the ability of language to soften the blow of a change in policy. The English have changed the debate by replacing the language "stem cell research" with the more benign "therapeutic cloning." The *New Scientist*, a British publication, puts it like this: "The focus of ethics and public policy has shifted from an alarmist and rather fanciful preoccupation with human reproductive cloning to an emphasis on 'therapeutic cloning' for cell and tissue replacement and repair."

Dictionary of the Future Predicts

4-Star Rat Hotels — rats and mice are now included under the Federal Animal Welfare Act, which means that whoever utilizes these animals will have to follow its guidelines for care and feeding, as well as pain relief. The term "4-Star Rat Hotels" will be used by cynics who see this as a waste of time and money, and symbolic of the extremes of animal rights activists. "We aren't feeding our children or educating them properly, and we're spending money to keep rats in 4-star hotels." See also *pets' rights.*

Bio-Freedom — the liberating behavior that comes from knowing that one is not at genetic risk for a particular condition. Bio-Freedom will give some individuals the license to smoke, to consume high-cholesterol foods, to drink, to refrain from exercise, to eat beef in the face of a Mad Cow epidemic (see also prion)—or to engage in whatever life-challenging practices they choose—with enormous public health and marketing consequences. It also is going to annoy—to say the least—all those who are Bio-Prisoners. See also *gene busters.*

Clinical Trial Scandals — not all people react in the same way to the same drugs. Recognizing that, and with their new ability to assess individual genetics, drug researchers will analyze the blood of volunteers before putting them into clinical trials, searching for genetic profiles that are more likely to yield a favorable outcome. This, of course, distorts the sample group and is completely unethical. *DOF* believes that, given the pressure to develop blockbuster drugs, clinical trial scandals will emerge, threatening our confidence in the pharmaceutical industry.

Do-It-Yourself Genetics — Americans love to work on our houses, so the next step could very well be to start tinkering with our bodies. Marvin Minskey, one of the founders of the MIT Media Lab, says that "Amateurs may be fooling around with black-market genetic manipulation . . . extending their lives by lengthening their own telemeres, the ends of chromosomes believed to control life span. Or they might, in fact, be growing new features in their brain." And you thought fixing the roof was dangerous.

Embryo Menus — the ultimate decision in our culture of multiple options. Advances in fertilization technology will give you your choice of the baby you want. A number of eggs will be fertilized simultaneously, and advanced genetic testing will let parents go well beyond the baby's sex and health to choose between the artist and the astronomer, the pediatrician and the statistician, Republican and Democrat. See also *pre-implantation genetic diagnoses.*

Gene Busters — a reaction to the increasingly widespread belief that our genes predetermine our fate. We will see nutritional supplements and stress-reduction clinics labeled as gene busters as well as other programs to help us transcend (and rewrite) our destiny.

Gene Cuisine — the tongue-in-cheek name that will be given to foods and meals that contain genetically modified organisms. See also *frankenfish.*

GENEology — while traditional genealogy is based on lineage, the new area of GENEology will be based on tracking the disease history of your family. In those cases where it is possible to conduct genetic research—based on hair or tissue samples for example—GENEology will include DNA testing. Some

Bb

people will be desperate to find out if they got Grandpa's gene for Alzheimer's along with his impressive nose. We expect a quiet but profound controversy to emerge as some dedicated GENEologists seek to exhume their diseased relatives to gain more genetic insight and information.

Genetocracy — the new genetic aristocracy; an elite based on either a uniquely valuable gene pool, or a successful gene transplant or manipulation. The process of creating this rarefied group, in the projective phrase of Lucas Hanft, is "genetrification." See also *genetic underclass.*

Thumbing — also *thumbed.* A colloquialism derived from the process of identifying oneself by inserting a thumb into a scanning device. (See also *biometrics.*) If you're accepted, you've been thumbed. If you're bounced, you've been de-thumbed, as in "I tried to get into the building, but I was de-thumbed at the door."

Womb Service — describes the controversial practice of out-of-body fertilization and gestation, still illegal in the United States. Precise womb-like conditions are replicated via an artificial placenta and other innovations. For a woman, age and child-bearing become independent; for a man, egg purchase plus Womb Service create the possibility of solo fatherhood.

The changing nature and shape of families—and the stresses they are enduring—are striking catalysts for the evolution of language. Ancient and never-ending battles like permissiveness vs. a firm hand give us "affirmative parenting," while new tensions—growing out of technology, competition and affluence—bring us to "financial parenting" and other newly minted terms that are both mirrors and engines of the debates. Similarly, the long and well-chronicled demise of the nuclear family takes us to a place where "skipped generation households" are newly important forces.

As we move forward, and continuing demographic shifts rush us to a more pluralistic and ethnically intense society, the *Dictionary of the Future* expects that we will also witness the rise of "comparative parenting." This discipline will examine ethnic differences with regard to child rearing, and how these cultural practices are influenced by the great leveling forces of American life.

Throughout all this, in the struggle between parents and children, each side says, "But you aren't listening to me." We hear language itself saying the very same thing, and by heeding it, we may better be able to mediate the complexities and inconsistencies of our lives.

Affirmative Parenting — a tough-parenting reaction to Dr. Spock and all his heirs. Dr. John Rosemond, who was trained as a family psychologist, is one of the leaders of this movement; *The New York Times* called him the "Johnny Appleseed of discipline" because he travels eight months of the year, planting the seeds of strictness as he lectures and hectors the public. He believes that parents are shirking their responsibilities in order to be their kids' friends, and that they must "properly assume the awesome power of parenthood." His Web site—www.rosemond.com—will tell you all you need to know. This debate—which sits at the sweet spot where politics, psychology and culture meet—will drive much of our national dialogue in the years to come. The net net: we may have made extraordinary strides in mapping our DNA, but when it comes to raising those unpredictable little collections of genomes, we're still in the dark.

Baby Signing — a controversial new practice that teaches babies how to communicate by "signing" before they are old enough to speak—as young as six months. Advocates argue that the practice—which was codified and promoted by Dr. Joseph Garcia—reduces frustration, gives babies a sense of control and lets parents communicate with their children earlier, and more successfully. Critics believe that the process has little value, and can actually slow the natural process of learning to speak. It seems to us that the pressure to turn babies into tiny communication factories is an outgrowth of our urgent need to accelerate the development of our children and make them smarter, faster. Many, like Neil Postman, author of the seminal *Disappearance of Childhood*, are highly critical of a society that over-programs and over-stimulates children. Nonetheless, baby signing is probably an unstoppable force, and it won't be long before a major baby products marketer, like J&J, jumps on the bandwagon, or before we see a whole industry of Signing-Friendly Day Care Centers. See also *free-range children*.

Boomerang Parents — we know about boomerang children—older kids who moved away, only to return to the nest due to divorce or financial distress. Boomerang parents, a term coined by Flora Hanft, are a different phenomenon entirely. They involve a parent—usually a father—who had no role—or a limited one—in raising his children after a divorce. Much later, this distant parent gets sick and finds himself with no choice but to move in with one of his children, thus creating all sorts of emotional fallout: between the missing dad and his child, his son- or daughter-in-law, and his grandchildren. Before the rise in the divorce rate, this situation rarely presented itself, but given the current divorce statistics—and the increasing age of those in the first great "divorce wave"—*DOF* predicts more boomerang parents than anyone ever expected.

The Delay Debate — the trend toward women having children later is being challenged by new evidence that suggests there are hidden health problems inherent in that decision— well beyond Down's syndrome (which can be tested for). A study in the journal *Epidemiology* found that certain cancers, including brain cancer and leukemia, show up more often in children born to older mothers. Other research has found that female offspring of some older mothers might be predisposed to breast cancer. Fathers don't get off the hook any easier. Older dads, it seems, correlate with a lowering of IQ. And both older dads and moms were linked in a British study to a higher risk of childhood diabetes—with moms, the risk increased 25 percent with each five-year age band. The irony is that as fertility research is making it easier for older parents to have babies, these new findings are shifting the debate. More to come.

Family Tech Guru — the person in the household, usually a child, who is the go-to computer expert. Computer manufacturers report that a surprising number of callers on the customer service line are kids. Researchers at Carnegie Mellon have put it nicely: "those with the least seniority have the most authority." *DOF* wonders why more hardware and software companies haven't marketed to the family tech guru—a mechanism to create customers today, and tomorrow. (As

EVEolution puts it, in terms of marketing to women: one generation will lead you to another.)

Filiarchy — coined by Prof. James McNeal at Texas A&M University to describe the growing power of children within the family to influence decisions such as where they go on vacation, what car they lease, what movies they see, what food they consume. (He also calls it "Kid-fluence.") This is driven by the guilt that working parents feel; Professor McNeal estimates that children under 12 directly influence $248.7 billion of spending by their parents. Previous generations were able to stand up to all sorts of global and domestic threats; today, we can't even stand up to our children.

Financial Parenting — teaching the newly wealthy how to raise children who aren't completely and utterly spoiled by their good fortune. Investment banks, who have helped create this wealth, are starting to offer Financial Parenting services to their clients. *Wired* magazine reports that "In the past two years, Merrill Lynch and Co. has seen growing demand for 'financial parenting' services that help with the problems some families face in dealing with sudden wealth." Lawrence Balter, an author and expert on parenting, weighs in with this advice: "Parents also should make a point to show children that many people are not as privileged. Go to a food drive. Even if your Range Rover drives you to the shelter, at least they can help dole out food and see people in need." That'll sure teach 'em compassion. See also *trust slugs*.

Free-Range Children — twenty-first-century kids who are raised in the spirit of an earlier era, without fear, without being chauffered from play-date to play-date, without being over-programmed. The opposite of "free-range children" is "battery children," and we are following the arc of this evocative and valuable language with great fascination. We've seen it used in Australia and England. From Australia: "The concept of 'battery children' as opposed to 'free range' children . . . escorted by car from home to school and so forth instead of independently transporting themselves as was the case 25 years ago, [has] negative impact on their personal development." From a column in the *London Times:* "If you believe that you will be judged by how clean you keep your children, how well you protect them, how many activities you lay on for them, then your children will end up battery-reared and hopelessly unprepared for adult life." And from our own *Entertainment Weekly,* in a review of the fine Barbara Kingsolver novel *Poisonwood Bible:* "In the beckoning kingdom of Kingsolver, thinking women . . . responsive men . . . and free-range children can live in harmony, breathe clean air, and listen to National Public Radio." Expect to see these polarities frame much of our debate about child-rearing in the battery-controlled years to come. See also *clean time, imagination therapists.*

Infantile Amnesia — once, we thought that babies couldn't remember anything before they turned three. Now, we are learning that they can. Andrew Melzoff of the University of Washington is quoted in *Newsweek* as saying, "We used to think that infantile amnesia was because memories were never laid down in the first place . . . now it seems more likely that early memories are laid down and we just can't access them." That should sound a cautionary note for parents. And it also holds forth the promise of psycho-restorative (our phrase) drugs that can help us, as adults, find those early neural pathways. But only if we want to. See also *pain memory.*

Intimate Terrorism — it's a notch below domestic abuse and violence, but captures another level of power and control within a relationship.

Little Emperor Syndrome — China's declining birthrate and its enforced single-child policy have created a situation where only children are being smothered by attention and spoiling. This is known as the Little Emperor Syndrome, for obvious reasons; it is also characterized as the 4-2-1 effect to reflect an upside-down pyramid of four grandparents and two parents focused obsessively on the wants, whims (and whines) of one child. Interestingly, the problem is spreading. Writing of the breakdown of discipline and respect for traditional authority in Japan, the *Washington Post* says that "Japan might also be experiencing the little emperor syndrome that has caused problems in Chinese schools. The Japanese birthrate has dropped to a historic low of 1.4 children per couple. Those children, especially in an affluent society, are more likely to be lavished with attention and material goods." As for America—the global leader in materialism—with our growing number of older and single parents we have our very own Little Emperor crisis.

Mannies — coined by *USA Today* to describe the unexpected growth of both domestic and foreign-born male nannies. The Intelligence Factory, a unit of ad agency Young & Rubicam, believes that "as more older men become fathers, a new breed of young, athletic male nannies will emerge to take on the more demanding aspects of the job . . . teaching a child to ride a bike, playing ball in the park." While it will take some cultural shifts to accept them, *DOF* concurs that the trend will continue. The cultural implications could be profound, and healthy—as men are increasingly seen in caregiver roles, young children will be less likely to fall into traditional male/female stereotyping. An anthropological twist driven by child-care supply and demand.

Media History — recognizing that the amount of time spent in front of the tube has profound emotional and physical effects on young people, the American Academy of Pediatrics now recommends that viewing habits be made part of a child's record. Though there is still some debate, experts are increasingly in agreement that social skills and neurological development can be influenced by violence and other visual assaults. Expect more and more attention to be paid to the subject, as the Internet increases the need for, and difficulty of, ensuring an optimum media history. And expect that the adults of the future will be telling their shrinks that they spent too much time watching "South Park" and not enough watching "Sesame Street."

Pets' Rights — a legal movement that is pressing courts to treat pets not as property or livestock, but as something akin to humans. The movement has had success: pet owners have won malpractice judgments, have collected for emotional distress and loss of companionship. As *Governing* magazine writes, the number of states that have designated animal cruelty a felony has quadrupled from seven in 1994 to 31 in 2000. Barry Herbeck, a Wisconsin resident, was slammed with a ten-year sentence for killing five cats. Daniel Lee Williams of Oakland, California, is serving four years for killing a Labrador (with a machete). New York has passed Buster's Law; New Mexico, a statute inspired by Dunkin the cat. Twelve law schools, including Georgetown and Harvard, now offer courses in animal law.

All this is to be expected given our national obsession with pets; pharmaceuticals for pets are projected to be a $3 billion market; there are even vacation tours for people and pets. And more than half of pet owners send their pet a birthday card. Will the next step be pets suing owners for complaints such as denial of table scraps? See also *4-star rat hotels.*

Skipped Generation Households — there are about 2.5 million families in America headed by grandparents, as a result of death, substance abuse, mental illness, jail, abandonment. Skipped generation households create all sorts of social complications, including legal issues, battles over grandparent rights, housing and day care. As we would expect, the government and the social service infrastructure has been slow to recognize this new unit, just as it has been slow to recognize other non-traditional family shapes. What will it take for us to come to terms with the fact that the nuclear family has been nuked?

Trust Slugs — the children of the wealthy who live off the accomplishments of others. As Scott Cooper, who runs Merrill Lynch's family office (for those with assets north of $100 million), says: "they fear their children will turn into 'trust-slugs' who are dependent on family money and have no incentive to follow a career." See also *financial parenting.*

Cc

Bamnesia — will be coined by defenders of video games and action movies to make the point that the temporary violence of these experiences is quickly forgotten by children, leaving no permanent impression or damage. See also *media history*.

Childhood Restorers — over-programmed, over–video gamed, and over-computered, today's children don't know how to stretch their imaginations and revel in their natural creativity. That's why *DOF* believes that a generation of play-deprived kids will need a new kind of childhood restorer to help them get in touch with their inner kid. As Alvin Rosenfeld, co-author of *The Over-Scheduled Child,* has observed, today's obsession with raising young Einsteins might have destroyed the real Einstein. See also *free-range children, natural kids*.

Clean Time — a higher level of free time. Recognizing that children are being overly programmed, parents will make sure that kids have enough clean time in their days. (We're actually seeing seven-year-olds with PalmPilots and Visors.) Expect to see books, Web sites, seminars and other cultural manifestations of this trend, which also is an outgrowth of the data smog that is choking the rest of us. See also *free-range children*.

Comparative Parenting — as America becomes more diverse—with moms and apple pie being complemented by mom and tortilla pie—a new discipline will emerge that examines the ways traditional, ethnic approaches to child rearing and family dynamics shape—and in turn, are shaped by—the greater culture.

Fight Chat — family counselors will soon discover an unexpected—and happy—marriage between the Internet and therapy. They will advise couples who are in the midst of a slugfest to separate, head for their separate computers (or wireless devices), and continue to fight via instant messaging: techno cool-down. The very act of communicating with each other in sequence lets each side get their message across, as opposed to yelling at the top of their lungs. Fight chat helps defuse the situation and let the couple return to rationality. Also, it's easy to say hurtful things, but it's different when you see that harshness on the screen in front of you.

Mariticide (also **mariticidal) —** derived from all the "cides" of our lives—fratricide, suicide, patricide. Describes the act of destroying a marriage, which can be immediate—infidelity comes to mind—or slow and insidious, as in "it turns out that moving from San Francisco to Omaha was an act of geographic mariticide."

Marriage Simulation — enterprising software geniuses, working with psychologists and family therapists, will develop a program that will help couples determine how compatible they are together. Each potential partner will enter attitudes, behavioral characteristics and belief systems, including politics and religion. The software will, in turn, present you with real-life scenarios about in-laws, children, money, sex. You and your prospective mate can see what it's like to live together, fight together, raise children together. Could be the best investment you ever make.

MUTTS — the rapid growth of immigration is changing the face of America: 40 percent of New York City residents were born outside the United States; the overall population of the country will be 30 percent Hispanic by 2010, and there are more than 15 subsets of Hispanic ethnicity. The result, children of diverse, multiracial backgrounds who will take to lightheartedly calling themselves MUTTS—for Multiple Upbringings Talking Together. See also *majority-minority society.*

National Parent Permits — you need a license to drive, of course. You also need a permit to become a beautician. Yet parenting requires no training or certification of any kind. In an attempt to address this, a movement will emerge to assure that parents are prepared, educated and capable of bringing up healthy and productive children. These nonprofits will require that parents take a course and a follow-up exam to get their National Parent Permits. The motivation? Major manufacturers and service providers, from Procter & Gamble to Allstate to Ford, will give discounts and special benefits to those who have their permits.

Natural Kids — a movement that seeks to eliminate the multiple dependencies that are victimizing millions of children. The Natural Kids movement will fight the power of behavioral drugs like Ritalin, of television and video games and other electronic baby-sitters, of a nutritionally bankrupt diet loaded with fast food and soft drinks (the average kid drinks 800 cans a year). Books, seminars, support groups and a grass-roots effort will make Natural Kids a national rallying cry that will attract politicians from both sides of the aisle. See also *clean time, free-range children.*

Pre-Custodial Arrangements — in the next (and logical) step after pre-nups, pre-custodial agreements will provide in-advance child custody guidelines (and this before the first place settings arrive via UPS). While it is less than romantic, the bitter custody fights that many couples get caught up in suggest that the concept is not without merit.

Second-Chance Theory — a sociological hypothesis which will argue that one of the most important differences between the children of the underclass and the children of the middle-class and upperclass is that the latter are granted a second chance. If a kid from the inner city is arrested for shoplifting, or drunk driving, or smoking a joint, it's just about impossible for him or her to bounce back. But if a kid with assets and influence goes astray, an armada of lawyers and psychologists rushes to his or her aid. Based on this theory, a number of nonprofit groups will emerge to take on the challenge of giving deserving kids of all economic groups a second chance.

The arrangement of people on the planet is shifting in ways that may not be as loud and unprecedented as the migration to the cities during the Industrial Revolution, but are still profound and complex. Indeed, when we stepped back from this section and inspected the totality of the entries, we were struck by one undeniable theme: the push and pull that results from increasing concentrations of people.

The intensity of human beings in closer proximity than ever before—which is closer, no doubt, than we are evolutionarily equipped to handle—creates the push: the heat-island effect, commute cancer, and sprawlout—as well as "O-squared" cities, a *DOF* coinage for places where over population will be exponential.

The pull, on the other hand, is an urge to withdraw and to separate, reflected in terms like lifestyle enclaves and open-space taxes—where people are happily voting to raise their taxes to preserve the little open space left. Trying to manage all these conflicts: the New Urbanists, who want to cope with development by changing the way we think about zoning. At the same time, the fast-growing Hispanic population is changing the sights, sounds and styles of American cities, creating a vibrant, emotionally charged Magical Urbanism.

In short, just as cities produce ideas, success, and despair, they produce words. And just as cities concentrate people, they hyper focus just about every aspect of life today, which is why the words that follow squeeze together everything from technology and demographics to retailing, immigration and the economics of the cemetery.

City Entry Fees — the mayor of Florence has proposed a tax on all visitors. As the British newspaper *The Guardian* reports: "Tourists who flock to Florence may soon be charged an admission fee to enter the city. Renaissance palaces and squares make it an open-sky museum meriting a tax on visitors, says the mayor, Leonardo Domenici. Money to maintain such treasures is running out." The fee would be added to hotel and restaurant bills, and would help to offset the enormous costs of maintenance and restoration. While the proposal may not succeed this time, *DOF* believes it is inevitable that fees of this kind will be charged in culture-rich but cash-hungry European cities. Further, some American destinations that are engulfed by tourists and have high levels of infrastructure costs—New Orleans, Key West, Aspen, Santa Fe—might also adopt similar measures. See also *tourist subsidies*.

City Trademarks — cities with less-than-appealing names are taking a lesson from Hollywood and changing their monikers to something with more marketing punch. Residents of Dania, Florida, approved a referendum to change their name to Dania Beach, and North Tarrytown, New York, became Sleepy Hollow, seeking to capture the romance of Washington Irving's books. In a much publicized move, the tiny town of Halfway, Oregon (population 360), changed its name to Half.com when the town and the Web site agreed to enter into a strategic partnership that included a donation of 20 computers to the school, and funds for civic improvement. *DOF* expects that we will see a flurry of these municipal name changes, both to create more powerful or romantic names for industry and tourism, and to escape the sins and scourges of the past. (Who'd want to live in Love Canal, even now?) It's to be expected from a society that idolizes change and worships at the shrine of re-invention. See *cool consultants*.

Commute Cancer — describes all the harmful effects of commuting, including the stress, the lost productivity, the stolen family time. With commutes getting longer, as sprawl forces families to move further from central cities, commute cancer is getting worse. The phrase was coined by a man named Jack

Niles, who is credited with dreaming up the phrase "telecommuting" when he was director of information technology at the University of Southern California. *DOF* wonders if all the publicity—and faith in—telecommuting as an option has caused us to lose sight of the need for improved mass transit—like light rail—to address commute cancer.

Conservation Communities — a new kind of low-density housing development in which just a few upscale homes are built in areas that otherwise remain preserved, albeit for marketing not altruistic reasons. *The Wall Street Journal* calls it a "rustic nature preserve with a few homes." These communities, which are located close to metropolitan centers, are supported by environmentalists and local authorities because they preserve open space. One such conservation community, in Irvine, California, will feature a "habitat-sensitive golf course" and will "preserve native grasses, rock outcroppings and coastal sage scrub"; others feature equestrian centers and all boast vast amounts of open space. It's yet another example of the trend in which the free market is made the friend—as opposed to the satanic foe—of the environment. See also *conservation concessions*.

Graves vs. Growth — as rural and suburban growth continues to march through the countryside, communities are faced with the problem of the cemeteries that stand in their way. It's a stunning crystallization of the struggle between the past and the present in the starkest of all terms. There is no easy solution as many planners don't even have access to maps that indicate the presence of these sacred areas. Recognizing this, Texas created the Official Historic Texas Cemetery Designation Program in 1998. But even with official support, so far they have designated only "130 cemeteries out of the 40,000 to 50,000 located in the state" according to *Governing* magazine. And that wasn't before two tiny cemeteries ended up squeezed between runways at the Austin-Bergstrom International Airport. *Governing* writes that "Cemeteries nationwide are threatened by burgeoning subdivisions, new shopping centers and other development that often comes to surround what were once peaceful havens." One solution: the "adopt-a-cemetery" program which is up for a vote in the Texas legislature in 2001. It's only logical that corporations and nonprofits will jump on this; what better way to show respect for the past?

Heat Island Effect — cities produce a lot of intellectual, literary and artistic heat—as well as just plain warmth. That is called the Heat Island Effect; temperatures in Los Angeles, for example, can soar to more than ten degrees higher than surrounding areas. This has implications for energy consumption, air pollution and, of course, the comfort and health of those who live there. The Heat Island Group is a collection of scientists whose solutions include the "Green Roof program," which has planted trees and gardens on top of Chicago's and Toronto's City Halls. Activist groups, such as TreePeople in Los Angeles, are also working to encourage community-based efforts at planting trees. We will be hearing a lot about the Heat Island effect as global warming intensifies the problem.

Hotel Reclamation — across the country, every variety of classic old building is being preserved and converted into luxury lodgings. The renovation of once-great hotels is easy, but developers have also converted an old molasses factory (in New Orleans), a City Hall annex (in Philadelphia), the original Citadel military school (in Charleston) and a classic courthouse (in St. Augustine). The trend marries the need for downtown hotel space with our growing desire to be simultaneously cool and classical. Plus, the conversions are cheaper than building new hotels, and developers get tax credits as well. See also *industrial cool.*

Immigrant Recruitment — there are areas in the United States where many workers are entering retirement and the population is stable or declining. As a result, local industry is having trouble filling the available jobs. To fill the void, Iowa has a program to attract Bosnian and Vietnamese refugees to cities that are 98 percent white and non-ethnic. We expect this trend to continue, and not just in America. Western countries that are experiencing low birth rates—and often negative population growth—will also have to rely on immigrants to keep their economies humming. Italy, for example, has the lowest birth rate in Western Europe; by the middle of the century its population will drop by 9 million people. Thus, irony of ironies, after years of restrictive policies and political struggles on the continent over immigration, countries will try to outdo each other with cash-rich "immigrant bounties" to attract foreign workers. See also *virtual immigrants*.

Infill — describes the redevelopment—and often reclamation—of decaying or abandoned areas in mature cities. For years, these areas went untouched. As the magazine *Scientific American* noted, there was a 30-year period when Detroit went without issuing a single new housing permit. Now, as increasing property values, gentrification, new cultural institutions and a return to the central city by both large businesses and start-ups makes neglected patches of the central city more attractive, mayors and urban planners are looking at the best ways to manage infill. See also *brownfields*.

JVC Cultural and Business Plan — this is a grand (if not grandiose) plan to create a new kind of city outside Guadalajara in Mexico. It is the vision of Mexican billionaire Jorge Vergara, who made his money selling nutritional supplements through a network marketing company called Omnilife (a company so large that more than one-tenth of Mexico's population are "distributors," or salespeople). Vergara has bought more than 600 acres of land for his vision of an integrated cultural, business and educational destination, and has managed to seduce and corral eleven of the world's leading architects to build his city—which he envisions will do for Guadalajara what the Guggenheim did for Bilbao, but on an even more stunning scale.

Philip Johnson, the legendary American architect, is included among those who will create JVC from the ground up, as is Daniel Libeskind—who is responsible for the widely hailed Jewish Museum in Berlin. Libeskind will be designing its "University of Success"—its buildings will give the illusion of smashing into one another, as a metaphor for inter-disciplinary studies. Skeptics abound—they automatically surface when any project of this scope is undertaken—but Vergara has already confounded them by buying the land and paying the architects. He expects to attract 25 million visitors a year (Las Vegas attracts 38 million). If JVC succeeds—and Vergara expects it to be finished in six years—it could be the beginning of a trend that finds visionary billionaires building cities, emerging as today's pharaohs.

Lifestyle Enclaves — named by sociologist Robert Bellah. He believes that we are replacing traditional communities, which are characterized by a true population diversity, with clusters of people who are linked by shared values and habits, and who seek the security of sameness. There is comfort to be derived when surrounded by people who watch the same Miramax movies as you do, wear the same khakis from the Gap and drive the same Ford Expedition. Even in urban areas, where there should be a coming together—even a healthy collision—of individuals from different experience zones, lifestyle enclaves are proliferating.

Magical Urbanism — a term coined by writer Mike Davis in his book of that title to describe the profound influence that the Hispanic population and its culture and values are having on urban life in America. Writing of the Latino influence on New York and L.A., Davis says that "New York and Los Angeles are, respectively, the second and third largest metropolitan economies on earth . . . and their ethnic transformation mirrors a decisive national trend with important international resonances . . . Salsa is becoming the predominant ethnic flavor—and rhythm—in major U.S. metropolitan areas." The changing nature of America's urbanscapes will have immense economic and social implications; they represent the multi-hued face of America's future. See also *majority-minority society; Neoyorquinos, Tejanos, MUTTS.*

New Urbanists — a group of urban planners with a new set of design principles. Their ideas are drawn from an ecological concept called the "transect"—the way that nature transitions gradually and effectively from one condition to another, wetland to upland, for example. New Urbanists want to apply those successful principles to urban and suburban design, and the movement from city to countryside. The idea is to replace a single standard—for example, street width, housing density, landscape design—with decisions that are appropriate for each section of the transect. This would make for more vibrant suburban towns that "unite the places of daily life—the dwellings, shops and workplaces" says Andres Duany, a New Urbanist and influential town planner. New Urbanists also have solutions for bankrupt shopping malls; one in Mountain View, California, was replaced with a mix of shops, homes and offices. For more information, go to the Web site of the Congress for the New Urbanism, www.cnu.org. See also *smart growth, sprawl out, telesprawl.*

Open Space Taxes — it's a way to fight sprawl with dollars. Confronted with developers who are swallowing up available land at every turn, homeowners are doing something they've never done before: actually voting to have their taxes raised so that remaining open space can be bought by their local governments. From New Jersey (where the program is known as "Green Acres") to Denver to L.A. to Chicago, voters have said yes to land preservation bonds. Phyllis Myers a leader in conservation financing, called it "definitely a striking trend." But *DOF* wonders: why don't local merchants, retailers and corporations join in to help, by allocating a percentage of every purchase to the open space movement? What better way to develop a relationship with your consumers then by helping them fight over-development? See also *conservation communities.*

Smart Growth — an urban planning philosophy which isn't about battling growth, but managing it sensibly and progressively. It was adopted early on by Maryland Gov. Paris Glendenning to "steer the state's infrastructure dollars . . . to discourage sprawl and encourage development or redevelopment in already settled communities." Since Maryland's focus on controlling unchecked expansion "Smart growth has been trumpeted nationally, by environmentalists, planners, slow-growth advocates, anti-sprawl enthusiasts . . . as one of the most compelling solutions yet devised . . . for the inequities and public expense created by sprawl." A long quote for an important trend—Smart Growth will become a catch-phrase of twenty-first-century politics, along with stem cell research and a woman's right to choose. See also *telesprawl* and *sprawl out.*

Sprawl Out — describes unchecked suburban growth, also called the sprawl brawl. In 1998, there were 200 sprawl initiatives on the ballot, including SOAR in Ventura County, California, short for Save Open Space and Agricultural Resources. See also *smart growth, telesprawl.*

Telesprawl — an unintended consequence of telecommuting. Freed from the daily grind, office-liberated workers relocate beyond typical commuting range, creating new kinds of environmental stresses and strains in formerly rural neighborhoods. When Agways are replaced by Starbucks, blame telesprawl.

Toxic Checks — for the first time, the Department of Housing and Urban Affairs and the EPA have gotten together to make it easy for homebuyers—or any concerned party, for that matter—to find out the dirty little secret of any neighborhood. Log onto www.hud.gov/emaps and zero in on the presence of superfund cleanup sites, brownfields, toxic release areas, waste-handling sites and other environmental assaults, in any zip code in the country. Never has location, location, location meant more, more, more.

UrbanAmerica — the first real estate investment company that deals exclusively with those urban areas that no developer wants to touch. According to *Time*, "So far, UrbanAmerica has acquired $110 million worth of commercial property." The company was founded by Richard McCoy, whose real estate management firm is the largest entity controlled by an African American. McCoy started by helping churches in poor neighborhoods develop their properties, and then sought to become a more dynamic change agent. UrbanAmerica is innovative beyond its location strategy: at one shopping center in Maryland, they are building a 22,000-square-foot police station which will reduce neighborhood crime—and increase property values. From developing properties to becoming a brand is the next step, and we imagine that UrbanAmerica will start putting its name on the concepts it develops, and then move beyond to other retail platforms—perhaps movie theaters or supermarkets—letting consumers know that they're putting money back into the community by shopping there.

Dictionary of the Future Predicts

Mom and Pop Rescue — threatened by malls and national chains, mom and pop stores—an icon of America's past—are an economic endangered species. *DOF* believes that those that remain, supported by local civic groups, will form a "Mom and Pop Rescue Campaign." The effort will celebrate the role that mom and pop stores play, and utilize advertising to encourage consumers to shop there. Talented designers will contribute their services to design a "Classic Mom and Pop" logo that member stores will feature. Credit card companies— which charge merchants based on volume—will make a special exception for Classic Mom and Pops, charging them less per transaction as a show of support. Local governments might also start offering tax abatements to help them survive. From hardware stores to bookstores to the local independent coffee house, mom and pops offer texture and eccentricity that are clearly under pressure in our homogenized age, and once lost, it cannot be recovered.

O-Squared Cities — stands for over-population, squared. By 2015, according to the United Nations, there will be 26 megacities around the world, with 22 of them in developing regions. They include Bombay, India, with a projected 26 million people; Lagos, Nigeria, with 24 million; and Dhaka, Bangladesh, with 19 million. This density will create a host of biological and environmental programs. Says Richard Preston, author of *The Hot Zone*, "Take all of California, cram those people into one city, remove most doctors and medical care, take away basic sanitation and hygiene, and what you have is a ticking biological time bomb. Now make eight or ten such bombs and plant them around the world." It's a scary thought, and certainly puts the inability to get a cab in rush hour into urban-nightmare perspective.

Reservoir Patrols — spurred by recent terrorist attacks, the thousands upon thousands of reservoirs around the country will soon be regularly patrolled by a combination of local police, private security and the military. But the sheer scope of the task, and the limited available resources, mean that thousands of miles of reservoir "shorelines" will remain unprotected. See also *terror entrepreneurs*.

Split City Living — affluent urbanites won't be satisfied with one place to live in their respective cities; they'll want two. One condo (or co-op, in New York) might be in a more conservative, established neighborhood, and the other in a funky, "downtown" location. For those who work at home, one apartment would be where the office is located, the other would be their urban getaway. The only problem: remembering where you left the dog (or the kids for that matter). See also *aging in place, reurbanize*.

Language, like computers themselves, is in a state of continual upgrade, improving its ability to process a changing world. Those who fretted over the allegedly chilling effect that computer technology would have on creativity couldn't have been more wrong.

What we have seen, in fact, is exactly the opposite. Under pressure from the explosion of computers at work and at home, the expansion of language—metaphorical and otherwise—has been nothing short of remarkable. Old words—"click," "memory," "mailbox," "icon"—have taken on bright new colors. Newer language – "download," "unstuff"— have become second nature. (Here, we must pause to pay tribute to John Turkey, a former statistics professor at Princeton who invented the word "bit" for binary digit in 1946, and gave us the earliest known use of software in 1958).

In this section we have sought to give you a window (there's another one) into what's next. They include computing revolutions in the works, everything from quantum and silicon-free computing, to the notion of community computing—which is attempting to consolidate the processing power of billions of individual computers into a giant brain, an immense planetary organ.

These words, of course, are just the beginning. Everyone who touches a computer—journalists, poets, grandparents, accountants—seems driven, almost ritualistically, to seek new words and phrases that define their experience, their relationship to this new force. As primitive cultures invented words and stories to contain and explain the unpredictable, change-making powers of nature, so too do we stretch language to help us name and proportion what is happening around us.

Affective Computing — a vast area of development which is focused on the creation of technology that can recognize human emotion, and adapt accordingly. Much of this work is going on at the MIT Media Lab (www.media.mit.edu/affect/), where such far-out ideas as affective wearables and affective jewelry are under development. Imbedded sensors in these items will monitor your biological signals and react—for example, recognizing your brain waves and delivering music to relieve stress or cheer you up—through Orpheus, the Affective CD player. Another kind of affective wearable, as MIT writes, would be a "fear detector" that works along with a WearCam; it would "capture a wide-angle view of the environment . . . and transmit the wearer's position, viewpoint, and fear state to a personal safety net," a community of friends or family with whom you felt secure. Used in still a different way, affective computing could enable teaching software to understand when you are frustrated, and then slow down the process or try a different teaching technique. All this sounds spectacular, but one might ask: If they can't write an instruction manual we can understand, how can they write software that can understand us?

Artificial Etiquette — computers and Web sites are being programmed to interact with people in a way that reflects the fundamentals of social relationships in the real world. As the *Financial Times* observes, "We follow the same social rules with computers that apply with people, and we expect the same of machines in return." The idea behind artificial etiquette is to create this same social contract on the Internet—and researchers argue that it's pivotal.

Blue Gene — nickname for a massive IBM project, launched in 1999 and budgeted at $100 million, to build the world's fastest supercomputer. Blue Gene, which will be 500 times more powerful than the fastest current computers, will be capable of more than one quadrillion calculations per second, which will make it able to take on some of the most complex tasks in computational biology. That includes understanding the mechanism of protein folding, which IBM has called a "grand challenge" and will "give scientists and doctors better insight into diseases and ways to combat them ... pharmaceutical companies could design high-tech prescription drugs customized to the specific needs of individual people." (See also *pharmacogenomics*.) Fifty people are working on Blue Gene, which IBM believes can be built in record time because it utilizes a new computer architecture called SMASH—Simple, Many and Self-Healing.

Brain-Machine Interfaces — based on a deep and unprecedented understanding of how the brain works, this technology will allow the mind to control a variety of devices—from a motorized wheelchair to even prosthetic limbs. Early results are demonstrating that this is more than elegant theory. Phillip Kennedy, a neurologist at Emory University, has developed a brain implant that has permitted paralyzed patients to move a cursor on a computer screen just by thinking. At MIT, scientists have sent electrical signals from the brain of an owl monkey to a robot, which was able to mimic the monkey's arm movements, in real time. As Miguel Nicolelis, one of the leaders in the field, puts it—tersely and provocatively: "Imagine if someone could do for the brain what the pacemaker did for the heart."

Community Computing — also called collaborative or distributed computing. A revolutionary concept that utilizes the processing power in the millions of Internet-connected computers when they aren't being used, community computing shares similarities with Napster—it leverages the power of the network, but it goes even further by creating a giant brain out of many smaller ones. ("Machines have no business sleeping," notes Richard Crandall, distinguished scientist at Apple.)

The process is simple: you download software that lets your networked computer crunch numbers when you're not working at it. Individuals can donate their computing power—there's a not-for-profit market emerging through an organization called distributed.net—or you can be compen-

Cc

sated. In fact, several companies, including Popular Power, are attempting to create markets where computing power can be purchased.

Community computing is ideal for huge processing tasks, like designing synthetic drugs or mapping the weather. The largest operation is SETI@Home—the Search for Extra-Terrestrial Intelligence at the University of California, where millions of linked global computers process information obtained from a radio telescope (http://www.setiathome.ssl.berkeley.edu/).

Fluid Documents — currently in development at PARC (Xerox's legendary Palo Alto Research Center), this technology could change the way documents are presented on the Internet. Rather than remaining a static page, fluid documents will change and morph as we look at them; as the *MIT Technology Review* writes, "elements of an electronic document smoothly rearrange themselves to make room for more information." So rather than having to go from one site to another, you could get a preview of the next site; it would politely elbow aside the text or graphics, or appear as an overlay. The growth of handheld devices, with screens the size of matchbooks, highlights the need for imaginative solutions for organizing content. See also *wet signature*.

Quantum Computing — an entirely new way of building computers that was once only a theoretical possibility, but has achieved practical reality. Quantum computing, as *The Wall Street Journal* puts it, "may achieve . . . unimagined speeds by figuring out all possible solutions to a problem simultaneously." The "computing" is done by molecules, which replace chips. These atomic particles—which are known as "qubits"—can be manipulated to represent "one" and "zero," which is the basis of all computing. A radio wave stimulates the molecules—functioning as the computer's "program," as we know it today—and the computing process begins. Using the laws of quantum mechanics, each qubit exchanges information with neighboring qubits, which is the quantum computing equivalent of what happens electronically in conventional computers. Expect to see the real revolution in five to ten years, when a "classical computer can't catch up with quantum computing anymore," says Raymond Laflamme, who heads a task force that is working on the technology at the Los Alamos laboratories.

Silicon-Free Computing — a technology that replaces silicon chips with microscopic carbon structures for a chemical-based computer that could be between one billion and 10 billion times more efficient than current alternatives. Such technology could have the "power of 50 of today's PC's" and "fit on the head of a pin" claims *Red Herring* magazine.

Unobtrusive Computing — coined by Neil Gershenfeld, research chief at MIT Media Lab, and also called ubicomputing. Describes a future in which computer power is seamlessly embedded in dozens of everyday objects from coffee cups to eyeglasses to clothing. Examples include a smart car that knows everything about the passenger so it can communicate with an airbag; file folders that use radio pulses to communicate with a smart filing cabinet; ink that can be activated/ deactivated by tiny computers in smart paper, so paper can change like a computer screen. Many of these digital information transactions will be enabled by Bluetooth (see listing). See also *pervasive computing, Internet iceberg effect.*

Dictionary of the Future Predicts

Counterbit — the practice of creating counterfeit software, which is a huge problem both here and abroad, and will grow more serious, causing a rift between the software companies— who want vigorous enforcement—and the government, who doesn't want to alienate our trading partners, notably China. (Coined by Simon Hanft.)

Ghost in the System — a reference to someone or something that lingers in one's life long after it is officially gone, e.g., "I'm doing my best to move on, but my old boyfriend is still a ghost in the system." The term comes from technology, specifically a data entry relating to a specific item (could be an individual or a company, for example) that is no longer valid. An individual dies, moves a number of times, changes his or her name (or sex), but the data memory remains in a main frame or hard drive or somebody's server—creating the impression that things haven't changed, when of course they have.

Page Memory — as computers and electronic books train us to read in a new way—via a fluid, pageless stream—and the physical dimensions of the printed page begin to disappear, we will lament the loss of what can best be called page memory. Page memory is both the experience of remembering where a specific passage resides on a page, as well as the satisfaction we get from finishing one chapter—savoring the literary epiphany—and starting the next. See also *fluid documents*.

Scroll-Reading — the online or downloaded equivalent of speed-reading; rapid scrolling down a computer screen (or the screen of a Web-enabled cell phone or PDA) enables the reader to capture the essence of a thesis or argument (or an email) without line-by-line processing. Scroll-reading techniques, classes and groups will quickly emerge, leading us to wonder: Where is the Evelyn Wood of the computer age?

For years, American business manufactured a lot of things—steel, automobiles, the Pet Rock—but it didn't produce a lot of words. That's because words come from the factory of change, and much of American business—despite protestations to the contrary—was fundamentally conservative in nature.

Times have certainly changed. Consider words like "Casual Friday," "downsizing" and "spin-outs." These are all reasonably new terms in the history of American business. Yet you won't find them here, because they're not new enough for *Dictionary of the Future*.

What you will find, though, are fresh and evocative words that reflect a business environment that has rebelled against the status quo. Change and nimbleness have become a religion and that religion has a new language, some of which is captured here.

Indeed, these terms shimmer with the shifts in the structure of corporate America. Instead of the man in the gray flannel suit we have "flexecutives" and "permalance." Instead of the corner office we have the "nonterritorial office." In addition to metrics like "profitability" and "ROI" we now have to consider "organizational health." And as a way to understand the many varieties of leadership we have "productive narcissists," who have to "manage the blood supply" of their respective companies.

Indeed, this tumble of new words mirrors a complex web of economic and management challenges that could drive even the best of us to take temporary refuge in a "nap tent."

A&D — stands for Acquisition & Development, the successor to Research & Development. As complex research challenges become more costly and risky, companies will buy the insights rather than struggle with inventing them. As John Seely Brown, who ran Xerox's PARC for ten years, put it, "Larger companies can buy the research they need and instantly acquire a diverse portfolio of research groups."

Adminisphere — used to describe the high and exalted levels of a company from whence emanate all manner of directives, edicts and pronouncements that have absolutely no connection with reality. "Of course he has no idea what's going on— he works in the adminisphere." Very much the world of Dilbert.

Bankrupt Words — when a big corporate project fails, they can fire the people but they can't fire the vocabulary that described and defined it. However, smart executives know which words are off-limits, because they instantly conjure up memories of failures past. Those are bankrupt words, and you use them at your own risk.

Boss Key — there you are, expanding your creativity and stretching the boundaries of your mind by playing a video game during office hours, and your boss has the nerve to walk into your office. No problem, just hit the boss key and you will return to a benign text page. Some sites also have a boss icon—a rendering of a grim-faced ogre that you hit to escape the game. The evil of the boss key has not escaped the attention of North Carolina's Republican Senator Lauch Fairchild, who cited it as yet another reason to ban computer games from the offices of civil servants.

Digital Decisions — crossroad business decisions that are fundamentally black and white in nature. The *Wall Street Journal* notes that Jurgen Schrempp, chairman and CEO of Daimler-Chrysler, described digital decisions as the kind of "uncompromising yes/no determinations that a computer might make." Digital decisions can only be made by a leader, not by committee, not by email votes, not by taking the temperature of the organization.

Employer of Choice — in a tight job market, employers create pro-active branding campaigns to convince current and potential employees that they are the right place to work—in other words, that they are employers of choice. *The New York Times* writes that these efforts are "part public relations campaign, part human resources experiment" and that they "seek to assure employees that no other workplace suits them better." See also *pleading economy*.

Exploding Offers — employment opportunities that are extended for a limited time, and are then withdrawn. Exploding offers are gaining in popularity; interestingly, they benefit employers both in times of high employment and recessions. In periods of high employment, employers force candidates to make up their minds quickly, thus creating urgency. During economic downturns, exploding offers give employers negotiating leverage.

Externs — a new kind of rotational employee "lent" by consultants to their clients for six to 24 months to give them operational experience and keep them happy. Mercer Management—recognizing that some of their most talented people don't just want to give advice, but want to execute— was one of the first to create externs, and others are following suit. It's also a function of an increasingly fluid economy marked by telecommuters, interim CEOs and other unorthodox structures. See also *pleading economy, trading employees*.

Flexecutives — also known as flex-execs, these are executives who run their businesses from wherever they happen to be at the moment: on a plane, at home, at a child's Little League game. Of course, technology enables this on a practical level. But for flexecutives to be truly successful they need to create a "culture of distance" by developing a support team that understands how to maximize their time and input.

Insourcing — every reaction has an equal and opposite reaction, viz Newton, and every business trend provokes an equal and opposite lurch. Now, after years of outsourcing being the reigning God of management, we are seeing the recurrence of insourcing. It has at least two meanings. The first deals with the current practice of outsourcing a vast range of systems and technology needs. The insourcing argument is that there are hidden costs and penalties associated with this: lack of continuity, demoralization of staff ("we aren't smart enough for the really big projects") and excessive costs. When they insource projects, companies maximize resources that are otherwise untapped, and gain real competitive advantages in the process through speed and marketing leadership. The second aspect of insourcing happens when an organization—for example, a manufacturing facility—takes in outside work during downtime. Moving beyond these parameters, insourcing has additional potential; in theory, why couldn't a corporate legal department take in outside work? It would make more sense to do this than to fire people when the work flow has dipped, only to have to rehire—at greater expense—when things pick up. Looking at every department as a revenue center is at the heart of the insourcing theory.

Managing the Blood Supply — making sure that management remains fresh and that new ideas continue to circulate throughout the corporate organism.

Marzipan Layer — an evocative metaphor that's passing through customs (from England) and should arrive here shortly. Cake-wise, the marzipan layer falls right below the icing—thus it describes a layer of management or influence close to the top, but not quite there. It also takes the form of the Marzipan Set. ("I know what's happening, but not what's going to happen. You see, I'm in the Marzipan layer.")

Nap Tents — Gould Evans Goodman, an architectural firm in Kansas City, is offering nap tents to its midnight-oil burning employees as an innovative perk (they call them Spent Tents). WRQ, a software company in Seattle, has nap rooms replete with futons. We expect this to catch on, given the growing recognition of the importance of the power nap, the need to keep employees happy and the coolness ambition that is driving companies to be different and act different. The motto of the fully rested organization: sometimes, the best way to get ahead is by falling asleep. See also *corporate comfy, pleading economy, work daze.*

Non-Territorial Offices — first we had traditional office configurations, and then open-space plans with workstations. The next step: non-territorial offices, where, as *The Wall Street Journal* writes, "no one, not even the boss, has his own desk." The Fraunhofer Institute in Germany is a productivity think tank that works on non-territorial concepts "that foster collaboration, communication, mobility and cost savings." Liberating workers does have practical and psychological benefits: wasted space is reduced (think how many desks and offices are empty when their occupants are traveling), and space can be configured around dedicated project teams. Additionally, creativity is spurred by changing environments. On the other hand, our nesting instinct—coffee mug, family photos, ugly paperweight—creates anxiety-reducing comfort. *DOF* believes territorial instincts are evolutionary, and office planners might not be able to undo what millions of years have wrought. Giving workers the ability to create a kind of "instant personalization"—using stored family pictures that would be downloaded to digital frames, for example—would help bridge this divide.

Organizational Health — a measure of the psychological state of a company. *The Wall Street Journal* writes that "Corporations are starting to realize that their 'psychological health' may be a major driver of costs." When companies are organizationally sick, one symptom is that employees jump ship; one study found that costs related to turnover have jumped to 37 percent of the total amount spent on health and productivity issues—up from 14 percent in 1997. Though critics will bash its New Age touchy-feelyness, *DOF* anticipates a growing focus on this concept of internal wellness, which will include organizational health as a CEO focus, the development of an accepted diagnostic system, the emergence of consultants who specialize in "healing" sick companies, and a new ratings system that ranks companies on their relative organizational health—just as it ranks them on measures such as productivity, ROI, philanthropy, and the percentage of revenue that gets invested in R&D. See *stock therapy, spot bonuses, ego audits.*

Permalance — the merger of permanent and freelance in the new economy, describing a new category of employee—usually a knowledge worker—who is both dedicated to the company, and a free agent at the same time. (At Microsoft they're called Permatemps.) In other words, you're not eligible for profit-sharing, but you know where the coffee machine is. See also *pleading economy.*

Presenteeism — fear of being laid off, or the desire to make the right impression, leads employees to adopt presenteeism, the opposite of absenteeism. Curiously, presenteeism results in decreased productivity, as the "make-work" it generates distracts attention from the issues that really matter. You probably know the shtick of those who practice presenteeism—they're the ones who show up early, stay late, let you know they were in on the weekend and send volleys of emails all day long—yet accomplish little. Reminds us of the famous Woody Allen quote, "98 percent of success is just showing up."

Productive Narcissists — a term coined by Michael Maccoby, an anthropologist and psychoanalyst, to define a certain kind of business leader who is aggressive, possesses a vision, and who can convince others to follow as he or she sets out to break the rules. The downside is that these narcissists are overly sensitive to criticism and impatient and thus have horrendous listening skills. According to Maccoby, Bill Gates, Jeffrey Bezos and Larry Ellison are productive narcissists, and their personality type is what reigns supreme in our business culture. In many ways—although they work in a less formal and more fluid environment—they are throwbacks to the Morgans and Carnegies and Rockefellers, and have less in common with the post-war, consensus-building, risk-averse leaders of the generation before them.

Reverse Mentoring — a new corporate practice that turns the traditional age-related roles upside down. Notes the *Economist*: "Big, traditional companies, from Procter & Gamble to Siemens have started reverse mentoring programmes in which middle-aged executives are tutored on the mysteries of the Internet by young newcomers." *DOF* expects this practice to widen as younger employees can also help middle-aged executives learn how to manage Gen X and Gen Y.

Scavenger Executives — individuals who are hired—often, but not exclusively—by media companies, to obsessively track the culture in search of off-the-grid ideas and properties ready for mainstreaming. *The New York Times* notes that MTV hired two scavenger executives for the purpose of "screening independent films, surfing the Internet, reading books and magazines by the scores seeking to identify people and ideas that might be turned into television shows." *DOF* predicts that scavenger executives will start to turn up in other fail-if-you're stale industries: fashion, food and beverage, home decor.

Spot Bonuses — the appeal of the scratch-off lottery comes to the human relations department. Increasingly, on-the-spot bonuses are being adopted by a number of high-tech companies as a way to motivate via the power of instant gratification. Cisco hands out $2,000 instant rewards; Exodus, the Web-hosting company, swoops down with PalmPilots and a weekend getaway. This unexpected generosity is in keeping with the culture of surprise that these companies embody, and we believe that the on-the-spot bonus will become a standard motivation tool of companies of all kinds. In a culture where everything else is wildly accelerated, why should recognition have to wait?

Submeetings — the explosion of wireless communication, including email enabled PDAs and next-generation wireless devices like the BlackBerry, have created the phenomenon of submeetings. Participants in one meeting are IM'ing (instant messaging) and emailing their co-workers or assistants in another meeting. Rather than increasing productivity, it de-concentrates everyone and raises distractions to a new level, thus resulting in two incomplete and unsuccessful meetings rather than one effective one. See also *attention slut, continuous personal attention.*

Trading Employees — the practice of swapping talent from one company to another, as a way of keeping restless employees from leaving the region altogether. One example of where this has worked is the area around Albany, New York, where local high-technology companies recognize that they need to collaborate or they will lose the best people to employers who want to seduce them to attractive destinations like California, North Carolina or Texas. See also *externs.*

Weightlessness — a desired corporate state, where you have shed capital-intensive manufacturing operations and can focus on the lighter load of marketing and sales. This is driven by our knowledge-economy focus. Proof of weightlessness: the weight of the gross domestic product in the United States was less in 1997 than 1999, even though its dollar value had grown by 70 percent. (Courtesy of an Ernst & Young Center for Business Innovative Study.)

Work Daze — increasing overtime is putting unprecedented pressure on workers, forcing many of them to work long hours without adequate sleep. *The New York Times* ran a front-page story on Brent Churchill, a 30-year-old lineman who worked two and half days with just five hours sleep, and as a result forgot to put on his insulating gloves and was electrocuted. Drowsy workers are a danger to others as well; Congress is under pressure to reduce the number of hours long-distance truckers can work without a break. As horror stories continue—James Maas, a psychology professor at Cornell, says that 100 million Americans, 40 percent of the population, are severely sleep deprived—look for this issue to wake up the public. See also *nap tents.*

Dictionary of the Future Predicts

Bodyguard Benefits — as high-profile kidnappings of wealthy executives proliferate, bodyguard benefits will be demanded, and granted, for current and even retired members of senior management.

Business Disbarment — lawyers can be disbarred and stockbrokers can also be restrained from practicing their trade. But what about business people who cross the line? Scott McNealy, founder and CEO of Sun Microsystems, is on record as saying that his archenemy Bill Gates should be disbarred from business. *DOF* believes that we will enter into a national dialogue about business disbarment—although its implications are ethical and not legal. After all, why should stockbrokers pay the price for behavior that violates the canons of their profession, while much more highly paid businesspeople who leave their ethics in the parking lot can simply move on and get another job?

Ceiling Tile Cultures — companies where power is measured by the size of one's office are those ruled by a ceiling tile culture. The term comes from the fact that by quickly counting the ceiling tiles you can instantly determine who's got the bigger position. While new economy, technology and media companies pretend to have flatter hierarchies, the truth is that more organizations are ceiling tile cultures than would like to admit it.

CoHo — short for corporate home office, a new form of officing in which corporations will actually fund all or a portion of the cost of constructing home offices. The benefits are numerous: for the employer, the cost of its real estate investment in expensive corporate headquarters can be reduced. And because employees appreciate the program, productivity is increased and loyalty cemented. Employees gain all the advantages of working at home—if they get fired, they get to keep the office; if they quit, they pay their employer a discounted amount.

Corporate Comfy — to attract desirable employees during a period when even the disgraced and the disbarred can find work, employers will accelerate the creation of workplaces that are comforting, away-from-home cocoons, featuring couches, microwaves, on-site day care. In other words, our homes are becoming more like work, and work is becoming more like home. See also *informalizing, nap tents, non-territorial offices.*

Corporate Ensembles — teams of senior executives will move from job to job as tough and focused problem-solving units. Unaffected by politics and legacy barriers, these corporate ensembles will be involved in tasks ranging from fixing technology problems, to managing the launch of a product, to re-engineering an entire division. Often, they will be recruited by frustrated boards of directors who recognize that current management has its limitations, and who can't wait to build a team on an individual-by-individual basis. Corporate ensembles will tackle projects lasting anywhere from three months to two years; some of them will develop their own brand names, others will grow by creating spin-offs concentrating on specific industries.

Corporate Term Limits — the appeal and popularity of limiting the time that someone can serve in elected office will be transported from the public to the private sector. CEOs, COOs and other senior management will be hired with non-renewable contracts for two-, four- or six-year maximum terms. The impetus for this will come from mutual funds, pension funds and other large stakeholder groups who know the damage that entrenched management can do. It's a logical way to protect against cronyism, but it doesn't recognize the fact that switching management can cause extensive short-term damage, and superior management often needs time to effect true business and cultural change.

Ego Audits — huge, unchecked management egos are the Achilles' heel of American business, resulting in major corporate blunders and billions of lost dollars. It happens when those in power refuse to take criticism or listen to (let alone accept) alternative options. As a defense against this ego damage, companies will institute ego audits, conducted by outside experts, who will interview senior management and report back on defensiveness, openness to new ideas, and refusal to back off an idea because "I thought of it." If you get a bad ego audit score, you might be sent for counseling, so you can get in touch with your inner consensus-builder. See also *productive narcissists.*

Flexpertise — when an individual possesses rich skills in multiple areas, and is adept at applying them from one category to the next. For example, a financial person who understands the intricacies (and intimacies) of consumer brand-building has flexpertise.

Groligarchy — describes the concentration of agriculture and food-production power in the hands of a few giants of agribusiness. With genetically modified foods being one of the most hotly debated issues on our radar, the groligarchy is being increasingly studied as a force even more intrusive and influential than the military-industrial complex of the 1950s. See also *foodopoly, plant genome project.*

Idea Harvesting — recognizing that the combined ingenuity of America is exponentially greater than the limitations of even the most well-funded R&D departments, companies will find ways to access this ambient communal creativity. (Consider that Napster and Linux were developed outside of conventional institutional structures.) The Internet will help, as well as local imagination fairs and other forms of idea harvesting. (A Web site called brightidea.com connects companies who need innovative ideas with grass-roots inventors who have them.) The only thing that can hold this back are executives who feel threatened. See also *Haystack Toys.*

Ignorientation — it's what happens when an employee is brought into a company and is immediately expected to perform brilliantly. TalentBanker Armato writes that "As competition forces even faster times-to-market . . . traditionally valued HR functions such as orientation, mentoring and jobs-skills training will be sacrificed by frantic managers." Those who survive will need "unprecedented flexibility, ingenuity, risk-taking and grace."

Karaoke Managers — a style of lip-synch management where you get ahead—or merely survive—by mouthing the buzzwords and platitudes of your superiors. A karaoke meeting is one in which the participants rush blindingly toward consensus; the trick to mastering karaoke managament is to rephrase the last statement so it sounds different, but adds nothing new. For example, the boss says "We need to look for global markets," and you say "I believe our domestic efforts will be inadequate to meet revenue goals." As companies grow larger—and it becomes easier to hide—we expect this kind of behavior to expand. Not only that, its incidence will be marked by a significant uptick.

Knowledge Blockage — the failure of knowledge (and information) to flow effortlessly within an organization, despite all the vast sums spent on intranets and other communications channels. A study by Korn/Ferry International found that "More than 70 percent of employees report knowledge is not reused across the company; 88 percent say they do not have access to lessons learned elsewhere in the organization." Knowledge blockage will be one of the greatest organizational challenges in the next decade, as availability of data confronts fear, anxiety and territorial defense zones that make even the tightest anti-missile defense seem like Swiss cheese. Experts will challenge themselves by saying: if we can only learn how rumors travel as fast as they do, we'd be home free. See also *knowledge membranes*.

Napkin — used as a verb to describe when a lower-level executive cleans up a mess made by his or her boss. "He said some really dumb things that pissed off the client, and I spent the rest of the day napkining up after him."

Stock Therapy — on-site psychological counseling which will soon be provided by public companies whose stock and option prices are depressed (along with their employees). It's hard to maintain motivation when those options you thought would buy you a beach house and a Porsche can now buy a mobile home and a Kia.

Supreme CEO — *DOF* foresees that after a decade or two of ascendancy, the era of the enlightened CEO—the consensus builder, the provider of yoga and meditation classes, the sensitive leader, will come to a close. Boards of directors, investors, even employees will feel the hunger (and nostalgia) for a Supreme CEO, a practitioner of Genghis Capitalism, of Ultimate Leadership. A boss who doesn't care about being liked, who sits proudly in the central office rather than in a democratic cubicle. (It's not different from the situation in Russia, where a majority of people miss the Communists.)

Title Choice — while unexpected titles are the rage—for example, Director of Great People (Intuit) or Director of Fun (Spring Paranet) or VP of Happiness (the position Donna DeGrande of FutureNext Consulting morphed her VP Organizational Development title into)—the next step is choose-your-own title. At Scitor, a project-management consulting firm, everybody gets to pick a title for his or job. Title choice is not a gimmick, it's a way to have employees shape their jobs and inspire their performance by giving them the power to define their role and influence in the organization. The traditional alternative is to put people in a box; when you do that, they remain there. A cautionary note, though: *DOF* reminds you to consider how your last title will look on your next resume.

CRIME AND TERRORISM

During our research we came upon the fact that the word "genocide," which many believe has long been in the language, was actually created by the philospher and historian Raphael Lemkin. In April of 1945, Lemkin prophetically wrote ". . . I took the liberty of inventing the word 'genocide' . . . [it] tragically enough must take its place in the dictionary of the future . . ."

The dark side of life has always been fertile ground for the generation of new language; it's why the patois of crime and the police is so colorful, so imaginative, so gaudy.

Today's dark side is, in large part driven by the chaos that comes from an accelerating world that is rapidly creating new winners and losers—and in turn, new threats and new risks. Some of these are age-old criminal attempts to profit illegally; others seem to be striving for a new level of destructiveness. Our entries include both "agro-terrorism" and "distance terrorism," which are enabled by technology—as well as "biopiracy," "denial of service attacks," and new kinds of illicit drugs like "ayahuasco" and "Ketaset."

Change, it seems, is like a drug. When it works its transformative magic in the right way, it can create stunning improvements in the body politic. When it works the other way, it can result in the dangerous side effects that follow.

Agro-Terrorism — a form of bioterrorism which involves attacks on crops and livestock. Intelligence experts are concerned about possible agro-terrorism attacks from both foreign nations and extremist groups. Before the Cold War ended, there were more than 10,000 Russians working on animal and plant toxins, according to Soviet scientists; this work included more than 200 "dangerous animal pathogens." (Many of the scientists who worked on these programs are being recruited by Iran.) These pathogens have lovely names like cow and sheep pox and blue tongue. The United States is upgrading our agro-terrorism and bioterrorism research labs as we debate how much of our civil liberties—if any—need to be compromised to protect our population from random acts of terror.

Attack Tree — the plans that hackers and terrorists use to stage an assault on a Web site or Internet server. By the same token, digital security forces study them to develop appropriate counter-measures. The metaphor is based on the fact that the Internet structure is tree-like, and attacks must be made on all components of the system: root, limbs, trunk, branches. If this is of interest, we direct your attention to Bruce Schneier's *Secrets and Lies: Digital Security in a Networked World.* See also *National Infrastructure Protection Center.*

Ayahuasco — a hallucinogenic plant, long used in religious ceremonies in Brazil, which is becoming part of the American drug culture; similarly salvia divinorum, a native Mexican plant that is chewed or smoked for the same effects, will gain popularity. Like the consumer marketplace, the drug marketplace thrives on new product introductions.

Biopiracy — when plants and botanicals are swiped from their natural habitat by drug companies seeking to capitalize on their genetic content in order to develop new drugs. It's stealing from nature's laboratory, and while some of these activities are governed by the Biodiversity Convention, experts wonder if the restrictions are adequate. "The flow of material from the gene-rich developing world to the gene-poor industrialized world is a form of biocolonialism" per Bronwyn Parry, Cambridge University research fellow. The ultimate irony of this: some of the richest repositories of these plants are the world's poorest countries, who will be unable to pay for the drugs that their natural resources were responsible for creating in the first place.

Brain Fingerprinting — a procedure for determining if someone is telling the truth that could very well become the new standard, replacing the unreliable polygraph and the controversial voice-stress analysis. (The old movie favorite of sodium pentothal is inadmissible.) Brain fingerprinting, developed by Dr. Lawrence Farrell, is based upon the fact that neurological responses do not lie. A series of electronic sensors read the subject's "brain fingerprint" as he or she responds to images flashed on a screen. Preliminary tests, conducted with federal agencies, have found it to be 100 percent accurate. See also *belief detectors*.

Capture Net — why chase a suspect down a dark alley when you can rely on a yellow, tennis ball–sized projectile filled with compressed string? Shot from a gun (of sorts), the device opens into a 16-foot net that doesn't harm the suspect and, at the same time, doesn't put any unnecessary cardiovascular stress on the police. It came out of research done by the National Institute of Justice, a little-known federal agency that funds research into public safety. Look for more innovations like this to emerge from them—after all, what's new since the gun, the nightstick and our personal favorite, the high-speed chase?

Cyber Posses — the Internet is creating a kind of amateur detective who, on occasion, is asked by the authorities to lend a hand. It has been reported that public investigators have asked for help from techno-whizzy PIs to track down virus creators and disseminators of child pornography, for example. It's not totally unprecedented; pre-Internet, detectives turned to psychics to locate kidnap victims. It's also in the same spirit as Linux and the "open source" software movement.

Denial of Service Attacks — when a Web site is brought down by hackers who flood the server with more requests than its infrastructure can handle. It is a curious inversion of the boycott which starves the enemy to death; with denial of service attacks, you overwhelm him. The ultimate embarrassment came when hacktivists (see listing)—in a display of their power—brought both the FBI and White House Web sites to their knees via denial of service attacks. See also *distance terrorism, National Infrastructure Protection Center.*

Earth Liberation Front — a group that practices environmental terrorism, which it believes is the only way to halt the destruction of the planet by government and corporate interests. (They are linked to the Animal Liberation Front, who shares the same philosophy.) The ELF has claimed credit for arson attacks on a U.S. Forest Service Ranger station, a portion of the Vail ski resort, as well as luxury homes under construction. The group has also sabotaged genetic engineering laboratories at the University of Minnesota and other places. See also *distance terrorism* and *terror entrepreneurs.*

Fusarium Oxysporum — forget your drug-sniffing dogs and your police sweeps. The real way to wipe out cocaine, marijuana and heroin is biological warfare. A fungus known as fusarium oxysporum is being tested as a devastatingly effective—and environmentally safe—way to destroy the growing fields. It's a bioherbicide, in other words; the stuff is so effective, reports *The New York Times,* that Montana State University suspended its research two years ago, afraid that they would be a target of drug cartels. It looks as though fusarium oxysporum could be the drug lords' worst nightmare. It's a narrative made for Hollywood: evil drug chief battles bioherbalist.

Hactivists — hacker activists, those who seek to bring down the Internet, or an individual Web site as a means of protest—or just for the techno-kicks of it. Hactivists have already targeted the privacy-invading Project Echleon (see listing) and have forced the Korean Ministry of Information's Web site to shut down for ten hours. Members of the Hong Kong Blondes, a covert group, claim to have hacked into Chinese military computers and shut down a communications satellite. Hactivists rely on the denial of service attack (see listing), but also have other techniques, including hacking past firewalls to mess with code, implanting viruses and making as much trouble as possible. With hactivists in an ongoing battle of cyber-upmanship with computer security experts, hactivism is an increasingly dangerous form of non-violent, surgical terrorism. See also *National Infrastructure Protection Center.*

Ketaset — the emerging party and street drug of choice. Designed to be an anesthetic, Ketaset causes hallucinations in high doses and a "fuzzy dissociation," in the words of *Time,* in lower ones. Recognizing its dangers, the Drug Enforcement Agency has put strict rules on the sale of the drug, but it is flowing into the country illegally, as you might expect: a gram of K sells for $80 in Manhattan. *DOF* predicts that Ketaset might be the next Ecstasy.

Koban — an innovative policing approach that began in Japan and is rapidly beginning to enter the U.S. mainstream. *Kobans* are mini-police stations that are set deep inside neighborhoods; policemen and policewomen actually live there. (They are largely credited with helping maintain Japan's low crime rate.) *The Economist* describes a *koban* in Columbia, South Carolina, as a two-story house where residents of the community are "encouraged to visit the carpeted first floor . . . to report crimes. The building is used for neighborhood meetings. It is intended to be a safe haven for youngsters and the elderly. It is also a work-station for social and educational services, with programs designed to teach literacy to both children and adults."

In Columbia, the crime rate initially rose as residents felt a new freedom to report crimes, and then it dropped. We believe that *kobans* will take off as an exciting and effective new form of community policing—and will attract a new generation of police officers who are thrilled by the challenge. Voters will start to demand them, politicians will start advocating them. We'll know they've broken through when real estate ads read: Lite brite 2BR apt. on *koban* blk.

Lolo — one of the drugs of choice of Brazil's thousands of street children (*meninoa da rua*), it is a combination, according to *The Economist*, of "shop-lifted solvents and medications, snorted with the aid of a perfume spray." Sadly, *DOF* believes that lolo, along with other drugs from Latin and South America, will make the journey north and become the cool alternatives for young people here, creating an unfolding series of public health problems.

Milk for Cocaine — an innovative drug-fighting plan being tested in Colombia. The United Nations has contributed $5.3 million to La Cristalina, a coca-growing area, for the purchase of dairy cows. The goal is see if 600 families can be encouraged to give up illegal crops, for an unexpected application of the "Got Milk" campaign. It seems to be working—the families are selling their milk to a local Nestlé factory. Though a small effort, the use of the free market as a competitive threat to coca-growing is enormously appealing, and far preferable to the alternatives, which include spraying cocoa fields with herbicides like glyphosphate. See also *fusarium oxysporum.*

National Infrastructure Protection Center — the official name of the FBI's cyber-crime unit. As countries and regions in conflict turn to "virtual violence" as a way to attack their enemies, we can expect to hear a lot more from the NIPC. For example, in the Israeli-Palestinian conflict, Web sites operated both by Israel's government and military and by pro-Palestinian Hezbollah and Hamas have been targeted, and both sides have posted instructions and attack tools. (In a symbolic gesture, Israeli hackers penetrated a Palestinian Web site and posted the Israeli flag.) The NIPC warns that American companies (or individuals) who are believed to be taking sides in this conflict—or any conflict—are also vulnerable, which adds a new dimension to the need for Web security and could create a national debate over the concept of "Internet self-defense." See also *distance terrorism, hactivists, terror entrepreneurs.*

Nazi Crank — an illegal drug described by the *London Times* as "home-cooked meth-amphetamine that is said to have originated in Hitler's Germany, where it was used as a stimulant . . . by battle-weary soldiers and factory workers." Produces a high greater than cocaine and longer-lasting for less money.

Pollution Time — rather than just punishing corporate polluters with hefty fines, courts have started to actually sentence key decision makers to time in jail. One company executive got a 14-year sentence for dumping pollutants into the water table in a suburb of Denver; the chairman of a Georgia chemical company was sentenced to nine years in prison for exposing his workers to hazardous chemicals. *USA Today* reports that federal prosecutors attribute the trend to a crackdown on white-collar crime and the fact that the courts are taking environmental crime far more seriously. Expect this to have the desired chilling effect. It's one thing for your company to pay a fine, even a multimillion dollar one—it's another to have to trade the health club for the exercise yard.

Pulse Wave Protection Device — a remarkably potent technology that is finding its way into self-defense weapons. One company incorporates this approach—which was developed for the FBI—into a device called the Pulse Wave Myotron. According to a Web site that sells it—www.securityplanet. com—the Myotron "intercepts and neutralizes brainwaves from the motorcortex (voluntary muscle control) and hypothalamic (aggression) regions of the brain within an amazing 1/1000th of a second! When the attacker is touched . . . they will instantly be immobilized and disoriented . . . they are also likely to collapse, lose bladder control and be completely immobilized for up to 30 minutes. They will remain conscious . . . but will be passive and unable to stand or walk. It will instantly stop any human or beast! Up to 10 times stronger than a stun gun!" It's interesting that during the last few years—while crime rates have been dropping—anti-crime technology has reached new heights. We believe that when the current reduction in crime turns the other way—as it inevitably will—devices like the Myotron will generate enormous interest and controversy. See also *lifestyle enclaves*.

Qat — one of the drugs of choice in the Middle East, qat is a psychoactive stimulant from a common shrub that is so pervasive in Yemen that the government issued a report asserting that 90 percent of adult men use it regularly. Qat is banned in Saudi Arabia, but is popular in North Africa and other countries in the region. *DOF* believes that qat will emerge as a popular drug in America, and because the plant isn't known here, authorities will have trouble identifying its cultivation.

Smart Sanctions — international attempts to punish rogue and outlaw states without putting the screws on the innocent people unlucky enough to live there. So rather than ban all trade, governments can (and should) impose selective restrictions that allow the flow of not just food and medical supplies, but books, music and even some computer hardware. Critics argue that it's impossible to realistically restrict trade in this way, and that a computer destined for a school could end up being deployed in a weapons facility. *DOF* suggestion: insert special code into the hard drive of computers that is able to detect any specialized scientific or engineering data that gets entered. Should that happen, the computer is instructed to immediately destroy the hard drive.

Superantigen — a toxic villain found in certain strains of streptococcus and staphylococcus, for example. While the body's immune system can dispose of antigens without harming healthy tissue, superantigens stimulate an abnormally strong reaction by the body's immune system. They can literally whip the body's immune system into a fatal frenzy, which is why they have been developed for use as biological weapons and why research into vaccines combating them is proceeding with exceptional urgency.

Web Site Cramming — a new kind of Internet fraud; crammers bill customers for Web-related telephone charges that were never incurred. The scam, which targets small businesses, is often successful because telephone bills often contain so many multiple charges from legitimate service providers that customers can't deconstruct all their complexity. *Fortune Small Business* magazine reports on one crammer, WebValley, which was found—according to court filings—to have "crammed 50,000 'customers' for $9 million in specious services." Check those phone bills carefully.

Wireless Virus — computer viruses that are spread by Web-enabled cell phones and personal digital assistants. Once these tools have enough power to open email attachments they will become vulnerable to infection. The Yankee Group, an industry research firm, projects that there will be 120 million people by 2005 with "infectable" devices, which creates a whole new opportunity for those who spread viruses, and a whole new market for the anti-virus software companies like McAfee.com. Consider that, at any given time, there are as many as 20,000 viruses flowing through the Internet's circulatory system. See also *F-Secure*.

Dictionary of the Future Predicts

Basuco — the impure by-product left by the manufacture of cocaine that is the South American equivalent of crack. Highly addictive, *DOF* believes that this drug will become a new drug of choice, as upscale abusers look for the next generation of illegal drugs as diligently as they seek out the next hot restaurant or bar.

Distance Terrorism — terrorist attacks once had to be perpetrated in person, but the Internet changes all that. Today, cyber-terrorists are capable of creating enormous damage without ever leaving their homes—from anywhere in the world. Christopher Kozlow, who is a counter-terrorism expert and the author of the authoritative book *Jane's Counter Terrorism*, warns of terrorism that can, for example, "cause large loss of life by remotely altering medication formulas at pharmaceutical manufacturing plants." He also notes that terrorists can "destroy an entire suburban block by remotely changing the pressure in natural gas lines, resulting in valve failure and escaping gas." Distance terrorism, which can "make certain that the population of a nation will not be able to eat, drink or move" will never be too far from our minds as we move into an uncertain and dangerous period.

Invisible Theft — a cluster of new technologies will emerge that allow the remote theft of information from a computer's hard drive. You will be able to point an infra-red transfer device at a computer, and the signal will beam instructions to the hard drive, telling the computer to send specific files back to the handheld device. This will have serious implications for industrial espionage and personal privacy.

Non-Cons — as DNA testing reveals that hundreds of people have been wrongly imprisoned, we will need language to describe those innocent people who have been released from jail. They're not ex-cons, and they are also clearly not ordinary citizens. *DOF* proposes "non-cons," which credits them for their pain and suffering while removing any stigma.

Prisoncam — *DOF* foresees that cameras will go into prisons, where shows put on by inmates will be viewed by the general public and entertainment pros. *DOF* believes that future singers, actors and comedians will be discovered this way.

Repro Terrorism — rumors will be flying over the Internet that terrorist groups have the ability—and are plotting to— poison our water supply with multiple kinds of bacteria, some with devastating virus strains spliced into them. One of the scariest cyber-rumors will spread word of a virus that is harmless to our immediate health, but will attack our reproductive systems and render us sterile—thus spelling the inevitable end of American civilization. This rumor will be driven by the power of the Internet to disseminate information (and disinformation) in a matter of hours, and the subterranean fear of terrorism that will only grow in the future as rogue groups continue to attack U.S. interests worldwide. See also *reservoir patrols.*

Terror Entrepreneurs — the increasing availability of low-cost weapons systems, and our vulnerability to technology attacks—both physical and virtual—will create a new kind of freelance terror entrepreneur. Unaffiliated with governments or even radical groups, these terror entrepreneurs will usually be acting out of extremely narrow and focused motivations. As the Terrorism Research Center has stated, "Access to weapons and methods of increasing lethality, or methods targeting digital information systems . . . could result in terrorist cells that are smaller, even familial, and thus harder to infiltrate, track or counter."

DEMOGRAPHICS

Demographics, once the province of geeky statisticians and tweedy scholars, has become a happening discipline. Everyone wants to understand who we are as a nation—and where we are headed.

Those answers are in motion, a point which was made many times over by the latest readings on our national change meter, also known as the census. The 2000 census—imperfect instrument that it is—made headlines by formalizing the growth of the Hispanic population, and the fact that whites are a minority in nearly half of the largest cities; correspondingly, 71 of the largest 100 cities lost white residents.

Demographic changes are of critical concern to public health experts, bankers, marketers, politicians and comedians (shared experience is the basis of all humor). They are also catalysts for all manner of innovation and insurgency in the language. The words and terms gathered together here include some that relate to new geographies, like "Cascadia," others that describe subsets of our ethnicity, such as "Cubanglos" and "Neoyorquinos"; and still others that define us by cultural, as opposed to ethnic, commonalities—be they shared values, as with "Bobos," or shared rootlessness, as with "Nowherians."

The entries in this section generally steer clear of the influence of foreign words and phrases on our vernacular—we leave that to the slang experts. (Although we have coined a word for the impact of demographic collisions on language: "clanguage.") And of course, not all demography is about blending—one term, "isopopulations," is about just the opposite: groups that—by virtue of geography—have remained isolated for so long that their genetic makeup is of great value to researchers who, ironically, are now able to understand different diseases through the perpetuation of sameness.

Dd

Afropean — an individual of mixed African and European ancestry; also describes a music style that fuses these traditions. Here's how PRI (Public Radio International) used it: "Having recruited the cream of British soul and acid jazz musicians, Les Nubians single-handedly declare the bold new genre of Afropean hip-hop."

Bachelor Herds — in societies where wealthy older men are allowed to acquire young new wives, the result is that younger men, who by all evolutionary rights should be pairing up with these younger women, become hostile and aggressive. According to *The New York Times*, anthropologists call them "bachelor herds . . . lots of young poor men without mates, who are prone to working out their frustrations through violence and crime."

Bobos — coined by David Brooks in his book *Bobos in Paradise*, the term is short for "bourgeois bohemians"—America's new elite. Bobos have merged "the rebellion of the '60s with the materialism of the '80s" in the words of *Newsweek*. That means they are consumers to the core, but *how* they spend their money separates them from previous elites. As Brooks puts it: "Bobos think that it's OK to lavishly spend money on anything that can be classified as a need, but it's vulgar to spend money on a mere want. So it's vulgar to spend $40,000 on a flashy sports car, but it's OK to spend $40,000 on a supposedly utilitarian Range Rover." A perfect marketing expression of Bobo-ism is the Montblanc pen called the Boheme, described by Eric Werner of BoHoCo as "a writing tool for today's bohemians, who work hard and play hard and appreciate the finer things in life." BoHoCo stands for Bohemian Home Colonial, more Bobo-ism in action. See also *bush lux*.

The Browning of the Midwest — few understand or appreciate the changing demographics of the Midwest; over the last generation, Latinos contributed to more than 50 percent of the population growth of ten central states. If we think of this farmland region as conservative bedrock America, we're wrong: the reverb effect of this has yet to be fully felt. In fact, down the road some of these cities and states could become the next majority-minority regions. Flapjacks, move over, the tortillas have arrived.

Cascadia — the geographical region defined by northern California, Washington, Oregon and British Columbia. This binational region contains many of the most advanced and enlightened cities on the continent, and they are working together on regional issues of transportation, trade, tourism, sprawl, the environment and technology (www.discovery.org/cascadia/). One thing they all might not have in common, however, is Seattle's coffee waste problem: recently caffeine has shown up in their water supply.

Cinco de Mayo — a Mexican holiday that is joining the pantheon of American days of celebration (which means plenty of shopping, drinking and barbecuing). May 5th commemorates an 1862 Mexican victory over French invaders and it's observed with what *The Wall Street Journal* calls "solemn restraint" in Mexico. Here, marketers have jumped on it—recognizing the growing Hispanic population. (A consultancy called Efficient Market Services estimates that the difference between a normal weekend and a "branded" one is $500 million in sales.) Estimates are that consumer spending has already reached $1 billion on Cinco de Mayo, and it is fast becoming a crossover holiday like Oktoberfest and Chinese New Year. Hallmark is testing a line of Cinco de Mayo cards, and marketers from Winn-Dixie to Frito Lay to the American Dairy Association have gotten behind it. It's the unstoppable arc of American life: from immigration to assimilation to branded holidays.

Crusties — an English term, just pushing into our language, which describes a subculture of street kids; some are itinerant, others live more mainstream lives. They are loosely associated with the environmental and New Age movements. The *Phoenix New Times* puts it like this: "Crusties. Squatters. Gutter punks. Street kids. Travelers. The young and transient in America go by and get called many names, and pass through

Dd

many places. There are dozens, or, in the case of cities like New York, Los Angeles and Seattle, hundreds of them in every major U.S. urban center." Though the term hasn't busted out yet, we expect it to do just that, as we will soon be hearing about crusty music, crusty fashion, crusty speak.

Cubanglo — coined by the writer Juan Flores to describe those residents of Miami's Cuban community who were born in the United States.

Cultural Abuse — used to describe the oppressive absorption of one culture by another; one example, native Aborigines by Australians. Another example: a group of Indians in Canada is suing both local churches and the government for not just cultural abuse, but what they are calling "cultural genocide." As PBS reported in its coverage of the story, early in the twentieth century "the government decided to take the Indian out of the Indian . . . and to turn red children into white adults." To enforce this, they took Indian children away from their parents—who were jailed if they didn't cooperate. The charge of "cultural abuse" will be heard often in the twenty-first century, as America struggles to come to grips with the growing diversity of its population.

Dem — to pinpoint a specific individual based on his or her demographic and psychographic characteristics. While this has always been done, sophisticated database marketers have dramatically elevated their ability to target with stunning precision, spurred by behavioral information gleaned from the Internet: they know who you are, where you live, what you buy, what groups you belong to, what magazines you read, how you like your coffee. In the future, we will all be demmed by a posse of observant marketers (not to mention political candidates and nonprofit groups) just about every day.

Edgewalkers — describes those of mixed background like Tiger Woods (Asian and African American) who are creating a new America. In her book *Edgewalkers*, Nina Boyd Krebs writes that they "do not shed one skin when they move from their cultures of origin to the mainstream and back. Edgewalkers maintain continuity wherever they go, walking the edge between two cultures in the same persona." The writer Walter Mignolo called this phenomen "bilanguaging." Basho Fujimoto, a young man who has an Irish-Welsh mother and a Japanese-American father, is quoted in the book as saying, "Our interest is not in taking traditional elements from our old cultures and mixing them all together, making a nice, evenly distributed multiculturalism. It is more like taking the consciousness of all our heritage . . . and working with that to create something new." This something new is going to be the most radical culture change we've seen since the great waves of early twentieth century immigration—influencing everything from food and literature to structures of thought. See also *magical urbanism, majority-minority society.*

Generation 1.5 — describes those Asians who came to the United States as children; the segment was named by Asia Link Consulting Group. Depending on when they immigrated and their family circumstances here, some Generation 1.5ers assimilate rapidly, others try to hold on to their roots.

Gold-Collar Workers — we have clearly moved beyond white-collar and blue-collar to gold-collar workers, although the definition of the term is somewhat ambiguous. Some use it to define the super-upscale knowledge worker, while others use it to define those who are particularly valuable because they know so much about so many aspects of a company's operations. Even the derivation is in dispute: *Information Week* says it was coined by Professor D. D. Warrick of the University of Colorado, yet Robert E. Kelley, a professor at Carnegie Mellon, used it in the title of a book *The Gold-Collar Worker: Harnessing the Power of the New Work Force,* he wrote back in 1985. But whether it's gold, white or blue, it's a collar nonetheless—and is thus in conflict with our irrepressible entrepreneurial, free-agent spirit.

H-1B Debate — H-1B is the category that the Immigration and Naturalization Service uses for visas that are issued to skilled foreign workers. The technology explosion has created great demand for these workers, and the tech industry keeps pushing to raise the ceiling; the current cap is 195,000 visas per year, but it is expected to go to even higher, since 850,000 tech jobs are open. Immigration has always been a hugely sensitive issue, as Americans are torn between our long history of welcoming newcomers and our desire to keep Americans employed. Clearly, there is a shortage of skilled tech workers now, but in a foreseeable future, when Americans are battling with foreign workers over jobs, a large national debate will erupt over H-1B and it will be on the tip of everyone's tongue. Also, with unemployment well over 10 percent among some minority groups, the growth in H-1B workers is an ongoing example of our own domestic educational failures. See also *virtual immigrant.*

Hispanos — a group of Hispanics from Northern New Mexico who call themselves Hispanos because they are descended from the original Spanish conquistadors and are not descendants of Latin American immigrants. Hispanos are the oldest remnants of early European culture within the United States, and their existence highlights the complex nature of ethnicity and ethnic definitions today. See also *Cubanglos, Neoyorquinos, Tejanos.*

The Long Black Boom — coined by Nat Irvin II, founder and president of Future Focus 2020 (www.futurefocus2020.org), an urban-futurist think tank based at Wake Forest University. Irvin sees buoyant times ahead for African Americans, believing that they are poised to benefit from the information economy in numbers not generally acknowledged. He writes, "A transformation of thinking will take place within the black community . . . black people will no longer be the monitors of social conscience in U.S. society . . . they will leave the public-sector and advocacy worlds, and they will enter business—in particular, e-commerce."

Majority-Minority Society — in 2000, California—following New Mexico—became the second state to be a majority-minority culture. In other words, no single ethnic group now represents a majority of the population. The radical nature of that shift is clear—white non-Hispanics, who were nearly 80 percent of the population in 1970, became a minority for the first time since the Gold Rush. The full implications of this socioquake have not yet been expressed or felt. And since California is a laboratory for the rest of the country—a tracking geography—we can study the impact of a majority-minority society there to better foresee our futures. See also *magical urbanism.*

Millennium Generation — used to describe those between 15 and 25; the most racially diverse group in American history; one third are black, Latino, Asian or Native American. While its predecessor generation was demographically consistent, the millennium generation is 60 percent more likely to be non-white than its parents' generation. They won't learn, shop or vote like any group we've seen, and—because they believe that rules aren't inherited, but invented—they will define the America to be.

Neoyorquinos — used to describe the polygot nature of Latino culture in the New York region. This dynamic, fast-growing group—which includes Puerto Ricans, Dominicans, Colombians and Cubans—makes it difficult, if not impossible, to generalize about Latino culture and politics. See also *Hispanos, magical urbanism, Tejanos.*

Nowherians — coined by writer—and nowherian himself—Pico Iyer to describe those born in one place—often from parents of diverse ethnicity—raised somewhere else, schooled in yet a different place and now engaged in a career in which they travel around the world. Nowherians, one could argue, are the citizens of the future, as they are increasingly dissociated from geography and are creatures of transport and motion. The mantra of previous generations was "there's no place like home"; for Nowherians it's "there's no place that is home." The open question: where will their loyalties and emotional center reside? For more on this, Pico Iyer's worthwhile book is called *Global Souls*. Walter Kirn's novel *Up in the Air* covers the same territory with sharp, satiric bite.

Off-the-Hyphen — coined by writer Juan Flores to describe the refusal of certain ethnic groups to use a hyphen to define their dual identities. Thus, for example, some Puerto Ricans insist on being Puerto Rican Americans. This is not just a punctuation debate; the old model of the "hyphenated American"—where dual heritages hang in the balance, a kind of cultural suspended animation—is being replaced by a fusion of identities. See *Edgewalkers* for a discussion of the same phenomenon.

Tejanos — describes those Mexican-Americans who live in Texas, as opposed to those who live in California, who are known as *"Californias."* Tejanos have long felt that their identity has been submerged by the larger, and more visible, *Californias* population. Many know Tejano music, which was popularized by the late Tejano icon Selena, but that's about it. A focus on Tejano identity is growing, however. One microcosm of this: the *San Antonio Business Journal* reports that the Tejano Hat Company has begun to market a line that is "tailored specifically to the Tejano culture." Says the company's founder, "It's a culture. It's the way you dress, what you eat, the music, what you believe." *DOF* believes that this culture—which has been in Texas for hundreds of years—is about to bust out more broadly, in food, fashion and design. As the *San Francisco Bay Guardian* noted, "Until now, the definers of hip Chicano culture (or any Chicano culture for that matter) have mostly been California-based writers and thinkers." Note to spellcheck editors: Tejanos doesn't appear in the Microsoft dictionary. See also *Neoyorquionos, Hispanos*.

Undercover Homeless — heard (by the authors) as part of a "fund-raising" pitch given by a homeless person on the R train in Manhattan. He maintained that there a lot of people who live with their parents, and don't make enough to live on their own. When their parents die, these "undercover homeless"

will be unable to afford their own homes or apartments, and will join the ranks of the official homeless. His point: don't shun me, I am closer to you than you may realize.

Dictionary of the Future Predicts

Alien Activism — while much attention is focused on the working conditions in the third world, there has been little focus on the exploitation of illegal aliens in America. *DOF* believes that's about to change, and predicts a wave of "Alien Activism." There are estimated to be 6 million below-minimum-wage illegal workers in America. The Cato Institute, a think tank, has calculated that the cost of fruits and vegetables would rise by 6 percent if growers didn't rely on illegal aliens. And rely they do—in Washington state, up to 70 percent of the pickers hired during growing season are illegal. *DOF* expects that Alien Activism will include a push for amnesty—the AFL-CIO has already endorsed it (believe it or not)—as well as pressure on growers to pay a fair wage and improve working conditions. Just as college students have protested the sale of apparel that is made by children, they will protest the sale of apples that are picked by children—here, in their own backyard.

Angel Island — we don't hear much about Angel Island, even though it was the Ellis Island of the west, the place where virtually every immigrant from Asia—mainly Chinese—passed through between 1910 and 1940. Unlike Ellis Island, Angel Island also functioned as a detention camp, and many immigrants were held there for months. This is a remarkable, basically untold story and we believe that as our Asian population continues to grow—and focuses on its roots in America— Angel Island will be the centerpiece of its efforts to claim its heritage. As a result of these efforts, Angel Island will move forward into our national consciousness. In the meantime, the Internet has many Web sites—including www.angelisland. org/immigr02.html—that tell the story.

Authethnic — whether it's food or literature or entertainment, authethnic describes the real thing: cultural expressions that are unadulterated, unmodified, uncompromised. These come from the pure heart of ethnic experience, as opposed to that which has been put through the homogenizing mill of American culture. When we seek out the Brazilian restaurant run by a family from Rio, buy tickets for a singer of Portugese *fado* in a part of town we've never been or track down a Russian émigré artist before her work gets swept up by the chic galleries, we are in pursuit of the authethnic. And it's getting much harder to find, even globally: *Travel & Leisure* magazine writes of sushi bars in Dublin, mariachi bands in Kathmandu and Thai hill people drinking bottles of Guinness.

BABOONS — baby boomers with no savings. It's what happens when you live in the moment—luxuriating in a house that's too expensive, wearing shoes that are too expensive and unwinding in the front seat of a car that's too expensive. BABOONS will have to work longer than they thought to preserve their lifestyles. See also *phased retirement* and *401-k'd*

Britafornia — while you might think that there are few places on earth as different as Britain and California, Britafornia describes the transformation of England in a manner that parallels the demographic shifts in California: How? Consider that a large and increasing number of Britain's college graduates and successful entrepreneurs are Asian newcomers. These recent immigrants, many from China, India and Pakistan, have achieved higher living standards than average whites, and the resulting demographic and income shifts will have profound (and not always positive) implications for British social life.

Clanguage — we've already got Spanglish (the merger of Spanish and English), and Franglais (the merger of French and English). Now, *DOF* introduces the term that describes the grand totality of recombinant language. Clanguage is driven by the growing diversity of the American population (as even casual readers of the last census are aware), the disrespect for borders that characterizes the Internet and the boundary-crossing that goes on in the arts. Clanguage is not just an American phenomenon; from France to China (where there is great national concern that the Internet is diluting the language) the spoken and written word is becoming as transgenic as the world itself.

Conservakids — years of a healthy economy and the buoyant consumerism that rides along with it have created Conservakids, a generation of young people between 15 and 25 who are anxious to preserve the status quo and the institutions that have created their personal prosperity. For them, a radical gesture is to mix Calvin Klein and Prada.

Isopopulations — isolated, undisturbed populations that are enormously valuable for researchers, because outside genetic material has not been introduced into their gene pool. Iceland is one such isopopulation (Ireland is another). An Icelandic biotech company called deCODE hopes to identify "genes, drugs and diagnostic targets" by using its "extensive Icelandic genealogical database to cluster patients with a particular disease into large extended families, sometimes comprising hundreds of individuals over more than ten generations." deCODE's database shows the relationship of all living Icelanders, and they have an agreement with the government to also assemble a database of blood samples. By being able to peer into a single sick individual's genes in the context of generations of his healthy relatives, researchers can zero in on mutations linked to the diseases far more easily than they could with patients whose genetic history is more clouded. What irony: from isolated populations can come breakthroughs that will influence the world. *DOF* expects other isopopulations—Madagascar, for example—to follow Iceland's model.

ECONOMIC CHANGES

Tectonic economic shifts are under way; as pundits have been punditizing, this is an electroshocked economy. The rapid reversal of technology fortune between the last years of the last century, and the beginning of this one, reminds us of the instability of any single point in time. Only in this era could you have a cable TV show "Business As Unusual."

But stay tuned, there's more. More includes "shock accounting," which argues that our traditional accounting practices are basically useless and outmoded; "dynamic pricing," which takes a definitive price and turns it into vapor; as well as a new generation of "micro-entrepreneurs" and an onslaught of "shareholder resolution votes" to challenge (and embarrass) management.

Add to that the implications of "buyer driven commerce"—which may be down, but is not out—and *DOF*'s predictions of "transparent mark-ups," and you'll see why all of our economics textbooks might be headed for sale on eBay.

Boutique Banks — of all the start-ups we might expect to see, new banks are low on the list. Yet *Inc.* magazine reports a trendlet: as a result of the massive consolidation of banks (9,143 vs. 13,000 a decade ago), there are "scores of bankers looking for work and some customers longing for what they imagine are kinder, gentler community banks." Along with a vigorous economy, these forces have created a strong cross-trend of emerging new banks that are "popping up all across the country." One thing *DOF* is sure of: few, if any, consumers are happy with the creation of mega-bank holding companies that vainly attempt to sell "relationships" but are as remote and inhospitable to consumers as the IRS on its worst day.

Buyer-driven Commerce — describes Web sites such as Priceline.com, where consumers establish the price they are willing to pay for products and services such as airline tickets, mortgages and hotel rooms. In a fundamental fashion, this shifts the balance of power from manufacturers and service providers—the old "take it or leave it model"—and swings it to the buyers. While Priceline.com has had its problems, *DOF* believes that the Internet has inevitably altered the relationship between buyers and sellers—and by extension labor and management—to create a post-capitalist equality that Marx never envisioned. See also *transparent mark-ups.*

Caveat Vendor — today's equivalent to *caveat emptor,* "let the seller beware," since eBay and other Internet auction sites can actually let aware buyers take advantage of naive sellers. Then there are shopbots—intelligent agents that compare prices—which force sellers to stay ahead of their competitors, or suffer the consequences. As Stan Davis and Christopher Meyer, the authors of *Blur,* so aptly put it: "If anything, a focused shopper is now better informed than the seller, who may have studied competitors more thoroughly."

Clusters — groups of interrelated companies that are geographically concentrated in order to energize a region with economic vitality. The model for clusters is Italy, where *distretti industri*—which are sprinkled around the country—produce a remarkable range of both consumer and industrial goods. A total of 2.2 million jobs, half of all the manufacturing in Italy, derives from these unique clusters. An example: in the region of Basilicata, 12,000 people are employed in the production of furniture involving more than 100 firms, including carpentry, fabric production, milling and other disciplines. Other *distretti industri* include the Sassuolo, where 80 percent of all Italian tiles are produced and Como, where 2,600 firms are involved in the silk industry.

The economic elegance of clusters is that they have grown and continue to thrive with little or no governmental intervention. Small wonder their model is being studied by economists around the world—the *Harvard Business Review* covered them in a major article—so that the learning can be exported broadly: to developing nations, and to regions in the United States, like West Virginia, that have been economically stymied for generations.

Design-on-Demand Retailing — inventory that's almost as fresh as the morning newspaper? It's possible thanks to a retailing concept that has been pioneered by the Spanish company Zara, and their innovative approach has ignited their expansion to 400-plus stores in 25 countries. Full integration—they control design and manufacturing—lets them track sales trends, and then manufacture and ship new production so swiftly that their stores have fresh inventory twice a week. Compare that to the lethargic six weeks that it takes their competitors to respond. As *Fortune* writes, "While the Gap and H&M outsource most of their manufacturing, Zara produces 60 percent of its merchandise in-house. Fabric—which comes from places like Spain, the Far East, India and Morocco—is cut and colored at the company's state-of-the-art factory." We expect many to follow this model—including department stores, whose calcified buying and sourcing process leaves them months behind more nimble competitors.

Dynamic Pricing — it's what hotels and the airlines have done for years—adjust pricing based on shifts in the supply and demand equation. While ecommerce theoretically enables every industry to become more price efficient, changing prices to optimize revenue is easier said than done: businesses need to study years of sales data to establish trends, while factoring in the costs of manufacturing and changing raw material prices. A new industry of price-optimization software engines is evolving to enable dynamic pricing, but *DOF* believes that the transition, though inevitable, will be rocky given the complexities—and risks—of implementation. If the software is off by even a small percentage, businesses could give away their margins, or sell below cost. Another obstacle is a backlash from customers who feel they are being taken advantage of. Coca-Cola was surprised by the outcry when they announced a vending machine that would charge more for a drink in the hot weather. Dynamic pricing will also be possible at brick and mortar retail locations, as electronic ink will allow prices to change instantly. Soon, you won't ask "how much is it" but "how much will it be at 2:30?" See also *transparent mark-ups, buyer-driven commerce.*

Emissions — a rather elegant euphemism for printing money, which is the convenient way that inflationary economies deal with shortages of cash. As reported in *The New York Times*, when asked how his teetering government would pay off its bank debts, Russian deputy Andrei Kozlov replied "Emissions, of course, emissions."

Green Accounting — a new way of looking at our gross domestic product (GDP) that takes into account not just the plus column, but also the minus column. Take your morning newspaper: GDP now includes the plus column, the revenue earned by the company that sells it. But it doesn't include the minus column, the tree that gave its life for your reading pleasure and the services it provides (shade, cooling, protection against global warming). Nor does GDP factor in any environmental costs involved in manufacturing (pollutants that are dumped into a local stream, for example). The National Research Council has published a book on this subject called *Nature's Numbers: Expanding the National Economic Accounts to Include the Environment,* which the magazine *The*

American Prospect has called "careful, intelligent and weighty."

It all sounds logical, but traditional accounting principles are so deeply systemic that changing them would require enormous, sustained public pressure. Thus, although *DOF* believes that green accounting can win some victories, to change GDP would require a rare convergence of timing and leadership. Perhaps a perfect role for post-retirement Jack Welch.

Hydrogen Economy — Iceland is a test case to see if an entire country can move its power supply to hydrogen power. Why Iceland? They have a pollution problem, and they also have a virtually unlimited supply of inexpensive geothermal and hydroelectric power; the geothermal power derives from the volcanic activity below the earth's surface, the hydroelectric power from water: both can be harnessed and converted to electricity by non-polluting power plants. The magazine *Red Herring* writes that, "If the hydrogen plan is carried out, Iceland could reduce its annual oil bill of $150 million to almost zero." Also, if Iceland is successful in harnessing its natural resources, they could "produce it by the megaton and ship it to mainland Europe." The result: Icelanders could become hydrogen sheiks. Also of note: Shell, DaimlerChrysler and the Icelandic government have formed a consortium called Vistorka to explore hydrogen power.

Micro-Entrepreneurs — low-income doers and dreamers who are starting their businesses against the most monumental of all odds—no MBA, no snazzy business plan, no Rolodex of VC connections. In fact, about 82 percent of them have never received a bank loan—usually the amounts are too small (often just a few hundred dollars) and the risks are too high. Even nonprofits tend not to fund these start-ups. There are 13 million micro-entrepreneurs, and we are just starting to recognize how their efforts can shatter the cycle of poverty. Micro-entrepreneurs and micro-finance are successful strategies around the world—the famous Bangladeshi Grameen Bank, for example has lent money to 2.3 million people, most of them women. Ironically, as *The New York Times* has noted, "Such financing, though often hard to obtain in the United

States, can be easier to find in countries like India and Colombia." *DOF* predicts that we will catch up and a new focus on micro-entrepreneurs will emerge: politicians will celebrate their virtues and start funding their efforts—perhaps with new equivalents to the Head Start program; banks will set up special lending programs; cause marketing efforts launched by financial services companies (including credit cards) will allocate funding to micro-entrepreneurs; nonprofits will suddenly wake up and start paying macro attention to these micro heroes.

New Economy Guilds — the medieval phenomenon of merchant guilds—collectives of workers that provided benefits and facilitated early economic structures—is being reborn as a concept that is perfectly suited to today's high-tech economy. Thomas Malone, professor at MIT, argues that the guild is the perfect vehicle for our freelance, free-agent work style. As the magazine *Fast Company* writes, "Malone . . . says that guilds offer talented workers an organizing principle by which they can associate with others who share an occupational affinity, develop professional skills, and share their need for new ways to provide for benefits and security." *DOF* expects to see guilds morph into consumer brands, as buyers of goods and services look to specific guilds as representations of superior quality and performance.

Personal Zoning — we've had personal zoning for a long time, except we haven't called it that. When we walk past the privileged first-class compartment in a plane, or watch people scoot down to the orchestra at the theater when we're in the balcony, those are all examples of personal zoning. *DOF* believes that as the wealthy continue to get wealthier, the carving up of space will be pushed to new levels. *The Wall Street Journal* reported that hotels are taking reservations just to be able to get into the lobby. We expect exclusive auto dealerships to move to an appointment-only basis, and luxury retailers will set aside territory that is off-limits to everyone who isn't on the A list. As the Internet democratizes the flow of information, the counter-trend is to create new hierarchies in what used to be public space.

Rooftop Management — revolutions turn the priceless into the dross, and create assets out of the unexpected. Witness the unglamorous rooftop, now so valuable that *Fortune* has reported that some New York City buildings are leasing their highest points for super-high prices: three times that of the office space below. Given all the satellite and telecommunications companies looking for places to plop their antennas there is fierce demand, and *Fortune* writes "The trend has created a cottage industry in the real estate business: rooftop management." At 20 Exchange Place in downtown New York, more than 80 antennas crowd the roof.

Shareholder Resolution Votes — these are not new, but their use by activists is. Many don't realize the SEC allows anyone who owns at least $1,000 worth of stock to file a shareholder resolution, which then appears on the company's proxy ballot and is voted on at the annual meeting. Simply put, a resolution can request that management adopt certain policies, or stop engaging in others. While management isn't bound by the vote, these resolutions are an effective way to draw attention to issues that an individual or group is passionate about: environmental practices, the use of child labor in foreign countries, the support of special interest groups through PACs. If a Shareholder Resolution has broad popular—and investor—appeal, management could be embarrassed by not implementing it. Amy Domini, who runs the oldest and largest socially responsible mutual fund, is leading a crusade to push the industry to post Shareholder Resolutions on their respective Web sites, making shareholders' viewpoints—and management responses—instantly visible. "It's outrageous that managers are not telling investors how they vote," Domini has said. *DOF* believes that mutual funds will eventually agree, and that corporate management will need to develop new strategies to manage an onslaught of visible, and popular, Shareholder Resolutions.

Shock Accounting — an increasingly influential group of theorists believe that our traditional methods of corporate accounting are inadequate for today's world. Shock accounting is *DOF*'s all-encompassing term to describe these emerging principles, which could up-end the fundamental way businesses report their performance and value their assets. In the words of *Fortune* magazine, traditional reporting (called GAAP, for "generally accepted accounting principles") "gives rotten information about the value, and performance, of modern, knowledge-intensive companies."

Accounting revolutionaries (how's that for an oxymoron?) like Robert Howell and Baruch Lev would toss out conventional balance sheets and replace them with an approach that captures the value of intellectual capital, of R&D, recruitment and training. Changing the way "profit" and "earnings" are calculated for P/E multiples would have radical implications, so changing it will require more than a few wise voices, but a grand sense of public will. *DOF* believes this could very well emerge, because Shock Accounting would add value to 401(K) investments and pension plans, which invest so much of their assets in technology companies that are undervalued by GAAP.

Slave Reparations — a serious movement to obtain compensation for the horrors and evils of slavery. Responsible parties include major insurance companies—from Aetna to New York Life—who wrote policies on the lives of slaves as "property" for slave-owners, and the federal government itself. We've paid reparations to Sioux Indians for property stolen from them, and to Japanese-Americans interned during World War II, but have never paid anything to descendants of former slaves. According to a study conducted by the University of Chicago and Harvard, 53 percent of African-Americans believe these payments are appropriate. Several legal cases are pending and more are planned, which means slave reparations could become a passionate, and probably divisive, national debate.

Sugar Parents Economy — *DOF*'s term for the money that flows from parents to their grown children to fund everything from buying a house or car to paying for vacations and education. To our knowledge no one has yet quantified this, but it represents a big chunk of the economy. As an example, W. Van Bussman, the corporate economist for Chrysler, has said that a significant portion of luxury car buyers are young people with wealthy parents and grandparents. *DOF* believes that more funds will be flowing through the sugar parents economy, and it will become increasingly studied as economists and marketers start to recognize there are two target audiences for many purchases: the user and the funder.

Virtual Close — the networked world is changing the way business looks at its finances. Rather than closing the books once a quarter, a corporation can look at where it stands instantly. This has been advocated by John Chambers, CEO of Cisco Systems, who describes the virtual close as: "the ability to close the financial books with a one-hour notice. By connecting the entire company via intranet, even one with dozens of operations in dozens of countries, what was once done quarterly can now be done anytime . . . the ability to close so quickly lets you spot problems and opportunities at any time." It's certainly theoretically possible and would be a powerful tool, but even sophisticated companies have a long way to go, which is why we keep hearing about those "earnings surprises."

Virtual Immigrants — technology workers who serve U.S. companies from their native countries—such as China, Russia and the Philippines—where they must remain because of immigration restrictions. (See *H-1B debate.*) Imagine the economic impact in these countries when you have some people making $35 an hour working for a U.S. company, and others making $35 a week working for a local one. A mini-industry is emerging to hook employers up with their virtual immigrants; it includes both headhunters and companies like Sunnyvale, California-based Angel Engineers who hires the programmers and then "leases" them to their clients. It's all an example of the efficiency—and complexity—of the global economy.

Dictionary of the Future Predicts

Barter Credits — *DOF* believes that the application of the Internet to the vast world of personal barter transactions hasn't even begun. We expect to see Web sites aggregating services offered, and services needed, by millions anxious to participate in the barter economy. Those with services to render will post their capabilities and the number of barter credits they will cost. You earn the credits by posting your own skills and capabilities, and rendering services to those who need them. The beauty of the barter exchange is that you don't have to earn your credits by rendering a service directly to the person you're swapping with. The quality control mechanism will start as self-policing, like eBay, but as it expands an informal judicial system may emerge—a Barter Court—to resolve differences.

Bonus Meters — employees will be able to log on to a corporate intranet and see how their performance-based bonus stands, based on how they, and their employer, are doing. *DOF* believes this technique will be an enormous daily motivator and boost to productivity.

Corportfolios — companies like Intel, Microsoft, Compaq, SmithKline Beecham and other 900-pound gorillas have invested in literally hundreds of start-ups. The numbers are staggering: Microsoft's stake in these companies was (once) worth as much as $20 billion; in the fourth quarter of 1999, 40 percent of Chase's profits came from its equity arm. While these numbers are not a secret, there is no convenient, standardized way of valuing this investment on a daily basis. This is an enormous oversight because the performance of the companies in the corportfolio has significant implications for the value of its stock. You should be able to check *The Wall Street Journal* and determine the corportfolio value, just like you check the P/E multiple. And one day, you will.

Patents vs. Profits — *DOF* sees this as the next big battleground for activists. When do compelling human rights issues

Ee

render the pursuit of profits no longer acceptable? The struggle over AIDS drugs in Africa is one such example, and we've seen some of the major pharmaceutical companies, under enormous pressure—and in an unprecedented step—relinquish some of their royalty rights and permit generic drug makers to manufacture and sell AIDS drugs at a fraction of the full cost. Anticipating this, some companies have decided to forgo patent protection in other areas. The journal *Nature* reports "Monsanto has announced royalty-free licenses to its technology for producing rice varieties with enhanced levels of provitamin A."

As technology breakthroughs become both more stunning and more expensive, the patents vs. profits debate will intensify. For example: What motivation do drug companies have to develop new treatments for diseases if they aren't permitted to make enough money to recapture their investment? After all, only three out of ten drugs ever make a profit. Many argue that the reason America leads in drug development is precisely the economic motivation that drives research, and that increased regulation would result in far less innovation.

Pleading Economy — a shift in the balance of power from employer to employee, driven by low unemployment and demographic changes. While the most exaggerated examples of this—pet-walking services for employees is one—are behind us, the fundamental reality has changed. Jeff Taylor, the founder of monster.com, has said, "I think we're in the beginning throes of a decade-long generational labor shortage. . . . People confuse a six-to-nine month correction with the reality . . . that we're going to have a huge skills shortage. . . . I predict that companies in this 10-year period will go out of business, not because they aren't good at providing products or services, but because they're not good at recruiting and retaining employees." See also *exploding offers*.

Transparent Mark-Ups — the next step in the full transparency wrought by the Internet revolution. We predict that you will be able to look at a product and see its entire economic biography—its cost of goods as well as the mark-up—so you know how much the manufacturer is making, and how much goes into the product itself. And if two cars each sell for $30,000, but one costs $23,000 to make and one costs $12,000, doesn't that tell you which vehicle gives you more for your money?

EDUCATION

It is the number one issue in the polls, it's not working as well as anyone wants, and everyone has an opinion—accompanied by a theory and an action plan—for how to improve it. (Followed closely by an excuse for why that much-trumpeted solution didn't work.)

All this heat has manufactured a schoolhouse full of words and phrases that document the pressures, debates and proposed innovations that are the verbal currency of this national exchange. As you would expect, some of this language is far from neutral, and is loaded—perhaps even burdened—with political ballast. Advocates have learned to wrap their positions with prespun language. You can't hear the phrase "woodwork children," for example, without your sympathy quotient rising for these ignored victims. Similarly, you can't hear a term like "educentives," with its happy ring of free-market solutions, and not believe that educational standards won't be served by a dose of competitive motivation.

We're also seeing the emergence of new teaching philosophies, including "just-in-time-education" and "minimally invasive education" that bear watching. Technology, of course, is also changing the way we teach, and the impact of computers and the Internet in the classroom are also touched on here—including a *DOF* prediction that parents will be able to review "teacher histories" online.

Occasionally, a term you're familiar with—like "charter schools"—may turn up. That's because its familiarity outstrips its comprehension, and even a dictionary of the future, occasionally, needs to do some remedial education.

Charter Schools — schools that offer an alternative to public school education by virtue of a "charter" they receive from a local jurisdiction. These charters are granted when parents and legislators seek to bring choice and accountability to education—particularly in areas where public school performance is sub-par. Thirty-six states, the District of Columbia and Puerto Rico have approved charter schools which are freed from many of the restrictions that public schools are bound by; and they receive government funding, but have contracts for just three to five years and, as a U.S. Department of Education report put it, "they are held accountable for improving student performance and achieving the goals of their charter contracts" (www.ed.gov/pubs/charter/execsum. html). Charter schools can be run by a for-profit company, like the Edison Group, or by a nonprofit group, and they can be for a specific purpose—e.g., vocational training—or they can serve a broader public school function.

Supporters believe that charter schools are the last, best hope for students—and neighborhoods—who have been failed by conventional public schools. Opponents argue that all of our efforts—financial and otherwise—should be put behind improving our public schools. One would think that as the track record of charter schools becomes clear, the debate would be self-answering. But there is enough smush in the numbers to give both sides in the argument something to grab hold of. A good source of reasonably objective background information can be found at www.uscharterschools. org

Ed-Flex — a concept which allows individual schools to adopt customized, innovative teaching approaches; by obtaining waivers they can continue to receive Federal funding. The debate is whether schools should have this much leeway. Critics say it will lower standards; supporters argue that creative teachers and administrators should be encouraged, that no single approach works in all cases. Also: ed-flex makes it easier to recruit exciting teachers who are unwilling to be handcuffed by rigid lesson plans. We predict that ed-flex will continue to gain popular support and expand nationally; the individualism and imagination it represents are squarely in the American grain.

Educentives — the hue and cry about our slipping educational standards is leading some municipalities to try a technique that's a free-market bonus to some, bribery to others. Terrorized by statewide exams that could result in funding cutbacks if districts don't measure up, local officials are offering cash incentives to motivate both teachers and students. In Concord, North Carolina, every teacher—not just those who teach any given class—stands to get a $1,500 bonus if the school's scores exceed the state minimum level. Students are motivated by gifts, as well: as *The New York Times* reports, those with high GPAs, or with grades that have improved substantially, "now carry gold, silver and white identification cards that entitle them to a $2 discount at Great Clips hair salon, free toppings at Ci-Ci's Pizza, and even a chit to skip a test or a homework assignment." *The Times* further reports that these radical ideas are spreading to places like Ohio, Kentucky and California. We expect this trend to catch fire.

Gap Year — the increasingly common practice of taking off a year between high school and college, either to accumulate the necessary funds, or to pad the resume with some kind of noble volunteer or public service work. Options have included building a boat in Russia, patrolling a beach in Costa Rica to secure the nests of leatherback turtles, and caring for penguins in Antarctica (Salary: $10,000). The gap year industry is poised to take off; already we've seen "The Center for Interim Studies" in Massachusetts, and www.whereyou headed.com. *DOF* believes that the direct high school-to-college track will eventually become as outdated as the one-job-for-life paradigm. See also *gap year counselors*.

Just-in-Time Education — a movement which is slowly transforming higher education—particularly in the technology area. We used to operate from the principle of "just-in-case" education ("Study this just in case you need to know it someday," as *Lingua Franca*, the magazine of academia, puts it). That was appropriate when the body of knowledge we had to master was, well, manageable. Consider that since 1950, the sum of all human knowledge has doubled. By the year 2020, that doubling will occur every 73 days. Just-in-time education teaches us what we need, when we need it. (Interestingly, it's the educational translation of the concept of "just-in-time manufacturing" which has brought new levels of efficiency to the economy. The analogy: Why warehouse useless information in our brains?) The downside of this—everything in life isn't about immediate application of learning, there is value in accumulated wisdom, and the most inspired problem-solving comes from the application of ideas that may not be (and usually aren't) immediately related to the task at hand.

K12 — a well-funded online school started by William Bennett, former Secretary of Education and outspoken advocate of traditional values. K12, which will stress back-to-basic principles like phonics and civics, will target—in large part—those families who are home-schooling their children; there are roughly 1.5 million of them nationwide, and, as *The Wall Street Journal* writes, "Once labeled a fringe group, home-schooled students are now sought after by publishers, which sell them textbooks and tests; public schools, which want them back; and colleges, which are recruiting them because of their generally high test scores." K12 plans to enroll 100,000 students by 2005, and its tuition will be around $2,000 per year. K12 is part of the larger online educational market; Merrill Lynch estimates that the kindergarten through twelfth-grade segment will soar from $1.9 billion in 1999 to $6.9 billion in 2003. K12 has taken a clear position in the educational wars, thus its success or failure is not necessarily a barometer for the future of electronic education.

Latent Semantic Analysis — a variant of artificial intelligence; utilized by Peter Foltz, professor at the University of New Mexico, for his program called "Intelligent Essay Advisor." It enables computers to grade high school or college essays based on previously inputted examples of "good" and "bad" essays, as well as data from encyclopedias, textbooks and other sources. It doesn't seem like this technology allows much room for creativity or innovation, and we suspect that this subject will be hotly debated in the years to come as this kind of assembly-line grading expands.

Minimally Invasive Education — a term coined by Sugata Mitra, head of research and development at NIIT, India's leading technology company. To demonstrate his theory that children can educate themselves, Mitra hooked up a PC to the Internet, and inserted the computer in a wall that separated his company from an area which poor people—who had no indoor plumbing—used as a toilet. Using a video camera, he monitored Internet use. Mitra, who won a Social Innovation award for his experiment, found that slum children, who had no education and could not speak English, learned to use a mouse, browse the Internet and draw on the computer in a matter of weeks.

Mitra maintains that if he had the funding for 100,000 kiosks he could allow 500 million Indian children to achieve computer literacy. *DOF* believes that the concept of minimally invasive education will get very hot, and that it will be studied as a pedagogical approach for both poor and affluent communities, as an alternative to our traditional belief that education is based solely on teacher/student interaction.

StudyPro — a laptop computer designed by NetSchools expressly for educational purposes. The computer has a magnesium case, is water resistant and—to make sure it isn't stolen—can only be used within a school's wireless network. Students take StudyPro from class to class, as they would a traditional notebook. In addition NetSchools (www.netschools. com), the parent company of StudyPro, has put together an innovative and integrated program that connects teachers, students and parents—and can be customized to meet the curricula of individual school districts. This is an innovative and affordable public/private symbiosis that will help many school districts—including those in less-affluent regions—

bring the advantages of Internet-based learning into their classrooms.

Universal Instructional Designs — a controversial educational approach that changes the classroom environment to make teaching more "dyslexia-friendly" as *Time* reports. This technique will use "visual aids like slides, repeat concepts several times, and allow more time for tests and note-taking." Since kids with dyslexia and other learning disabilities have to work twice as hard to keep up with their peers, advocates say this levels the playing field. But we can expect a firestorm of controversy from those who say it's penalizing (and frustrating) kids who want to move ahead. This is a cultural debate distilled down to its raw essentials, and it's just the beginning of other arguments along the same fault lines.

Unschooling — a home-schooling method based on the belief that kids learn best when they're allowed to pursue their natural curiosities and interests—a field trip to Disneyland, or a comparative study of Nintendo, perhaps. There is no curriculum or master plan—it's a free-form approach to learning controlled by children themselves. One Web site describes it this way: "Unschooling, child-led learning, interest based learning or child delighted learning. No matter what you call it, it is a wonderful way to raise a child. I say 'raise a child' rather than 'homeschool' because for most unschoolers, all of life is education and worthy of notice and discovery." See also *affirmative parenting, free-range children.*

Woodwork Children — the average child, the one in the middle who is prone to fading into the woodwork. Woodwork children are a product of the fact that educational spending is increasingly diverted to gifted children on one end of the spectrum, and children with learning problems on the other. Thus, funding for "average education" is down from 86 percent of school budgets in 1975 to less than 60 percent today. Woodwork children are also spurring the market for supplemental education—more than $4 billion and growing.

Dictionary of the Future Predicts

Cheat Searches — mini-wireless technology, from Internet-enabled watches to smart pens, is making it easier than ever to cheat on exams—from the SATs to civil service tests to the law boards. To prevent this, testing services will have to search all incoming test-takers, using the sophisticated devices designed to catch terrorists at airports and border crossings. But relax, kids—they are still working on brain scans to detect overnight cramming.

Counter-Schooling — driven by the competitive educational environment and the failure of public schools, the counter-schooling movement will emerge. For-profit companies will sell supplementary educational services that are "counter-programmed" to school vacations, providing back-up and enriched programs during vacations and breaks.

Ivy Brands — recognizing that they are sitting on branding assets of incalculable value, *DOF* predicts that Yale, Harvard, Princeton and other elite institutions will begin to extend their names—some of them more than 300 years old—into the consumer and B2B marketplaces. Expect to see tutoring centers, educational toys, CDs, medical centers, seminars and other branded products and services. Which means that you may not be able to get into Yale, but you can buy Yale's very own brand of Ginkgo biloba. See also *museum getting*.

Kinder Krisis — with all the talk about education, the emerging crisis in America is our shabby record with pre-school education. In France, thanks to their *ecole maternelle,* three year olds, according to *The New York Times,* "bake pies in a science lab and learn to count and read." Here—even though pre-school education is recognized as a precursor to later academic success—only 55 percent of children between three and five are in a program, and 79 percent of them are from families earning $75,000 or more. It's a complicated issue that involves funding, unions and the role of day-care centers. But the problem is real, and many believe that if we're serious about educating our children, the federal government would mandate pre-school for all. In fact, *DOF* believes that this will become our next great educational crusade, and that given the shortage of K and pre-K classes—and the time it takes to establish them—vouchers will be used to help parents pay for private school alternatives. This will drive people like Disney and CTW (Children's Television Workshop) into the business.

Madmissions — the competitive frenzy over getting your kid into an elite private school, college, law school, medical school or—as affluent urbanites know, the most grueling of all—pre-K. That's right, it's no longer an admission process, it's a *madmission* process. The signs of madmission are all over: extra tutoring sessions, college counselors, the dirty little secret of paying people to ghost write college essays and Web sites like www.achieve.com. The competition is heightened by more people with more money battling over the same number of places. And it starts early; with two and three year olds being subject to accelerated learning programs. Expect a counter-trend, as in *natural kids, clean time* (see listings).

Seminar Royalties — the deepening relationship between the Internet and education, along with the growth of broadband and streaming media, will find major universities webcasting the seminars of their most famous and popular professors, e.g. Yale's Harold Bloom on Shakespeare. Universities will charge "admission" to these seminars—either live or on an archived basis—and therein lies the rub. How do the professors get a piece of the action, since this kind of Internet revenue is a whole new concept? We anticipate that seminar royalties will evolve as the solution; the professors will negotiate a royalty split, just as movie stars have points in a film.

Teacher History — in an era of increased accountability, teachers will not escape more intense scrutiny. Soon, you will be able to check a teacher's pedagogical portfolio on the Internet. Find out how his or her students did on standardized tests, review parent comments, check homework assignments and grading philosophy. Also learn how the teacher's class does in the subsequent grades, the true measure of classroom success. The teachers' unions will fight it, but public demand will prevail.

Wired to Failure — the unintended result of Internet access in the majority of American classrooms—"Webucation"—will spell further problems for schools. Kids are becoming even less able to think independently and critically, to connect patterns, to move in abstract realms. Also called the Empty Luggage Syndrome, as in computers in the classrooms appear to deliver a great deal, but actually contain nothing inside. *DOF* wonders if a reaction to our latest obsession with wiring classrooms is forthcoming—in the 1950s, after all, a TV set in every class was considered the answer to educational reform—which suggests that a refocus on interaction between kids and a teacher, not computer skills, is in the wind.

This section turned out to be as long and nuanced as it is because the
environment is, and will be, seizing more of our time and brain-space.
The word "environment" itself is moving from what it was—a relatively
narrow sphere that focused on single-issue initiatives like recycling and
pollution—to a far-reaching conversation that involves complex,
interrelated subjects from agriculture to urban planning to
pharmaceuticals.

This section attempts to move from the narrow but indicative, like
"arborcide" laws that punish the illegal removal of a tree by up to a year
in jail, to more involved concepts like "designer waste streams,"
"industrial reincarnation," and "ecological footprints." Innovative
solutions to horrific problems like global warming and the destruction of
rainforests are tendered by "carbon sinks," "low emission farming," and
"conservation concessions."

New threats, like "pharmaceutical pollution," the "circle of poison"—
involving exported pesticides—and light pollution, which is creating the
need for "dark sky preserves" also find their way into this section. So do
free-market approaches to environmental stresses, including "green
premiums," new materials like the recyclable carpet "Solenium," and
Polyactide, a natural plastic. And we must not forget the "Viridian
Greens," whose manifesto sets forth a plan to use status marketing to
save the world from environmental doom.

Arborcide — a telling linguistic victory for environmentalism is when trees become equated with human beings. That is precisely what the term "arborcide" does, turning what George Washington did when he chopped down the legendary cherry tree into an offense that might stop someone, today, from becoming president. In New York City, arborcide can get you up to a year in the slammer, plus a $15,000 fine. Other municipalities, we believe, will enact similar legislation. It's part of the trend that finds activists turning to sympathetic courts for support. See also *pets' rights*.

BANANA — acronym for "Build Absolutely Nothing Anywhere Near Anything." A reaction to sprawl and over-development—a radical kind of geographic isolationism—and an outgrowth of the NIMBY ("Not In My Backyard") phenomenon, the term is taking on international resonance: a reference even turns up on the Prince of Wales's Web page (www.princeofwales.gov.uk/speeches/architecture_17021999. html). As the livability of cities and suburbs reaches the breaking point, the next decade will witness an unprecedented struggle between BANANA activists, and those on the other side: developers, business leaders, hospital and university presidents who—although they talk the environmentally sensitive talk—are becoming the twenty-first-century version of the nineteenth century's evil industrialists. See also *smart growth, sprawl out, telesprawl*.

Bioneers — a loosely knit group of activists—biological pioneers—who believe that biological methods are our best way of dealing with environmental problems. The *Utne Reader* writes that they include "farmers, students, priests, lawyers, teachers, ecologists, designers, writers, artists." One bioneer, Paul Stamets, is a mycologist (mushroom expert) who found that these fungi are capable of breaking down contaminants such as diesel oil and E. coli bacteria. Another bioneer is the famed architect William McDonough, who built the Gap's headquarters in California (a prototype of sustainability) and is now turning Ford's notorious Rouge River factory into an "ecological industrial facility." Bioneers have created a radio series that airs on 120 stations in the United States (and, remarkably, 390 in Australia); learn more at www.bioneers. org. *DOF* believes that just as the pioneers helped create one vision of America, bioneers will lead the way to another. See also *ecological medicine.*

Brownfields — they're not as toxic as Superfund cleanup sites, but they sure aren't on any Chamber of Commerce tours. Brownfield is a catchall term for abandoned factories, dumps, landfills and other neglected areas, most between 10 and 50 acres. Estimates are that there are over 100,000 brownfields, many of them in valuable areas within city centers. Undeveloped for years because of liability issues, there is a brownfield revival movement underway thanks to the confluence of a number of factors: legislation limiting the liability of developers; new insurance policies to protect them; new technology for measuring and remediating the pollution; and the economic boom which is forcing developers to turn their attention to long-overlooked properties.

Carbon Sinks — the burning of fossil fuels, and the carbon dioxide they release, have created the global warming mess. What many don't realize is that half of the carbon dioxide that's released eventually gets absorbed by plants, soil and forests. These are called carbon sinks, and one theory is that global warming can be addressed by increasing the number of them in industrialized countries by planting trees, changing farming methods, and other approaches. Some environmentalists are against this, believing that reducing emissions is the only real answer. There is also some evidence that "terrestrial sinks may become net producers of carbon dioxide within 50 years" according to the journal *Nature.* Meanwhile, the Kyoto Protocol—the international global warming treaty—requires that emissions be cut to 5 percent below the 1990 level by 2010. For us to accomplish that will require both reduction and an increase in carbon sinks, the environmental equivalent of raising revenue and cutting expenses. Down the road: carbon removal technology that will capture CO_2 before it's released and sequestering it—perhaps storing it in undersea fields.

Ee

One thing we do know: the future had better not be a carbon dioxide copy of the past. See also *iron fertilization*.

Caulerpa Taxifola — an invasive algae that has had devastating effects in the Mediterranean Sea, and has been found off the California coast. In Europe, a small colony of the algae released from a public aquarium now covers more than 6,000 hectares and, according to the journal *Nature*, it "out competes native species and seriously reduces diversity." Research has shown the California algae to be the same strain, which led *Nature* to call for "rapid eradication to prevent a new invasion." This is one of those environmental issues that tends to get ignored until it's vastly more expensive to fix. Or just too late.

Circle of Poison — here's how this scary circle works. Each year, about 100 million pounds of banned or unregistered pesticides are manufactured in the United States, for export. Foreign agricultural workers are exposed to them, spraying pollutes the area, runoff ends up creating toxic water supplies. At the same time, these workers arrive home with pesticides all over their clothes. Animals that graze on pesticide-soaked fields are slaughtered and eaten. Lastly, foods treated with these pesticides (which are not approved by the EPA) are exported back to America, where we consume them. (This description draws significantly from a fact sheet published by the National Campaign for Pesticide Policy Reform.) Although this has been known for years, it has not yet—but shortly will—capture our imagination. We see consumers and retailers getting together to "break the poison circle" and predict that consumers will avoid fruits and vegetables that are part of the chain. See also *toxic bouquets*.

Conservation Concessions — an innovative way to preserve wilderness areas, given that emerging nations are motivated to sell their environmentally sensitive lands to rich developers, rather than donate them to well-intentioned, but poor environmentalists. Conservation concessions enable these nations to lease these lands to environmental groups—thus generating revenue, and preventing destructive development. For example, the Conservation International Foundation—as reported in *The New York Times*—is buying the long-term logging rights to 200,000 acres of a rain forest in southern Guyana, and they expect to expand into Peru, Bolivia and Cambodia. It's a really smart solution—the government gets compensated for lost revenue, and the environment is spared. The Conservation International Foundation includes the likes of Craig McCaw, visionary cell phone billionaire; Gordon Moore, one of the founders of Intel; and Disney's Michael Eisner: innovative philanthropists looking for new solutions to age-old problems.

Dark Sky Preserve — areas that have been set aside for the peaceful contemplation of the heavens, a kind of visual quiet. It is necessary for municipalities to impose these restrictions because of light pollution, which destroys the spiritual and meditative glory of a dark night sky. Everything from commercial and residential lighting to night Little League games combine to create the problem. Lake Palmer in Arizona was an early dark sky preserve; in New Mexico, the governor has signed the Night Sky Protection Act; a local preservation group lists the state's night skies as one of New Mexico's most endangered symbols. Lighting manufacturers are trying to cooperate, by designing fixtures that project down, not up. As the life-congestion of the future creates an even greater need for contemplation—and as development creates additional sources of over-illumination—battles for dark sky preserves will erupt across the country. Proving that pollution takes many forms, and that even light can be toxic. To learn more, there is www.darksky.org.

Designer Waste Streams — coined by Reid Lifset, editor of the *Journal of Industrial Ecology*, this takes current recycling efforts up some very big notches. Biotechnology and genetic engineering would assure that much of our waste has *built-in* recyclable qualities. For example, as *Time* magazine reports,

"Scientists at Monsanto and Heartland Fiber are working toward engineering corn plants with the kind of fiber content that paper companies would find attractive; that approach could tap into a huge stream of agricultural waste, turning some of it into an industrial ingredient." *DOF* believes that soon, designer waste stream products will be identified proudly, just as those made from recycled paper boast about it.

Eco-Industrial Parks — traditional industrial parks are collections of faceless office complexes, taking from the environment and returning nothing. Eco-industrial parks, like the one in Kalundborg, Denmark, have a reciprocal relationship with their surroundings. *Time* magazine writes that "Within the park, a power company, a pharmaceuticals firm, a wallboard producer and an oil refinery share in the production and use of steam, gas and cooling water. Excess heat warms nearby homes and agricultural greenhouses. One company's waste becomes another's resources. The power plant sells the sulfur dioxide it scrubs from its smokestacks to the wallboard company, which uses the compound as raw material." *DOF* predicts that governments and local municipalities will begin to create favorable tax and zoning laws to allow these eco–industrial parks to flourish. See also *clusters green accounting*.

Ecological Footprint — every moment, our presence on the planet has an environmental impact, the calculation of which is one's ecological footprint. (It could be for an individual, a group or even a product). Ecological footprints are compelling because they reveal the *net effect* of our behavior. They also measure current consumption patterns against projected supply, to project depletion and sustainability. (If you're interested in calculating your own personal environmental impact, go to www.lead.org/leadnet/footprint/food.cfm.) *DOF* predicts that the concept will gain in visibility as a marker for a company's commitment to the environment. Product labels will reference ecological footprints—like cars reference their gas mileage ratings—and corporations will conduct "green marketing" campaigns touting their collective global footprint. Similarly, individuals will gain status based on their own personal footprints, as a badge of social awareness. See also *biotecture, polyactide.*

Environ — a substance made of soy flour and recycled newsprint possessing the properties of wood and the physical appearance of granite. It is manufactured by Phenix Biocomposites, a company dedicated to sustainable building; they also make "Biofiber" soy and wheat industrial panels that use renewable fiber from American farms—www.phenixbiocom posites.com. (Which means that while you're bouncing off the walls you can also be eating them.) If marketed properly, we believe that the new status symbol will be the use of sustainable building materials. See also *biotecture, polylactide Viridian Greens.*

ESU — biological shorthand for "evolutionarily significant unit" and technical as it sounds, it sits at the heart of much environmental policy and debate. That's because species will be defined—and thus protected—based upon how narrow or wide the definition of an ESU is. While one working definition incorporates the phrase "distinct population segment," others disagree. *Science News* notes that this very narrow definition would mean that an ESU would include not just a species, but—say in the case of salmon—each distinct breeding ground. The fear is that overly narrow ESUs are too complicated to enforce and will actually backfire, giving anti-environmentalists an argument that we can't "protect every creek around the world"; the debate shows how complex a seemingly simple issue like species identification can be. See also *Red List.*

Frankenfish — derived from frankenfood, which is what the anti-GMO (genetically modified organism) forces call any foodstuff whose DNA has been altered. Frankenfish are farmbred, but some of them—especially salmon—are escaping into the oceans and mating with wild salmon. Their offspring lack the full complement of natural defenses, and thus

Ee

frankenfish are weakening the gene pool and contributing to the direct decline in the number of the wild fish. This has huge consequences for the ecosystem, as you can imagine. See also *conservation genetics*.

Green Premiums — as more and more drugs use plant materials, there is a race to harvest the raw materials despite the environmental consequences. For example, bark poachers are killing so many evergreens of the genus *Prunus Africanus*—which is used as a prostate remedy—that the *Economist* reports it will be extinct within 10 years. Certain sustainable techniques will preserve the trees, but cost more. Groups like ICRAF (the International Center for Research in Agroforestry) want farmers who use these sustainable techniques to be able to charge green premiums at the market. There's plenty of room in the price structure: farmers get less than a dollar per kilogram of bark they harvest, less than a hundredth of the retail price. We predict that sooner or later, green premiums will become a term we all know, as shoppers will be asked to pay a step-up for sustainably grown herbs (both medicinal and culinary), fruits, vegetables and garden plants.

Greenwashing — consumers are anxious to support companies that are good corporate citizens. Surveys show that more than 60 percent of consumers, in fact, would choose to buy from a company that supports causes they believe in. This is no surprise to corporations, some of whom exaggerate their green credentials to mislead consumers into thinking they are on the side of the angels (these are also called "Astroturf" companies because they are artificially green). How do these great pretenders use greenwashing strategies? They might run ads that talk about how they give a percentage (usually a tiny one) of sales or profits to environmental causes—when they are polluting the air and releasing tons of greenhouse gases at the same time. We predict that a couple of greenwashing sites will pop up on the Internet, giving consumers the full environmental report card of companies that wrap themselves in a mantle of faux green.

Grow-It-Yourself Furniture — the re-popularization of a technique, which goes back as far as the Egyptians and the Greeks, for training trees to take the shape of furniture. This ancient form of furniture topiary is also sustainable and environmentally friendly; the approach has been taken up in England by Chris Cattle (www.buckscol.ac.uk/research/resdescc.htm), who believes the technique can be commercialized, envisioning "furniture orchards." Likewise Richard Reames, also in the U.K. at www.arborsmith.com/index.html, describes his farm as "the place where houses are planted, chairs are watered, tables are pruned and fences grow taller and stronger as the years go by." We expect this to become a hot new design trend—the next step beyond the gardening craze—as we start to grow our end tables along with our endive

Hard Green — an environmental turn in the road that will increasingly define the eco-debate. The term was coined by Peter Huber to describe adherents of a more pragmatic view of environmental issues. Hard Greens look at the full range of the implications of a particular decision; for example, Huber maintains that "It's greener to live in Trump Tower than a 40 acre farm in Vermont." (When you live in Manhattan you use public transportation and recycle; in Vermont your wood-burning stove, pickup truck and tractor pollute the air, and your fertilizer—even if it's organic—runs off and damages marine life.) Opposed to the Hard Greens: Soft Greens, who never met a solar panel they didn't like.

Industrial Reincarnation — there are hundreds of ways that industrial materials can be re-used rather than discarded, and new applications are turning up all the time. There's even a Web site that lists a lot of them: www.dpiwe.tas.gov.au/env/waste_exchange/potential_reuses.html. *DOF* predicts that soon, products will automatically list the recycled materials they were derived from—on the package and on their Web sites—to give consumers a chance to buy products that started off as something else, like the vest that came into the world as a snowtire. See also *eco-industrial parks, natural capital.*

Ee

Iron Fertilization — a controversial but potentially breakthrough method of removing carbon dioxide from the atmosphere. Supertankers start the process by distributing millions of tons of iron in the ocean. The iron encourages the growth of algae that feed on carbon dioxide. When the algae die (of overeating) they sink, bloated, to the bottom of the ocean, taking the carbon dioxide with them. To restabilize the balance, the ocean then withdraws carbon dioxide from the atmosphere, making up for what the algae consumed. It seems logical, but opponents argue that the environmental consequences of dropping millions of tons of iron are still an open question. See also *carbon sinks*.

Low-Emission Farming — studies are finding that changes in agricultural practices can actually reduce or eliminate a significant portion of the greenhouse gases that are responsible for global warming. Farmers need to reduce fertilizer use, grow so-called "cover crops" in winter like alfalfa, and plow their fields less frequently. This allows the farmlands to "trap" more carbon, thus keeping it out of the atmosphere. If these studies are accurate, why not encourage farmers via subsidies to adopt these ozone-safe practices? And let's use marketing to encourage consumers to spend more for products that were grown this way—with special "Low-Emission" stickers. It's time to use the considerable power of the free market to reduce greenhouse gases, employing a new kind of economic judo. See also *carbon sinks, iron fertilization, Viridian Greens*.

Network Farming — a technique advocated by David Cole, technology entrepreneur turned organic gardener. At his Sunnyside Farms in Virginia (www.sunnysidefarms.com), Cole is developing a system where, according to *The New York Times*, "a large central farm is the hub, with smaller nearby farms the spokes, their production marketed to the hub." If it works, network farming (it's what you'd expect from someone who worked at AOL) will enable small organic farms to flourish, and will protect land from developers. Cole is attempting to marry marketing, technology and the principles of organic farming; his innovations include mobile chicken units—

portable structures that move chickens from place to place, letting them eat bugs and eliminating the need for pesticides. This experimental farm, into which Cole has sunk more than $11 million, isn't a charity—he expects it to become profitable by 2004. Learning from Sunnyside Farms could have a profound effect on the entire industry.

Pharmaceutical Pollution — when drugs taken by patients pass through their digestive systems and end up in the waste stream. Studies in Canada, Louisiana and Minnesota have turned up the by-products of cholesterol drugs, the pain reliever naproxen and estrogen. This means these drugs end up in the drinking water, and are also consumed by fish as part of the food chain. While some studies suggest that fish have been made sterile by these discharges, more investigating needs to be done. As drug consumption increases, *DOF* expects that pharmaceutical pollution will become a significant problem. The consequences are pretty scary; drug interaction problems, and healthy people taking medicine they don't need. It's a surprising, uninvited result of our over-medicated society.

Polylactide (PLA) — a plastic derived from corn and wheat, known as "natural plastic." The result of a joint venture of Dow Chemical and Cargill Inc., the plastic will be marketed under the name "NatureWorks" and will be used to make carpet fibers, packaging, clothing and other products. Cargill Dow claims that PLA, unlike petroleum-based plastics, is made completely from renewable resources and is biodegradable. In addition, it is immune from the cyclical price swings oil-based products are subject to, and is claimed to be strong enough to compete with other plastics. Plastic has already escaped its cheesy heritage and has become a sophisticated design material, thanks to advances like translucent polycarbonates, in the hands of designers like Karim Rashid. Nature Works, we believe, will accelerate plastic even further into high-end decoration and design.

The Red List — the master list, so to speak, of endangered species, the Red List is put out by the World Conservation

Union. The 2000 edition had some shocking news: the situation is worse than we thought. Of the 18,276 organisms investigated—and that's a tiny fraction of the 175 million known species—11,046 are in danger of extinction. That includes 24 percent of all mammals (the number of critically threatened primates has risen 50 percent) and 12 percent of all birds. While the Red List is virtually unknown outside of the environmental movement, we expect it to gain a wide currency as activists push corporations to avoid practices—from fishing to oil exploration—that further endanger these species. We also foresee a push behind Red List protection efforts, such as marketers "adopting" endangered species and raising money on their behalf. So expect to see the Asian Tree-Striped Box Turtles on your cereal box, and the Wandering Albatross on your yogurt containers. See also *conservation genetics, ESU.*

Solenium — a revolutionary, environmentally-friendly carpet that is true to principles of *Embodied Energy* (see listing). In other words, it is created with as little energy, and as many sustainable materials as possible. This is a radical shift within an industry that is notoriously riddled with hazards—as the *Financial Times* pointed out, "Much carpet is literally toxic: petroleum is turned into nylon, which is then fastened into glass fiber and PVC, two known carcinogens." Ray Anderson is founder and chairman of Interface, the company that makes Solenium. In 1994 he turned his organization inside out and pledged to "make the entire organization sustainable" as *the Financial Times* reports. As an example, Interface will come and pick up your existing carpet—even if you aren't replacing it with one of their products—and will, as they put it, "either recycle, downcycle, or repurpose it. We guarantee that your old carpet won't end up in a landfill, period." Interface is also the company behind Terratex, the fabric made out of recycled soda bottles. See also *natural capital, polylactide.*

Terratex — a fabric made of recycled soda bottles. If fashion designers were really the environmentalists they claim to be, they would be wearing Terratex and designing their next collections around it, rather than using unsustainable synthetics.

We believe that this will be the next step in the environmental movement, although we doubt if we will be seeing a fall Mountain Dew collection anytime soon. See also *Viridian Greens.*

Viridian Greens — an interesting movement that was officially "launched" on the Whole Earth Web site on January 3, 2000, with the "Viridian Manifesto" (www.wholeearthmag.com/ ArticleBin/246.html). Their manifesto insists that previous green movements failed because they were "too pure" and didn't recognize the realities of our consumer economy; in other words, if you can't beat them, join them. Thus, they argue, pragmatically, for a "form of Green high fashion so appallingly seductive and glamorous that it can literally save people's lives. We have to gratify people's desires much better than the current system does."

The Viridian Greens will come to influence mainstream environmentalism movements because they are so alert to the need to work within the system; they even want to turn electric meters into fashion objects to encourage conservation. We love the savvy of: "We are not hip, underground, bohemian, or alternative in any way. If anyone asks you, tell them you are engaged in corporate futurism and product development." See also *ecological footprint, environ.*

Wave Power — a new technology that uses the power of the oceans to create electricity, efficiently and cleanly. An English company called Wavegen (www.wavegen.co.uk) has been the first to turn the tides. They are currently generating energy in Islay, a small island off Scotland with a simple process: water rushes into a chamber and displaces air, which is forced into a pair of turbines that generate the power. When the water ebbs, air re-fills the chamber, ready for the next rush of water. How practical is this? About 50 percent of the earth's population lives within 40 miles of an ocean, claims David Langston, Wavegen's president. And there is no shortage of water power—the company's Web site writes "it has been estimated that if less than 0.1 percent of the renewable energy available within the oceans could be converted into electricity, it would satisfy the present world demand for energy more than five times over."

Wind Farms — groups of windmills used to generate electricity. Windmills are experiencing a boom, and they will continue to flourish because they are finally able to compete with other sources of power on an economic basis. (On an environmental basis, they have always been the winner: windmills produce no emissions, are renewable, and unlike hydroelectric power—which also harnesses nature—require no dams.) *The New York Times* reports that globally, the wind generation of electric power grew by 39 percent in 1999 alone; Denmark generates 10 percent of its power that way, and one of Germany's provinces has achieved a level of 14 percent. In America, wind farms have appeared from New York and Pennsylvania to Minnesota. Charles Lindermann, who directs energy supply policy at the Edison Institute, says, "My belief is the current boom will continue." The *Times* reports that in South Dakota, which has no wind farms yet, "brokers have begun to make their way from farm to farm, offering royalties for wind rights." Tax incentives favor the creation of wind farms, and California's highly publicized electric crisis will certainly put more pressure on wind farming development. *DOF* predicts that consumers will eventually be able to choose their sources of power—wind, coal, nuclear—as de-regulation opens the power grids to multiple competitors.

Dictionary of the Future Predicts

Ecological Equations — converting abstract environmental statistics into relationships that are immediately understandable. Because of their eye-opening quality they will be used by environmental advocates as they seek to sound the alarm during the early years of the twenty-first century. Consider that it takes the equivalent of 40 showers with a reduced-flow showerhead to produce enough grain to feed a cow enough food to produce a single hamburger. And it might change the way you think about agriculture—and the food you eat—when you realize that the amount of sewage produced by the city of Los Angeles is actually less than the production of a single hog farm in Utah. See also *guilt credits*.

Extinction Savings Bank — at the current rate, about 30,000 species of plants and animals become extinct each year as a result of pollution, over-fishing and other environmental assaults. Genetic techniques now allow us to preserve the raw material of these endangered species, which can be preserved until such time that cloning and recombinant DNA techniques allow them to be economically re-created. While there is a great deal of independent activity in this area, *DOF* believes that the next step is extinction saving banks, created by the leading scientific and environmental groups, with the support of a number of nations and the U.N. Money will be raised to both save the DNA and to fund research into cloning extinct species. The area is not without controversy, however; see *conservation genetics.*

Home Water Treatment — recognizing that current light-duty water filters are inadequate to the task, an industry of sophisticated water purification installers will emerge. (Consider that a recent EPA audit of 170,000 water systems revealed that nearly 90 percent of all violations of the Safe Drinking Water Act never find their way into the government database—which means millions of consumers are unable to identify the hazards of the water they're drinking.) Driven by society's growing fear of water safety, companies with names like HomePure and Drink Easy will deliver, install and maintain industrial-grade water monitoring and purification systems in consumers' homes; the bottled water companies, like Evian, will get into this as well, either directly or by licensing their names.

Interruptive Conservation — as our homes become networked (see *Bluetooth*) innovative nonprofits will find a way to make conservation (and philanthropy, for that matter) active rather than passive forces. A tiny early example: the experimental Stump Project, developed by Natalie Jeremijenko at NYU's Center for Advanced Technology, turns a laser printer into a conservation advocate. In her words, a "memory-resonant program ... watches your printer queue, counting the number of pages you print. When you've consumed a tree's worth of pulp, the printer prints out an image of tree rings. Eventually, the pages of the ring images accumulate into a stump." *DOF* envisions trash receptacles that prompt you to recycle, cars that tell you the damage to the ozone your trip to the mall has resulted in and refrigerators that remind you about starving children in Africa. See also *environmental footprint.*

Leadfills — the Information Age, and our world of technology "upgradesmanship," create a problem as old as civilization itself: too much trash. It is estimated that 315 million computers will become obsolete by 2004—and all those abandoned monitors will result in 600,000 tons of lead to dispose of. (The average cathode ray tube contains five to eight pounds of it.) Where will most of it end up? Landfills, which will become leadfills. Expect to see computer recycling stations emerge to help address the problem, where old computers get rehabbed and sent to schools in disadvantaged areas, or charities. Major computer makers like Dell and Gateway will get behind this.

FASHION AND STYLE

Language itself is, in many ways, a fashion—we wear it, show it off, and discard it when it is no longer stylish (or no longer fits). For that reason, the interaction of language and fashion is a particularly fertile growing medium.

But fashion also resides at the intersection of much else in our lives. The environment, for one, which is expressed through new (and newly rediscovered) fibers such as "sorona" and "banana fiber," and accessories like the "Batbelt." Fashion also expresses the diversity of America—witness "mehndi" and "waki"—as well as our seemingly unstoppable desire to fuse luxury with rusticity, as in "Bush Lux." And just as we are rejecting the mass control of our entertainment choices— witness the popularity of independent movies—fashion has its own corresponding trend of "locouture."

Technology, as you might guess is as inseparable from fashion as it is from everything else, which is why *DOF* foresees the emergence of "designtists" who will lead the way with wired clothing that runs the gamut from cloth keyboards to health-monitoring systems.

What's particularly engaging about fashion language is the way that it sharpens our cultural eyesight; just saying the words "mini skirt," "spats," and "Nehru jacket" brings entire worlds of the past to mind. We have every reason to believe that the terms that follow will, eventually, have similar conjuring powers.

Ff

Banana Fiber — the search for sustainable alternatives takes us to banana fiber, which will be the next new thing in the world of natural fabrics. In the nineteenth century, there was a thriving banana fiber trade in Jamaica, but it is only now being rediscovered as an inexpensive, quite beautiful textile for clothing, accessories and home furnishings—even paper. In Japan, silk and cotton were reserved for the nobility, while banana fiber was for the common folk. *DOF* believes that major fashion, interior, and industrial designers will incorporate banana fiber into their most innovative efforts. Expect banana fiber lines, boutiques, catalogs.

Batbelt — Batman had all kinds of futuristic tools, weapons and propellants hanging from his batbelt. Computer hackers have latched on to this term, because they carry so much stuff around their waists. Starting with the obligatory cell phone clip, Batbelts are starting to move into the mainstream—expect to see versions, many by top designers, incorporating hooks, clips and other devices for all the technoware we'll be techno-wearing.

Bush Lux — roughing it, with style. Writing in the *Financial Times* of his experience in a private game reserve, a reporter notes "Ngala's 'tents' are large, comfortable structures in stone, timber and canvas, complete with doors, beds, basins, toilet and shower. Not for nothing do they call it 'bush lux.' " This fusion of the rustic and the luxurious is visible across the landscape, from well-appointed, bush-lux SUVs to home furnishings. See also *bobos, informalizing*.

Bruise Palette — people who come to New York City invariably ask "Do New Yorkers own anything that isn't black?" Now, thanks to the trendy *New York Observer*, the predominance of black, purple and brown fashion has a name—and what could be more perfectly tongue-in-cheek than the bruise palette—particularly because of the tendency of chic New Yorkers to always feel wounded by something or other.

Color-Shifting Paint — the idea of a single, unchanging paint color is changing, as new technologies allow paints to adopt a continuum of shades and hues under different lighting and viewing angles. These new color-shifting paints are "coming closer to matching nature's palette with a synthetic iridescence," reports *The New York Times*. These effects are achieved by the use of additives that range from microscopic glass beads, to mirror chips, to volcanic dust and aluminum flakes treated with metal oxides. We've seen from the iMac how color can differentiate products, which is why the *Times* says that these color-shift paints "are likely to appear first on cell phones, golf clubs . . . helmets, textiles and faux leather." A product called ChromaFlair, which has made it to the new $20 bill (look at the lower right), uses a five-layer sandwich of color that reflects the light in stages, as the object and the viewer move; they call it "color by physics" technology. In a world where nothing is fixed anymore, why should paint be any different?

Locouture — though the Gap may have spread its khaki tentacles around the world, there is still a local fashion culture and it's called locouture: local + couture. Riding the same trend-wave that has us supporting and falling in love with independent films, these small-scale locouture boutiques are springing up in emerging downtown areas. It's a whole new opportunity for neighborhoods to be reborn, and for unknown designers to get their start. Another benefit of locouture: it's sparking a return to old-fashioned cottage industries, since the quantities are too small for mass production. *DOF* predicts that locouture will become America's fashion laboratory, and will change the way fashion trends are introduced. From downtown to up-market, in moments.

Mehndi — a fashion movement, based on a tradition found in places as diverse as India and Morocco, of decoratively painting one's body with complex and beautiful designs—using a paste made from henna leaves. Already, Madonna and Prince have been seen wearing beautiful, intricate mehndi patterns. *DOF* believes that mehndi will spark an entire cosmetics segment, and in the future there will be brands of mehndi paint, mehndi salons, mehndi artists, mehndi Web sites. It's moving beyond tattoos to a whole new level of the body as art.

Ff

Restylane — technically known as hyaluronic acid, Restylane is a synthetic form of collagen, which means it fills wrinkles and fine lines without side effects. As *DOF* goes to press, Restylane—which is being injected by all the *skinerati* of Europe and South America—is still not FDA approved for anything other than cataract surgery. But doctors can still write what are called "off-label" prescriptions, which means that in our ongoing fight against gravity, the sun and our genes, Restylane—which of course is not covered by insurance—will become another way to pay more than you should to look younger than you are.

Sorona — a new kind of polymer manufactured by DuPont that—in its application as a fabric—is claimed to be more breathable, softer and have a better "hand" than other synthetics. (Sorona can also be used in home furnishings and packaging.) What's fascinating is that DuPont has known about 3GT, the key component in Sorona, for about 50 years. (It's a waste product, actually, of the bacteria E. coli.) But it took the biotechnology revolution to figure out a cost-efficient way to manufacture it. (Note that this fact is wisely omitted from the DuPont Web site, which merely says that Sorona is made from 1.3 Propanediol.) *DOF* expects that Sorona will be as much a part of our language as nylon and lycra, as well as a boon to lyricists who've been desperate for a new word to rhyme with "Jonah" and "corona."

Triple Point Ceramic — a new fabric created to meet the most extreme conditions. It uses multiple layers and ceramic particles; under a high-pressure manufacturing process, tiny pores form around the particles creating breathability without reducing its waterproofing and windproofing attributes. Triple point itself is a scientific term—the point at which a substance exists in three states: solid, liquid, gas. Of course, most people who wear Triple Point Ceramic clothing aren't going anywhere near the Arctic; see also *IMB*.

Waki — armpit art. *The Daily Candy*—www.dailycandy.com—an arbiter of what's cool and what's coming, reports that waki is "the hippest in street wear from Japan . . . underarms are decorated with multi-hued paintings and glitter." It's a deep reflection of a subculture (if not a culture) that believes any part of the body can be beautiful.

Workday Saturday — the line between work and life continues to smudge, and fashion marketers aren't far behind. So let's welcome workday Saturday, a style of dressing that bridges the gap between office and (even) less casual weekend clothing, as reported by *Zoom on Fashion Trends*

Dictionary of the Future Predicts

Athleisure — so much of that cool stuff from L. L. Bean and Eastern Mountain Sports, with all that advanced wicking and breathable outer polyshells designed for trekking in the Himalayas, is actually bought by "visual adventurers" whose most dangerous adventure is getting into an SUV without hurting their back. This studiously misleading kind of deceptive dress: athleisure. See also *bobos, IMB.*

Designtists — no longer will fashion designers be able to sit and create in splendid isolation. The merger of fashion and technology—which includes innovations such as smart fabrics, wearable computers, cloth keyboards and health monitoring systems—means that designers will have to be technology experts too. Hence designtists. See also *affective computing, smart T-Shirt.*

Disability Chic — after years of fashion pretending that everyone in the universe is healthy and gorgeous, we will begin to see a recognition of a less-than-perfect world by designers. Case in point: the legendary (and 90 +) Pauline Trigère has introduced a line of chic accessories including pillboxes, hearing aid cases and canes. Ms. Trigère—on www.Goldviolin.com, the Web site that offers her merchandise—says that her objective was to design products for "people like myself, people who need a little assistance, but who haven't lost their sense of style." She continues, "I noticed, especially at the theater, how many people walk with canes and how unstylish they are. Just because we are getting older, doesn't mean that we have to look it." Look for others to follow. See also *ear electronics*.

Fash — will become the shorthand for a certain kind of fashionable, as glam has become for glamour. Fash refers to the trend of cheap chic, which we see in furniture—witness Ikea—and in fashion, with H&M (Hennes & Maurittz), the hugely successful Swedish retailer that is only now beginning its march to the United States. H&M has 600 fash stores throughout Europe; their first American location, in New York, had shoppers waiting on line to buy $35 flared-bottom jeans and $9 fake pony-hair bags. Like Ikea, H&M tracks street fashion and the downtown scene to catch the first bubbles of a trend. Another fash leader is the Japanese retailer Muji (www.mujionline.com) with 270 stores in Japan, the U.K. and France. While once you had to choose between expensive fashion or tacky, style-free alternatives, now you can go fash. Expect to see fash style colonize other categories, like fash motels, fash cosmetics. See also *apocope*.

IMB — a coming acroynm for "I mean business." When consumers choose the most industrial-strength option when a far more modest solution will do. Covers a trend that ranges from four-wheel drive vehicles and pickup trucks driven by faux adventurers to restaurant stoves purchased by people who eat out more than they cook, to those who buy computers powerful enough to analyze the recent census for nothing more chip-stretching than sending email. And IMB shows no signs of waning: GM plans to introduce a small version of the Hummer in 2002, and DaimlerChrysler will be selling a consumer version of its Geleandewagon, designed as a vehicle for the German military. See also *bobo*.

Lipoids — a term of derision that will be used to describe those who have lost weight the easy way, via liposuction. Of course, there is also a measure of jealousy. Losing weight this way is the aesthetic equivalent of inheriting a fortune; you didn't have to sweat for it.

Populast — in our trend-obsessed age, the popular remains on the radar screen for only a few moments, or the equivalent thereof, after which point it becomes decidedly uncool. By contrast, when a trendy spot—a restaurant, a club, a neighborhood—maintains its ineffable chicness over time, it has achieved populast status. "Some places come and go, but the Royalton Hotel, that's populast."

Preservation Jewelry — historic but endangered buildings and monuments—and there are hundreds of them in the United States and globally—will raise money by selling jewelry and other accessories that incorporates tiny fragments of these structures. We will see earrings using shards of terracotta from Roman ruins, pins and necklaces using damaged mosaics from Russian churches, paperweights made of ancient Venetian stone. The World Monument Fund could be one of the sponsors of this movement, selling these certified items over the Internet or through retail stores. These unique items satisfy our hunger for authenticity while putting the power of the free market to work for a worthwhile cause. See also *authethnic.*

FEAR, FRUSTRATION AND DESIRE

While it might seem that this section is more suited to a study of the emotional conditions of the Middle Ages, we are seeing more and more expressions of a culture under psychological siege. Rapid technological and social change create as many spirals of anxiety as it does gusts of optimism, and language gropes for new ways to adequately express these new longings, urges, and paralyzing doubts.

The growing ability to predict our destinies based on our genes imposes a controversial "burden of knowledge" on us. We are afraid of our food—both because it could harbor strains of disease like "campylobacter jejuni" and because it's loaded with unhealthy fat and cholesterol, leading to an eating disorder that is being called "orthorexia."

While some of our fears are well-founded, like "C-scare"—millions of smoldering cases of hepatitis C—many of them are concocted by what we call "scarevoyants," who elevate our anxiety levels until more sober voices prevail and the perceived threats experience "climbdown." Along the way we are bombarded by others who are more successful or more accomplished than we are, creating "admirenvy" a *DOF* term that names, for what might be the first time, the peculiar combination of admiration and envy that is a function of a society that is at once competitive, narcissistic, and honest.

Ff

AgION — a compound which has the ability to suppress the growth of hundreds of different strains of bacteria. A prototype house in California is being built that uses AgION to coat virtually every metallic surface possible. *The New York Times* writes that "all the ducts and vents, as well as such 'high-touch zones' as handrails, doorknobs, faucets, [and] food-preparation surfaces" will be treated. The company behind AgION is also "working on ways to embed it in virtually everything else found in the house: furniture, fabrics, carpeting, linens, drywall, wallpaper and paint, grout . . . toilet seats and telephone receivers." While certainly obsessive, this reflects our growing fear of microbes, and *DOF* fully expects that AgION will end up in hundreds of consumer applications.

Burden of Knowledge — genetic and diagnostic testing can give us more information than we need to know, want to know or can handle. The results of DNA mapping, and of increasingly sophisticated testing, tell us a lot—but not everything—about our likelihood of developing chronic diseases like cancer or Alzheimer's, as well as the chances of passing these on to our children. Murky and unprecedented ethical and psychological issues result. Some argue, strenuously, that we must be very careful about assuming the burden of knowledge, and that, conversely, we have a "right to ignorance." We will be hearing both these terms a great deal.

Campylobacter Jejuni — move over salmonella—our old food-poisoning standby has been replaced by this infection which now represents a greater risk to public health. Usually communicated through chicken, infections caused by campylobacter are particularly dangerous because they are increasingly drug-resistant; a survey of poultry products showed that 20 percent of the campylobacter strains tested were immune to antibiotic therapies. An aging population—combined with those with compromised immune systems—creates a recipe for serious complications from campylobacter and other foodborne pathogens.

Ff

Climbdown — after the Chicken Littles scare us to death about a problem, experts re-assess the scope of the crisis and find, lo and behold, that it isn't that bad after all. The lowering of risk levels that results from this is called climbdown. The risk of butter, eggs and chocolate, for example, have experienced climbdown. The fear of automation putting people out of work—so dominant in the 1950s and '60s, has experienced climbdown. As the *Economist* describes it, "Without fanfare, the official consensus estimate of the size of the problem is shrunk." But some risks won't be lowered, and there are many times when we must also heed the prophetic minority, as they are called. What about those who warned about AIDS in the early days, or global warming, or the risks of smoking?

C-Scare — a public health crisis regarding hepatitis C that is waiting to blossom. Here's the drill: silent infections are brewing in four million Americans who carry the virus but don't know it. The source of the infection is contaminated blood—from transfusions or injected illegal drugs, or even from cocaine—since cocaine straws can contain virus-infected blood droplets. While new drug treatments—a combination of interferon and ribavarin—can sometimes clear the virus and prevent liver damage, many people who received tainted blood before screening started in 1992 don't have any idea that they were exposed. Dr. Michael Mirg has stated on www.personalmd.com that "If we don't slow this disease soon, it is predicted more people will succumb to hepatitis C than AIDS."

CyberSteam — letting off steam via the Internet. It's never been as easy to share your frustration, or to join with the collective frustrations of others in the same boat as you. And just as it's therapeutic to vent, it's an instructive cultural experience to find out what's frustrating people. To get a glimpse of it, go to www.bitchaboutit.com, www.disgruntledhousewife.com, www.bitterwaitress.com, www.vault.com (where employees rant and rave about their employers) or www.PassengerRights. com. Of course, some have found revenue opportunities in the midst of all this venting: David Horowitz of "Fight Back" fame brings us www.fightback.com where he will investigate your beef for $50.

Freeway Fury — coined by *USA Today* to describe a higher form of road rage. They predict that with speeding and congestion racing ahead, and with cell phone distractions causing thousands of accidents and close calls—it's going to get worse before it gets better. Expect more and more municipalities to legislate restrictions on cell phones and other techno-distractions, as we move to a new kind of DWI (Driving While Internetting).

H.A.C.C.P. — shorthand for "hazard analysis critical control point," the acronym that describes a strategy for assessing and controlling the risks of food-borne illness. The idea is to map and track all the points in the production, shipping, storage and handling chain, which could provide an access point for contamination. Surveillance of H.A.C.C.P. could reduce the risk of bacteria and other infectious agents entering the food supply. *DOF* expects that consumers will become conversant with this term, and will say "I hope this passed H.A.C.C.P.," or "Haycip."

Orthorexia — full name: Orthorexia nervosa. Condition: an unhealthy obsession with eating healthy and avoiding even the slightest bit of fat, preservatives or salt. Dr. Steven Bratman has coined the word—which is derived from the Greek words "orthos" meaning correct and "orexis" for appetite (and which is cleverly close to "anorexia.") Bratman, who has written a book on the condition (*Health Food Junkies: Orthorexia Nervosa*) believes that orthorexia is an example of a good idea—eating healthy, avoiding dietary villains—gone dangerously off track. *USA Weekend* quotes an expert as saying "I have no numbers, but orthorexic behavior is probably as common as the other eating disorders. Perhaps more common, as it is less extreme and promoted as allegedly good behavior." *DOF* believes that orthorexia will sidle into our speech—"Go ahead, have the French fries, don't be an orthorexic"—both because it is a real medical phenomenon, and because it functions as a pointed metaphor for all the extremist, exaggerated aspects of American life.

Rabbit Hemorrhagic Disease — a virus-born disease, RHD has killed hundreds of millions of rabbits in China, Asia, Australia and Europe since the first epidemic in 1984. Experts believe that the virus has been around for a while, but "started to emerge from nowhere to start killing Chinese rabbits," writes the *Financial Times*. Thus far, there are no examples of the virus jumping to other species, but a researcher at Oxford University has said that this evidence is only "provisional," and there is a "remote possibility" of "an exchange of genes between RHD viruses and related caliciviruses that infect humans." Of course, AIDS, Mad Cow disease and other scourges were also once "remote." In fact, given the unexpected epidemic of Mad Cow disease, and the uncertainties about cross-species infection, *DOF* believes that we will be hearing much more about RHD as a threat to other animal populations, and beyond.

Dictionary of the Future Predicts

Admirenvy — it is remarkable that our rich language offers no word to describe the common feeling that blends admiration and envy. A writer who reads a terrific book by another feels admirenvy, as does a parent who observes a friend's child sitting quietly at a restaurant while theirs is throwing Jell-O at the waiter.

Bacterroria — the panic that ensues from the fear, or reality, of a terrorist attack using bacteria or viruses.

Cubicle Fever — the feeling of entrapment that cubicle workers are overcome with. Cubicle fever will mount, as economic pressures and rents are forcing employers to stack workers in smaller and smaller workplace. Consider that the newest cubicle size, according to *Wired* magazine, is five by six, or 30 square feet. By contrast, a taxpayer-funded, spacious prison cell in San Quentin, *Wired* notes, is 70 square feet.

Desire Gap — the difference between intention and behavior. Examples are scattered all over the culture—we buy cookbooks, watch cooking shows and invest in luxury French cookware—but we seldom prepare a meal, and actually plan to cook even less (see *museum kitchens*). We join health clubs and drink oceans of diet soda, but we're fatter than ever. Young girls are confronted with images of beauty that are unachievable, and an epidemic of eating disorders erupts. Across the culture, the frustration that the desire gap triggers is real and deep, as the unreachable aspirations of the consumer economy eventually weaken our spirit and lead to many varieties of emotional disrepair—which is expressed in depression, psychosomatic complaints, and violence.

Forwarded — the act of damaging someone's reputation by forwarding hurtful information via email, whether it be police files or credit reports. The Internet makes it easy to collect this dossier of dirt, which can be used in romantic entanglements, or to discredit a competitor. Language like "He lost the contract because he was forwarded" and "If you don't watch out, I'll forward you" will soon ring throughout the land. See also *carry a Drudge*.

Mindwash — a term that will be used to describe the impact of psycho-pharmacological agents on the way we think and feel. Whatever bad stuff grips us—all those demons of gloom, anxiety, doubt and fear— simply gets washed out in a wondrous kind of cranial irrigation. See also *pharma factor.*

Posterity Anxiety — as technologies that enable us to document our lives advance in sophistication (see *personal archivist*) we will begin to recognize that everything we do and say—not just the big and important moments—will be there for generations to come. This new posterity anxiety will have disparate effects: we will fight the invasion of these recording technologies, and our behavior will be influenced by a new "posterity politeness."

The "Right, But" Club — people who did the right thing, but for whom life didn't work out as ordained. "I exercised but got heart disease"; "I took anti-oxidants but got cancer"; "I spent quality time with my kids but their SAT scores stink"; "I went to an Ivy League school but I'm stuck in middle-management quicksand." It shouldn't be surprising that life isn't predictable, but our consumer society, the self-help industry and the media have all conspired to have us believe that we can actually micromanage our destinies. See also *desire gap*.

Scarevoyants — those who warn of upcoming cultural, environmental and political dangers. While scarevoyants are not always right, they have plenty to work with—for example, the 60 unknown viral agents in the world that could cause the next AIDS epidemic, as was noted in the last chapter of *AIDS in the World*, ominously headed "The Next Epidemic." See also *climbdown*.

Stop-Coms — protestors are just beginning to learn how to use the Internet, and it's a powerful weapon. To see the future, log onto www.stopdrlaura.com and see what we mean.

Successism — the belief—almost religious in its intensity— that you cannot fail, that you are destined for success. A common condition—even in the years after the Internet bubble burst—among recent college graduates who have been lucky enough to move into a low-unemployment economy. Only when you've been cured of successism do you realize the very short distance from being toasted to being toast.

These expressions are the propellants of conversation, our folk metaphors, the turns-of-phrase that capture a truth about our lives with a compressed and irresistible poetry. We've tried to bring you a sampling from across the culture, because the language factory has tiny branches in every corner of our lives. Taken together, the vitality, humor and witty compression of these figures of speech reflect a people delighted with the possibilities of expression, and acutely aware of the intense time in which they live.

As for our own invented language, we concede that it takes a full quotient of linguistic hubris to attempt to create the clichés of the future, but we did so by using our ongoing trend research, and our work on this dictionary, to lead us to these new word packages. If any of our inventions manage to survive in the unforgiving world of the vernacular test track, it is only because they succeed in expressing something that hasn't been said quite the same way before. Accuracy, in language, can only be road-tested by those who know it best: its users.

Airport Test — used by executive recruiters. In its simplest terms: Could you stand being stuck in an airport, with this candidate, for hours on end? We even found this in an Indian Web site (www.expressindia.com) so the fear of hiring someone who can bore you to death obviously has global implications. We think this neat little phrase could have a life beyond human resources; someone you don't want to date, or live next to, could also fail the airport test.

Anticipointment — an all-too-common experience, the feeling of disappointment you get when the reality is a mere shadow of the promise. It's not clear who dreamed it up, but one of the Beatles is taking some sort of ownership: As *GQ* reported, "Paul McCartney has a term for the letdown the public feels when a new song by an old group fails to make them feel young again: anticipointment." We assume that he's not referring to himself, of course. With everyone from movie studios to software pushers promising the next big thing, be prepared for years of anticipointment to come.

Apocope — this is a very old (and seldom used) word that we are dusting off because it is so relevant today. Apocope, from the Greek, refers to the dropping off of a syllable (or two) from the end of a word. We are creating a torrent of apocopes today, possibly because we're living (and talking) too fast to get the whole word out (BrainReserve's 99 Lives Trend, linguistically speaking). Current examples include "glam" for glamour, "mag" for magazine, "no prob" for no problem, "goth" for gothic, "endo" for end over end (mountain bike lingo), "fab" for fabulous and of course, "cred" for credibility. What other apocopes can we expect in a time-crunched age that doesn't have a moment for full syllabic presentation? Perhaps auth for authentic, imp for impossible. Let us know on our Web site, www.dictionaryofthefuture.com.

Banana Problem — derived from the apocryphal story of the little child who says, "I know how to spell banana, I just don't know where to stop." From this comes the banana problem, which in its narrowest usage is an algorithm with an unclear termination point. In its broader and vastly more imaginative context, it is any example where somebody doesn't know where to stop. An over-designed computer program for one, or David Foster Wallace's telephone book–sized novel *Infinite Jest*, or a skit on "Saturday Night Live" that the writers can't figure out how to end. In our society of excess, the banana problem shows no signs of splitting.

Bang On — used in the software industry as a synonym for a stress test. This expression is so colorful and resonant that we expect it to break into the greater language: "I banged on this term paper all night, and now I'm ready to submit it."

Beaded Up — overly stressed or excited, from pilot lingo. "Don't get beaded up" will be the next version of "Don't freak out" or "Don't sweat it."

Blue Screen of Death — *The New Republic* writes, "Every PC user is familiar with the notorious 'blue screen of death,' the azure void that appears when Windows crashes." *DOF* expects that this tidy little expression will wander more broadly into the language: "Staring at the double fudge chocolate cake with Creme Anglais, I knew I was looking straight into the eye of the blue screen of death."

Brain Bag — a particularly roomy laptop case that not only holds a computer, but a PDA, cell phone, Evian water and copy of *Gravity's Rainbow*.

Buried Shovel — a technology successor to Joseph Heller's magnificent phrase, "Catch-22." Buried shovels are instructions that are implicitly impossible to access—for example, instructions for installing a modem that are only available once the modem has been installed. We found an Internet user group comment which captures the frustration of this paradox: "I like an install that I don't need to get an ulcer wondering if I'll get a buried shovel." The winsome self-contradictory nature of this expression is likely to propel it into the slipstream of our vernacular— "It's a buried shovel situation—if I knew how to find the answer, I would have the answer."

Buy It with Both Hands — Wall Street speak for an opportunity to buy something aggressively.

Cammunity — the way in which the thousands of Webcams across the world give us an extended sense of community by letting us all get on the view. They range from the deeply personal and broadly public to the cultural, spiritual and quirky. Cammunity can be found all over the Web, and AltaVista's site has an entire area dedicated to it. *DOF* believes that we haven't even scratched the surface of the unexpected ways in which cammunity will be an enormous influence in acclerating globalization, ironing out differences and celebrating diversity at its most authentic level. See also *face translation*.

Camoflanguage — a contradiction in terms—language that seeks to hide rather than illuminate.

Chart Abuse — the use of misleading or manipulative charts and graphs to prove a point. It's done by politicians, scientists, companies, just about anyone who's got a Magic Marker and a calculator.

Clear Blue Water — an English expression that should catch on here because it's such a non-threatening way of expressing disagreement. (Leave it to the British to make an argument seem like a Caribbean vacation.) Clear blue water is the wide, and sometimes unbridgeable difference between two parties; here, we see it coming to mean any kind of parting of the ways. "There is so much clear blue water between us that I can't imagine myself agreeing with you."

CLM — shorthand for Career Limiting Move; can include making an inappropriate comment in a meeting, the refusal to take on a new position or to be relocated.

Cold Water Historian — someone who refuses to accept the conventional wisdom, and, in fact, exults in splashing cold water on received truths. John Patrick Diggins, who has gone his own way as a conservative chronicler of the past, has described himself as a "cold water historian" and we think the phrase could take on a life of its own in other areas. There is so much half-baked, ill-considered theorizing going on that *DOF* could easily imagine cold water scientists, cold water politicians, cold water journalists.

Continuous Partial Attention — coined by Linda Stone, a researcher at Microsoft, to describe the way that today's computers and wireless devices render us ever-vigilant about the flow of information, but never fully engaged in any one subject. (See also *two-tasking* and *submeetings*.) Continuous partial attention results in halfway thinking, uncompleted tasks and a decline in productivity—all from the very tools that were supposed to make us more efficient. A book that takes a provocative look at this phenomenon is *Why Things Bite Back: Technology and the Revenge of Unintended Consequences* by Edward Tenner.

Cusping — when a personality is about to break through and occupy a set of coordinates on our radar grid. *The New York Times* describes E. Elias Merhige as "the cusping film director."

Decimal Dust — very small amounts of anything, usually money, e.g., "For all the controversy, the budget of the National Endowment for the Arts is decimal dust."

Dropping Packets — when a baby boomer forgets something momentarily, it's a Senior Moment; when a Gen X or Y'er does it, it's a far more charming (and less threatening) problem, known as dropping packets. It is derived from packet transmission, which is the way that data is shipped over the Internet; packet loss is why it can take so long for information to download.

Drownloading — downloading so many files in rapid succession that your computer, submerged by data, crashes. Also describes a situation when your own brain is overloaded with information.

Economy-Class Syndrome — initially used to describe the medical condition know as DVT—deep venous thrombosis—potentially fatal blood clots caused by being cramped into a small airline seat, with no legroom, for hours on end. (Airlines, by the way, are attempting to deal with the problem with on-board excerises they call "flyrobics.") But *DOF* spots a logical extension of this characterization: any problem caused by taking the low-cost way out. A sweater that pills after the first dry cleaning session? Blame it on economy-class syndrome. You bought the cheap laser printer and it now only recognizes every other vowel? Economy-class syndrome strikes again.

Eternity Leave — when you take off (paid or unpaid) to care for a terminally ill relative or friend. *The National Post,* a Canadian newspaper, writes of an activist in the Alzheimer's community who is fighting for eternity leave for caregivers.

Future Shock Absorbers — created by the Nigerian writer Kodwo Eshwa, this describes those who hold the past and present in place, keeping everything and everyone safe. They include religious figures, writers and poets, and sages of all stripes. With time moving so fast that we tend to forget our history, future shock absorbers play a critical social role.

Good Dish — describes someone who's wired in, based on the ability of a satellite dish to pull in signals from everywhere. "Ask Flora, she's got good dish."

Green Shoots — uses the metaphor of new plant growth to capture the moment when something—a system, a country, an approach—is showing signs of rebirth. We are finding the reference in many, many places. A NATO document states: "In other words, beneath the permafrost there are some green shoots of democratic recovery." Other sources use it to describe new vitality in places as diverse as China and Tanzania. Since "rebirth," "resurrection" and "fresh start" are all beaten-down cliches, we see a bright future for green shoots.

High-Contrast Living — our tendency to explore extremes in daily life, bouncing from hours in the gym to indulging in fabulously rich desserts, going from reading Manga—Japanese comic books—to Proust; coined by singer k.d. lang.

Human Chauvinist — those who hold out for the superiority of human beings, as computers approach and exceed human potentiality. "I was rooting for Kasparov, human chauvinist that I am," Sir Roger Penrose was quoted as saying in *The New York Times*, January 19, 1999. A next-century version of the Luddites, this movement will gain force and influence spawning movements such as the "Inkists"—those who insist on generating all their documents and correspondence using traditional ink and paper methods. See also *wet signature*.

Ivory Basement — scholars, detached from reality, labor in an Ivory Tower. Techies, geeks and silicon wizards labor in Ivory Basements, tucked in windowless offices below massive computer installations. When technology that is too complex and appallingly user-unfriendly appears on the market, it's because there are people working in Ivory Basements who forget what it's like for real people—without technical support standing by—to take a new computer out of its box and try valiantly to set it up.

Knee of the Curve — describes the period of exponential growth of a market, a concept, or a phenomenon. Think of a graph that moves horizontally and then shoots up, in a knee-shaped fashion. It was coined by Ray Kurzweil in *The Age of the Spiritual Traveler* and is based on the idea that for long periods of time change happens slowly; in other times—like today's technology revolution—"the exponential nature of the curve of time explodes." When we are located in the knee of the curve, rules change; opportunities and risks are exaggerated, and judgment is often suspended.

Ff

Long — from Wall Street to your street. Any statement of optimism about the future—"My second semester grades weren't good, but I'm still long on the Ivies."

Meth-Paced — faster than fast. A pharmaceutical metaphor for the ever-increasing speed of life and work. A personal Web site we found describes the "meth-paced frenzy on which most teenaged girls seem to thrive."

Modelizer — perhaps the first word to emerge from "Sex and the City"—and it describes, what else, a man who dates models or fantasizes about it.

On or Off the Zipper — its original meaning came from the furniture arrangement in Internet offices; working on the zipper describes desks in close, ritualized proximity. Working off the zipper is when desks are separated and unrelated to each other. Will come to describe those who are close to the decision-making process—"I'm working on the zipper"— and those on the margins of the organization—"I'm the last to find out, I'm off the zipper."

Prebuttal — formulating the response to an objection before it is even raised. Political candidates, as part of their spin control, develop prebuttals. But almost all of us who try to stay a step ahead of the conversational flow also use this tactic.

Reader's Block — the inability to read or fully concentrate due to our shortened attention spans. What's interesting to us is that this isn't limited to those for whom reading was never important. The writer Alyce Miller in the *Chicago Tribune* captured this paradox in a piece titled "Reader's Block; How a Lifetime's Activity of Pure Enjoyment Became a Chore." Coping with reader's block, publishers are rushing to put out less daunting volumes that still offer intellectual nourishment. Case in point: the popular Penguin Lives series—slim biographies of famous individuals by notable writers that, at less than 200 pages, are easily consumed. What's next? Reader's Block sections at Barnes & Noble next to Oprah's Books?

Reality-Distortion Field — a psychological space into which we enter when yielding to the truth is too painful, and the perpetuation of illusion too rich with pleasure. *The New York Times* quoted John Shock, a venture capitalist, as follows: "The valley is now divided into two camps . . . there are those people who are firmly inside a reality-distortion field and there are the rest of us who realize that this is going to end."

Reboot — so much of computer language has been pilfered from non-technical English (mouse, desktop, windows) that it's interesting to see the other migration. "Reboot" is being used to describe the act of refreshing or rebooting a person or a system. From *Paper* magazine: "Favoritism, anarchic and impromptu, is the vital strategy that reboots the arts within the individual human."

Rep Surfing — a response to the contemporary torture that is also known as customer service. Rep surfing is the practice of repeatedly calling the same customer service line until you get a friendly voice that is actually interested in helping you. From *Experience* magazine: "Yvonne hit redial, hoping that rep surfing would get her a response this millennium."

Sarchasm — the gulf between the author of sarcastic wit and the recipient who is completely in the dark about the intent. (Entry from *The Washington Post* Style Invitational.)

Self-Unfulfilling Prophecies — when our fears provoke a reaction that reduces or eliminates the threat they pose. We found this in an article by John Seely Brown and Paul Duguid, and thought it had the potential to join its predecessor (the self-fulfilling prophecy) in our vernacular. Brown, who was chief scientist at Xerox and director of their Palo Alto laboratory, and Duguid, who is a researcher at the University of California at Berkley, believe that self-unfulfilling prophecies will prevent technology from running rampant and invading our privacy because effective and appropriate responses will be triggered. "Once warned, society could galvanize itself into action" is how they put it, much as the threat of the world's

Ff

population outrunning the food supply created the agricultural revolution that transformed our ability to feed the planet.

Shouting Heads — as the media raises its voice to get our attention, the talking heads reach a new decibel level and become shouting heads; shouters include John McLaughlin and Chris Matthews.

SITCOM — single income, two children, oppressive mortgage.

Snap to Grid — from the world of graphic design comes this evocative expression which describes the process by which a computer replaces hand-drawn lines and angles with precise, sharp representations. *DOF* has noted that the term is being used to mark the transformation of a hazy idea into a clear plan of action: "It's time we stopped talking about this idea and snapped it to grid."

Talk Spurt — an eruption of buzz around what is believed to be the next new thing.

Tarmacked — from the experience of being stuck on a plane that is stuck on the runway, tarmacked is gaining wider acceptance as a way to describe being shunted aside. "It was a great idea, but they tarmacked it because they were afraid of it."

Toggling — used to describe the way in which a user can go from one computer application to another. Is also taking on a greater meaning, to describe darting from one reality to another. Lynn Harris, a writer and comedian who developed the Internet heroine Breakup Girl, has this to say about the possibility of turning her comic strip figure into a situation comedy persona: "What would be ultra cool is to show the internal tension by toggling between the real character and the superhero." The question is, of course: What is real? Hence the glory of the toggle.

Trailer Visits — a recent euphemism for having sex; based upon the prison language that describes a conjugal visit between a prisoner and a spouse or significant other. Trailer visits are described as the "ultimate carrot" by *U.S. News & World Report.* And because we are a culture that romanticizes the marginal elements of society—what the French call *nostalgie de la boue*—we fully expect this phrase to stroll into our mainstream language. "After dinner, how about a trailer visit?"

Unobtanium — tongue-in-cheek term used by enthusiasts in categories as diverse as technology, sailing and auto-racing to describe something leading-edge, expensive and for all intents and purposes, unavailable. (It's one step short of Jetsonian technology, which doesn't exist as of yet, in any form.) A combination of "unobtainable" and "titanium." As one sailing aficionado notes on his Web site: "You don't need the latest in zircon-encrusted widgetry or unobtanium sailcloth to have a great time out on the water with your friends." Of course, unobtanium is just what premature adopters and *neophiles* (see listing) fantasize over.

Videorazzi — paparazzi with video cameras instead of still cameras. With the potential to sell their footage via streaming video on the Internet, expect to see more of them.

Wet Signature — technology doesn't just create new language to describe itself, it forces our vocabulary to recast what was. In that way, the existence of digital signatures—now legally binding—forces us to relook at the traditional ink-stained variety, and rename them wet signatures. "Give me a big wet one" may take on a whole new meaning.

Work the Seam — when someone—a manager, a politician, a child—finds a way to successfully accommodate two strong, often opposing personalities. William Safire, writing in *The New York Times* of Secretary of State Colin Powell, and Secretary of Defense Donald Rumsfeld, says that "Condi Rice . . . is not yet in their power league, but will work the seam."

Ff

Yes, Minus — we've been hearing this a lot lately, and have gotten emails alerting us to it as well. "Yes, minus" is agreement-lite, a soft approval. It's the cousin of the "definite maybe."

Dictionary of the Future Predicts

Airport Fiction — while once the phrase described the frothy, superficial reading that one does on an airplane, it will soon come to mean any escapist truth that gives us an excuse to put reality aside. "Don't believe what Phillip tells you about the fourth-quarter revenue numbers, it's just airport fiction."

Ambient Ideas — have you ever noticed how, all of a sudden, everyone seems to have the same idea? We've heard this, dozens of times, from people in just about every industry. Movies and books about the same subject appear in the same year, after years of neglect, for example. We call this phenomenon "ambient ideas" and we believe that it's not an accident; it's what happens when creative people are exposed to and process the same cultural input, yielding a similar end result.

Amphibian — someone who is at home in the world of technology and the world of the humanities. Increasingly, more value is being and will be placed on amphibians. Medical schools, for example, are looking for physicians who have a broad-gauge sensibility and are fluent in the language of the smallest particles of our being, as well as the largest.

Anti-Magnetic — a person with no charisma.

Birthwrong — the opposite of your birthright. Everything you got stuck with from the moment the doctor slapped you, from the wrong genes to the wrong parents to the wrong hometown. See also *genetic underclass* and *"right, but."*

Blanquilized — when someone is so loaded up with tranquilizers that they go through the day in a medicinal fog, e.g. "Don't bother to ask Jeff anything, he's been blanquilized for the last two weeks." New generations of anti-depressants making their way through the FDA approval process will create more Jeffs in the future.

Burn — one's available cash. The term began its linguistic voyage as a way to describe the funding of beginning businesses; *The New York Times* quotes an entrepreneur as saying "Start-ups are great until they run out of burn." *DOF* believes that the word is so vivid and handy it will soon come to mean the sum total of cash on hand in any situation. "Can't go to the show this weekend, don't have enough burn."

Carry a Drudge — to retain incriminating information on someone for later use, inspired by—of course—*The Drudge Report*, an Internet gossip site that rose to prominence during the Monica Lewinsky scandal. See also *forwarded*.

Carry-Ons — lifted from the language of airplanes, describes the emotional and real-world baggage we take forward into our lives, e.g. "I can't get involved with him, he has too many carry-ons."

Carve — in ski lingo it means to handle a twisting trail with particular agility. *DOF* believes it will take on a second life as a description for any complex procedure that has been executed with particular elegance and effortlessness. "She had only one night to write that contract and she carved it beautifully."

Crash Dummy — the state of data deprivation caused by a crash of a hard drive on a computer, a personal organizer or any device which has not been backed up. The loss of this data can trigger depression and other reactions; expect support groups and self-help programs for "rebuilding" the lost dimensions of one's existence.

Decal Value — status, pure and simple, and shamelessly stuck-on and stuck-up. Derived from the college decals that proud parents slap onto their rear windows. Anything can have decal value: jobs, houses, children, bodies, IRAs, relationships.

Ff

DNA'd — the act by which a prospective spouse breaks off an engagement or a planned marriage based upon unfavorable DNA research into a potential mate, e.g., "The wedding is off. My genes for future financial success scored low, and I was DNA'd." With DNA testing becoming faster, cheaper and more accurate, we see this as an onrushing reality. See also *GENEology, genetic underclass.*

ERR — stands for Excessively Rapid Response, usually by email. You hit the send button (or, even more humiliatingly, the "reply all" button) too fast, and the consequences can be ugly—which leaves you no choice than to follow-up, appropriately chagrined, and apologize by saying "Sorry about that, I ERRed."

Espeak — the migration of email shorthand to conversation. We expect to hear people actually saying BTW (by the way), IMHO (in my humble opinion), TMOT (trust me on this) and g2g (got to go) as our time-pressed lives don't even allow us to get a full phrase out. There are precedents for this: we say ASAP and RSVP without thinking twice. See also *apocope* and *iMode.*

First Blood — in mountain bike speak it's a way to credit the first in a group to fall. But like other rich niche language it's poised for broader, celebrity status. "First blood" will be used to celebrate the individual who is the first to take any bold step: "He drew first blood. He opened his mouth while everyone else was rapidly nodding yes and told the CEO that the acquisition was a terrible idea."

Get to the Top of It — for hundreds of years we've been satisfied with "get to the bottom of it" as a colloquial way to describe the act of resolving a mystery. But who wants to end up at the bottom? The metaphor involves peeling away the surface to find the fundamentals of truth. But for some problems, success comes from reaching a higher level where you don't see *into* something, but see *further*. For those moments of aerial satisfaction *DOF* offers "get to the top of it." Accomplished men and women—in a variety of fields—have said the equivalent of "If I have seen further, it is because I have stood on the shoulders of giants." They have gotten to the top of it.

Gravel — used as a verb, "to gravel" describes breaking a concept down into its smallest constituent parts, e.g., "She was terrific at gravelling the problem until it became instantly clear to all how to solve it." It's the next step after "granular" and "drilling down," two current buzzword favorites.

Greedership — a negative kind of leadership, highlighted by greed and selfishness. Each of us have our exemplars of greedership; for example, Donald Trump might be on your list.

Hard Bounce — a direct and painful rejection. "I really wanted the job but got a hard bounce." Derives from email marketing, where a hard bounce is when an email message is returned because it was sent to a bad email address. (A soft bounce, in case you're curious, is an email message that's returned for technical reasons.)

Heat-Seekers — those who have an uncanny ability to identify and seek the company and approval of those who have power and influence. "Jennifer immediately knows who to spend time with at a press party. She's a real heat-seeker."

High-Altitude People — those with high-level brain power, who function at an elevated level. Brain surgeons, rocket scientists and people who know the difference between RAM and ROM are high-altitude people.

Idea Cuisine — the practice of cooking up innovative thinking; brainstorming at the highest of all levels. See also *idea harvesting*.

Imbas — an ancient Irish term for a state of inspiration or heightened consciousness, what the poet Yeats called "fire in the head." Because our culture is always on the hunt for new language to describe these kinds of epiphanies, *DOF* predicts

Ff

that we will adopt the word as we try to achieve a state of imbas through meditation, exercise, aesthetic experiences, or other kinds of stimulation.

Immersant — borrowed from virtual reality and other immersion technologies, this word will take on an ambidextrous life, as it will also come to mean one who is immersed in any high-stakes situation, from labor negotiation to a crime scheme to serious office politics.

Kawari — "change," in Japanese. *DOF* believes it will gain global currency as a way to describe sudden, almost violent change as opposed to the incremental, almost unnoticeable variety.

Lamping — will come to describe the act of identifying hypocrisy and cant by shedding light on it, e.g., "The reporter from *The Wall Street Journal* went lamping and discovered the unfair information exchange between analysts and investment bankers that undermines the fundamental integrity of the IPO process." Derived from an English term that describes a kind of hunting, done at night, that uses a bright light to identify and stun an animal.

The Lunch Lob — when you need to call someone back, but don't really want to speak with them, you call them at lunch with the hope that they won't be there and you can leave a voice mail message—hence, the lunch lob.

Make It into the Wild — originally, tech-speak to describe the process by which a computer virus actually breaks out into the wider universe. The language will broaden to describe any kind of mass pathway. Writers, painters and ideas can make it into the wild, an unknown artist about to have her first big show will be described as "poised to make it into the wild."

Make It to the Trailer — the most potent and successful moments of a film are the ones that end up in the trailer; this will become synonymous with any idea or moment that is worth preserving: "That line of vegetable flavored waters is not going to make it to the trailer."

Mix Tape — this started as a description of the customized tapes that DJs prepare for us in clubs, but *DOF* has spotted the very beginnings of its journey to an adjective that describes any individualized expression of personal taste: mix tape meal, mix tape reading list, mix tape vacation. It's a kind of fusion, but on an individual, not a cultural level.

Nemawashi — a wonderful Japanese gardening term that means tending to the roots, but also describes the way decisions in Japanese business tend to be bottom up, rather than top down. We can foresee this term taking on wide use, as a way to describe the need for sensitivity to those at the level of implementation—where things succeed or fail. It doesn't matter what the home office proclaims, nemawashi reminds us; it matters what happens at the local level.

Neophile — one who adores the future, welcomes it and advocates new technology, ideas, concepts. The neophile's opposition: the neophobe. Neophiles are not just early adopters, they are change-makers—indeed, change junkies—in their businesses, their lives, their communities.

Neurcotic — a neurotic who remains on a prescription drug for a long time. Coined by Lucas Hanft.

Next Guard — beyond Old Guard and New Guard, describes the up-and-comers who will soon be running any given world or subculture. In today's rapid-replacement society, the New Guard becomes the Next Guard before the former even realizes it has been booted out. An example of Next Guard success: The tiny Hidden Beach record label with just eight employees garnered three Grammy nominations in 2001.

No-Fly Zone — off-limits conversational areas; when people say "don't go there," the *there* is a no-fly zone.

Ff

Over-Bookers — those who chronically over-commit themselves, either socially, in business, or both.

Phlux — a new middle ground between *phile* and *phobe*. If you vascillate between adoring and reviling England, for example, that makes you Anglophluxic.

Pilotable — worthy information, derived from the PalmPilot. "I took his business card. It was Pilotable."

Post-Classic — for previous cultures, the goal was to become a classic; for art or literature or a restaurant to enter into the rarefied category of the legendary. Today, we are entering a post-classic period, where anything that strives to achieve an enduring reputation is working too hard—and is, as a result, unappealing, undesirable, uncool. In a post-classic culture, the goal is to catch fire and flame out, leaving nothing substantial behind in a gesture of complete combustion. See also *populast*.

Re-Setters — the game re-set button is a wonderful, liberating fantasy. If only it were this easy to start over in our lives. Those who try it—with relationships, careers, self-image or any other utter transformation—will be called re-setters.

Saviorize — the process of turning someone into a savior—of an institution, a company, a family. The build-up to some sort of a rescue mission. "They saviorized the new CEO so much that by the time he arrived, not even Jesus and Mohammed could have lived up to the anticipation."

Secondhand Speech — the cell phone equivalent of secondhand smoke. Not as dangerous, but more annoying, and definitely hazardous to your peace of mind.

Sell-By Date — any date which signals the end, or the perceived end, of someone's marketability—as an employee, spouse, professional athlete, artist, you name it. ("I would have hired him three years ago, but he's past his sell-by date.") After all, in one way or another we are all for sale, and in our youth-obsessed society, there are sell-by dates every step of the way.

Sendtriloquist — one who assumes the identity of another on the Internet, either as a prank or for nefarious purposes. See also *identity theft*.

Shake-Up Call — a wake-up call to the tenth power. The difference between heartburn and a heart attack.

Speech Wreckognition — when your cool and whizzy speech recognition technology gets something totally wrong. "Get my wife on the phone" becomes "My life is on loan."

Suburbane — the word "urban" has a lovely and evocative adjectival form that describes the sophisticates who live there: urbane. But what about suburb-dwellers? Tired of being cast as being a step behind, they will adopt and proliferate a new adjective to describe their own growing coolness: suburbane.

Swiped Out — taken from the credit card world—and describing those times when the magnetic strip isn't picked up by the reader—the term will come to characterize a circumstance when someone's utility has vanished. "It won't help for me to talk to David about this. I'm swiped out with him."

Techlish — the merger of technical-speak and English. Everytime you hear someone say PDA or WAP or LAN or DSL, they are speaking techlish.

Trophy Time — if time is the new currency, as experts have maintained, then we will come to admire those who have enough free time on their hands to do the things they truly enjoy. Trophy houses, trophy kids and trophy wives will be replaced by this new kind of temporal status as in "Phil's out this week; he's taking some trophy time."

Ff

Turning Time — a measure of the importance of a subject by our investment of time in turning the pages required to read about it. (Coined by Flora Hanft.) "I have no interest in the Taliban, they're not worth my turning time."

Two-Tasking — derived from Two-Timing—the act of checking email, or performing another technology function while on a phone conversation or even in a meeting. Two-Taskers are also known as attention sluts; the phenomenon has also been described as backgrounding. See also *continuous partial attention* and *submeetings,*.

UV-Blocked — borrowed from the world of sun protection to describe people who are resistant to new ideas, new thinking. "I tried to convince him, but he was UV-blocked."

Word Burger — as in grinding perfectly good words into chopped meat; garbling a phrase in a public speaking environment, courtesy of our friend Peter King Hunsinger, publisher of *Architectural Digest*.

Xenophilia — those who love and seek out the exotic. While the global culture makes some withdraw into a deeper sense of nationalism and isolation, others celebrate the opportunity to embrace the new and different. Those are the xenophiles, fueled by the allure of inexpensive foreign travel, the culture-probing power of the Internet and the fear of creeping sameness. These include many of the so-called early adopters, which is why this psychographic target will be important to all kinds of marketers in the future.

FOOD AND ENTERTAINING

If the predictions of the fifties and sixties had come to pass, by now we'd all be eating like astronauts, consuming our meals in little nutrient-packed pills. Instead, we have become a food-obsessed culture; hundreds if not thousands of new cookbooks are published each year, exotic fruits, spices, and meats that used be relegated to the "gourmet" section have moved front and center. Consider the portobello mushroom, which—from produce section obscurity—has achieved near ubiquity in culinary record time.

It is to be expected that given our interest in all things food, new news is breaking all the time, and our vocabulary needs to be microwave fast in responding. The entries in this section point to the multiple ways that food serves the culture, and the culture serves food. Our need for the cutting-board edge is reflected in argan oil from Morocco; the warp speed of our lives is responsible for both "eating amnesia" and "hyperconvenience foods." Our quest for a kind of spiritual purity in what we eat brings us to "heirloom grains" and "clean label foods," and our parallel fear of the evils that food can harbor is what animates language like "stealth fat" along with technology like the "smart dipstick."

What's also telling as we read through these terms is the way that food, like fashion, is a series of cues that reveal a great deal about who were are, a menu of social and cultural distinctions. If we asked you, for example, to describe someone who only bought "pastured poultry," who practices "farm sharing," and goes "fooding" in their spare time, you would have a clear idea of their politics, what they wear, and the car they drive. We have moved from "you are what you eat" to "what you eat is who you are."

Ff

Argan Oil — move (slide) over virgin, cold-pressed olive oil, the choice of foodies will soon be argan oil, straight out of the Souss Valley in southern Morocco. According to *New York* magazine, it has a "powerful fragrance and pungent, nutty flavor . . . made by the Berbers for a thousand years from the pits of the olive-like fruit of the argan tree, found only in this region." It takes 250 pounds of argan fruit to yield enough seeds for one liter of oil; the fruit is hand-harvested, the seeds are roasted over charcoal and stone-ground into a thick paste, which is kneaded by hand to produce the precious oil.

Body Clock Cuisine — new food concept created by Sheraton to "help you fight jet lag while traveling through different time zones." Their menu promises an "array of gourmet recipes developed by our nutritional experts to re-adjust your inner clock."

Clean Label Foods — natural and preservative-free aren't enough anymore. The next trend is clean label foods—a larger promise that includes products that are free of genetically-modified ingredients, that aren't overly processed or packaged and that run no risk of contamination. The latter is a major challenge for manufacturers: no preservatives, but high levels of freshness. As *Prepared Foods* magazine puts it, "The call for clean labels has prompted food processors to seek 'natural' antimicrobials and shelf-life extenders." Spices are being studied for this purpose, as well as friendly bacteria that kill food pathogens. While consumers might be initially skeptical of bacteria in their foods, *DOF* believes that these innovations will eventually be accepted (just as active yogurt cultures finally became a benefit)—and that products will be marketed as clean label, with consumers actively seeking them out.

Cuisine Mirage — a sophisticated form of vegetarian cooking where the preparation—using ingredients like tofu and tempeh—simulate the taste and texture of meat. But turning tofu into filet mignon requires more of a miracle than a mirage.

Culinarian — someone who devotes their professional life to food—perhaps as a chef, restaurant owner, reviewer, operator of truffle-hunting tours or an importer. Some call it elitist, but culinarians enable us to stay in touch with a time when food was grown on small farms and prepared in small batches. Expect to see more and more young people become culinarians, as they reject the clinical, clean-room environment of technology careers.

Culinambulator — one (of the many) who eat on the run.

DIM — better known as diidolylmethane, for you chemistry majors. This is a phytonutrient that appears naturally in broccoli, cauliflower and brussels sprouts—but, expectedly, not in caviar, champagne or foie gras. DIM works by encouraging the production of enzymes that control estrogen production, and you know what that means: reduced PMS, easier menopause. Some experts say that DIM also reduces the risks of estrogen-dependent cancers, because it works to lower the levels of "bad" estrogen. Fortunately, rather than having to down a half-pound of broccoli a day, there are DIM supplements available.

Eating Amnesia — when we forget what we eat, because we're moving too fast and doing too many things at the same time. Studies have shown the devastating impact of the time crunch on the meal ritual: the average lunch takes about 20 minutes today, and with 30 percent of all meals consumed in the car, we're barely paying any attention at all to what we consume. Some argue that eating amnesia accounts for our national obesity epidemic—we don't think about and savor our food, so we are never truly satisfied. One reaction to this: the Slow Food Movement, started in Italy, which now has dozens of local chapters worldwide encouraging members to slow down and restore mealtime to the sacred role it once had.

Edible Wraps — The U.S. Department of Agriculture has developed a food wrap—made of fruits and vegetables—that's

Ff

also a food. So it doesn't just keep your leftovers alive longer, it can actually add vitamins and minerals to them because it "melts down to a glaze during cooking" according to *Wired* magazine. The product has been approved by the FDA, which means it will be showing up in the market soon.

Five-Meal Day — Christopher Wolf, a food writer, predicts that the combination of our fast-paced lives (many little breaks, few longer ones) and nutritional re-programming will lead to a new habit of five meals per day, including daystart, a pulsebreak at 10 A.M., a holdmeal at 4 P.M. and an evesnack at 8 P.M. Our current three-meal structure is a relatively recent development—and, in fact, runs counter to the way our ancestors survived and evolved—so there is no reason that changing structures of work and family life shouldn't influence meal patterning.

Flash-Bake Oven — a new cooking technology that uses visible and near-visible light—tungsten/halogen lightwave technology—to yield conventional oven results at a speed that's 60 percent faster. The technology was developed by Quadlux (www.flashbake.com), and is being licensed to GE and others. Just as the microwave revolution spawned a generation of cookbooks and special foods (microwave popcorn, everyone's favorite) so too will flash-bake ovens create a brigade of new, supporting industries.

Food Bars — springing up in upscale restaurants across the country, food bars are communal counters or "share tables" where single diners or groups gather at one big, long table. While the idea of strangers eating together isn't new—cafeterias, including New York City's famed Automat, introduced this more than 50 years ago—what is unexpected is the upscaling of the phenomenon; now you can pay $20 for a tuna tartare appetizer and sit next to someone you don't know. Food bars force us to become social—and we seem to like it. After working alone all day at our computers, we even welcome the opportunity to schmooze with strangers.

Fooding — a word coined in early 1999 by Alexandre Cammas in *Nova*, a trendy Parisian culture magazine. The word—used as *le fooding* in France—is intended to capture the combustion of the two key elements of the dining experience: the food itself and the environment. This combination creates what Mr. Cammas calls "the universe of the table." He notes that "to eat with feeling in France is to eat with your head and your spirit, with your nose, your eyes, your ears, not simply your palate." Since the word was born, *The Wall Street Journal* reports "le fooding has been on every Paris gastronome's lips, as well as on food-oriented pages from *Elle* to the Air France in-flight magazine." Going "fooding" will soon be on our lips, here, as it captures our fascination with both dining out, and the search for higher experiential levels.

Food Spas — more and more, spas are using foods and beverages as part of their de-stressing, immune-boosting, purifying regimens. This notion of "topical nutrition," as *DOF* calls it, includes the therapy at the Arizona Biltmore, which starts with a "rub of wheat germ, moving on to a cactus-juice wrap and concluding with a vanilla-yogurt cleanse," according to *The Wall Street Journal*. In California's wine country you can get an olive oil and crushed grape scrub. The next step will be "home delivery" of these food spa treatments, as places like the Golden Door and Canyon Ranch recognize that if you can't go to the spa, there are enormous opportunities for the spa to come to you.

Genetically Engineered Decaf — researchers have found the gene that produces caffeine—and it is one jittery bundle of DNA. "We have cloned the gene encoding caffeine synthase from young leaves of tea, opening up the possibility of creating tea and coffee plants that are naturally deficient in caffeine," reported researchers in Japan and Scotland. Because these plants will be transgenic, the decaf brews they produce should be identical in taste to the fully loaded versions.

Heirloom Grains — agriculture is undergoing a mini heirloom revolution. Heirloom seeds, flowers and vegetables are gaining in popularity, as these classic strains are thought to be better than today's over-bred, obsessively hybridized varieties. Now, this trend is moving to heirloom grains. As *Food & Wine* magazine reported, "today, more and more farmers are growing heirloom varieties of wheat, rice and barley, including some grains that were practically on the brink of extinction."

In addition to standard grains, heirloom varieties include Kamut (which is derived from seeds that were supposedly found in one of the pyramids), red posole and many kinds of quinoa. A large part of this cycle of rediscovery are the "seed banks" which are dedicated to finding and preserving these grains. One of the more important ones is the Kusa Seed Research Foundation, which has collected more than 2,000 varieties of these "folk cereals." Expect "made with heirloom grains" to appear on restaurant menus and on the breads and cereals we buy.

Holistic Herding — a new cattle-raising technique. Although we're not sure if you'll find many cowboys in adult-ed psychology courses, *The Wall Street Journal* writes, "forget the whooping, whip-cracking Stetson-waving cowboys" because holistic herding involves "exploiting bovine concepts of 'space' and 'respect.' " Cattle who are managed with this strategy do less damage to the range, and also gain more weight—an extra pound a day, some argue—which makes them more valuable. Holistically herded cows are permitted to graze naturally; when it's time to move on, rather than using the old "round 'em up" approach, the cowboy approaches an animal from the front, never from the blind spot, and urges it gently, appearing as a "friend" and not a "predator." *DOF* predicts that we will start seeing "holistically herded" appear in the marketing of beef, the equivalent of free-range chickens. See also *pastured poultry*.

Hyperconvenience Food — faster than fast food, it's a new category that cuts as much time off a meal as possible from every angle: preparation, packaging, eating. Breakway Foods puts macaroni and cheese onto a stick and into a cardboard tube that gets microwaved and eaten with one hand. (The line is called IncrEdibles.) Frito-Lay nestles corn chips in the same package as chili; 7-Eleven has introduced a line called "dashboard dining." They're the latest manifestations of the Brain-Reserve Trend, 99 Lives. See also *crashboard crisis, gaze trackers.*

Jabugo Ham — a legendary—and costly—ham, produced in the Andalusia region of Spain, that is, according to the food writer Nicholas Lander, a "cult product, a national gastronomic obsession." There is, apparently, good reason for this. The black pigs used to make Jabugo are coddled and cosseted, with two and half acres of forest per pig; according to *Saveur* magazine they are "free-range and acorn-fed." There is also a health benefit lurking here; the technical director of the largest Jabugo ham curing house believes that "the high levels of fat in Jabugo hams are also healthy—like olive oil . . . it lowers cholesterol." While Jabugo ham might never achieve the popularity here that is has in Spain—where there are Jabugo bars and a special wine-like vocabulary to describe the flavors—*DOF* believes that it will become a culinary rage. One thing has to happen first, though: the government has to sort through all those trade disputes and let it into the country. Perhaps *DOF* readers will write to their representatives in Washington and demand their Jabugo ham.

Late Plate — as our daily schedules become even more inconsistent, restaurants are finally learning to adapt. The Late Plate is the meal that's served after the traditional dinner, for entrepreneurs who set their own pace, for knowledge workers who have never been introduced to the wonders of nine-to-five, for couples who want a quiet dinner after the kids go to sleep, for time-shifters, for dictionary writers. See also *five-meal day.*

Liquid Ice — a breakthrough created by Brunnar, an Icelandic company, for use initially on fishing boats. Liquid Ice, which is a flowing gel—and which is converted from water in five minutes—totally surrounds the fish, or anything else for that matter. This ice embrace, not possible with conventional flaked ice, eliminates air spaces and thus reduces the risk of bacterial contamination. Applications are enormous—food processing, supermarkets, even air-conditioning. *DOF* predicts that

Ff

"packed in Liquid Ice" will become a consumer marketing hook, much as "farm-raised" has become, and pasteurized has been for generations.

Pastured Poultry — move over free-range chickens, the next rage of "the way it used to be" set will be pastured poultry. As the wise and warm *The Art of Eating* newsletter informs us, "Few people have heard of pastured chicken, but the American Pastured Poultry Producers Association says it has nearly 500 members and estimates . . . at least three or four times that many producers in the U.S." Chickens raised by pastured poultry are moved from field to field, which advocates claim produces a finer flavor. These chickens also feast on a highly selective diet, including organic feed. Expect to see "pastured poultry" claims in supermarkets and gourmet stores at some point in the future. Of course, this is yet another example of our schizophrenia—we cherish these natural, "hand-crafted" approaches, yet support policies and practices that favor the *groligarchy* (see listing). See also *holistic herding*.

Pescatarian — a new kind of flexible vegetarian (flex-veg?), pescatarians consume fish, including shellfish, but not meat or poultry. Traditional vegetarians, who are acting out of moral and ethical—as opposed to health—reasons, scoff at pescatarians, who are usually motivated by personal (read selfish) health concerns, as opposed to any strong philosophical principles. But in an era when we tend to justify our behavior by creating finer and finer gradations of everything—it's to be expected that we are slicing and dicing the definition of vegetarianism. *DOF* wouldn't be surprised if still narrower and narrower constructs emerge, i.e., quasitarians: people who eat chicken only three times a week.

Schizo — coffee made with half regular and half decaf.

Smart Dipstick — technology that analyzes foodstuffs to determine whether they were produced with any products that were genetically modified. Originally developed to allow manufacturers to test their sources, the technology will eventually be made available to consumers for personal use, given the publicized problems that manfacturers have had with keeping GMOs out of the food chain.

Stealth Fat — you read the labels diligently, but that's not enough. Because trans fat—found in French fries, chips, cookies and deep-fried delights—doesn't show up. While hydrogenated oil—which is listed on labels—contains trans fat, you can't get a full accounting on the label. One journalist wrote that "Nutritionists say this omission could have deadly consequences because trans fat is significantly more harmful than other fats." A study done by Dr. Walter Willets at the Harvard School of Public Health found that people can reduce their risk of heart diseases by 53 percent, by simply replacing two percent of their total caloric intake with unsaturated, instead of trans fats. The FDA has introduced a proposal that would force manufacturers to list trans fat content on their labels—but it is years from implementation. Till then, don't let stealth fat sneak up on you.

Tea Sommelier — recognizing the soaring popularity of teas—for health reasons, taste reasons and because its ritual and spirituality are an antidote to an increasingly soul-less world—restaurants (the Heartbeat at the W Hotel in New York City being the first) will start to offer wider varieties of the beverage, and a tea sommelier to educate diners and help them choose. *Newsweek* writes of a "Tea Tender" who is the equivalent of a coffee "barista" and "often brings an hourglass to your table, so you can watch the sand run out before decanting." With sales of premium teas expected to grow 30–50 percent a year, *DOF* expects to see, finally, a national tea bar alternative to Starbucks.

Toaster Cookies — pre-baked cookies that are finished in your toaster oven. They are pre-coated with flavors that release the scent of fresh-baking when heated. Pop them in and in a few minutes they emerge warm, moist and ready to eat. If your appetite is whetted, you'll need some patience. ConAgra holds the patent, but they have not yet commercialized this kitchen-shaking technology.

Tyrian — cross cabernet sauvignon and a Spanish grape called Sumoll and you get Tyrian, a variety designed for Australia's wine-growing conditions. These wines, which will be released as the decade progresses, will be plentiful and affordable, thus creating a new wine cliché to pick up where chardonnay and merlot leave off.

Dictionary of the Future Predicts

Bankaurants — as cash machines and the Internet continue to draw business from traditional banks, they will look to find new uses for their largest branches. Their best ones—fine architectural examples that are dormant from three o'clock on—will be turned into chic restaurants in the evening.

CafeFearia — growing concern will develop over food-borne illnesses that are spread through school cafeterias. The reason for the problem: fast food restaurants have demanded strong safety standards from the food processors they buy from, but much lower standards govern what goes into our third graders' meatloaf. *DOF* predicts that a few well-publicized outbreaks of CafeFearia (which is a subset of the BrainReserve trend AtmosFear) will trigger major changes in the regulation of school lunches nationally, giving the term "school safety" a whole new meaning.

Farm Sharing — a food-sourcing innovation through which individuals purchase a protected, organically farmed portion of a specific crop, or of livestock or poultry production. Based on the time-share vacation model, farm sharing will be increasingly popular as the food chain grows more and more suspect. Individuals can check out their farm sharing plot in person on the Internet.

Food Macho — the courage to consume foods that others find objectionable. For example, it takes food macho to chow down on insects in America, even though *entomophagy*—consumption of bugs—is enjoyed worldwide. Peruvians relish dryopoid beetles, which are ground and used in a peppery sauce. Cultures that enjoy caterpillars and crickets and locusts are well known. With so many exotic foods now staples, those who pride themselves on food macho may have to move on to insects, and we expect a few adventurous restaurants—always prowling for newness—to start featuring insect-based dishes. In fact if we all become less insect-phobic, American farmers would be able to use far less pesticides. For more, there's the Food Insects Newsletter: www.hollowtop.com/finl_html/finl.html

Foodopoly — when global agriculture is controlled by just a few companies who own the patent on seeds and superior strains of crops. *The New York Times* writes of the possibility that companies like Syngenta and Myriad Genetics could "own the food staple for over half the world's population." See also *consolidation studies* and *groligarchy*.

Frost-Proof Fruits — fruits and vegetables that are genetically engineered to be resistant to cold. By expanding the growing seasons, frost-proof fruits will have a profound impact on global agribusiness, and will provoke massive trade wars with countries that currently export fruits and vegetables during the off-season. It will also enable you to freeze fruits and have them retain their taste and texture for months on end.

Mobile Prep — increasingly, restaurants that deliver to the home will prepare meals en route, enabling them to deliver a fresh, better-tasting product. Instead of beat-up Celicas loaded with dinners that are in the process of slowly turning to mush, sophisticated "KitchiVans" will roam the roads, complete with pizza ovens and grills. A favorite prediction of ours: a chain called Wok and Road. The only downside—hungry drivers might begin a rash of foodjackings.

New Hawaiian — *DOF* predicts that the next cuisine to capture our culinary imagination will be from the last state: Hawaii. Hawaii is nothing less than America's fusion state, and as R. W. Apple of *The New York Times* notes, its foods combine

Ff

"a dozen culinary cultures from Portugal's to China's to Thailand's." French, Greek and Vietnamese influences also touch the table. New Hawaiian food is marked by witty twists on the familiar—a burger finished with Maui onion and avocado, ahi tuna with an Asian remoulade. *DOF* expects to see New Hawaiian restaurants—from upscale to fast food—explode on the scene, as well as a focus on Hawaiian produce in supermarkets, New Hawaiian cookbooks and cooking shows and all the other signs of culinary hotness.

Rawganic — the best possible thing to eat: raw, whether it's vegetables (or anything else that can be consumed without cooking), because it preserves nutrients, vitamins and co-factors that are destroyed by heating. Plus all the benefits of a pesticide-free organic existence. Rawganic diets and rawganic menu items will appear.

Risotto-to-Go — the next dish to catch fire nationally will be risotto. We expect to see a rush of trendy, upscale "risotto bars" using new cooking technologies. The arborio rice will be prepared in special pots imported from Italy, and the ingredients will be added individually for each customer. Breakfast risotto will include chopped eggs and ham; other kinds of risotto will use seafood, vegetables, meat and traditional ingredients. For dessert, what else—fruit risotto.

Subscription Restaurants — a concept that will take the private club one step further. Celebrity chefs will open cool, hip restaurants that are by subscription only. Food and status-obsessed customers will fund the restaurant by investing in a "food bond" in advance; depending upon the amount, you're entitled to a certain number of meals per month—for you or your guest—which you have to pay for, of course. Food bonds will also have liquidity; you can sell them to someone else, and transfer the privilege. If you're lucky, and your restaurant impresses the right reviewers and the fooderati, you might even be able to sell your bond for a meaty profit.

GOVERNMENT, POLITICS AND WORLD AFFAIRS

The politics of the post-war era were a great furnace for language creation. Just reciting these colorful coinages brings to mind the urgent zeitgeist of the era—"Cold War" (courtesy of Churchill), "fallout shelters," "spooks," "mutually assured destruction," and the "Evil Empire."

Our post–Cold War period consigns those colorful coinages to the dustbin of history as it launches us into a new world of virulent terrorism, regional conflicts, warfare that will utilize technology to a level not seen before, and new kinds of economic combat that grow out of an increasingly globalized planet.

In the years to come, military correspondents will write of attacks by insect robots, the deployment of burn weapons, and the unfolding of Net Wars. Business reporters will follow the government's curious role as a venture capitalist (what *DOF* calls "DC/VC") and other journalists will be covering issues like "global pillage," the economic importance of the "Caricom" region, and the improvements that the Internet brings to the way that government relates to its constituents, courtesy of "CRM"— Citizen Relationship Management.

Karl Clausewitz—the nineteenth-century thinker—famously said that war is the continuation of politics by other means. To that we add: Language is the continuation of change by other means.

Access Capitalist — beyond fund-raisers, access capitalists are those wealthy individuals—according to *The American Prospect*—who are political junkies and love raising money for the access it gives them as much as the worthiness of the cause.

Back-Channel Media — when politicians choose pop culture vehicles like MTV, "Saturday Night Live," and "Late Night with David Letterman" to reach the public. The advantages are two-fold: it marks them as cool and hip, and it makes it less likely for any tough, hardball questions to emerge. It represents the ultimate smudging of news and entertainment, and the creation of an era of what we call poli-tainment—only possible in an era of relative peace and prosperity.

Burn Weapons — a new Pentagon approach for dispersing crowds. It uses high-frequency electromagnetic waves—what's called an "active denial system" to create a burning sensation without injury. The waves penetrate the skin just 1/64th of an inch, so burn weapons make you feel like you've been hit with 120-degree heat, but cause no injury. The Pentagon believes that burn weapons could replace tear gas and rubber bullets (longer range, less chance of injury) and expects full deployment by 2006.

Caricom — the Caribbean Economic Community. Ten countries have joined together, following the model of the European Union, to work on issues of trade and tourism, and to create an economic force more powerful than the sum of its parts. Expect to hear more from Caricom as the century rolls on, particularly when in the inevitable post-Castro period Cuba becomes a regional economic powerhouse.

Concrete Bombs — used as an "innovative weapon" against Iraq—according to *The New York Times*—2,000-pound concrete bombs are a new military option. The beauty, if you can call it that, of the concrete bomb is that it can destroy a target while inflicting a minimal amount of collateral damage upon civilians. We expect continued research in civilian-sensitive weapons technology, as we need to combat terrorism in population-dense areas of the world.

CRM — short for Citizen Relationship Management, it is an emerging attempt by government to improve constituent service. As ACS—a software company which markets to municipalities—puts it, "when practiced correctly, CRM improves a person's experience with government and positively influences his perception of it." CRM includes tracking letters, emails and faxes to create a contact history, so that when you call your local building department, for example, you don't have to start from scratch each time. Why is government non-responsiveness almost never brought up as an issue in political campaigns? Why should it be easier to communicate with your credit card company than your congressional representative? CRM says it doesn't have to be that way, and if effective it will make the notion of "government of the people, by the people, and for the people" translate into "people who will return your phone call."

DC/VC — a *DOF* term that describes the surprising role of the federal government as venture capitalist. In-Q-Tel, a VC offshoot of the CIA ("in" and "tel" are for intelligence, the "Q" a droll nod to James Bond's tech guru) invests in early stage companies that are engaged in technology that the CIA can use in its operations. As they so delicately put it on their Web site: "In-Q-Tel's areas of interest focus on leading edge information technology issues of great value to American citizens, corporations, infrastructure, and the government."

This is just the start of Uncle Sam reaching into his (our) pockets as a VC investor, and though it's fraught with issues, we believe it's a valuable practice, on balance. (Why should the private—but not the public sector—be able to leverage its assets into higher levels of return?) Expect the Defense Department, the Agriculture Department, the National Institutes of Health and many branches of the government to start their own seed capital programs.

Feebates — a marriage of the fee and the rebate—or the carrot and stick—used by governments to encourage us to adopt socially beneficial habits, and reject bad behavior. An example: you pay an extra fee when you buy a gasaholic sport utility vehicle, or you get a bonus when you buy a gas-respectful vehicle. The neutral no-fee, no-bonus position is reached with a car that delivers the average miles-per-gallon. Similarly, feebates could be used to reduce water consumption by household, or even to influence public health—a fee for Ben & Jerry's, a bonus for tofu.

Girlcott — the act of women joining together to boycott products and organizations that are discriminatory or that stereotype. For example, female tennis players have considered, but have not yet girlcotted, Grand Slam events that award more prize money to men. The Media + Women Project have girlcotted the movie industry, based on "a lack of stories featuring inspiring, heroic women, especially compared to the number of heroic and interesting men found onscreen." *DOF* expects more girlcotts in the years to come, as women become more active and linked as a result of the Internet—where they already represent over 50 percent of users.

Global Pillage — describes the looting of the global village from an archeological or economic perspective. As the Web site for "Village or Pillage" (www.villageorpillage.org) puts it: "Today's global economy lets corporations pit workers and communities against each other to see who will provide the lowest wages, most abusable workers, cheapest environmental costs, and biggest subsidies for corporations." Global Pillaging also describes the way in which indigenous cultural products (music and fashion) are appropriated by the first world design-industrial complex. See also *virtual immigrants*.

Indigenization — it's what's happening all over the world. Russians are turning inward to their native roots (the Cossacks are heroes again); there is a return to Hindu tradition in India, where young Oxford and Cambridge graduates are reverting to their ancestral names and dress. This force will continue to change the world in the twenty-first century and create new stresses and conflicts. For more on this, we recommend Samuel Huntington's *The Clash of Civilizations: Remaking of the World Order.* It's polemical but irresistible.

Insect Robots — a tiny insect army that is currently in development could help transform the way battles are fought. Bugs were chosen as the model for this robotic technology because they are energy-efficient and their movements are easily simulated by ceramic-coated wafers that expand and contract when current is sent through them. These insect robots—hundreds or thousands at a time—could carry "infrared detectors, acoustic sensors, video cameras and possibly lethal toxins," according to *Time.* Remarkably, further down the road, these could cost as little as $10 per critter. At some point, insect-configured micro-aerial vehicles may also be developed. These robotic spiders and dragonflies could "free future American troops from the terror of the unknown," says *Time.*

JTRS — short for Joint Tactical Radio system, this is a software-based radio that the Pentagon is developing to replace the traditional battlefield version (which hasn't changed that much since World War II). JTRS will transmit voice, video and data, and will connect all those engaged in combat at any given time—a military intranet. *Scientific American* quotes Col. Michael C. Cox, deputy program manager, as saying, "It's going to completely redo the way that [military] people will use communication devices in the future." JTRS should start being phased in by 2002, and as many as 750,000 radios could be replaced within 10 years. Beyond the armed forces JTRS could revolutionize emergency response—police, fire, ambulances—where some vehicles now have to carry as many as seven different radios in order to communicate and coordinate with all the different services involved in any one event.

Low-Burn Warfare — the combat equivalent of a chronic infection. Writing in the *New Republic*, Peter Hirschberg offers "low-burn war-fare" as one of the possible scenarios for the Middle East, but *DOF* sees the phrase having utility beyond the region, to describe not just the relations between countries, but between people. "Ira and Bruce have pulled back from open hostility, but there's still a low-burn war going on."

Multitary Use — the use of technology developed by the military for other applications. This is an increasingly widespread phenomenon, but as of yet there has been no way to quantify this benefit, and relate it back to the value of our overall defense budget. Case in point: a system that was designed to prevent enemies from jamming our radar is now being tested as a breast cancer treatment. In preliminary trials, it shrank tumors by 50 percent in 10 days—the equivalent of months of debilitating chemotherapy or radiation. Celsion (www.celsion.com) has licensed the technology, which might also have application for prostate, lung, liver and pancreatic cancer.

Net Wars — political struggles fought on the Internet. One example: on May 1, 2001—the anniversary of the accidental American bombing of the Chinese embassy in Yugoslavia— Chinese hackers broke into a number of American Web sites, including one for the clerk of the House of Representatives, where a hacker posted a message "What happened to this American site?" And those logging onto a site run by the mayor of Philadelphia found a message that said, "Beat down Imperialism of America." While these Net Wars are essentially harmless, they do point up the weakness of our Internet security measures; in that way, they could actually be helping us by focusing attention on our porous digital borders. See also *distance terrorism*.

Placebo Politics — when a politician addresses a serious national problem with heightened rhetoric but with no real intention of making any kind of meaningful change. (In England it's called "gesture politics.") It's a political sugar pill that gets an elected official off the hook by satisfying constituents with the illusion of action on one hand, and not alienating special interest groups by maintaining the status quo on the other.

Plaintiff's Diplomacy — when aggrieved individuals, such as Holocaust survivors, torture victims, or the families of those killed by terrorists, turn to the U.S. Courts for help. In September 2000, a judge in Manhattan found Radovan Karadzic, the former Serbian dictator, guilty of torture and ordered him to pay $14.5 billion in damages to victims of rape, torture and genocide. A controversial yet expanding trend, it uses a legal loophole that permits the courts to get involved in matters that happen outside the country.

RMA — Revolution in Military Affairs, a NATO acronym (how's that, an acronym from an acronym?) for a military strategy that reduces the risk that combat troops face by substituting technology such as unmanned aircraft and robots as a peace-keeping force. RMA is tied into the "maneuverist" philosophy which the *Financial Times* describes as "being at the heart of modern military thinking." Rather than advancing on a single front you employ a "panoply of methods to strike at an enemy and overwhelm his decision-making cycles." See also *insect robots*.

Rollforward — the opposite of a price rollback is a rollforward. An example: German "competition regulators" forced Wal-Mart to raise its prices, under pressure from local retailers who claimed that the retail giant's prices were too low and unfair to local chains. As American retailers from Wal-Mart to Home Depot seek to maintain their growth by expanding globally, this issue of prices being "too low" will trigger some brutal trade wars. The need for "rollforwards" to compensate for prices being "too low" will, of course, strike Americans as preposterous, given that we obsess over discounts, and in fact have supported an entire Internet industry that finds the lowest price wherever it might be hiding.

Gg

Selective Purchasing Laws — a kind of sanction; these are state laws that restrict local governments from purchasing from countries whose policies are found objectionable—either directly or through third parties. For example, when San Francisco passed a selective purchasing law outlawing transactions with Burma, this encouraged Motorola—who did business there—to pull out of the country so they could continue to sell products to the city. Similarly, when Massachusetts passed its law, Kodak and Apple also packed their bags and left Burma. The key question: Is it Constitutional? The federal government has the sole right to conduct foreign policy, and these Selective Purchasing Laws are viewed as an effort to subvert that authority.

Silicon Republic — they were banana republics back when banana exports dominated their economies. Now, Latin American countries are becoming silicon republics, as high technology manufacturers are moving in. Indeed, local governments are courting these companies, because they are a quick route to better economic times. *Newsweek* used the term in its coverage of Costa Rica, reporting that about 40 percent of the country's exports are now controlled by Intel (thus giving new geo-political meaning to the phrase "Intel inside").

Soft Authoritarianism — a form of government that is, according to the Carnegie Endowment for International Peace, a "mixture of strong political control, limited popular participation and economic liberalization that allows for a strong state role in regulating the market—South Korea, Taiwan and even Singapore are viewed as models to be emulated." This shows how far economic—as opposed to democratic—principles guide, and will continue to shape, our thinking in a world governed by free-market considerations.

Three-Block War — a twenty-first century military likelihood for which American soldiers are preparing. As the *Economist* describes a potential conflict situation, it will be "an operation in which they would simultaneously be distributing food and medicine to frantic civilians in one part of a city, quelling rioters and maintaining order in another, and fighting guerillas in a third." With nationalist struggles the most explosive threats on the horizon, three-block wars may become more than theory sooner than later.

Tourist Subsidies — as Starbucks and the Gap take over the world, the local institutions that define a city—and that tourists put up with endless travel delays to experience—are coming under financial pressure. Given the economic importance of tourism, governments will be forced to subsidize these unique, privately owned restaurants and shops—and it's happening already. Take Buenos Aires, which was witnessing the decline of its once-grand cafes that served the same role in the city's intellectual life as the cafes on the Left Bank of Paris. To rescue them and maintain the tourist viability of the city, the Commission for the Protection and Promotion of the City's Notable Cafes, Bars and Billiard Halls (that's the actual name, folks) decided to subsidize the restoration costs for 15 of these Buenos Aires landmarks. Other cities with similar problems—from Vienna to Budapest—will follow suit.

Unmanned Vehicles — the future of combat. Aircraft and ground vehicles that can fight and win battles without anyone piloting or driving them—or risking their lives. The *Financial Times* has reported that Senator John Warner, chairman of the Senate Armed Services Committee, believes that "one-third of deep strike aircraft could be unmanned in 10 years, and one-third of ground-combat vehicles in 15 years." According to the definitive *Shephards's Unmanned Vehicles Handbook,* there are 62 kinds in production, including six-inch "micro" aircraft. See also *RMA.*

Bureauclout — bureaucrats with clout. For example, a number of states in New England are getting together to pool their resources and put pressure on drug companies to lower their prices. The combined efforts of several state attorneys-general in the anti-tobacco litigation is another case in point. We expect to see much more of this activism—against polluters, against record companies who sell X-rated material—as local elected officials become far more expansive and aggressive in the way they define their jobs.

Department of Technology — recognizing that profound changes in information technology require a dedicated federal agency, Congress will pass and the president will sign a measure to create a Department of Technology, led by a Secretary of Technology. The DOT will help set technology policy, and will coordinate efforts that are now disbursed across the existing agencies; currently there is no real sharing of ideas, or of best practices and innovations.

Government Test Marketing — every serious corporation test markets its products and services—or researches them in other ways—before spending a fortune on introducing them. The government doesn't. But *DOF* believes that this basic marketing precept will finally take hold in federal and state governments, and we will see small-scale, modest tests of programs ranging from education, agriculture and environmental protection before local and national roll-out. It's another example of private sector disciplines coming—albeit belatedly—to the public sector.

Hyber-Nation — neo-isolationism; although we are more a part of the world economy than ever before (witness the global business reports on CNBC each morning), we will nonetheless reach a point where we rebel against the interdependency and stress that come from lack of control.

Restorative Justice — an inclusive term which captures a trend we're seeing in the criminal justice system; it includes both victim's rights and alternative sentencing which requires that criminals perform community service. Its core principle is that justice should not just punish the offender, but should attempt to offset the damage, treating society like an ecosystem where the balance needs to be restored.

The panorama of this section unspools the extent that health-related issues dominate what we think about, worry about and argue about—as well as how we spend our money, personally and as a nation. (One-third of our Gross National Product goes to health care.) It also reflects the feverish activity that is underway to diagnose, prevent, and treat the most intractable and implacable conditions we face.

On the diagnostic front we have "pill-cam"—the test you swallow; "Three-Dimensional Coronary Magnetic Resonance"—which could replace the angiogram; and "PEPSI"—a new kind of brain scan. On the vaccine front we have: "DNA vaccines"; a cancer approach called "telomerase vaccines" and what *DOF* has labeled "crackcines"— vaccines against drug addiction. On the treatment front, there is far too much activity to even hint at completeness, but "resynchronization devices" for congestive heart failure, and "EGF" (epidermal growth factors), which are yielding startling advances in cancer therapy, warrant inclusion.

The traditional and non-traditional cohabit this section as well; in the case of "PC-SPES," they are one and the same: this traditional Chinese approach for prostate cancer has withstood the bright light of clinical studies at the renowned University of California at San Francisco. *Time* magazine has noted that of the 350 new compounds and molecules undergoing human trials, more than half are "based on innovative, sometimes bizarre-sounding ways of homing in on tumors." Purists pay heed: if scientists are open to the possibilities of the unexpected, so should those who are the guardians of our language.

Animal Assisted Therapy — increasing attention is being paid to the role of animals in a variety of therapies. Research is being done, for example, with seizure-alert animals—including potbellied pigs—who are capable of detecting epileptic seizures *before* they happen, and can be trained to use a footpad telephone to summon help. (They seem to be responsive to changes in brain waves.) The University of Florida's College of Veterinary Medicine is studying the sense of smell that seems to enable dogs to identify illnesses that manifest themselves with slight changes in odor: one dog kept licking a mole on his owner's leg and eventually tried to bite it off. The mole was biopsied and found to be cancerous. These healing or "therapy" animals will become an increasingly important part of the health care system, and while there are many wonderful nonprofits working in the field, *DOF* expects that we will soon see the first for-profit entity that attempts to commercialize the area.

Antibiotic Gum Therapy — new drugs and new research might offer an alternative to surgery for the millions of us with periodontal disease. Dr. Rick Niederman, who is in charge of Harvard's office of evidence-based dentistry, maintains that the profession is in "transition" from surgery as a first-line treatment to drugs. And not a moment too soon.

Astaxanthin — a little-known, but extremely powerful antioxidant that is "purported to be 100 times stronger than Vitamin E" according to *Let's Live* magazine. An antioxidant this potent could be enormously valuable, which is why astaxanthin is being studied in a number of areas. Early animal research shows it to be a potent cancer fighter and booster of immune strength. Some believe it can also slow the progress of auto-immune diseases (these include rheumatoid arthritis and lupus); a study in the *Journal of Dermatological Science* found that astaxanthin can offer protection against ultraviolet oxidative stress, which leads to skin cancer. Of course, effective antioxidants can have significant cardio-protective benefits, so astaxanthin's most important use could be in preventing heart attacks.

Awareness Episodes — a surprisingly common but little-reported condition where patients remain aware of what's happening to them despite being under anesthesia. During cardiac surgery, for example, 23 percent of patients recall becoming aware of the procedure; during surgery for major trauma the percentage soars to 43 percent. These incidents have serious consequences, as one report found that "Some patients suffered from a post-traumatic neurotic syndrome marked by anxiety and irritability, preoccupation with death, repetitive nightmares and reluctance to discuss symptoms." In development: the FACE monitor, which detects micro-expressions, reactions that are virtually unnoticeable without the electrodes the system employs. We foresee that awareness of these awareness episodes will grow and will become yet another issue in the ongoing patient's rights movement; surgical patients will demand more extensive monitoring.

Bigorexia — the opposite form of anorexia—but like it, a focus on an unattainable body type. Bigorexia, which is usually found in men but also appears in women, is a body-building obsession that drives sufferers to get as big and "ripped" as possible, resulting in hours spent in the gym, and often involving illegal steroids—although there is a "natural" body-building movement as well. See also *orthorexia*.

Breathwalk — a new exercise strategy that combines breathing, walking, yoga and meditation into a single, integrated activity that alleviates complaints like depression, back pain, high blood pressure and stress. Advocates believe it can also help break addictions. Dr. Candace Royer, director of Physical Education at MIT, raves about it, saying "Breathwalk is a simple but elegant method for altering moods and state of mind . . . I use it in my general walking . . . almost every time I walk anywhere, for an exercise or relaxation effect."

Cernilton — an extract of flower pollen that has a long history in the alternative medicine community of being an effective treatment for an enlarged prostate. More disciplined research seems to suggest this folk medicine tradition has clinical value.

Channeling — the practice by which HMOs "use incentives and plan design to encourage members to utilize network providers." (Definition courtesy of the USA Managed Care Organization Web site.) In other words, your doctor is paid bonuses if he or she manages to refer you to doctors in the network, and discourages you from your freedom to choose the doctor you want. Similarly, doctors are often penalized if too many of their patients wander out of the network. *DOF* expects that consumer pressure will force doctors and HMOs to publish their channeling policies.

Chinese Spoon Massage — a stress-relieving and purifying procedure (called *gua sha*) that is part of Traditional Chinese Medicine (TCM). The blunt end of a porcelain spoon—the kind you see in Chinese restaurants all the time—is pressed against the spine in a skilled fashion, which relieves tensions and toxins. Often, you will break into a rash, which signifies that the sha—or toxins—are leaving the body. *DOF* believes that this is just one of many practices of TCM that will be finding their way into the American mainstream, just as acupuncture has. See also *Chinese string facial, massage menus.*

Chinese String Facial — a traditional beauty regimen that is only beginning its journey to cosmetic necessity here in America. A Chinese string facial is the mechanical version of the harsh chemical peel, which aggressively removes the dead layers of skin to create a more luminous and glowing appearance. With the string facial, a flax string is gently rolled from side to side across the patient's face, slowly scraping the skin without causing any wrinkling—which chemical peels tend to do. Vivienne Tam, the Chinese fashion designer, calls the Chinese string facial—and other ancient beauty techniques—"the cosmetic equivalent of feng shui, clearing a path for chi, or energy, to flow." See also *Chinese spoon massage.*

Clean Embryo — an embryo that has been created in vitro, has passed genetic testing and is ready for implantation. See *embryo adoption, pre-implantation genetic diagnosis.*

Hh

Closure Treatment — a new way to treat varicose veins, which are an aesthetic—and often a health—problem for 25 million Americans. The traditional treatment, called "vein stripping," is invasive; it requires general anesthesia and four weeks' recovery. No wonder that of those 25 million, only 150,000 a year opt for the procedure. Closure treatment works in a whole different way: it requires only local anesthesia and a small incision with no stitches. The "interventional radiologist" identifies the offending vein by ultrasound and a small catheter is inserted behind the knee and threaded to the site; radio-frequency bursts are then sent to heat the vein, causing it to collapse. With the cost at around $2,000, we expect closure treatment to join the ranks of tooth whitening, eye lifts and lasik surgery as the personal improvement strategy of choice.

Cord Blood Banking — cord blood, which is what remains in the umbilical cord after a baby is born, contains stem cells. At some point in the future these stem cells might be required for a transplant—either for the child, or a close family member—which is why, as *PregnancyWeekly.com* has noted, "more and more expecting parents are choosing to privately store their baby's cord blood." The costs range from $500 to $1,500, and while cord banks market their services as "biological insurance," the odds are substantial—from 1 in 10,000 to 1 in 200,000, depending on whose numbers you believe—that a child will never need his or her stem cells. That's why the American Academy of Pediatrics has come out *against* banking and *for* donation—unless there is a family history of a blood disorder. (But if the blood is banked, who owns it legally—child, mother or father?) The implications are mind-boggling, but so are the potential rewards.

Counter-Detailing — detailing is the marketing practice that pharmaceutical companies engage in to convince doctors to prescribe their drugs. Counter-detailing is an emerging, cost-saving practice which seeks to neutralize these sales efforts by spreading the gospel of lower-cost and generic options. According to a newsletter published by the investment bank of W. R. Hambrecht, it includes "counter measures . . . to promote drugs that are less expensive, yet produce equal or better outcomes." The Vermont legislature is actually reviewing a bill that would "educate physicians and consumers . . . to counteract the marketing efforts of pharmaceutical companies directed at physicians, and to counteract direct-to-consumer advertising." It's a blunt attack on what's called Big Pharma, and with the cost of prescription drugs such a huge social issue, *DOF* expects counter-detailing to become a rather significant trend. See *bureauclout.*

Crackcines — crack + vaccine, coined by *DOF.* There are vaccines in development which work by stimulating the body to produce antibodies that block the effects of drugs like cocaine, PCP, methamphetamine and even nicotine. The concept is not without its ethical implications. As the British publication *New Scientist* put some of them: "Should people be vaccinated simply because they belong to a group thought to be particularly at risk of becoming addicted? Should parents be allowed to make that decision for their children?" A Boston company, Addiction Therapies (www.addictiontherapies.com) is forging ahead anyway on a cocaine vaccine. *DOF* believes that the debate over who should be crackcinated, and who shouldn't, will be one of the great bioethical divides of the next decade.

Cyberchondria — coined by Humphrey Taylor, the dangerous zone where hypochondria meets the Internet. With health-related information a click away, even those who aren't health-obsessed often find it difficult to fight the temptation to indulge their worst fears. As www.healthscout.com points out, the Web "offers sites such as the 'Wonderful World of Disease,' which tells in explicit detail what happens to the body when struck by rare diseases like hantavirus, dengue fever and the ebola virus."

Delta Sleep — the deepest, most restful stage of sleep, essential to human health. As awareness of the widespread public health implications of sleep deprivation increases and the problem is exacerbated by the continuing extension of working hours, research into how to achieve delta sleep will grow and therapies and medications will be developed to insure a good night's delta sleep. Luxury hotels will introduce "Delta Sleep" rooms with special mattresses, curtains and aromatherapy. See also *lucid dreaming, nap tents, REM-up* and *work daze.*

DNA Vaccines — an emerging vaccine technology which could someday replace the traditional method with an ouchless delivery system. In one application, the DNA from the hepatitis B virus gets applied with a cream that is absorbed through the hair follicles, which then turns hepatitis DNA into an antigen. Next in the cycle, the body's immune system recognizes the antigen as foreign proteins and stimulates the lymph nodes to produce antibodies to it. Voila, you're vaccinated! Thus far, the approach has worked with mice. "It's an exciting development because it shows that DNA vaccination will get simpler and simpler," said Dr. Stephen Albert, who directs the Center for Biomedical Inventions at the University of Texas. Down the road, DNA vaccines could be incorporated into shampoo, sprays or food. Importantly, DNA technology could enable vaccines to be developed against a wider variety of pathogens than we can now protect against. The delivery system would also make it far more economical to protect people—particularly children—in third world countries (DNA vaccines don't require refrigeration or specially trained personnel). See also *GAVI.*

DOT — Directly Observed Therapy, used to assure that patients with conditions from AIDS to tuberculosis remain on their drug therapy. Estimates are that from 20 percent to 50 percent of AIDS patients do not comply with their prescription regimens; surprisingly, the cost of using trained healthcare workers to monitor these patients is actually far less than the health-care costs involved if the patients fail to follow their treatment and get sicker. DOT will be a big public health debate in the years to come as Web-cams increase the ability of health care practictioners to raise the intrusiveness of DOT.

Ductal Lavage — an innovative diagnostic test for breast cancer, which has received FDA approval. A catheter is inserted into the nipple and withdraws cells from the milk ducts, where 95 percent of breast cancers begin. These cells are then analyzed for atypical and malignant cells. (Ductal lavage resembles a Pap smear in that it detects early cellular changes eight to 10 years before a cancer is large enough to show up on a mammogram.) Research among 500 high-risk women found that 17 percent had atypical cells, and 7 percent had suspicious or malignant ones. *DOF* anticipates a rush of at-risk women for this procedure, and hopefully, there will soon be enough surgeons and pathologists to handle the demand. Like many other sophisticated diagnostic modalities, ductal lavage can give us more information than we know what to do with. Should a woman with suspicious cells automatically have a prophylactic mastectomy, for example? See also *burden of knowledge.*

EGF — a new class of exciting anti-cancer drugs called epidermal growth factors. They work differently than conventional chemotherapy by attaching themselves to cellular receptors and "jamming" the messages sent by rogue proteins that instruct cells to divide and become cancerous. The first drug that works in this way, Gleevec—developed by Novartis—was given fast-track approval by the FDA for chronic myelogenous leukemia; it is also showing success in a form of gastro-intestinal cancer where, in the words of *The Wall Street Journal,* it "essentially melted large stromal cancers." Unlike conventional treatments—which also damage healthy cells—the elegance of EGF is that it targets only cancerous ones. (Although some of the emerging EGF drugs are being tested, along with chemotherapy, as a cocktail.)

Some physicians believe that by targeting cellular mechanisms cancer may not be eliminated from the body, but controlled—turning it into a chronic disease like diabetes, or like AIDS is becoming. This creates a great deal of complexity for researchers, since cancer drugs have traditionally been evaluated on their effectiveness at shrinking tumors, rather than their ability to stabilize cancer and make it a "livable" condition.

Electronic Smog — the soup of electromagnetic radiation we live in, created by computer screens, cell phones and other electronic devices. Controversy rages about the health impact of all this exposure. Ross Adley, a distinguished professor of neurology at Loma Linda University School of Medicine, was quoted in *Fortune* as saying, "It is not a good thing to proceed toward a world of ubiquitous wireless communication in a totally uncontrolled fashion." But, that's just what we're doing, as questions about cancer, brain chemistry, allergies, immune capacity reduction, ADD and other health issues are being debated. If you're concerned, there are some devices that claim to offset the electromagnetic radiation, like Radbusters (www.radbusters.com/index.html). See also *SAR.*

Emu Oil — oil from the emu, which has been used by the Australian aborigines for thousands of years, is emerging as a new natural remedy of choice for everything from burns to arthritis due to its anti-bacterial, anti-microbial and anti-inflammatory properties.

Ergonomic Audit — according to the Occupational Safety and Health Administration (OSHA), 1.8 million U.S. workers develop work-related musculoskeletal disorders each year—everything from repetitive motion injury to carpal tunnel syndrome to back problems. OSHA has proposed a controversial measure requiring employers to conduct ergonomic audits, to be conducted by an outside expert who analyzes jobs and their related stresses. The results of these audits are supposed to help companies increase productivity and avoid costly leaves of absence and even lawsuits. Needless to say, it is being attacked as an example of governmental over-regulation.

Fat Virus — researchers at the University of Wisconsin have found that mice and chickens that are infected with a common human virus gain more weight. The same virus is also found in overweight people to a greater extent than others, leading scientists to believe that there could be a fat virus. (That's right—you didn't gain ten pounds, you caught a bad case of it.) Don't hold your breath—any drugs that might emerge from this discovery are still years away.

Feldenkrais — a form of therapy that uses the idea of "awareness through movement" to reprogram the nervous system to help overcome pain, stress, anxiety and other conditions of twenty-first century existence. We believe that Feldenkrais is moving up to a new level of popularity and acceptance, and that many people will move from yoga to this less psychologically intense approach that is more focused on physical end-benefits (www.feldenkrais.com).

Fenretinide — a vitamin A derivative that has been found to have some effect at preventing the progression of breast cancer in pre-menopausal women. The initial work was done by Dr. Alberto Costa of the European Institute of Oncology in Milan.

Futile Care Theory — medical jargon for the practice of denying care to the massively disabled or terminally ill. While the trend over recent years has been to find ethically acceptable ways to end life, *DOF* has detected the beginning of a reaction to this approach. The counterargument is captured in Wesley J. Smith's book *The Culture of Death*, in which he argues, essentially, that we have become too quick to pull the plug: "Some doctors now report a rush to write off newly unconscious patients as disposable, and consign them to death by cutting off life support before they have a chance to recover." Smith believes that bioethicists have abandoned the sanctity of life principle, often driven by costs and a need to quickly harvest organs for transplantation. As the future holds new possibilities for sustaining life—along with higher standards for what we know as quality of life—we can be certain that there is no easy answer for how gently we go, in Dylan Thomas's words, into that good night.

Guggul — an herb used in Indian ayurvedic medicine that has been shown to have some potent cholesterol-lowering properties. Guggul is reported to lower triglycerides by 30 percent, and can also reduce LDL cholesterol and raise HDL levels. *Yoga Journal* brings our attention to an ancient ayurvedic text, the *Sushrita Samhita*, which describes a condition called *medoroga*—which resembles atherosclerosis—and has been, for generations, treated successfully with guggul. *DOF* believes that ayurvedic medicine is poised to move into mainstream acceptance—it has been largely neglected in America by all but a few devotees—and that guggul will become the subject of intense scrutiny by traditional medicine and the mainstream pharmaceutical companies.

Happiness Set Point — just as we are genetically programmed with a weight set point, so too is our happiness level established for us. So goes a theory promulgated by psychologist David Lykken. To help validate his hypothesis, Lykken—who has been researching 300 identical twins, including some who were raised separately—asked them each a series of questions about their state of happiness; to rule out day-to-day fluctuations, he repeated the questions nine years later. Lykken could predict the twins' level of happiness with 90 percent accuracy, including those raised apart. So are we stuck with our happiness quota forever? Lykken says we can work to achieve a condition "slightly above" our natural level; if we choose not to work at it there are always drugs. In fact the happiness set point theory will probably be used to justify the increasing use of Prozac and other mood-altering brain innovations. See also *VNS*.

Heart Pollution — it's more than our lungs that are threatened by dirty air; even moderate air pollution raises the risk of heart attacks for those who already have cardiovascular disease. The *Los Angeles Times* reports: "more than a dozen studies on humans and animals suggest that heart attacks, not lung disease, may be the most serious medical threat posed by air pollution." What's the mechanism of destructive action? Particulates—small by-products of air pollution—can actually create unnatural rhythms and interfere with the heart's ability to adjust its rate. Estimates are that 10,000 people a year die this way.

hs-CRP — stands for high-sensitivity C-reactive protein, and it could be the hot new diagnostic test of the century's first decade. The presence of hs-CRP is a marker for inflamed arteries, which are more likely to be closely linked to heart attacks than cholesterol. *Time* reports that a study of 28,000 healthy women found "those with high blood levels of hs-CRP are four and half times more likely to suffer a heart attack or a stroke even if their cholesterol count is normal." The test is inexpensive and has been approved since late 1999. This means you can stop worrying about your cholesterol level and start fretting about your hs-CRP; like so much else today, we aren't lowering our burden of anxiety, just re-allocating it.

Hygiene Hypothesis — a theory which holds that our focus (obsession, perhaps) on cleanliness, as well as increased antibiotic use, is actually responsible for the dramatic increase in allergies, ranging from asthma to hayfever. Some advocates even believe that the hygiene hypothesis can account for auto-immune diseases such as rheumatoid arthritis and Type 1 diabetes. The argument, according to the *Science News* Web site, is that by "stamping out innocuous organisms we have weakened some parts of children's immune systems." We know, for sure, that the growth of asthma has been significant and unexplained—it's more than two and a half times greater for children under four today, than in 1980. We also know that in logical asthma "centers," i.e., East Germany, rates of asthma are lower than elsewhere. Nonetheless, there are scientists who question the hygiene hypothesis, and there are studies on both sides. On the germ exposure side of the aisle: one Canadian study of 1,314 children followed from birth to age seven found that children who had two or more upper respiratory infections had half the risk of asthma. There are even vaccines in development to expose children to the harmless bacteria that have been scrubbed, boiled and otherwise sent scurrying from our environment, in order to strengthen their immune systems.

Hh

Iatronic Injuries — describes any condition that was caused as a result of medical injury, by medical personnel. Numbers are difficult to obtain, but in some hospitals, as many as 17 percent of all patients have been shown to suffer from some kind of iatronic injury. Many believe that with the increased workloads that doctors face, driven by HMO economics, the number of iatronic incidents will increase. They also insist that the number of incidents is under-reported because of the *white wall of silence* (see listing). The statistic that shocks the most: the fourth leading cause of death is medical injury.

Insulin-Resistance Syndrome — the inability of cells to absorb insulin readily, causing a build-up of insulin and glucose in the blood. Long known to be a precursor of adult-onset diabetes, insulin resistance is now believed to be linked to a variety of other diseases, including atherosclerosis and breast and colon cancer. The condition is still the subject of great debate, regarding its symptoms, risk factors and genetic basis. Nonetheless—recognizing the marketing power of the word "insulin"— diets that claim to be able to modulate or control the syndrome are becoming increasingly popular.

Intuitive Surgical — an innovative medical device company whose da Vinci surgical system enables bypass procedures to live up to their name, because they bypass the old-fashioned rip-open-the-chest approach. A tiny, one-centimeter incision is made, and a robotic endowrist performs the procedure, including the necessary cutting, clamping and suturing. The cardiac surgeon simply manipulates the endowrist from a computer console, using a joystick. (All those Nintendo-defenders who talked about the value of improved hand-eye coordination have been redeemed.) See also *bio-bypass*.

Laughter Clubs — started in Bombay by Dr. Madan Kataria, these groups took off in India and now have offshoots in the United States and around the world (www.worldlaughter tour.com). Laughter Clubs are a form of therapy, utilizing elements of yoga to help overcome health problems, reduce stress and put the body's natural systems in balance.

Lucid Dreaming — a state in which you are dreaming yet are simultaneously aware of it. Believers hold that it liberates you to imagine, fully and richly, any possibility. As the Web site of the Lucidity Institute puts it (www.lucidity.com), "A large part of the extraordinary pleasure . . . comes from the exhilarating feeling of utter freedom that accompanies the realization that you are in a dream and there will be no social or physical consequences of your actions." Other, more functional uses include healing, preparation for events (performances, athletic challenges). This same Web site provides details on how one can achieve the dream state, which include special training in dream recall and other exercises. *DOF* believes that lucid dreaming will surge in popularity as it invades the last frontier—our sleep—with the guilt-free hedonism that can even exceed that which dominates our waking hours.

Microneedles — tiny silicon needles—no more than 150 microns long—that make microscopic holes in the skin's outer layer, which (unlike the ego) is not sensitive to pain. This innovation could be used to deliver drugs through the skin, including new substances derived from bio-tech that are destroyed by digestion and thus cannot be taken orally. Further down the road: microprocessors measure your blood sugar, and microneedles deliver just the right amount of insulin. Our skin is our largest organ, and its role as a drug delivery system is just beginning to be explored. See also *sonophoresis*.

Nicastrin — a recently discovered protein which could play a key role in Alzheimer's. Named after Nicastro, an Italian village whose residents gave physicians some early insights into the nature of the disease, Nicastrin is believed to be part of the bio-chemical process that creates the brain "plaque" which is responsible for the symptoms and progression of Alzheimer's. The discovery of the protein gives drug developers an important new molecular target. See also *isopopulations*.

Oleuropein — the active ingredient in olive leaf extract, which is removed from green olives when they are processed and has been found to have enormous antiviral, antifungal, antibacterial, antiparasitic and heart benefits. The antimicrobial properties of olive leaf have been known for 6,000 years in the Mediterranean region, including ancient Egypt, where the extract was used to mummify their kings. Olive leaf extract is now available as a supplement, and we expect it to become one of the "hero nutrients" of the future.

Pain Memory — do infants feel pain? For years, it was believed that they didn't. However, a study done with infant rats found that those exposed to pain ended up as hypersensitive to pain as adults. If applicable to humans—and many studies of this kind are—the implications are profound for the way that babies and premature infants are treated, often without painkillers. There is debate in the medical community; some say that children are resilient, others, according to *The New York Times*, that "injury and pain will damage a child for life." *DOF* predicts that this research will be extended beyond lasting pain sensitivity, to the link between early pain exposure, and the onset of behavioral conditions such as autism.

Patient Poaching — the international hospital competition for wealthy patients. With sophisticated medical care now available in many places worldwide, and with hospital overcapacity an issue, the fight is on for the rich and the sick. *The Wall Street Journal* writes that the Auguste-Viktoria hospital in Berlin "recently launched a virtual Internet tour featuring fancy hospital suites, swimming pools, [and] sculpture gardens." A private company called International Patient Service (www.int-patient-services.com/) was created to help foreign nationals (and foreign corporations) identify the best American hospitals for any given medical need. The flow will be in every direction: Saudis to London, Germans to Texas, New Yorkers to Paris (for those who want real food, not the hospital variety).

PC-SPES — a herbal formula—containing eight ingredients which are part of traditional Chinese medicine—that is gaining increasing attention as a possible natural treatment for prostate cancer. The "PC" stands for prostate cancer, the

"Spes" means hope in Latin. The Web site www.pc-spes.com is filled with useful information, including a link to the prestigious UCSF (University of California at San Francisco) Medical School, where clinicals have been done, and are continuing. While the medical establishment is usually super-skeptical about alternative treatments, here's what the UCSF Web site says: "our findings suggest that patients who have never been treated with hormones will virtually all have a significant response to PC-SPES. One hundred percent of patients had a decline in their PSA, and 56 percent of patients achieved an undetectable PSA . . . we were surprised that in hormone-resistant prostate cancer patients approximately 60 percent had a significant drop in their PSA . . . Furthermore, in those patients who were tested, some had improvement in bone scans and other measures of disease. Thus, we believe that PC-SPES probably has some activity in patients with hormone-resistant prostate cancer." The product can be purchased over the counter, although UCSF strongly advises that it be taken under the supervision of a physician.

PEPSI — short for proton echo-planar spectroscopic imaging, a new kind of brain scan that's 32 times faster than an MRI, which allows for more detailed brain functioning to be captured. PEPSI scans can monitor brain activity in real time; recent work has found, for example, that the brains of dyslexic children actually work harder at processing information than the brains of other children, which confirms that dyslexia is a condition that is based on problems with brain wiring. In the future, PEPSI scans could be used to diagnose and monitor the treatment of a variety of neurological conditions, although their expense, once again, will focus attentions on the cost/benefit issues that are presented by sophisticated diagnostic technology.

Peregrine — a new technology for improving the use of radiation in cancer treatments, which was developed at the Lawrence Livermore Laboratory. A company called Nomos (www.nomos.com) has obtained a license for the technology, and has received FDA clearance for it. Peregrine uses

Hh

three-dimensional modeling technology developed for the military (see *multitary use*) in order to focus the radiation, thus enabling doctors to deliver high doses without damaging healthy tissue.

Pill-Cam — also video pill, two shorthand names for the FM2A capsule camera—the diagnostic device you swallow. The size of a large vitamin, it contains a tiny light, video camera and transmitter. The patient wears a Walkman-sized recorder on his or her belt, and as the pill-cam moves efficiently through your body it captures accurate and detailed images of your colon and other parts of your insides. When it's finished, the disposable device passes naturally through your digestive system. Pill-cam will eventually replace endoscopy and colonoscopy—it causes far less discomfort, and covers more territory besides. The product, which was developed by Dr. Paul Swain of the Royal London Hospital, and Given Imaging (www.givenimaging.com), an Israeli company, has worked in early trials. It should be moving through the digestive system of the FDA approval process when *DOF* goes to press.

POMC — a natural substance whose full name is proopomelanocortin. Early research indicates that POMC signals the brain that it's time to stop eating. When plump mice were treated with POMC boosters, they dropped 40 percent of their weight in just two weeks—and they weren't working out on tiny treadmills, either. Because there are many substances that work in mice but don't work in people, we shouldn't get overly excited. Nonetheless, it's within the realm of possibility to imagine POMC therapy, perhaps in the form of injections. See also *fat virus*.

Portable Defibrillators — the fire extinguishers of the next decade, portable defibrillators are devices that can re-establish a normal heart rhythm in people who suffer incidents of sudden cardiac arrest. The statistics tell the story: a patient has a 90 percent chance of survival if he or she receives a shock from a defibrillator in the first minute. With each passing minute, the chances of surviving decrease by 7 to 10 percent. Ambulances reach these patients within a minute less than 10 percent of the time. These devices are now being sold to airlines, the police and other obvious places. While about 25 percent are being sold to individuals, *DOF* predicts that a larger consumer market for these devices will emerge—for homes, cars, offices, stores, just about everywhere. We also anticipate that wireless technology will be incorporated in them, to notify hospitals, physicians and families when and where the cardiac event happened, and to send a cardiogram at the same time.

Renal Assist Device — this could be the salvation for the 40,000 people waiting for kidney transplants. Created by David Humes using cells from the kidneys of pigs (posing an interesting medical and ethical dilemma for Moslems and Jews), the renal assist device is far better than dialysis because it is able to reclaim the salts, sugars and water that the body requires. It accomplishes this by arranging the pig cells to reabsorb parts of the ultrafiltrite, which is the waste stream before the formation of urine. The dream is a bioartifical organ that, according to *Wired*, could be worn on a belt. Human trials could start sometime in 2001.

Resynchronization Devices — a new generation of medical devices to treat congestive heart failure, which is second to childbirth in total hospital admissions. A device from Medtronic—called, ironically, Insynch—and one named Contak, from Guidant, are currently awaiting FDA approval, which may have happened by the time you read this. That would be great news, because if these devices live up to their promise, they could be—according to *The Wall Street Journal*— "one of the biggest developments ever in heart failure treatment." Currently, half of those with congestive heart failure die within five years—and there are five million Americans so afflicted. The only existing treatments are pharmaceutical, so let's hope that the language of resynchronization devices enters our vocabulary for good: "I'm feeling great since I've been resynched."

Hh

Reverse Geometry Lenses — charlatans have long promised you could learn a foreign language, or lose weight, while you sleep. Now a legitimate sleep activity has emerged. Research has shown that those who are mildly nearsighted (myopic), might be able to improve their vision simply by sleeping with reverse geometry lenses, a new kind of contact lens. While traditional contacts are convex, these new lenses are shaped in the opposite manner, putting gentle pressure on the cornea and flattening it in a way that mimics what happens during refractive surgery. In a small study, subjects who slept with these lenses were able to improve their vision enough to go without glasses or contact lenses during the day. If further studies confirm this, the next ocular controversy could very well be sleep vs. surgery.

R.O.S. — short for a substance called "reactive oxygen species" that is believed to be involved with a number of biological functions, including muscle contraction, cell growth and brain activity. Recent research has found that therapeutic light—the kind used to treat SAD, or seasonal affective disorder—stimulates R.O.S. production (20 million Americans suffer from SAD, which is marked by depression and lethargy during the winter months). For a long time it was believed that therapeutic light had to stimulate the vision system in order to relieve SAD symptoms, but Dr. Dan Oren, working at Yale, has found otherwise. Oren's research found that a "light band" wrapped around the knee raised R.O.S. levels, and that the body somehow absorbs and processes this light through the skin. If further research confirms this, we can expect physicians to be measuring our R.O.S. levels, and an explosion of smaller, portable light bands.

Roobois — an intriguing herbal tea that is only grown within a small area in South Africa. Roobois is being investigated for a number of therapeutic properties. *Alternative Medicine* magazine writes that "studies show that the tea relieves insomnia, nervous tension, mild depression, stomach cramps (including colic), constipation, and allergic symptoms." Roobois has also been found to contain as much as 50 times the antioxidant properties of green tea. *DOF* expects to see roobois approach the popularity of green tea—which means it will be appearing in supplements, in beverages and even in ice cream.

Sentinel Event — it sounds innocuous, but is far from it: sentinel events are those which could have been prevented or avoided with timely or adequate medical attention. When one occurs, hospitals are obligated to perform what's called "root cause analysis." These terms will become known to more than the medical community, because with the increasing cost-containment pressure that doctors and hospitals are subject to, there are going to be more and more of these. *DOF* also believes there will be pressure for hospitals to post their "sentinel events" and "root cause" analysis on their Web sites—so consumers can decide where they want elective treatments to be made—much as physicians are now being forced to reveal their malpractice histories. See also *iatronic injuries, white wall of silence.*

Skin Cholesterol — researchers at the prestigious Cleveland Clinic found that a three-minute cholesterol test using the outer layer of skin appears to be accurate. Those with the highest levels of skin cholesterol also had the largest number of diseased arteries. In fact, measuring skin cholesterol this way could be more accurate than through the blood, because it reflects the actual level of cholesterol that is built up in tissues and artery walls. *DOF* envisions that this will open up a new generation of do-it-yourself home cholesterol tests because it doesn't involve drawing blood.

Skin-to-Site — *DOF*'s term for a range of health monitoring systems that use the Internet and wireless technology to transmit real-time diagnostic information from the wearer to a Web site. One such example is Bodymedia (www.bodymedia.com), whose "senseware," according to *Wired* magazine, includes "chest straps, arm bands and smart rings that monitor the

Hh

wearer's heart rate, respiration and other physiological data." The information is captured and ends up on a personalized Web page. A similar company, although from more of a fitness-related perspective, is Sportbrain (www.sportbrain.com). *DOF* expects a deluge of companies to appear in this space, but the question is how many people—beyond the seriously ill—will want to be monitored this closely? If an economic motivation can be built in—for example, saving on your insurance, just as non-smokers get a lower rate—the dynamics could shift.

Skyrad — if you want a scientific way to get a safe tan, you might want to be on the lookout for the Skyrad sticker. It's a tiny dosage meter (disposable and reusable varieties will be available) that changes color to let you know that you've reached the permissible level of UV exposure for your skin type. Photochromic elements in the sticker absorb the UV radiation; when they turn red, it's a signal to apply more sunscreen. When they turn orange, it's time to pack up the cooler and head for home. The technology—which was incubated at Technion (part of Israel's Institute of Technology)—can be in the form of a sticker or wristband; it can even be made part of the trim of your clothing. Wherever it ends up, we should pay attention, because our chances of getting skin cancer are 15 times higher than 60 years ago, thanks to the depletion of the protective ozone layer.

Sleep Hygiene — the proper disciplines for the development and practice of healthful sleep rituals. The *Financial Times* describes them as "restful, regular bedtime routines, waking at the same time each day, removing work and noise from the bedroom, cutting out caffeine, avoiding day-time naps, and going to bed only when one is sleepy." We expect to hear lots of talk about sleep hygiene in the days to come, because sleep deprivation has become a serious national and global issue (see also *work daze*.) Insomnia alone costs the U.S. economy an estimated $100 billion a year. Expect to see sleep hygiene appear in hotel marketing ("our luxury rooms feature the ultimate in sleep hygiene appointments"), in corporate well-ness programs ("we encourage all our employees to practice proper sleep hygiene") and in-home decor as Martha Stewart asks: "Is your bedroom a sleep hygiene nightmare?"

Smad3 — a protein that is the subject of increasing investigation because of its pivotal role in wound healing. When the protein is inhibited—in mice, anyway—wounds have been shown to heal more rapidly. In a few years, doctors might be able to suppress this protein and encourage the rapid healing of chronic conditions such as diabetic ulcers.

Smart T-Shirt — developed by the government for military use (see *multitary*), the smart T-shirt was designed so that sensors could tell if a soldier had been shot, where the bullet or shrapnel entered and then transmit the data to a field center. It works via optical fibers that are actually sewn into the shirt; as researcher Sundaresan Jayaraman put it in *USA Today*, the shirt is simply a "computer motherboard." At a projected price of less than $30, the shirt has many non-military uses: keeping track of recent surgery patients, monitoring babies for signals of sudden infant death syndrome, tracking cardiac patients.

SNPS— single nucleotide polymorphisms. These are the DNA variations that separate one individual from another—and though they represent a tiny portion of the human genome, less than 0.1 percent—they are vital to the future of genetically engineered medicines (see also *pharmacogenomics*). Because identifying SNPS is such a daunting task—with such potentially high rewards—13 competitive drug manufacturers got together to form the SNP Consortium to map SNPS and post the findings on the Internet so all researchers can benefit. There are up to 30 million SNPS, but not all are important; the *MIT Technology Review* writes that experts believe the number of key SNPS, those "that account for the genetic contribution to virtually all aspects of our potential health outcomes, from how we metabolize drugs, to the pace of aging, to our cells' susceptibility to cancer" are in the low thousands. If you want to help identify SNPS, you can contribute your own DNA samples and family health history at *www.dna.com*—a little known and simple way to join an effort that can change the world. In other words, painless philanthropy.

Sonophoresis — a process that exposes skin to low-frequency ultrasound, which, when combined with a vacuum, renders it super-permeable. In this state, where fluids can easily pass out of the skin—and large molecules can enter—a number of science fiction-like treatments approach reality. Diabetics, for example, would be able to remove fluid and test their glucose levels without needle sticks. They would also be able to pump drugs across the skin—what's called transdermal delivery—and into the body, without needles. Using sonophoresis, the combination of measurement and delivery could mean that diabetics could manage their condition through a simple, wristwatch-sized unit that would measure blood sugar and deliver insulin without even being aware of it. Sontra Medical of Cambridge, Massachusetts, is working to commercialize the concept. See also *microneedles*.

Sertoli Cells — cells located in the testes that are being studied for their ability to prevent damage in stroke victims. The first step was to prove, in vitro, that sertoli cells protected brain cells from dying after the effects of a stroke were simulated. It worked. Next, rats injected with sertoli cells within a day of a stroke were found to have less damage, and fewer movement handicaps than rats that were untreated. Further research needs to be done, but an encouraging start has been made. Additional good news: because sertoli cells don't trigger an immune response, they can be used in both women and men.

Super-Antibiotics — as mutant, drug-resistant bacteria continue to present a significant health threat—particularly in hospitals—a number of companies are developing a class of "super-antibiotics" to fight them. Cubist Pharmaceuticals (www.cubist.com) is the only one of them dedicated to these super new drugs. The prime reason for the growing problem: antibiotics are prescribed too frequently, giving bacteria the chance to mutate into stronger strains. We are creating our own enemies—but it's certainly not the first time. See also *hygiene hypothesis.*

Synvisc — a treatment for knees hobbled by arthritis and sports injuries. The injection, which has been approved by the American College of Rheumatology, is called "visco supplementation" because Synvisc comes close to replicating the body's own lubricating fluid. The gel is actually made from rooster combs, which contain the same hyaluronic acid that appears in the knee. If Synvisc doesn't do the trick for the trick knee, another high-tech possibility is to grow-your-own cartilage. Doctors take a small sample of healthy cartilage— about 200,000 cells—and whisk it off to Genzyme Tissue Repair. There, it is grown to more than 12 million cells, which are returned to the knee, along with a small temporary patch that replaces the defective cartilage. The new cells continue to multiply, and gradually replace the patch. As stunning as these developments seem, they are only the beginning of a new era of replacement medicine: genetic engineering will enable us to grow bone on biodegradable scaffolds (see also *scaffolds*), to regenerate nerves from stem cells, and even to connect prosthetics to the peripheral nervous system and the brain—all as routinely as what goes on in an auto body shop. See also *bone growth factors, brain-machine interfaces.*

T-20 — a promising AIDS drug (developed by Trimeris) that is in human trials, and could be the precursor to a new generation of drugs that block the virus from entering a human cell. The company (www.trimeris.com) calls it a "viral fusion inhibitor"; *USA Today* writes that the drug "essentially handcuffs a segment of HIV's surface membrane, GP 41, that is required for the virus to enter a human cell." While one researcher calls T-20 more "proof of concept" than a drug, the fact is that there is great hope in the not-too-distant future for the 20–30 percent of AIDS patients for whom the current drugs don't work or stop working—or who cannot tolerate their toxicity.

Telomerase Vaccines — telomerase is an enzyme that is responsible for the natural death of cells by maintaining normal chromosomal length; when telomerase is over-expressed, cells replicate in an uncontrolled fashion and cancer begins. That's why telomerase is found in all major cancers. Much research is underway to knock out telomerase; one approach is to use telomerase to boost the immune system's response—encouraging it to produce more of the body's own killer cells (CTLs)—that would in turn wipe out the excess telomerase and destroy the cancer. The test worked in vitro, and, happily, it didn't have any effect on stem cells, which also contain telomerase. Clearly, these are the early stages of development, but among the reasons for optimism is that while it was once thought that a different vaccine would have to be developed for each kind of cancer, the presence of telomerase is present in many different kinds of the disease suggests that a universal vaccine is theoretically possible.

Therajuana — *DOF*'s term for the use of medical marijuana, a subject of increasing controversy. Researchers are searching for ways to deliver the therapeutic benefits of marijuana—such as reducing the nausea associated with chemotherapy—without the high. Techniques under investigation include suppositories, pills, shots and sprays. The challenge is that many of the 60 psychoactive components of marijuana are the same ones that have medicinal value. (One company, Atlantic Technology Ventures [www.atlanc.com] claims to have synthesized THC—the most psychoactive of all the cannabinoids.) If researchers are able to separate the high from the help, it would encourage additional investigation into the therapeutic potential of marijuana, a field of study that does not have much investment behind it because of the political implications—and because as a natural product, cannabis cannot be patented.

Theratope — no promises, of course, but a breast cancer vaccine called Theratope was given fast-track status by the FDA. If the current trial works, we can expect it to be marketed sometime in 2002. It's made by a Canadian company called Bio-mira: www.biomira.com.

Three-Dimensional Coronary Magnetic Resonance — a non-invasive method of diagnosing the same cardiac problems (in greater detail) that an angiogram is used to detect. Angiograms, which have been around for decades, inject dye into the blood vessels and use X-rays to look for blockages. 3D coronary magnetic resonance works on the MRI model, using immensely powerful magnets to "provide detailed images of blood flow" according to *Circulation,* the journal of the American Heart Association. It takes just 30 minutes, and even better, is safe and reasonably inexpensive. Its ease could revolutionize the diagnosis of heart disease, while simultaneously leading to a national diagnostic neurosis; see also *scanosis.*

Thrivers — HIV-positive men and women who continue to flourish.

Vanity Financing — ever alert to new opportunities for lending money, banks and other financial institutions are just starting to introduce products to help you fund your plastic surgery, and *DOF* calls the emerging concept "Vanity Financing." Surgery.com is doing this right now, but we believe this trend will explode, as these kinds of procedures, which include laser eye correction, continue to take off. It's the perfect conflation of two of America's gifts to the world: easy credit, and the obsession with looking younger. See also *closure treatment.*

VEGF2 — short for vascular endothelial growth factor, a synthetic gene that "manufactures" a protein which stimulates blood vessel growth. VEGF2 has had success in returning circulation to the legs of diabetics, but—more theatrically—it has been able to stimulate the growth of new blood vessels in those suffering from advanced heart disease. Proteins like VEGF2 could (and should) lead to drugs that repair so many disease conditions that, as Randall Tobias, the former head of

Eli Lilly, put it, "The day will come when we regard all surgeries, except treatment of trauma—as failures of the pharmaceutical industry." See also *pharmacogenomics.*

VNS — short for vagus nerve stimulation. This technique for treating epilepsy via an implanted device has been approved since 1997, but is currently being investigated for treatment-resistant depression. If this pacemaker-like pulse generator is successful—and the pilot study suggests that VNS stimulation can work—it could open the door to an entirely new, non-pharmaceutical way to treat serious depression. You can keep up with the latest clinical findings at www.cyberonics.com. *DOF* believes that VNS is the first of many kinds of brain stimulation that will be investigated to alter our moods and our behavior (drug abuse, obsessive/compulsive disorder).

White Wall of Silence — the tendency of doctors and nurses to cover-up incidents where patients were harmed by medical mistakes. Derived from "Blue Wall of Silence," which describes the same closing of ranks in the police department. See also *iatronic injuries, sentinel events.*

Dictionary of the Future Predicts:

Breatheman — a portable air-filtration device that will be initially launched in Mexico City and other regions suffering from serious pollution problems; it will then become a chic accessory in New York and Los Angeles.

Cosmetic Underclass — those who can't afford plastic surgery and are thus forced to forever look their age.

Death Divide — there are enormous gaps in medical treatment across the country—both by demographic group and by geography. Physicians and epidemiologists know this—but it has not hit the public's radar . . . yet. For example, African Americans simply do not receive the same quality of care as whites do. Women are under-treated for cardiovascular conditions. And regardless of race and gender, there are many hospitals that can't deliver life-saving treatments which have been universally accepted. Scary example: dispensing TPA (tissue plasminogen activator) to stroke victims is recommended, but only 2–3 percent of patients get the treatment. Far more important than the so-called digital divide, which is already closing, the death divide will become a major political and policy issue as we move into the twenty-first century—the health-care equivalent of the Civil Rights and Women's Movements of the last century.

Experimental Drug Coverage — the much publicized battles over whether HMOs will cover experimental and emerging diagnostic treatments—for example, digital mammograms and bone marrow transplants for certain cancers—leaves a marketing opportunity. *DOF* believes that insurers will soon start offering a special policy to fund any "reasonable" experimental diagnostic tests or treatments that an HMO refuses to cover. The coverage won't be cheap, but many individuals will sign on, and some employers will offer it as a benefit to show how enlightened they are.

Germography — in the future, everyone will have a personal record of all the bacteria and viruses they have been exposed to—a germography. This will be identified by blood work, and by tiny, nanotechnology-derived germ monitors circulating in our bloodstream. Germographies will be helpful in diagnosing your individual condition, and in constructing large-scale epidemiological models to help understand the development of chronic conditions. Your germography will be accessible via computer to doctors all around the world so you'll always be able to get the appropriate treatment.

Pathology Paranoia — studies are showing that as many as 5 percent of pathology opinions are wrong. This will create a need for, and an industry that serves, pathology second opinions. One early indicator: a Web site called www.findsecond opinions.com.

Hh

Pixelache — a headache triggered by exposure to too many pixels, from a computer screen or other display. Courtesy of Mark Lehr, via the BrainReserve Web site.

Policosanol — a dietary supplement that has been studied in Cuba since the mid-1990s. Policosanol, an extract of sugar cane wax and beeswax, has "been found to lower cholesterol, decrease the risk of blood clots, enhance blood function and improve blood flow to extremities that have been impaired by hardened arteries," according to *Let's Live* magazine. *DOF* predicts that policosanol will become one of the most popular supplement products—an effective, natural way to lower cholesterol—and that the major pharmaceutical companies will explore ways to incorporate its chemistry within their own prescription "statin" drugs to achieve new levels of safe and effective cholesterol therapy.

Post-Scriptions — increasingly and surprisingly, researchers are finding that drugs approved for one use can be effective for another. The most famous example, of course, is the hypertensive drug Minoxidil which was reborn as Rogaine, for hair-regrowth. Prozac has been found to ease the symptoms of PMS and has been relaunched as Sarafem. Botox injections (botulinium Toxin A), used cosmetically to reduce wrinkles, are being shown to also ease migraine pain, according to a study published in the journal *Headache*. Propranolol, long used to treat high blood pressure, along with Amantadin, used to treat Parkinson's disease, are both being used to help cocaine addicts in withdrawal. Sometimes, failed drugs are found to have a second life. Thalidomide is being used to treat AIDS, and Atrasentan, an experimental heart drug that failed in early clinicals, is being tested as a promising treatment for prostate cancer.

Another area where this trend holds: human drugs with pet applications. Anafranil, used to treat obsessive behavior in humans, is terrific for anxiety in dogs. Anipryl, derived from Deprenyl—used to treat Parkinson's—restores memory and improves cognition in older pets. We expect more of these curious dualities to emerge, which is good news for the lucky pharmaceutical company that finds its marketplace doubled overnight.

Prehab — also prehabilitation. A transitional program where substance abusers, primarily of alcohol, will begin the process of self-awareness and recovery without the pain and stigma of being treated like they have hit the bottom. Savvy psychologists and treatment marketers will create an entirely new category of prehab, attracting millions of the "gently addicted" who would rather not believe they require full rehab and are thus not ready to pack up for a trip to Betty Ford.

Re-Abled — a term that will be used to describe the way in which previously disabled men and women regain (or gain) functionality through technological innovation. Could involve implants for sight and sound (cochlear implants, stem cell therapy for corneal scarring). Could also involve brain implants to stimulate or replace damaged neurological assets. See also *bone growth factors, brain-machine interfaces.*

REM-Up — a kind of power sleep, where your REMs (rapid eye movements) put you in a state of maximum restfulness. Rather than the last century's "I'm going to get some z's," we will be saying, "I'm going to REM-up." (Coined by Simon Hanft.)

Retro-Medicine — while the medicines and therapies of the past are studied on an individual basis, there is no disciplined approach to re-investigating and assessing these modalities on an integrated basis. Retro-medicine will be just that. The past can be ancient, including leeches (the subject of increasing study and utility) or, for example, chewing sticks, which have been used as a form of oral hygiene for thousands of years in the Middle East, Africa and Asia. When university scientists analyzed these twigs—commonly known as "muthala"—they isolated six compounds which had antimicrobial activity. Retro-medicine will also look at discredited drugs of recent years—this approach led AIDS researchers to discover that Thalidomide, responsible for tragic birth defects in the 1960s and warehoused since then, could be beneficial to HIV-positive patients. *DOF* sees a sub-specialty of retro-medicine emerging, and a column, before you know it, in the *New England Journal of Medicine* featuring the latest retro-medicine discovery.

Scanosis — scan + neurosis, describing a group of patients who will become obsessed with the new medical screening and imaging techniques available. These screen addicts will pay to have ongoing full-body MRIs and other diagnostic modalities with the intention of catching the smallest possible threat—whether it's a few cancer cells, a weakness that can lead to an aneurysm, or other such warnings. Cost/benefit ratio aside, physicians warn that a new kind of hypochondria is emerging, (see also *cyberchondria*) and since they don't have a great deal of experience with these screenings, much of the information they get is useless. Even so, a generation of screen addicts will emerge, and medical entrepreneurs will be right behind, opening and promoting full-body screening centers and clinics that feel less like hospitals and more like hotels.

Screenside Manner — the analogue to bedside manner in the era of telemedicine. We expect medical schools to start teaching fledgling doctors how to communicate through this vehicle, which is essentially limited in its capacity for empathy. See *email coaches*, which is not unrelated.

Subscription Hospitals — driven by the affluence of baby boomers and the decline in health care, subscription hospitals will be private facilities with membership sold by subscription only. Some of these will be linked to specific HMOs, others will be branded by existing powerhouse health care names, e.g. Cornell, Mayo Clinic, Memorial Sloan-Kettering. Additionally, subscription hospitals can be created by entrepreneurs who purchase failing community hospitals. Over the last decade, 10 percent of these hospitals have closed, and hundreds are in precarious shape. Many are in affluent areas, too—perfect for subscription conversion.

Hh

HOMES AND GARDENS

Today, our homes are more than our castles. They are our consciousnesses. All our fantasies, anxieties, tensions, and obsessions are bound up in the way we construct and ornament the places in which we live.

When we think beyond our narrow self-interests, we arrive at "biotecture," which describes a new intersection of environmentalism and our homes. On the other hand, when our homes reflect our fears, we build "neo-fortresses," design "God-forbid rooms" and withdraw to "privatopias." When we want to display a new kind of status—a curious form of uselessness—we build expensive "museum kitchens"—which remind us that status can be expressed not only by what we own and use, but by what we own yet merely observe. We're also seeing a tension between technology's invasion of the home, and a need for a more tactile and unruly experience, which is reflected in a gardening trend called "naturescaping."

So potent is the influence of our homes on the greater culture that it pops up elsewhere in *Dictionary of the Future*, as our offices are becoming more homelike—through "corporate comfy"—and hotels are attempting to evoke domestic imagery to soothe our travel-induced sense of placelessness.

As we move into the century, *DOF* expects that one of the controlling metaphors will be the home, as places from banks to houses of worship to airports will seek to convey—through architecture and design—the implicit security and emotional anchor so famously described by Robert Frost when he wrote "Home is the place where, when you have to go there,/They have to take you in."

Bamboo Flooring — the next rage in floor covering, bamboo is tough, attractive and environmentally sensitive, since it is grown and harvested in protected forests. It is also on-trend with our design fascination with all things Asian. Go to www.bamtex.com and be the first on your block to go bamboo.

Biotecture — the use of plants to create buildings, primarily homes, that are environmentally sound and sustainable. By using exterior landscaping, including plantings, vines and trellises, biotecture creates a natural form of insulation that can reduce our fossil fuel reliance when it comes to both heating and cooling. We expect tax credits and other incentives for biotecture, and for leading architects to begin to incorporate this practice into their work.

Boatominiums — floating condominiums, used by the wealthy, who own their own cabins as vacation homes. They will include swimming pools, casinos, tennis courts, as well as stores selling luxuries and necessities (a fragile distinction for the retired rich). Also called Floatominiums.

Fit Furniture — combination furniture and exercise equipment for crowded apartments. *Bare* magazine reports that a Dutch company, Do Create, has come up with a line of fit furniture: Do Swing is a sleek chandelier that doubles as a pull-up bar; the Do/Droog is a chair that begins life as a hollow metal cube; you work out by bashing it into any shape you choose. *DOF* sees fit furniture as an emerging trend in home design; just as the kitchen broke out of its shell and blended with our living space, so will the home gym.

God-Forbid Room — new upscale homes are being built with safe rooms where residents can seal themselves in, should they be threatened by criminals or hostage-takers. Mark Dery, in his book *Pyrotechnic Insanitarium: American Culture on the Brink*, dubbed these "God-forbid Rooms." *DOF* expects to see these become almost standard equipment; they are already commonplace in many parts of the world.

Hh

Home Vineyards — the new status symbol in California is a home vineyard, and *DOF* believes that the trend will spread to wherever it is climate-appropriate. You don't need as much property as you might think; if you have two acres and $60,000—expensive, but not all that much when you consider the cost of landscaping—you can start your very own chateau and give new meaning to the term "local wine." We see an entire mini-industry of suppliers emerging to help these virgin vintners, and wouldn't be surprised to see a few chic retail stores emerge, Pottery Barn and Smith & Hawken style.

Naturescaping — a trend that has us replacing manicured lawns and gardens with untamed, natural habitats that are designed to attract birds and other wildlife, thus replicating a more natural environment. As Sara Stein writes in *Noah's Garden: Restoring the Ecology of Our Own Back Yards:* "Yards and gardens patched with grass and stitched with hedges all across America constitute a vast, nearly continuous, and terribly impoverished ecosystem for which we ourselves are responsible. We cannot in fairness rail against those who destroy the rainforest or threaten the spotted owl when we have made our own yards uninhabitable."

Neo-Fortress — an architectural style in which homes are built around walled courtyards featuring turrets, smaller windows and a real sense of withdrawal from the world. In describing one such house, the *Florida South Coast Times* writes "the neo-fortress movement . . . expresses a general mood these days: 'Keep out.'" *The Wall Street Journal* concurs; its piece on the trend maintained that "the neo-fortress style reflects concerns about privacy and security." Paradoxically, these security concerns continue to grow in the face of rapidly declining crime rates. So the question is, are we turning inward for safety reasons, or simply because the world is too swift, too complex, too stressful? Perhaps, as the Internet invades our privacy in one way, we seek it in another.

Personal Aroma Center — appliances that are capable of re-creating just about any smell in the universe—from an apple pie in the oven to a Parisian flower market to the beach after a rain. This is possible because technology whizzes are now able to encode smells as software. Once these aromas are expressed digitally, they can be sent over a computer—to a device that reproduces that smell in your home or office. Alternatively, CD-ROMs can be sold that contain the same information. The applications are endless: imagine a whole new level of sensory flexibility in your home, car or office. Internet marketers will be able to let you smell their new bath gel, filmmakers will be able to add a "scent track" (*DOF*'s term) to their sound track. Digiscents (www.digiscents.com) is the current leader, with their proprietary "scentology," but we expect this marketplace to become much more crowded.

Portable Furniture — a company called "it" designs furniture for what it calls "urban nomads." Their "it" bed, for example, is made out of cardboard and folds into a small package (www.tarabox.com). In an era when everything else is portable, it's about time that furniture was equally movable, and *DOF* expects to see dozens of companies enter this market. See also *couch surfers*.

Privatopia — the allure of security, homogeneity and hot-and-cold running luxury in privately governed, gated, patrolled communities. As far as we know, the word was coined by Evan McKenzie, who used it in the title of his worthwhile book *Privatopia: Homeowner Associations and the Rise of Residential Private Government*. See also *lifestyle enclaves*.

Roble — a tropical wood that is an environmentally sensitive alternative to teak, which is often harvested using unsound ecological methods. Gardener's Supply has stopped selling teak altogether and replaced it with benches and other garden furniture made from roble (pronounced RO-blay.) *USA Today* quotes a representative as saying "roble . . . is a golden,

Hh

honey-colored wood from a sustainably managed indigenous forest in Bolivia that is actually harder than teak . . . and cheaper." Expect roble to become the wood of choice for the environmentally sensitive consumer.

Sick Home Syndrome — the residential version of sick building syndrome, except it is a combination of spiritual (bad feng shui) and physical problems (chemical fumes from glues and resins, including sheetrock and plastic allergens lead). A new category of sick home therapists, who combine technical and psychic skills, will emerge to fix the problems.

Starter Castles — a slap at the new wealthy who are building outsized homes for their outsized egos. Economist Barton Biggs wrote to clients of his at Morgan Stanley: "In Greenwich, Connecticut, where I have lived for some time, the older citizens are appalled by the size of the mansions ('starter castles') that are being added to the landscape by wealthy young investment bankers." A couple of thousand miles away, the *Boise Weekly* is similarly incensed, writing that "Developers are building 'starter castles' at a phenomenal rate in the 'foothills' above Boise. These elitists are making life miserable for those who live in the established neighborhoods of Boise." When the same term pops up in Greenwich and Boise, you know you're onto something.

Winter Landscaping — gardeners are increasingly focused on how their backyards look when the trees are bare and the rose bushes straggly. Enter winter landscaping, the search for trees and shrubs that can add color to a barren season. *The Wall Street Journal* reports that gardeners are "Searching the Internet, books and catalogs . . . and turning up relatively obscure perennials that flower in winter, bushes with brightly colored leaves, not to mention bark and berries as bright as a box of crayons." Try *dragon's-eye pine*, a Japanese native with red bark; *pasque flower*, a perennial with lavender and yellow flowers; *blackberry lily*, a show-stopper with apricot flowers in summer and seedpods in winter that resemble lush blackberries.

Dictionary of the Future Predicts

Branded Housing — the last un-branded luxury territory is housing. Of course, there are famous architects, but they build their houses patron-by-patron. That's the way couture clothing used to be, before designers discovered the financial brilliance of ready-to-wear. We imagine that Frank Gehry, Michael Graves, Robert A. M. Stern and Cesar Pelli will discover what Oscar de la Renta, Armani and Christian Dior realized decades ago: you don't have to be limited to customization. Enter the brand-name home—the world's leading architects, working with high-end builders. Together, they will produce limited-editon house plans built to exacting specifications. Architect-designed furniture will fill the rooms, much like Frank Lloyd Wright did. After a specified number of houses are constructed, the plans are embargoed forever.

Bubbling — low-cost technology, including breakthroughs in plastic technology and solar panels, will enable homeowners to install heated bubbles in their backyards. They will become the next must-have status item, as they allow year-round use of the outdoors.

Content Rooms — replacements for traditional living rooms —or merely additional space—these will be places where content is accessed from computers, televisions and other information appliances. It will also be the room where the digital operation of the home is centralized. This will create the need for new kinds of furniture and accessories—for example, a computer desk that can accommodate multiple people for shared viewing and video-gaming.

Museum Kitchens — beautifully designed sacred spaces with high-tech refrigerators that cost as much as automobiles—yet like museum exhibitions, we admire them but don't touch. It's no surprise: close to 40 percent of the total amount we spend on food goes to restaurants, and 59 percent of the population reports that they buy takeout or prepared food "sometimes" or "often." Further, of those who do cook, 70 percent

Hh

spend a half hour or less in the kitchen. Add to that the explosion of home delivery, and the kitchen becomes increasingly vestigial. Yet we keep investing a fortune in more and more renovations—even though nearly half the population imagines themselves cooking even less in the next five years. See also *desire gap*.

Repair Patrols — a new homeowner service consisting of a small fleet of vans capable of performing—or arranging for—relatively small tasks such as carpentry, electrical repairs, roof work, installing air-conditioners. Some of these patrols will be branded (Sears, for example, would be a logical entrant into the market) and some will be provided by upscale home developers as an added benefit to purchasers. (Look at it this way: you buy a $30,000 BMW and get roadside assistance, why shouldn't a $750,000 house come with "lotside" assistance?) With busy working families and older Americans who choose to remain in their homes (see *aging in place*) as a market, *DOF* expects that repair patrols will be a familiar sight in upscale and upper-middle-class neighborhoods.

Storage Chic — with the explosive growth of self-service storage facilities—which are no less than mini-museums of consumerism, as Americans run out of room at home to store the stuff they buy—*DOF* believes that we will be seeing a new generation of upscaled locations. These will include storage rooms that can function as small offices, along with coffee bars, "lite" office services like copying and binding and other amenities available on premises.

Subscription Appliances — a replacement for the outright purchase model of appliance ownership that has been the standard since the first Frigidaire. *DOF* anticipates that we will be leasing our appliances—from dishwashers to stoves—just like we lease our cars and businesses lease their computers. This will be driven by the changing nature of the appliance business; manufacturers are desperately trying to shorten the purchase cycle by innovating more rapidly, as they hope to convince consumers to upgrade more often than once every fifteen years. The answer: a subscription structure that encourages consumers to think about their appliances as "temporary"—like they think about automobiles and technology products. See also *cradle-to-cradle, natural capital.*

Toxic Bouquets — we're alert to pesticides in our fruits and vegetables, but what about that innocent-looking bouquet of flowers on your dining room table? Virtually no attention has been paid to these toxic bouquets yet—but awareness is growing. Reporting on an investigation by the World Resources Institute, the *Utne Reader* writes that "growers use any means at their disposal—including banned and unregistered pesticides; heavy loads of synthetic growth hormones and fertilizers; and an illiterate, underpaid workforce." The Environmental Working Group found that "California-grown roses had 1,000 times the level of cancer-causing pesticides as comparable food products." True, we don't eat flowers—but we handle them, kids smell them, and the reality of exploited workers handling poisonous chemicals—usually without gloves or masks—for our own aesthetic appreciation, is a bitter irony that will not escape us. *DOF* predicts that there will be a movement to compel the U.S. government to set standards for pesticide residue, and that we will see a new category of pesticide-free flowers in our supermarkets, florists and direct-to-consumer purveyors like 1-800-FLOWERS.

INTERNET

Given that there are entire dictionaries and glossaries dedicated to the Internet on the Internet, we had to surrender the notion of completeness before we even started this section. Our editing principles were range and provocative sparkle, focusing not just on the technical future of the Internet, but on the social, personal, and business implications of its future development. (Given the Internet's pushy behavior, you will also come across these implications as you read through the many other sections of *DOF*.)

Some of the entries deal with exciting new applications of the Internet— and dot-com collapse or not, we are at the end of the beginning rather than the beginning of the end of Web innovation. One of them is "BTO"—for "build-to-order"—an internet-based business that hopes to do for cars what Dell did for computers. BTO might not make it, but the concept eventually will, which is why they have been included: the risk of failure is trumped by the importance of exposing our readers to this idea in its earliest form.

You'll also note a slice of words that deals with the growing and inevitable ubiquity of the Internet; these include the "Internet iceberg effect" and "webidemics." Another slice grapples with the risks of a network this vast, including a plan for battling viruses by conceptualizing the Internet as a "digital immune system."

Throughout this book—and sections that deal with fast-changing areas of technology in particular—we had to be vigilant about the fact that new language becomes history's cliché in the same compressed time frame that innovations spring forth. With that in mind, we attempted to strike an acrobatic balance between utility to our readers, and the risk of defining what has already been launched into familiarity.

403 — we all know (or some of us do) that 404 means clueless, from the Internet error message "404 not found." Now, those code-writing sadists have a new term for us: Forbidden 403, meaning access is denied. Thus, 403 will come to mean off-limits, as in "Sorry, I can't tell you that. It's 403."

Bluetooth — the wireless protocol, accepted by virtually every manufacturer, that permits devices around your home to connect to each other. Bluetooth is the ultimate enabler of the smart house that has been the darling of futurists since the 1939 World's Fair. Using thousands of embedded microprocessors, (see also *pervasive computing* and *internet iceberg effect*) Bluetooth will let your alarm system talk to your coffeemaker and your DVD player converse with your cell phone. It is estimated that there will be 200 million items connected by Bluetooth in 2003.

BTO — stands for Build To Order, and it's a revolutionary automobile start-up that intends to manufacture cars with "build-to-order precision and craftsmanship." This new brand, which expects to launch "a portfolio of new vehicles" by 2004, says it will leverage the power of the Internet for integrating design, engineering, manufacturing and distribution, and will invite consumers to "collaborate with the program team in designing their cars." This takes the concept of "mass customization" to the highest of all levels, and although it remains to be seen if BTO (www.btoauto.com) can realize its ambitions, there is no question that creating products for an audience of one is an unstoppable force, whether it's drugs (see *pharmacogenomics*), publishing (see *mygazines*), shampoo (as reflect.com has done), or clothing, as the Interactive Custom Clothes Company is doing (www.ic3d.com/2001/index.html.) Skeptics: consider how Dell has changed the computer industry.

Cobweb — a Web site that never, ever changes.

Combinatorial Auctions — online auctions where companies bid for items in combination, based on their needs. It's based on the theory that you'd pay one price for peanut butter, one price for jelly and another price for bread, but might pay a different price in total for peanut butter, jelly and bread at the same time. Currently, software is being developed to allow these combinatorial auctions, which is the next step in the refinement of the online auction marketplace.

Cookie Management — an upgrade to Microsoft's Internet Explorer that will allow Web surfers to repel cookies from third parties. (Cookies are tiny files inserted by marketers into your hard drive in order to track your habits so they can target you most effectively.) You'll have the ability to choose between rejecting cookies launched by a Web site, and by advertisers. Microsoft's decision is clearly a result of the noise made by privacy advocates and consumers who don't want to be part of a vast national Truman Show. It's one small chapter in the large national privacy debate.

Cyberia — a Web site that you want to escape from as soon as possible. It can be a bleak landscape badly designed, boring, useless, too slow or populated with dated text. If marketers don't continually update and keep their Web sites fresh and vital, they will be imprisoning their customers in a brand cyberia. Not good for business. See also *cobweb* and *Web gardeners*.

Deep Web — if the amount of data on the Internet overwhelms you, it might not be with great joy that you greet the deep Web, or the iceberg that's below the tip which comes up on your search engine. In fact, the firm BrightPlanet has estimated that the deep Web is no less than 500 times bigger than the surface Web. Eventually (and sooner, not later), the deep Web—which is rich in valuable information—will start being indexed by search engines, which will in turn put more demands on them to organize and present their information in smarter and more intuitive ways. See also *taxonomists*.

Digital Immune System — researchers at IBM are attempting to defeat computer viruses by looking at the Internet as one large organism, and finding ways to boost its immune system. In other words, attack a computer virus using the same tactics that the body employs when a foreign invader appears. As one of IBM's developers has stated: "We . . . have found the biological analogy to be helpful in understanding the propagation of computer viruses on a global scale, and inspirational in our development of defenses against them." A similar biological approach is Artis, created by Stephanie Forrest and her colleagues at the University of New Mexico. Artis parallels the structure of the human immune system—complete with the software equivalent of lymphocytes, the body's virus-attacking cells. As the English magazine *Prospect* neatly puts it, "The future of computing lies in biology, and that of biology in computing."

Evernet — coined by Tom Friedman of *The New York Times* to describe our ability to get on the Internet everywhere and anywhere.

Face Translation — Internet translation is advancing at a rapid pace, but the Holy Grail is face translation—the merger of autotranslation and video. With face translation—as anthropologist Robert Wright puts it in *Time*—"Your face is morphed so that you seem to be pronouncing the words of the language you don't really speak." Wright believes that this isn't just a gimmick, but could have profoundly positive global implications. He writes, "True international friendship, now available mainly to business big shots, can in principle become a middle-class indulgence. Stamp collecting, environmental activism—all kinds of interests can kindle the citizen-to-citizen amity that makes war politically different." And he's right: the more we know each other, the more difficult it becomes to demonize an enemy.

Give Us a Click — the Internet version of "give us a call." A radio commercial in New York for www.myhomekey.com urges consumers to "give us a click." Teenagers are saying "I'll give you a click when I get home from school." The proliferation of mobile devices like the BlackBerry will increase the opportunities to give—and get—a click.

Global Hell — the name of a hacker group that has created major problems for the government (they're the ones who broke into the White House and the FBI Web sites). The FBI has cracked down on them, several members have pled guilty, and they appear to be "going legit." But where they stop, others will continue, and the more dependent on technology we become, the more vulnerable we are. Expect to see the FBI's "10 Most Wanted Cyber-Criminals" site—until it falls victim to a denial-of-service attack, of course. See also *distance terrorism, National Infrastructure, terror entrepreneur.*

Haptics — the Greek word means contact, but in the world of computers it involves a system that gives tactile feedback to the user. As one Web site puts it: "A haptic interface would allow the user of a virtual space to perceive physical characteristics of the space and interact with those characteristics." For video gamers, it means a joystick that pushes back as you get closer to the target. For anyone who uses the Internet, it means a mouse that lets you feel a wide range of physical sensations. For physicians, it could (and will) mean the ability to learn a technique remotely by "feeling" the procedure; eventually haptics will facilitate tele-diagnosis and even robotic tele-surgery. All those who believe that the computer revolution is essentially completed—and all that remains are marginal improvements—should recognize that the haptics revolution is only just beginning: it is the touch of the future.

Internet Iceberg Effect — coined by Alex Lightman, co-founder of Charmed.com, an MIT Media Lab spinoff. Alex believes that "Internet connections to things, particularly sensors, that are not used directly by humans will outnumber human subscriptions, leaving 90 percent of Internet growth nearly invisible, like an iceberg." These "things" will include toasters, Sonicare toothbrushes, wallpaper, window-shades, mattresses. This hypothesis is confirmed by the English futurist Michael Dempsey (his book, *The Wired Society*, predicted our networked world 20 years ago), who is quoted in the *Financial Times* as saying, "Homes will be full of addressable processors—you could have thousands of Internet addresses in one house." See also *blue tooth, unobtrusive computing.*

Internet2 — 180 universities and 60 companies have decided the Internet isn't fast enough, isn't a wide enough pipe, isn't cool enough. So they've gotten together to create a public/private consortium that is building Internet2. It won't replace or make the current Internet obsolete, but will expand its potential. (To learn more, go to www.internet2.edu/html/faqs.html). Internet2 will allow innovations like tele-immersion (see listing), virtual libraries and long-distance learning to become more effective and elegant realities. If you haven't lost enough money in Internet stocks, just think what opportunities will present themselves with Internet2.

Open Building Movement — as apartment buildings, office buildings and corporate campuses get wired for the Internet, a debate has emerged about whether or not the property owner has the right to restrict Internet access to a single service provider. *DOF* sees it like this: although real estate interests (read landlords) want to generate as much profit as they can, the momentum of tenants—who want a free market and lower Internet costs—will prevail. It will be increasingly rare in the future for closed-access advocates to carry the day.

Rijndael — pronounced rhine-doll, this is the data-scrambling technique that has been chosen by the National Institute of Standards and Technology as the official cryptography solution. (How perfect that our new encryption technology happens to be impossible to spell.) Rijndael was chosen after computer experts from around the world entered a contest to replace the existing standard—DES—which was far from impenetrable. (Two years ago, a computer built by researchers precisely for the task cracked the code and recovered a secret message in just hours.) Rijndael is impossible to crack and easy to implement, which makes it perfect for protecting the data in our national security system, but far more important, the info in our cell phones, smart cards and computers. One thing that the inventors couldn't crack, though, is how to make a buck: by competing in the contest, they agreed to make their encryption algorithm available at no cost.

The Skim Project — we are quite fascinated by www.skim.com. They are trying to link people through the "street" and the Internet. For example, as part of their Skim Project, every item of clothing that they sell has a unique email address, worn on the outside—skimming the surface, if you will. When you activate it, you can communicate with everyone else in the Skim Project. As they put it: "When the street meets digital expression, the possibilities are endless." The idea hasn't been fully thought out, frankly, but there is something relentlessly intriguing about connecting people in this way—and about selling products that are uniquely encoded. The fashion we choose to wear has always sent a message, in one way or another—now it can do that literally.

Skin — a new metaphor, describing a pervasive layer of net-worked nodes, using broadband optical connections, that will cover the earth and will "give the world a new communications 'skin' within the next two or three decades" the *Financial Times* has said, quoting Arun Netravali, president of Bell Labs. The *FT* also tells us that "Like the human skin, it will develop senses: ubiquitous devices to measure pollution, climatic conditions and road traffic will feed a central nervous system." See also *unobtrusive computing*.

Skip Tracers — today's version of the bounty hunter. Using Internet search capabilities, you can hire skip tracers to find virtually anybody, anywhere. As one Web site puts it: "Can't find that lost 'dead beat'? You have a court judgment; he owes you a lot of money, he's left town with your collateral (car, boat, RV, airplane?) and if you can just locate him you can recover the item, or money. Or by now, it's been so long, maybe it's just the principle of the thing?" Gives new meaning to the phrase "you can run, but you can't hide."

Sniffers — also Sniffing. Technology that enables an Internet service provider to detect specific characteristics of the user, e.g., the speed of the connection, or the source. If the ISP "sniffs" out that the user is accessing the Internet from a wireless source, it will deliver data that will have the appropriate configuration, and the right content. That means if you're calling from your cell phone, and you happen to be near a Starbucks, you'll be sniffed out—and will get an instant offer for a discount.

Stegotext — ordinary looking Web text that is actually anything but, because it hides encoded information. This clever masquerade is made possible by steganographic programs that essentially allow data to disappear in a crowd. As *USA Today* has reported, Osama bin Laden doesn't go to any great efforts to conceal his plans from public view. On the contrary, they are "hidden" within sports chat rooms, family pictures and other apparently harmless Web sites. When you log onto the site you see an ordinary-looking Web page, but a terrorist, using a program to decode the stegotext, sees blueprints and instructions for bombs. While satellite telephones can be tapped, the unruly enormity of Web traffic makes it virtually impossible to identify stegotext. *DOF* believes stegotext will invade our vocabulary, as we will come to know it as both a terrorist tool and a mechanism for spreading viruses.

UNL — Universal Networking Language, an innovative way to make the Internet truly multilingual. Developed by Dr. Hiroshi Uchida, UNL is an intermediary, a kind of linguistic switching station. Languages get translated into UNL ("enconverting") and then get translated from UNL into another tongue ("deconverting"). As the *Financial Times* describes it, "Language servers that reside in the network of the Internet provide this process . . . for example, a home page written in Arabic can be translated into Spanish using Arabic and Spanish language servers." The communication and commercial applications of UNL are nothing short of massive. Dr. Uchida, by the way, worked on Atlas, the first mechanized translation system from Japanese into English back in 1984. See also *face translation.*

Versioning — the process by which content is sliced and diced into smaller units which can then be sold on the Internet for a per-item price. Versioning applies to newspapers, magazines, archives of all kinds—for example, a single entry from the *Encyclopedia Britannica* or the price of an Ansel Adams photograph from a Sotheby's auction in 1985—even software. To put versioning in perspective, in 1986 you had to spend $10,000 to buy a CD-ROM copy of the New York telephone book—even if you just needed the number of your neighborhood pizzeria. There are still hundreds of examples where we pay for more content than we need; versioning takes that inefficiency, and cost, out of the system.

Viral Wars — a debate between those who believe that it is possible to create "good" computer viruses, and those who strongly (and urgently) oppose it. Advocates believe that a virus is merely a technology, and like all technologies it can be used for good or evil. Beneficial viruses, the theory goes, would be able to fix and improve software, and seek out and destroy bad viral strains, a kind of Internet antibody. Opponents believe that while this seems intuitive, it's just plain wrong. Objections are vast: it's unethical to send even a good virus, uninvited, into someone's hard drive; a slight flaw in any one of them could mean that they damage or delete the very software they are trying to fix or install; a good virus can mutate and become an evil one; so-called beneficial viruses would tie up valuable memory resources; and once released, no one has any control where the virus goes and what systems it will end up in. Supporters say that there are technology solutions for all of these objections. Stay tuned for the next episode of the Viral Wars.

Walled Garden — a term wrested out of horticulture to describe the way in which AOL, for example—or any portal— can build a digital moat around its content. In other words, once you are within the AOL system, you have easy access to their sponsors and a more difficult time otherwise. A PBS story put it like this: "Keeping the viewer inside the 'walled garden' means that ad revenue and transaction fees also stay within the portal organization." At the center of this is a fundamental debate between the free-spirited, democratic nature of the Internet and the need to build compelling revenue models. It's refreshing to see an eighteenth century gardening term suddenly gain fresh relevance in the digital age; the rebirth and recapture of lost language enriches current language as much as coinages and new turns of phrase do.

Webidemics — cultural phenomena, including massively adhesive rumors, that start from nowhere and rapidly assume epidemic proportions due to the "viral" nature of the Internet to disseminate information without the traditional social brakes (also called "word of mouse"). Before the Web, it took a long time for one person to tell 20 people, and for those 20 people to tell another 20. With email address books, it happens in the click of an eye. Like Mark Twain once said, a "lie travels around the world while the truth is still putting on its shoes." See also *meme, viral marketing*.

Dictionary of the Future Predicts

Air Internet — in an attempt to reduce shipping costs—which are slowing the growth of consumer e-commerce—*DOF* predicts that the largest Internet etailers will form a consortium and buy (or start) an air-express company.

Comparative Anxiety — the Internet creates a networked world that allows everybody to compare everything, instantly. How much money are you making compared to people your own age who graduated from the same college you did? How many words does your baby know versus millions of babies her exact age, around the world? This ability to benchmark yourself in seconds will create an epidemic of comparative anxiety—a national wave of insecurity.

E-Commerce War — also e-commerce assaults. Activists will attempt to disrupt companies and cost them money through what they will argue is the perfectly legal practice of ordering large quantities of merchandise, and then returning it. (The protest can only work with an e-commerce site that offers free shipping and guaranteed satisfaction—and there are lots of them.)

Let's assume that anti-gun groups want to punish a retailer for continuing to sell guns. Protestors would click over to the retailer's Web site, and make 20 $25 purchases. When they receive their merchandise, they simply return it—and since the retailer guarantees satisfaction, they have to pay for shipping on the return side. If 100,000 people make 20 purchases, that's 2 million individual purchases; at a $5 cost each way, or $10 roundtrip, this little e-commerce assault would cost the retailer victim $10 million—not counting the internal administration charges. The damage mounts quickly, which is why *DOF* believes this will become a highly controversial protest tool in the years to come. And to make it even easier, some Web sites are letting consumers print out their own return shipping labels at home!

Everywood — as it becomes easier and more inexpensive to create your own digital movies, and distribute them on the Internet, everyone can have access to the power of Hollywood to create an alternative world: hence Everywood. See also *microcinema.*

IDD — short for Internet Deficit Disorder. Think Attention Deficit Disorder exaggerated by the power of the Internet to bring a child from one site to another in a flash. The result: an inability to follow a logical, narrative pattern and an impatience with any structured reasoning.

IDI — short for Internet Distraction Index. With so much employee time spent surfing the Web for personal fun and frolic, economists will devise a measurement to calculate time lost to these digital pursuits, much as they can measure the productivity loss due to absenteeism, back problems and other human failings.

Intellectual Shoplifting — a new phrase that will offset the "freedom of the Internet" argument that advocates of Napster and MP3 use to justify their dissemination and usage of music without paying the copyright owner.

IPI — short for Internet Productivity Index, a new metric for investors, analysts, and others that will track the extent to which a company is deriving the optimum level of efficiency from shifting its business—sourcing, logistics, etc.—to the Internet. Companies that have a low IPI are in a position to generate a great deal of profit from improved productivity in the future, while companies with a high index have already benefited from these productivity enhancements and will have to create profit growth from other sources.

Netlag — the kind of dissociation that comes from spending so much time on fast Internet connections that we expect the rest of life to be that way. Characterized by restlessness, impatience and an inability to stay focused.

Participlaytion — an Internet phenomenon which has consumers both playing a game and participating in its development at the same time. It blurs the distinction between a consumer and consultant, and is very much in keeping with the co-parenting model that was advanced in the book *EVEolution: The Eight Truths of Marketing to Women.*

Search and Impress Missions — the Internet makes it so easy to find people from one's past that we are seeking out old friends, old boyfriends, and girlfriends (only the less successful ones of course) to show them how rich and famous we've become. "Hi, remember when you wouldn't let me into that club? Boy, did you blow it." See also *comparative anxiety.*

Wristicuffs — fighting via email. Wristicuffs are breaking out all over, as it's easy to be keyboard-tough. (But then there's that awkward moment when you're face-to-face with that person to whom you've shown no email mercy.) See also *email coaches, ERR.*

MARKETING AND THE CONSUMER ECONOMY

Our society is one in which consumerism is more than the king. It is the entire royal family, some might argue. After all, a large portion of the listings in *Dictionary of the Future* could, in some way, fit under "consumer economy," since beyond the king, it is the judiciary—ruling on the technology that gets pursued, the research that gets funded, the entertainment that gets devoured—a vast web of investment and public policy decisions driven by its free-market implications.

Given the breadth of its influence, we have limited ourselves in this section to language that pinpoints the tip of the consumer economy's growing iceberg. We have "ad creep," to describe the fact that no stone today goes unbranded; we have the lovely term "ergonarchy" which describes a society in which it is our duty to consume; and we have "attention economics," which maintains that our greatest natural scarcity is attention.

You'll also come across "sponsored weddings," where couples save money on their special day by letting their "vendors" insert branding messages in visible places. Tucked at the end of this chapter, like the others, are *DOF*'s predictions for the next branding colonies, which we imagine will be blood (there are six kinds of artificial blood in development) and pets— why isn't there a national brand (or franchise) of pet breeders rather than hundreds of mom and pops? We also believe that marketers will start to look at "brand mythologies," studying the great folkloric myths to appropriate strategies for welcoming consumers into their brands—and keeping them there—through "conversion ceremonies" and the construction of powerful narratives that satisfy the deepest of all needs.

Ad Creep — also called commercial creep; the gradual expansion of advertising into our entire visual field. Coffee cups, the sides of buildings, the bottoms of golf holes, even entire cars: "Three California start-up companies are racing to turn the average person's car into an advertising vehicle. . . . Not everyone is thrilled with this phenomenon. It's part of ad creep," says Gary Ruskin of the nonprofit awareness group Commercial Alert, in *The Wall Street Journal. DOF* also calls it ambient advertising, and it includes phenomena like the Taco Bell Distinguished Professor of Hotel and Restaurant Administration at Washington State University. The question is, are we reaching the point of diminishing return by creating an environment that is, effectively, an advertising theme park? The more we see, the less we observe.

Advertrapment — when the lure of something for nothing traps you into being the recipient of advertising messages. There are many—and will be more—examples of this. You get a free or discounted PC if you are willing to accept advertising embedded in your normal functionality—e.g., screensavers, word processing programs. You get discounts on regular phone calls for listening to a 10-second commercial before your call goes through, or on cell phone calls if you are willing to accept location-specific messages: a Taco Bell ad on your cell phone when you are in smelling distance of a burrito. And of course, there are hundreds of Web sites where you get discounts in exchange for accepting Web banners.

Eventually, it seems like we will reach the point of message overload—but until then, expect this trend to continue. The paradox: it seems like Americans like being recognized as much as they resent being followed.

Armored Packaging — impenetrable packages that we need assault weapons to open, from fast-food condiments to aspirin to CD packages. Although this form of packaging started as a response to tamperings, many argue it has gone too far and has become the scourge of environmentalists. Thus, we expect to see a move from armored packaging to what *DOF* calls low-defense packaging.

Attention Economics — a theory, also called Attention Mechanics, which maintains that the most limited of all resources is attention, well beyond natural scarcity. As Tom Portante of Ernst and Young puts it, "The notion has immediate, visceral appeal. In a world of information overload, anyone can identify with the need to allocate attention judiciously." With the demands on our time expanding virus-like, and with commercial messages fighting a Darwinian survival-of-the-fittest battle, attention economics will become a lens through which companies view their marketing strategies—and decisions.

Consumer Serfs — describes the way that retailers—restaurants included—turn customers into workers. We clear our own tables, add our own condiments, bag our purchases to speed our way out of the store. (George Ritzer originally called them "consumer workers," but we prefer our language of consumer serfs.) Other examples of how we are turned into unpaid workers: at the drive-thru, we pay the same price as inside, but take the trash away for them; telephone voice mail substitutes the caller for a paid operator; and at ATM machines we become our own unsalaried tellers—and often have to pay extra for the privilege. What's more, new technology will create new opportunities for serfdom: a supermarket self-check-out system designed by Optimal Robotics—called the U-Scan Express—is being tested by Kroger and WalMart. The U.S. market alone is estimated at $2 billion to $3 billion—a market that exists only because retailers fail at service-delivery and force consumers to take matters into our own hands.

Ergonarchy — a system in which working to accumulate has become the engine of our lives; it has almost become a "duty" to consume goods. Author Fay Weldon describes this phenomenon in the *New Statesman*: "Alas, we live in an ergonarchy: rule by work . . . Where once we worked in order to make things, and thus keep warm and fed, now we work in order to earn, and earn in order to spend in order to work."

Esearch — a *DOF* term that includes all forms of online research, including polls, surveys, focus groups and consumer use tests. While consumer research was once done sporadically, esearch enables companies to be in constant touch with their consumers—asking, analyzing, assessing. Some have said that we don't have markets any more, but conversations. This changes the fundamental way products and services are developed and brought to market—but like any kind of sophisticated diagnostics, sometimes we can pay too much attention to research findings. And some of the most successful products of all time—the Sony Walkman, for example—were introduced even though consumers said they hated them. See also *random research.*

Geo-targeting — when your wireless phone, with a cookie tucked securely in its browser, lets a marketer know where you are. (Also called location specific marketing.) Once they have that knowledge, be prepared to get barraged with messages about the Old Navy around the corner or Krispy Kreme across the street. Big Brother, in the form of geosynchronously orbiting satellites, is watching. See also *E-911, sniffers.*

Gouge Gap — originally used to characterize the spread between the cost of a brand name and a private label alternative. But *DOF* foresees that the comparative shopping ability of the Internet will widen the usage of the term to include any unjustifiable price differential—between online and offline stores, from country-to-country, within a city.

Haystack Toys — an innovative toy company whose products are developed by kitchen-table inventors around the country. As they describe it on their Web site, "Founded by banker-turned-toy-inventor Dan Lauer, Haystack Toys knows firsthand the challenges, frustrations and joys associated with bringing a new toy concept to market. Our commitment is to dignify and honor the invention process." *DOF* believes that this will be a model for other industries—from consumer products to software—as companies realize the fertile imaginings of the mil-

Mm

lions of entrepreneurial and creative Americans. See also *idea harvesting*.

HempWorld — a group of wealthy investors believes that the next big global brand could be HempWorld. After all, hemp is an environmentalist's dream: safe, plentiful and flexible. With this in mind they are planning a chain of HempWorld hotels—in Paris, Tokyo, Toronto and other cities. From hotels, the HempWorld brand is intended to move to a range of products and services—restaurants, shops, health and beauty products and food—all hemp-based (but not the mind-altering, psycho-active kind). The appeal is to all those who seek a sustainable, eco-friendly brand. Nothing could possibly say it as well as their own Web site (www.hempworld.com): "Can you imagine a most hospitable and atmospheric place where all is made from hemp? Where one can sleep, bathe and clothe in hemp? Have a hemp oil massage, then a hemp dish with hemp beer or hemp wine and hemp ice-cream or hemp cheesecake for dessert?"

Hometels — a new sub-category of luxury hotels, like the W chain, that make an effort to literally bring you all the comforts of home, including a rubber ducky in your bathroom, plus down comforters and VCRs/DVD players in your bedroom. It's an attempt to take the stress and strain out of traveling. By re-defining luxury as a savvy re-creation of the familiar, rather than a fantasy of ultimate pampering, it's yet another example of the blurring that is permeating our culture: here travel blurs with life-at-home, just as the work environment is attempting to simulate those same comforts. (See *corporate comfy*.) What better testimony to the enduring power of Cocooning, which Faith Popcorn's BrainReserve first identified and defined back in 1981.

J-Pop — Japanese pop culture, a huge industry in Japan. It's a broad-brush term that includes all the curious, cult-like and often luxuriously trashy manifestations of Japanese style. While previous generations turned to the West for their cultural cues, the youth today are looking inward: at *atsuzko*, shoes with enormous platforms that have been pioneered by fashion tribes like the yamanba; at *manga*, which are comics "as thick as telephone directories," as the *Economist* writes— with the most popular racking up sales of four million copies a week; at the "character business," defined by the unaccountably beloved Hello Kitty franchise of which sales are $1.3 billion annually. We believe that J-Pop, already here, will mushroom in its influence, and that Japanese youth and street culture will have the same transformative influence that British mod culture did in the 1960s.

LIVS — a virtual product placement technology, winningly pronounced Elvis. LIVS allows marketers to re-insert their products in movies and TV shows, as if they were there at the creation. Producers will sell this "real estate" for lavish fees. So imagine you're watching *Casablanca* and a bottle of Dom Perignon champagne appears on the table in front of Rick and Ilsa—or you're watching a re-run of "Friends" and there are little packs of Altoids wherever you look. The possibilities are endless, and—to purists—endlessly depressing. What's fascinating from a cultural point-of-view is the ability to retroactively change our cultural memories. When the past can be so gracefully manipulated, the distance between what was and what is becomes fuzzy, and each generation can come to hold its very own, and personal, sense of history.

Neovintage — a once popular brand that fell into neglect and abandonment, and has suddenly been resurrected as cool. In fashion we've seen Gucci rocket back, thanks to the designer Tom Ford. Lilly Pulitzer and Pucci have similarly been reborn. But neovintage isn't limited to fashion. The VW Bug is part of the resurrection crowd, as is Altoids and its metal tin. Restoration Hardware, which sells your grandmother's cleaning products—like Fels Naptha soap—trades off neovintage chic. The question is whether these mummy-fresh brands can reappear and endure, vs. reappear and disappear for the same reasons they faded from memory the first time.

Phonespace — coined by Philp Nobel in *The New York Times* to describe the open airtime that is ripe for "sonic branding." Phonespace is the tiny territory into which AT&T crams its famous one second "sparkle tone"—heard no less than 28 million times a day. With increasing phone use, we can expect the phonespace, like every other open territory, to become increasingly branded. We can also expect marketers to hire well-known composers to work their magic in this, the smallest of all concert halls. See also *earcon*.

Shockwave Marketing — when a product or a movie crashes through the walls of indifference and becomes a phenomenon based upon many media platforms coming together. Win Farrell, who wrote *How Hits Happen*, appears to have coined the term. In describing the success of *Austin Powers*, Farrell said "It's shockwave marketing . . . a word-of-mouth generated by a confluence of marketing messages which all peaked at the same time. While Mike Myers is on the *Today Show*, you see Virgin ads on billboards, Heineken displays in grocery stores, clips on the news, promotions on TV Land—you get a catalytic reaction of conversations: Have you seen? Did you see?" See also *meme, word of click*.

Sponsored Weddings — couples get free or reduced-cost wedding services—flowers, caterers, limos, photographers—in exchange for allowing providers to discreetly promote their businesses during the affair. According to *The New York Times*, the idea "can be traced to Tom Anderson, an entrepreneur living outside Philadelphia." He "approached 80 local businesses . . . and eventually convinced 24 to foot almost the entire $30,000 bill including the use of a castle . . . and a white stretch limousine." The couple ended up on "Oprah," which, the *Times* writes, "set off a chain reaction." Sponsors can get their names listed on the invitations, mentioned in the programs, and can also get visibility on the couple's Web site. Sponsored weddings are the ultimate incursion of branding into our lives. (We're waiting for a band to bring us the special moment by playing "Here comes the bride, dressed in a white chiffon dress courtesy of Murray of Englewood.") *DOF* expects this idea to expand to sponsored baby showers (think of the sampling opportunities), sponsored sweet sixteen parties, and beyond.

Viral Marketing — the holy grail of Internet marketing, it happens when your customers become your unpaid salespeople. The classic example is Hotmail (which was bought by Yahoo in the good old Internet days for $400 million). Hotmail offered free email service—but every message you sent contained an embedded Hotmail message—recruiting others for the free service. It brought Hotmail millions of customers in record time—and since Hotmail makes its money by selling advertising on its site, the idea soared.

Another kind of viral marketing is when an application is so cool—a game, for example—that you can't resist emailing it to your entire address book. Think about the math: ten to the sixth power, possibly in a matter of hours or days. If you're selling advertising on this game—or if the game involves your own e-commerce business or brand—your name is in front of millions, for virtually nothing. That's a virus every marketer we know wants to catch. See also *Webidemics*.

Dictionary of the Future Predicts

Altered States — with the number of people gaining weight and losing weight—plus the volume of clothing purchased at discount retailers that don't offer tailoring—the opportunity is palpable for the first national chain of tailor/alteration shops. We've named it Altered States, but the real point is the opportunity; this new source of reliable alteration would bring expertise (computer-aided fitting) and standardization to a fragmented industry. Of course, the move to lower cost, mass market custom-made clothing is the next step.

Blood Brands — at least six companies are rushing to develop their own artificial blood substitutes. It isn't just the fear of HIV that's driving this—there's an ongoing issue of blood banks being at the emergency level, as well as anxieties about contaminants that haven't even been identified yet. We expect that sooner than later, these technologies will have their own brands and marketing campaigns attached to them, and patients will specify the brand of blood they want. The fluids we put *into* our bodies—from water to beverages—are the most branded items on the planet, so it's logical that the fluids *in* our bodies get the same treatment.

Branded Floors — in an attempt to create ever-finer gradations of status, hotels currently segment their floors by designations like Concierge Floors and Club Floors. What *DOF* predicts is a more transcendent level of marketing in this area, as hotels will partner with third-parties to further differentiate themselves. We can expect, for example, someone like Hyatt or Marriott to bring us a Ralph Lauren floor, a Martha Stewart floor, a Cartier Floor or even an Amazon floor (filled with the latest books in each room) and a Sony floor—a virtual laboratory of technology. For the hotels it's a way to create luxury space that isn't cookie cutter—funded by their partners who are happy to provide their products, either for nothing or at cost, for the distinct privilege of sampling to the wealthy.

Brandlash — the backlash against the excessive branding of every inch of space and time in our lives will be expressed by a rush to use generic, unbranded products—and raw materials—whenever possible. This will be a replay of the 1920s, when it became fashionable to brush your teeth with baking soda, for example. Of course, brandlash—the absence of branding—is less about declaring our independence from marketing, and more about finding another mechanism for self-identification.

Brand Mythology — the gold standard of branding, where the written and unwritten history of a brand fuse to create an appealing and resonant myth. (Myths, like successful brands, satisfy our deepest needs through construction of a gripping narrative.) Apple possesses a rich brand mythology, Compaq doesn't. Sony has a brand mythology (fed by the original

Tummy TV, Trinitron and Walkman), while Panasonic does not. *DOF* predicts that experts will work to identify the ways in which they can construct a mythology in and around their brands, applying the relevant cultural icons and archetypes in the process.

Brandparents — it's what happens when an established brand spins off an offspring for the next generation. Vogue is the brandparent of *Vogue Teen*, *Cosmo* is the brandparent of *Cosmo Girl* and Sony the brandparent of Playstation. When Jeep licenses its name to a bicycle company, that's also brand-parenting. *DOF* anticipates more and more brandparents, as marketers seek to win over the next generation before its pref-erences are signed, sealed and delivered. (This trend was anticipated in *EVEolution* and its Sixth Truth: "This genera-tion of female consumers will lead you to the next.") More big brands, from IBM to Amazon, will try to become brand-parents.

Brandrogeny — as we wear brand names on our clothes and speak in brand lingo, we are increasingly inseparable from them, a fusion we call brandrogeny. Case in point: a classified ad that actually recruits candidates with the language "MTV Types" and "Vogue Attitude."

BuySexuals — describes those who cross-shop at status stores—like Prada and Vuitton and Tiffany—and mass mar-keters like Target and Wal-Mart. This is driven not just by eco-nomics—as many BuySexuals can afford to shop only at prestige retailers—but a cheeky sense of independence. It says, "See, I'm not just about badge value." The need to make a personal statement in an era of great wealth (any millionaire can be decked out in Dolce and Gabbana) is predominant. In a parallel trend, be alert to what *DOF* has dubbed the Schizoid Home—home decor as defined by flea market finds co-habitating with $7,500 couches.

Cheeze Appeal — the curious, irresistible and significant cultural appeal of the kitsch and the trashy. (*Viewpoint* maga-

Mm

zine calls it "high-tack.") Elements of this diverse fixation are everywhere, and it's only the beginning: the attraction of old sit-coms, the return of the pink flamingo to front yards, John Waters movies, the popularity of '70s disco style and fashion, the new trend of collecting '50s and '60s paint-by-numbers drawings. Also included: the fascination with the Mentoes "Freshmaker" advertising, and gloriously tacky Web sites like thespark.com where thousands click to view rotting meat. Cheeze appeal is particularly fascinating to the young; as the *San Jose Mercury News* put it, "the generation that grew up on 'South Park' likes its Web sites loud . . . and crass." We believe that all this is driven by a rebellion against political correctness (as in I don't care what is supposed to be good taste and what isn't) and by a need for an aesthetic shock to the system.

Cruelty-Free — language to describe products that are produced without either having animals suffer, or—worst case— surrender their lives. One example: *Ethical Culture* magazine writes of "cruelty-free" condoms that don't use casein, a milk protein. The Vegan Society has okayed these condoms, but that is only the beginning of what *DOF* sees as the proliferation of "cruelty-free" as a branding (and packaging) element. Think about it—which is more compelling, replacing leather with material that is a polymer resin, or is cruelty-free?

First National Bark — Even water is branded today, but what about dogs and cats? It's still a mom and pop industry, with thousands of tiny breeders around the country. *DOF* predicts that national brands of pet breeders will emerge, guaranteeing not just the blood line, but that the puppies are in good health. They will also provide luxury pet transportation to bring the puppies to potential buyers. These larger breeding entities (a perfect opportunity for Ralston-Purina, by the way) will also have a wider population to choose from, and using special software and gene mapping, will be able to create the best pairings, reducing the likelihood of negative traits that comes from pedigree inbreeding.

Green Stores — we expect to see large dedicated retailers who specialize in natural products for the home—Home Depot meets Whole Foods Market. These will be driven by health, environmental and psychographic concerns—the persistence of allergies, the steadily growing problem of chemical sensitivities, environmental respect and the need to feel good about what we buy.

Green Label Strategy — the tactical use of scarcity to build consumer demand. It comes from the success of Jack Daniel's Green Label—a lower-priced and lower-proof version of the classic, which is in limited distribution in the South, "particularly around military bases," *Newsweek* quotes the company as saying. This scrunched window of availability is making Green Label cool and hip in the latest bars. The marketing lesson: produce a lower-priced version of your premium brand and restrict distribution. You generate incremental revenue and create a cult following, all without undermining the image of the premium mother brand—the implicit fear in all low-price line extensions.

Hospital Brands — the great American hospitals, like the Mayo Clinic, Johns Hopkins, Children's Hospital and the Dana Farber Cancer Center, will extend their brand names via licensing to generate revenue and increase awareness. Pharmaceutical companies will license these brands for drug lines, e.g., Dana Farber oncology drugs; similarly, OTC manufacturers will do the same for products like analgesics and cold/flu preparations, e.g., Mayo Clinic Winter Stress products. And why not? It's better than complex drug names like neurloxamine. A further iteration of this: veterinary clinics like the famed Animal Medical Center in New York City will put their names on pet medicine and pet foods. See also *Ivy brands, subscription hospitals.*

Indentured Studenthood — students raise money for their education by selling a portion of their future earnings to investors. Method for allocating percentages is covered by U.S. Patent No. 5,809,484. See also *creative futures.*

Independent Products — soon we'll have just about smart everything: smart stoves, smart shoes, smart fireplaces, smart lives, in fact. The question is, how will we describe those objects that aren't bristling with imbedded microchips—the poor lonely toothbrush that can't talk to the toothpaste, for example? "Dumb" isn't quite the right word, because something isn't stupid just because it isn't smart. We think "independent" could become the antonym of choice for "smart;" e.g., would you like your toaster to be smart or independent? Independence is a real benefit, too. When the system crashes, a microwave that is independent of the great processing oligarchy will still be able to make your popcorn.

Info Gourmets — sophisticated consumers of information. They read *The New Yorker* and *The New Republic,* watch PBS and listen to NPR; on the Internet they find their way to Slate and Salon and aldaily.com. These info gourmets are part of the desirable audience that marketers like Volvo and Williams-Sonoma want to reach. But not all affluents are info gourmets— many are junk-food info consumers. Similarly, not all info gourmets are going to be affluent—making life complicated for marketers.

Intrusion Sponsorship — when sponsors actively—and more to the point, unexpectedly—enter our lives. As an example, Microsoft could decide to treat an entire city to ride the subway for a day, as a way to introduce a new version of Windows. Or, alternatively, you order a Domino's pizza, and when it shows up at your house you find out it's free—courtesy of Ford, who is doing this as part of the introduction of its latest minivan. Of course, the vehicle is right outside your door for you to check out in person. The potent power of these sponsorships is their out-of-the-blueness, and *DOF* expects we will be seeing a great deal of intrusion sponsorship as marketers keep struggling to capture our attention. See also *attention economics.*

Make-Up Marketing — recognizing the importance of a loyal customer, marketers will go out of their way to make up for any relationship glitches. Efforts will include cash make-up gifts, extended warranties, special offers, house calls (if the item is expensive enough), dedicated service numbers for future inquiries and other dramatic steps. (A supermarket in Ireland pays customers when they spot a problem.) It's taking the Nieman Marcus and Four Seasons Hotels' models of ultimate consumer service into the broader marketplace. If you love me, show me, consumers are saying.

Price-Unconscious — the way wealthy people shop a lot of the time, or the way less-than-wealthy shop on occasion. We read about them in *InStyle* magazine, the movie stars who earn $12 million a film and can drop $50,000 in an hour—before they even warm up. But it's us, too: "I was depressed so I went shopping and had an episode of price-unconsciousness."

Product Contracts — an entirely new kind of relationship between consumers and the products they buy. You agree to purchase a specified amount—e.g., 5,000 Pampers—over a period of time. In return, you are given a discounted price (in effect, the manufacturer is treating you like a retailer, by aggregating your future purchases). Once you make the deal—over the Internet, of course—you get a card with a UPC number that is swiped at the point of sale, and recognized by the scanner (Internet purchases get credited as well). What happens if you don't live up to your side of the deal? Your credit card number gets debited for the difference. Product contracts are a way to guarantee consumer loyalty (great for manufacturers) and lower prices (great for consumers).

Programmable Horns — a way to personalize your car's beep-beep, borrowed from the programmable rings available on cell phones (see *digital autograph*). Choose your favorite pop song, your favorite jingle, your favorite hip-hop sampling or even write your own. When cars come Web-enabled, you'll be able to download a melody straight from the Internet. And you can change the tune as often as you want. There's no greater pleasure than serenading someone who cut you off a

Mm

mile back, and is now in the process of getting a ticket, with "Who's Sorry Now?"

Random Research — a new kind of research methodology that is the polar opposite of traditional, structured approaches. Random research leverages the power of the Internet to let marketers, politicians—anyone interested in unmediated consumer response—tune in to what's really going on in the culture, and with their brand. What makes random research possible is that at any time, there are undoubtedly people talking about your product—or about the world in which your product exists—on the Internet. (And that's not even taking into account the vast tonnage of archived information.) You can learn more about your consumer in this way than in any other. To help facilitate random research, we envision a random research search engine, to help you find the conversations you're looking for. See also *esearch*.

Smart Store — a chain of retail stores, physical and virtual, that will sell the full complement of "smart," technologically enabled and networked products—from smart tires, to smart clothing, smart paint, smart sneakers, smart appliances, smart kitchen countertops, smart everything in fact. (See *bluetooth*.) A single sales team, with cross-category knowledge, can also sell home networking products to tie all these fragmented household brains together. It's only a matter of time before not just a smart, but a wise retailer moves into this market. See also *Internet iceberg effect*.

Stock Loyalty Programs — companies will attempt to create loyalty among consumers by linking repeat purchases to free or discounted stock or stock options in the company. For example, for each GM car you buy, you get 20 shares of stock in GM—worth about $800 as we go to press. The program works on two levels—consumers buy products to earn the stock, and then feel financially (and emotionally) committed to the company, so they continue to buy more. Can also be linked to *product contracts* (see listing).

Super-Sizing — borrowed from the fast-food world, it describes the trend towards extra-large everything. That means cars, like the Ford Excursion and the new GM Hummer; coffees, like the reservoir-sized Starbucks "Vente"; portions like the platter-busting amounts we're seeing at family-style restaurants; houses, like the castle-sized 12,000-square-foot extravaganzas that the wealthy are building (what civic leaders call "mansionizaton"); home theater screens, and more. It's a manifestation of our need to feel powerful and important in an increasingly complex world.

Wage-to-Cost Ratio — a new metric that will be used by human rights advocates to highlight sweatshop manufacturing conditions. For example, if a Haitian worker is paid ten cents to make a shirt that sells for $20 (a real statistic, by the way), then the wage-to-cost ratio is 200. The higher the ratio, the greater the exploitation. *DOF* believes that this measurement will emerge as way to let consumers know if they are participating in the economic abuse of foreign workers. Web sites that list excessively high ratios will be started, and some retailers and manufacturers will establish corporate policies that set wage/cost limits, and will feature them in advertising, on labels, and at the point-of-sale.

ZipZones — guaranteed no-waiting sections in restaurants, banks, stores and other places where lines are inevitable—and getting longer. You pay a little more, and get a smart card with a yearly fee that lets you sail past everyone else. The check-out process is actually outsourced from the retailer (or merchant) to ZipZone, much as the NYCE network of cash machines works.

Mm

MEDIA AND ENTERTAINMENT

We are a society driven by, and to some extent created by, the media. That is no surprise. Nor is it a surprise that media consolidation has created a handful of giants that control much of what we hear, read and watch.

What is revealing, though, is that much of the language we're tracking doesn't reflect this economic consolidation, but is more indicative of a society that is splitting apart. Thus the section that follows includes "decentralized music," reflecting the continued—and projected—lack of a defining national musical taste; "microcinema," a phenomenon driven by low-cost video cameras and essentially free Internet distribution; and "house concerts," which utilize the smallest and most intimate venue of all: the private home.

You'll also find "pop genome," which is a witty take on the media's lack of originality, and "culture jamming," which reflects our ambivalence about the media's power and dominance—it's what happens when performers leverage the media while attempting to subvert its influence at the same time.

Whether its power is used to serve an increasingly fissiparous culture, or to homogenize us, the media's influence will continue to grow; indeed it is almost its own judiciary, as you'll find when you read *DOF*'s notion of "media justice."

Commentariat — used disparagingly, with its obvious Soviet subtext, to describe television and radio commentators and the control they wield over public opinion. See also *shouting heads.*

Culture Jamming — when members of the alternative culture use the mainstream media to subvert accepted mass ideas. *The New York Times* writes that the phrase was "coined by the art-punk band Negativland to describe its parodic defacements of billboards and other mass-media outlets" and that it "encompasses any act of media sabotage, from newspaper hoaxes to computer hacking." In short, "culture jamming is the act of infecting the mainstream from within." An example of this is when Rage Against the Machine seems to have "sold out" by appearing on MTV's "Total Request Live." But Tom Morello, their guitarist, justified his presence on the show by saying, "We're going to do our best to terrify them." We expect the term to gain a larger foothold, describing any act of "biting the hand that feeds you," for example, when a university professor attacks his employer. The question, however, is whether taking the media's money and then spitting on it is revolutionary—or merely opportunistic?

Decentralized Music — used to describe the fact that music is balkanizing into dozens of genres and subgenres, and that the period when one or two musical styles united the country has vanished. (Consider that in the summer of 2001, no single record held the number one position for more than one week, and each best-seller was from a completely different genre, from pop to reggae to metal, an unprecedented continuum of change.) The phenomenon is due to our increasing demographic diversity, as well as the explosion of alternative channels of distribution which allow for the indulgence of every rhythmic whim. Some (and this is just some) of these include: rapso (built on rap and Caribbean calypso); drum base (Brit-based renegade music crosses with Chicago house); screamadelic (neo-psychdelic); cosmic country (country with psychedelic flavorings); gloom rock (blending glam rock, goth and punk); sampladelic (retro '70s funk with a worldbeat feel); and grindcore (super-fast guitar-driven pop).

Digital Autographs — DJs at dance clubs take their signature sound and program it into cell phones and pagers for friends and fans. *Interview* magazine writes, "It's so new that phone manufacturers have no idea DJs are trying to use them like keyboards. But when they figure out it's a selling point . . . they'll make phones that have more sophisticated tone capabilities." See also *programmable horns*.

Distributed Mode Loudspeakers — created by NXT, an English company, they use new technology that is capable of producing sound from a flat panel, rather than the conventional bulky and boxy units. They have many applications; at home, they can be as small as wings on a computer, or as large as a living room wall (where they could also incorporate graphic elements and function as artwork). In large venues, they can give billboards and other signage speaking roles.

DVD-Audio — a radically new approach to recorded music. Backed by Panasonic, it plays DVDs and uses a 24-bit recording to deliver a far richer and more layered sound than traditional CDs. See also *super audio CD*.

Excitement About the Excitement — coined by novelist David Foster Wallace to describe the media frenzy over his own novel, the phrase will gain acceptance as a way of capturing the way in which media attention feeds upon, and incrementalizes, itself.

Farmclub.com — started by music industry veterans Doug Morris and Jimmy Iovine as a place where unknown musicians get a chance to be heard and possibly break through. On www.farmclub.com, your music gets exposed to a large (and potentially important) audience; industry professionals and fans have the chance to listen, provide feedback and vote on their favorites. We don't know if farmclub.com will succeed but we do know that it is exemplary of the power of the Internet to change industries with new pathways of exposure, whether it's music or art or literature. See also *micro-cinema*.

FEDS Magazine — stands for Finally Every Dimension of the Street. Started by Antoine Clark, this unvarnished publication that reflects the truth of urban life is becoming a phenomenon. At the end of 1999, it had a circulation of just 9,000—most of it in prisons, where the raw tone struck home. Clark, himself a high school drop-out who has been shot in the back and leg, doesn't glorify violence but neither does he hesitate to run photographs of murder victims and high-living gangsters. Today, its circulation is approaching 100,000, and a publishing deal is in the works. *FEDS* could become the next Phat Farm, a licensed property that finds its way into fashion and music.

House Concerts — Cocooning meets live entertainment. Homeowners are opening their living rooms to live mini-concerts, giving them the opportunity to make a couple of bucks—guests pay a small fee that's split between the "house" and the entertainers while also giving performers the opportunity to build a following. Made possible by the Internet, *The New York Times* has written that house concerts "have blossomed into a full-fledged national movement" and that while live performance outlets are "drying up," house concerts are "becoming the most exciting and vital alternative-performance circuit around for acoustic musicians." It's also a reflection of our need to create connections and community. Of course, commercial sponsorship isn't far behind; Jim Beam sponsored 32-year-old Kimberli Ransom, whom the *Times* described as "queen of house concerts."

Japanimation — Japanese-style animation. Yoshitaka Amano, who is perhaps Japan's most famous artist, is the hand behind the enormously popular video game "Final Fantasy" and the best-selling *Sandman* comics. The look and style of Japanimation will continue to influence American art, design and fashion.

Lean-Forward Entertainment — programming on TV that draws you to the action of the screen, meaning the couch potato will soon end decades of tuberous vegetation. This transformation will be triggered by sophisticated immersive techniques including three-dimensional animation and astoundingly realistic special effects. "We're moving into a period of what I call lean-forward entertainment, as opposed to lean-back entertainment," said Fred Angelopolos, a software executive, in *The New York Times*. For example, a technology called haptics (see listing) adds what's called "force-feedback" to a joystick or mouse. In many ways, it will further blur the distinction between reality and fantasy; it might even encourage us to lean forward toward Descartes and other philosophers who examined the differences between perception and reality.

Mandopop — Mandarin pop music, which is "making a big splash in the United States," according to *The Wall Street Journal*. "Mandopop icons such as Mr. Lau and singer Jacky Cheung—the Chinese equivalents of Latin heartthrob Ricky Martin—are playing to capacity crowds," they go on to say. The trend has even caught the attention of highbrow *Commentary* magazine, which describes a recent issue of *A.* (for Asian) magazine as follows: "in between features on Asian-American fashion designers, you'll find the hottest Mandopop (as in Mandarin) CD."

Microcinema — fueled by inexpensive digital video cameras and editing equipment, and the ability of the Internet to provide what is essentially no-cost exposure and distribution, an entirely new culture of low-budget cinema is emerging. The technology is also creating new kinds of digital experiences and storytelling that exploit the power of the medium, and its non-linear capabilities, to go beyond traditional film structures. As broadband access rolls out, microcinema will become even more macro in importance. Like any new medium, it will create enough self-indulgent foot-age to fill a large self-service storage facility—but never before has it been as easy for true talent to find an audience quickly. Check out www.atomfilms.com, www.bijoucafe.com, www.ifilm.com and www.dfilm.com. See also *everywood, farmclub.com*.

Open Publication License — mechanism which allows those who create copyrighted material to release those works into the public domain—the Internet for example—while simultaneously preserving their ownership and their right to commercialize the property at some point in the future.

Pop Genome — appropriating the language of genetic engineering to describe the irresistible urge of popular culture to copy itself. *The New York Times* has described the nearly identical nature of the Backstreet Boys, 'N Sync, 98 Degrees and O-Town as a Pop Genome Project. With success so difficult to achieve, it's no wonder that imagination and innovation lose out to Xeroxing. This term strikes us as elegantly on the money, and we won't be surprised to start hearing about this band or this movie or this TV show as a pop genome.

Puerto Rock — the fusion of Latino music and hip-hop; there's a whole sociology of this in Juan Flores's book, *From Bomba to Hip-Hop: Puerto Rican Culture and Latino Identity.*

Satellite Radio — the radio equivalent of cable TV. Two companies, XM and Sirius, will be battling for market share. To receive satellite radio, you will need a special unit—around $300 and going down—and will have to sign up for a monthly package, for around $10. As with cable, there will be dozens of programming options, including every genre and subgenre of music, talk, sports and ferret ownership. Because we spend so much time in our automobiles—collectively 700 million hours a week—car radios will be among the first applications. GM and Honda will be offering XM; Ford, DaimlerChrysler and BMW have lined up behind Sirius. *DOF* expects that corporations and universities will buy or lease their own channels for training, education and other applications.

Siliwood — also referred to as Hollywired; the coming together of the Internet and Hollywood. Thus far, it's been more talk than triumph, but there is no question that new entertainment concepts will emerge; new technology always creates new explosions of creativity (impressionist landscape painting emerged from the technological innovation of oil paints in tubes, which made them portable).

Mm

Super Audio CD — just what we needed, another audio format—and another format war. (Where is the United Nations when we need it?) Super Audio CD, backed by Sony and Phillips, uses a technology called direct stream digital (DSD) to create sound that is noticeably better than traditional CDs. DSD re-creates an analog sound wave—yes, like the old 33 rpm vinyls—by sampling the sound wave far more often than previous generations of hardware. The result addresses the criticism that CDs are harsh, untextured, lacking depth. *The New York Times* reviewer was blown away, saying "the difference between conventional CDs and Super Audio CDs was like the difference between sparkling cider and Piper Heidseck champagne." But it will take years for the transition to be made, and once again you'll have to buy another music library. See also *DVD-audio.*

Dictionary of the Future Predicts

Conflict of Interest Police — because we are down to just a few massive media companies, and the potential for conflict of interest is vast—*Fortune* has to cover AOL-Time Warner, for example—*DOF* predicts that these mega-giants will establish an internal conflict-of-interest squad. The primary motivation: to reassure regulators and consumer watchdogs. This group will be dispersed throughout the operation, looking for examples where stories are squashed, where full and open reporting is discouraged. George Carlin, in his book *Napalm & Silly Putty,* puts the need like this: "Keep in mind, the news media are not independent; they are a sort of bulletin board and public relations firm for the ruling class . . . Those who decide what news you will or will not hear are paid by, and tolerated purely at the whim of, those who hold economic power. If the parent corporation doesn't want you to know something, it won't be on the news. Period. Or, at the very least, it will be slanted to suit them, and then rarely followed up."

Ear Cones — the ultimate surround sound, a simple triumph over sophisticated speakers, digital signal processing and other technology breakthroughs. Ear cones, as we predict them, will be small cone-shaped devices—fitted with tiny receivers and amplifiers—that are inserted into the ear and pick up the signal from your stereo system. The proximity of the source of amplification to the eardrum creates an amazing response. Even a reasonably okay sound system can be instantly transformed into a stunning surround sound experience.

Media Justice — describes the way in which the public reaches its decision about the guilt or innocence of public figures—from O. J. Simpson to President Clinton to Gary Condit—based on the media presentation of the "facts."

Mygazine — magazines that will combine their generic editorial with customized content for distribution over the Internet; for example, a *Gourmet* mygazine would contain articles, reviews and recipes created around a personal profile of your interests and passions—along with some of its regular features. If you don't want recipes with meat, you won't get them. If you're only interested in the Mediterranean region, your mygazine will reflect your interest. Mygazines will be enabled by high speed color printers and home binders that will emerge along with the electronic book industry. Of course, it won't be economical for magazines to create mygazines from scratch for each person—they will need to create clusters of interest, using the same technology—called "collaborative filtering" that Amazon (and other Web sites) use so successfully to make their individual recommendations.

Venture Production — with the volatility in the technology and IPO markets, and driven by the natural attraction between the wealthy and Hollywood, venture capitalists will begin to fund film production. Studios will offload some of their risks to pools of VC money; entrepreneurial producers will also begin to peddle their projects to venture capitalists. After all, a film is very much like a start-up business: you need a great idea, people with a track record and a willing marketplace. And, of course, it's a lot more fun to hang around with Sharon Stone and Tom Cruise than software designers.

Mm

MODIFIERS, PREFIXES, SUFFIXES

As social and cultural change is often recombinant—re-arranging existing elements in new patterns—language also evolves in the same way. Bolting on new prefixes, lassoing new modifiers and caboosing new suffixes is how language recasts the familiar in a new way. To us, it's the linguistic application of the principles of cubism—taking an object apart and putting it back together from different perspectives. The new word or phrase that results forces us to simultaneously look backward— to the original sense of the term—and forward, to apprehend the new meaning. The synthesis of these subtexts is what makes so many of the words manufactured through this process glittery with wit and layers of references. These hybrids are often great fun, and as we read through them—and revel in their tightly-packed explosions of commentary—you might be encouraged to create your own new language menu combinations. Go for it. You'll also note that in this category we've woven our "*DOF* predictions" into each individual entry; it seemed to work better that way.

Alpha — we're being over-run with alpha as a prefix to denote the first or most important and powerful in a group. We've got alpha rich and alpha male, which led, inevitably, to alpha mom, and alpha geek—to identify the most technologically proficient individual in an office (courtesy of *Wired* magazine). We are fully confident that we will also see: alpha chef, alpha jock, alpha drinker (big in fraternities), alpha bidder (in the show-off world of auctions) and—given the competitive world of parenting—alpha infant.

Capital — used in combination with a range of different descriptors, it references the sum total of the value of an intangible asset. One of the first examples was social capital, to describe those reservoirs of civic associations, communal norms and bonds of social trust that—taken together—allow people to solve shared problems. Kevin Thomson has written a book called *Emotional Capital* about the connection between employees and their company, and argues that a shortage of this asset is responsible for poor customer service and low productivity. In a review of the novel *Iguana Love* by Vicki Hendricks, the reviewer writes, "Mona possesses the rare freedom of looking at men as promising hunks of sexual capital." And Pierre Bourdieu, one of France's leading intellectuals, believes that when you add up all the "capitals" possessed by an individual, you've got his or her "symbolic capital," the ultimate measure of status.

DOF sees a range of emerging capitals, including genealogical capital—the total of our genetic assets; verbal capital—our vocabularies, knowledge of foreign languages, ability to respond quickly and articulately; and mechanical capital—those skills that allow us to assemble anything . . . without looking at an instruction manual.

Challenged — this is a not very PC extrapolation of the phrase "physically challenged" but nonetheless (to our surprise) its usage has exfoliated throughout the culture. A therapist offers services for the relationship-challenged; a sports columnist called Mike Tyson's baiting of Andrew Gulota "courage challenged"; *Electronic Design* magazine writes of "innovation challenged multi-national firms." Just about any glitch or slip-up is an occasion for a self-deprecating remark.

Creep — from the military we get mission creep, from our friends at the IRS we get bracket creep, from Tom Friedman in *The New York Times* we get device creep. *DOF* has already brought you ad creep. It's a perfect way to capture the essence of a slow, and often—but not necessarily—insidious expansion of something. All of which brings us to: remodeling creep, romantic creep, wireless creep, anxiety creep.

Disorder — our tendency to want to make the world perfect, and give everything a name, creates a culture of "disorders." For example, when children display resistance to authority for six months or more, you may call it the terrible twos but the American Psychiatric Association calls it Oppositional Defiance Disorder. Similarly, what was once simply bad behavior is now Conduct Disorder. *DOF* predicts that we will soon be seeing Parental Deficit Disorder (brought on by over-worked, inattentive parents); First Child Disorder; Post-Wealth Disorder (depression caused by losing money in the stock market); Vacation Deficit Disorder (irritability and lack of creativity caused by too many months on the job). When is a disorder merely an excuse in an elegant wardrobe? It's a question we will be asking well into the future.

Drive-Through — a synonym for anything fast, routinized and implicitly a reckless short-cut. In terms of health care we've already seen drive-through delivery and drive-through mastectomy used in the media. What's next? Drive-through education, drive-through sex, drive-through relationships and weddings, drive-through investing?

Fatigue — used to capture the sense of being overwhelmed by a relentless focus on a subject, either by the media or by marketers. (Sometimes, the word "syndrome" is added as a reference to Chronic Fatigue Syndrome.) We've had donor fatigue, Internet fatigue and media fatigue (there are actually mathematical studies being made of it). Testimony before the House of Lords spoke of "consultant fatigue." *DOF* envisions luxury fatigue (see listing) and also blame fatigue (we're getting tired of being made to feel guilty), lecturing fatigue (a reaction to political correctness), cool fatigue (utter exhaustion from the effort of trying to think cool, buy cool, be cool) environmental fatigue, bottled water fatigue.

Geno — the astounding rate of change in the world of genetics will hurl "geno" into front-row prefix status. *DOF* predicts genoluck, for those blessed with terrific gene pools; genofault, to explain those instances when we can't perform up the level we want to—or is expected of us ("Don't blame me for not being able to do solid geometry, it's a genofault"); genofuture, the bright new world promised by genetic manipulation; genoskeptic, those who see the genofuture somewhat differently.

Imperialism — the new shorthand for any kind of overly aggressive behavior; shipping our trash is garbage imperialism, for example. We also have seen media imperialism and design imperialism (in a course at Columbia). What we see next: grandparent imperialism (from control-freak baby boomers), software imperialism (when we are forced to do what the technology wants) and neighbor imperialism. A spin-out of this: colonialism. France and China, for example, are fighting the domination of Microsoft, and are considering making open-source codes a part of all government codes, to fight "information technology colonialism."

Inner — psychologist John Bradshaw helped popularize the notion of the inner child, one who hungers for the love and attention he or she was denied growing up. This has become a way to communicate—often but not always in jest—either a sense of genuine truth, or thwarted desire. As we are encouraged to get in touch with our inner child (an ad for Riders jeans reminds us "your inner child is calling"), we will be exhorted to get in touch with our: inner romantic, inner jerk, inner adulterer, inner entrepreneur, inner artist, inner thinker. Canadian bishop Anthony Burton writes "Some people have an inner child: I have an inner bureaucrat."

Mm

Megaly — a suffix that means big or enlarged, and is commonly used in medicine, e.g., acromegaly. *DOF* predicts that in our overblown and oversized culture, this convenient term will be grabbed as the suffix of choice in new catchphrases like: egomegaly (a condition of insufferably self-important people); technomegaly (products—or software—with puffed up, useless features); heteromegaly (aggressively sexual male/female or gay couples who feel the need to demonstrate that in public); biomegaly (800-page biographies of minor figures that only scholars and those with bare coffee tables ever purchase). See also *super-sizing*.

Mother-of-All — suddenly, the modifier "mother of all" has become the descriptor of choice. One search engine lists over 176,000 hits, for Web sites that include the mother-of-all brain cells, the mother-of-all excuses, the mother-of-all conspiracies, the mother-of-all viruses. We are also beginning to see some support for "father-of-all" as well, particularly in the U.K.; the *Guardian* in the U.K. has referred to a Tony Blair statement as the "father of all spins," for example. *DOF* also thinks that the phrases "son-of-all" and "daughter-of-all" will wander into the language to describe the transition to a successful next generation, e.g., "The son-of-all laptops."

Nazi — graft it onto a word and, lo and behold, you get a way to characterize, with humor but edge, anyone (or any group) that practices a form of overly punishing enforcement. *Seinfeld* brought us the Soup Nazi, but the construction was around before, as in Health Nazis and Body Nazis. We've already spotted Napster Nazi, and as the culture develops new ways of punishing ourselves (or others), this is surely a handy way to categorize them. (Expect our renewed focus on education to bring us Homework Nazis, SAT Nazis, Spelling Nazis.)

Noir — for decades, it seems, all we had was film noir. Suddenly, noir is being used for anything that embodies the same low-budget, tough-guy, unromantic spirit. The imagery is deeply appealing in our overly manufactured, glossy culture; thus we find a whole generation of "noir" spin-offs: *Vanity Fair*

described *The Way of the Gun* as buddy noir; *Entertainment Weekly* has used the term gangster noir. One reviewer, writing of a film called *Pigalle*, said it is "very stylish in a docu-noir way." Another critic, writing of the novelist James Ellroy, says that "The 'mystery' that drives the plot is secondary; Ellroy's work is mood heavy, the novel noir." There is also a band called *Cafe Noir*. Heard on National Public Radio: surf noir. What's next? Name your noir: food (or cuisine) noir, vacation noir, decorating noir.

Pollution —*DOF* notes that we've gone beyond air and water pollution, passed noise pollution and visual pollution, and have entered into a place where any evil—large or merely annoying—is being retailed as a kind of pollution. "Poll pollution . . . is poisoning our collective psyche, clogging up our thought processes, turning our poor brains into pulp," rages Alan Abelson in *Barrons*. "Poetry pollution gnarls the Net," writes Chris Kidler in *Florida Today*. Yahoo! message boards encourage us to "stop email pollution." *DOF* expects to see logo pollution—from too many logos on too many objects; guilt pollution—from too much media focus on our bad behavior; cable pollution—from the hundreds of barely differentiated cable channels. See also *heart pollution*.

Porn — there are two related uses of porn that *DOF* is seeing. One variant describes a kind of guilty pleasure, such as real estate porn (spending inordinate amounts of time with magazines that show fabulous houses); *job porn* (see listing); wine porn (one Web site writes that "the world's wine press pumps out voluminous quantities of 'wine porn'"). The other variant relates to the way that the media manipulates us, as in the online magazine *Salon* describing network coverage of the Olympics as "soft-core emotional porn." *DOF* expects a continued growth of this expressive term, such as golf porn, auction porn, computer porn, vacation porn (dozens of cable TV shows, Web sites and magazines about places we'll never go) and the controversial philanthropy porn (all those images of starving children, which are called for, however, to offset charity fatigue).

Mm

Potato — made its first popular appearance with couch potato, and then mouse potato, but we haven't seen anything close to the end of this carbo invasion; expect: desk potato (those who work all day); spouse potato (someone who stays married out of inertia); plane potato (frequent travelers); auto potatoes (those who spend hours in their cars, mostly commuting).

Rage — we all know road rage, the mother-of-all-rage expressions. (See *mother-of-all.*) We've also noted rain rage (launched by impolite umbrella utilization); age rage (when senior citizens are ignored and treated with condescension, see listing); steroid or "roid rage," and low-fat rage, which has been exhibited by those whose moods are influenced by sustained low-fat diets. The popularity of this phrase springs out of the multiple—and growing—frustrations of contemporary life. We imagine the next explosions will be: success rage (unprovoked violence against obviously successful people); customer service rage; delay rage (courtesy of Lucas Hanft), directed at all those who slow us up, from the checkout line to the golf course.

Serial — for a long time this was reserved for serial murderers, but the usage has moved to serial entrepreneur (describing those like Jim Clark who helped start Silicon Graphics, Netscape and WebMD); serial exaggerators; serial failures (a British consultancy promises to "monitor the activities of companies and directors/managements which have a history of serial failures"); serial disappointers (stocks that always let you down, per money.com). *Travel and Leisure* magazine writes of spas for "attracting idle women who lounge around the pool trading stories about serial husbands." We also expect to see serial disasters (a tornado followed by an earthquake), serial athletes, serial collectors.

Stealth — well-disguised, but real, threats, attacks, insults or small thefts. Stealth bombers, which are undetectable (in theory) by missile defense systems helped give the term its currency. We now have *stealth fat* (see listing) and stealth tax increases, which raise taxes without actually raising rates (for example, by capping the limit on itemized deductions). *DOF* sees boom years ahead for stealth activities, and we envision stealth demotions (you get a new title, a small raise, but report to a new, lower-ranking boss); stealth romances (someone who keeps a relationship going because they need a date for a wedding or a party); stealth software (a "free" upgrade that, in fact, leads you to the purchase of additional, more expensive options); stealth art (paintings and sculpture that draw you in based on their aesthetic appeal, then jolt you with a political agenda).

Tainment — we know that much of society has been turned into entertainment (see Michael Wolf's *The Entertainment Economy*). That's why the language is overflowing with permutations and combinations of the word. We have infotainment, edutainment, retailtainment, sportainment (used in *Variety*), shoptainment, cybertainment, irritainment (media spectacles like the O. J. trial that we resist but watch anyway), and religiotainment. There is also agritainment, which is a strategy being adopted by family farms as a way of remaining in business (see listing for *agritourism*). So far, though, we haven't seen healthtainment (doctors' offices and hospitals that feel like medical theme parks): walk through the human heart before having yours operated on—or why not turn diagnostics into a video game—fun and therapeutic—called cardiotainment?

Voodoo Everything — we've already had voodoo economics (courtesy of the first President Bush) and voodoo science. (It's the title of a provocative book by Robert L. Park.) We expect this prefix to grow in usage over the years to come, as critics, cynics and skeptics use it to dismiss anything they disagree with as bogus or specious. Thus, expect to see voodoo art, voodoo education, voodoo technology, voodoo real estate, vodoo logic.

Mm

NEW BEHAVIORS

This is a section that could easily be redistributed across the *Dictionary of the Future*, because these new behaviors also fit neatly into the multiple modes and precincts of our lives. "BizVacs," for example—a new kind of blended business trip and vacation—could have lodged itself in "Children and Families" or "Economic Changes." Similarly, "controlled drinking"—a controversial alternative to Alcoholic's Anonymous—could easily have found a home in "Crime and Terrorism."

We decided, however, to bundle (now there's a word that has taken on a whole new vitality since the Microsoft trial) them here, because they tell a larger story when viewed in their totality, a story that often reflects the schizophrenia within our culture. For example, we have "horizontal ambition"—which drives us to seek higher values than just traditional "vertical" success—doing battle with "premature pragmatism," which finds young people inordinately focused on the economics of their future.

These tensions grow out of the fact that our society is moving so fast. There is a curious co-dependency between the forces of change and these new behaviors: each needs the other to feel good about itself. Without new behaviors, change is having no real impact. And without change, new behaviors are frivolous and narcissistic.

Adulescent — our youth obsession creates the phenomenon of men and women who refuse to live their age. (In the 1980s this was called the "Peter Pan Syndrome," based on a 1983 book by Dr. Dan Kiley.) Today it's more desperate, more widespread and not limited to men. It's visible in the way adulescents think, dress, talk, avoid responsibility and—since the advent of scooters—the way they get around town. It's even becoming the subject of scholarly investigation; a recent seminar at the University of East London was titled: "The Adulescent Society: The Quest for 'Youth.' "

Agonism — an academic term that is rapidly expanding in usage. Britannica defines "agonistic behavior" in the animal world as "aggression, defense and avoidance." Its new colloquial currency relates to the nature of political and social discourse today. When confronted by those we disagree with, we don't listen with an open mind, we simply withdraw into our preconceived views. In reviewing Deborah Tannen's book *The Argument Culture,* Jonathan Rauch writes, "Too often, in her view, American culture engages in 'agonism,' ritual verbal contact, in which people reflexively boil down complicated questions to two crudely polarized positions." See also *rage.*

Agritourism — a new travel trend—also known as Green Travel—that includes stays at working farms or any agricultural or horticultural venue. Popular in Europe and Latin America (particularly Costa Rica) for a while, agritourism is just now being promoted in California, Vermont, and other states as a means of providing extra income to small farmers and creating a bridge between urban and rural life. (The University of California Web site on the subject can be found at www.sfc.ucdavis.edu/agritourism/agritour.html.) Agritourism is one of those curious phenomena that can be destroyed by success. If everyone wants to visit the same farm, then it expands its accommodations and amenities, becoming less of a real farm and more of a farm theme park.

Allerednic Syndrome — Cinderella, backward. As the *Independent,* an English newspaper, describes it: "identified by Professor Jonathan Gershuny of the University of Essex . . . an Allerednic is a Cinderella in reverse . . . a man marries a clever, successful, achieving woman and in so doing rips the glass slipper from her foot, condemning her thereafter to a life of kitchen drudgery and child-rearing." While not yet on our radar screen here in America, *DOF* expects this term to land here and take off—as it succinctly captures a real social reversal.

Bibliotherapy — the use of writing as a therapeutic tool; the explosion in memoir writing we have seen, from the work of Mary Carr, to J. D. Salinger's daughter's deeply personal reflections, to Frank McCourt's amazingly successful *Angela's Ashes*. (This categorization, by the way, comes directly from the Library of Congress's cataloging system.) We expect bibliotherapy to become a favored tool for non-writers as well; expect workshops, online groups, seminars and Web sites, like the extraordinary www.openletters.net which sadly was forced to close for lack of funding (the wonderful archives are still available). After all, what better way to get something out of our system than to get it down on paper?

BizVacs — increasingly, in our combine-all society, we are merging business trips and vacations, hence the BizVac, a *DOF* coinage. A recent study by MCI/Worldcom found that one third of all vacations are built around the nucleus of a business trip. The risk is that we never fully cut the cord—or, in a wireless world, cut the connection. Another study, this one by Anderson Consulting, found that 83 percent of us stayed in touch with the office—60 percent took their cell phones, and more than half not only checked email, but responded.

Brivo — after generations of "leave it inside the screen door or on the porch," a new solution for accepting deliveries when you're not at home has been developed by the folks at Brivo (www.brivo.com). Brivo is a secure, steel-reinforced container that is, needless to point out, networked. The company calls it "a system that enables the unattended exchange of goods." Brivo links the merchant, the shipper and the container; whoever is dropping off the package enters a code into the keypad and gains access. There are also commercial uses: companies with tele-commuters and large sales forces. With the Internet changing the way goods are bought, sold and distributed, Brivo—and others who are working on competitive solutions—fill a huge need. What they eliminate, of course, are those small interactions with deliverypeople that add texture and dimension to our daily lives.

Controlled Drinking — a radical new approach to the long-term, traditional treatment for alcoholism. Rather than total, lifetime abstinence—as was pioneered by AA, and remains their unyielding position—advocates argue that controlled drinking offers a workable alternative. But this middle ground is a battleground to those who believe the AA way is the only way, and that anything else is a slippery slope that enables ongoing denial. It's no surprise that this struggle has emerged: in an era when we want (and expect) more of everything, it's to be expected that the theory of "a little can't hurt" would become seductively appealing.

Couch Surfers — a group of young men who have everything except a place to live. As *The New York Times* defined it, these "yuppie vagabonds" are a "nomadic subculture of young professionals in their late 20's, 30's and even 40's who appear to live normal, prosperous lives but in fact are couch-surfers who rely on the kindness of friends, seek shelter in their sport utility vehicles, or list about in all-night coffee shops." The phenomenon is driven by a tight rental market, for sure, but also by the fact that many of these nomads spend everything they make, and thus are economically lost when they are downsized out of a job or are in a relationship that went south. It's the underbelly of the growth economy, in many ways, and bound to get worse given the dot-com collapse.

Cybersex Addiction — a relatively new psychological condition. The addictive and compulsive use of the Internet for sexual stimulation—driven by the easy access of provocative material and chats—is becoming a real problem. Indeed,

Nn

according to Dr. Mark Schwartz of the Masters and Johnson Institute, sufferers can achieve "Intense orgasms from the minimal investment of a few key strokes." Experts report that there are a minimum of 200,000 people who are afflicted to the point where jobs and marriages suffer. Expect the problem to intensify, and new treatment modalities to be developed and tested. Wireless access to the Internet will exacerbate the crisis, creating a new kind of portable addiction.

Dating Dossier — an online project planned by Germaine Greer to help women share information and experiences about individual men. While this might not get off the ground, the "trend energy" behind it is very real, and we fully expect that the communal utilization of the Internet as a clearinghouse of acceptable and unacceptable alternatives in every category—from man to machine—will continue to explode.

Desire Line — we've all seen a paved path in a park or other public place, along with an informal path created by people who've chosen their own way of journeying from point A to point B. That personal pathway has been given the lovely and lyrical name, by urban planners, of the desire line. (To see some streaming video of the desire line in action go to www.gsd.harvard.edu/~gsd98sl2/MAS965/final/movie/line.html.) To us, what is most telling about the desire line is the power of human inclination over the routes laid out by the theoreticians. It's also a great metaphor that deserves further use. If you are feeling frustrated, just say to someone, "You're standing in the middle of my desire line. Get out of the way."

Divorce Showers — an emerging ritual; friends throw one to commemorate the end of a painful divorce process and the beginning of the next stage of life.

The Dump Book — a subcategory of self-help books that celebrates "the art of female revenge" as it is described in the publication *City Journal.* They report the genre as including: *Dumped: A Survival Guide for the Woman Who's Been Left by the Man She Loved; The Heartbreak Handbook; Getting Over Him; How*

to Heal the Hurt by Hating: The Woman's Book of Revenge. It's all part of a trend that celebrates, optimizes and otherwise manages the state of female singlehood. Previous best-sellers, including the Bridget Jones books and Melissa Banks's *Girl's Guide to Hunting and Fishing,* are part of this ongoing personal management process, as is, of course, "Sex and the City."

Earworm — a tune or melody that rapidly "infects" the culture—so that we can't shake it. It is attributed to Howard Rheingold, creator of the original Internet community the WELL, and is an audio example of *meme;* see listing.

Ego Surfing — the guilty practice of putting your name into search engines to see where, and how often, you appear. One of our favorite descriptions appears on ZDNet as the "Narcissist's Guide to Ego Surfing." The author reads: "Fire up your browser and follow this step-by-step guide to finding every cyber-reference to your favorite subject: you." The posting also talks about "seeing your name in links" which we love.

Hi and Bye — describes marginal relationships where you know the person well enough to say "hi" and "bye" but not much else. Sometimes, these relationships are meant to remain where they are, without turning the flame up.

Horizontal Ambition — not ambition in the traditional, vertical sense of more money and power, but in the sense of creating a life rich in relationships and experiences, believing that success will follow. As the magazine *Arena* describes it: "Horizontal ambition means that instead of committing to anything, you gather experiences of different people and places that feel authentic—and this then makes you feel a broader person. You multi-lifestyle, just as you multi-task at work."

Itinerant Rich — coined by inventor Bob Metcalf to describe himself and other affluent men and women who choose to live and work wherever they want, and are probably the first truly global citizens. They have movable roots. Metcalf was the inventor of Ethernet and theorist behind Metcalf's Law—which maintains that the value of a network expands exponentially with the addition of each node—so when he talks about the itinerant rich spreading all over the world, he is creating a human metaphor for a digital network.

Job Porn — when you are drawn, obsessively and repeatedly, to check out Web sites offering jobs in your industry—to look for opportunities or to validate that you are being woefully underpaid. It's to be expected when around 60 percent of all workers report that they don't expect to stay in their current job more than a year. Job porn, by the way, is just one example of the way in which the use of "porn" to describe any kind of guilty pleasure is racing headlong into the language. For more on this, check under *porn* in the Modifiers, Prefixes and Suffixes section.

Junking — going through the trash and garbage of wealthy homeowners; a social by-product of rampant consumerism which relentlessly replaces the new with the newest. It's not just about saving money, it's about the thrill of discovery and also has some philosophical implications as well. One Web site puts it like this: "Junking is a way of redefining the usage of things . . . not to mention . . . a way of cleaning up our polluted Earth." Would Junking Day capture more of the public's imagination than Earth Day?

Oversharing — when someone tells you more, far more than you want to know. We've all experienced oversharing, and technology doesn't help. As Julia Sleik, who sent us this word, wrote in her very to-the-point email: "Who hasn't had an email that you have skimmed because the writer chronically overshares." Even worse, as Julia points out, is when you plunge too deeply into the personal: "On Monday, our co-worker John was oversharing about his weekend escapades. We all now have vivid mental pictures we wish we didn't have." It's a symptom of a society which has become so remote that we crave intimacy, even from relative strangers.

Premature Pragmatism — coined by the writer Barbara Ehrenrich to describe the propensity of college students and recent graduates to plan for the future; research has found that 31 percent of students actually invest in the financial markets. Not that long ago they were picketing against Dow Chemical; now, they're buying futures in it.

Privileging of Distance — coined by *Prospect*, the English magazine of ideas, it describes what happens when someone with a cell phone insensitively invades the personal space of those in the vicinity. In other words, the person 1,000 miles away has more rights than the person ten inches away.

Swarms — unstructured replacements for traditional meetings, as far from the formal "board room" as one can imagine. This term is wonderfully visual and accurate; we found it in an interview with Christos Cotsakos, founder of E*Trade, where he was quoted as saying that he avoids formal meetings for what he calls " 'swarms,' more informal sessions in which employees buzz briefly about dealing with a problem." As more and more offices move to open plan arrangements, expect the swarms to be buzzing all across the many hives of American business. See also *informalizing*.

Vampire — in pilot lingo it's someone who flies at night, and it's entering the language as a way to describe someone who works similar midnight hours, most often in the computer and technology worlds, but also freelancers and other entrepreneurs.

Dictionary of the Future Predicts:

Address Book Activism — when individuals forward an urgent email to their entire address book in an attempt to call attention to a cause, issue or concern. The Internet makes it easy, of course, for individuals—as well as special interest groups—to quickly harness the power of great numbers of people, almost overnight. Of course, many of us resent these

Nn

intrusions, which creates the counter-term: address book aggression. See also *meme, mind virus.*

Binding Public Arbitration — a new form of alternative dispute resolution that will resolve controversies without litigation, by using the power of the Internet—and the public's faith in the combined wisdom of many over the possibly skewed judgment of one. The process is simple: a Web site—www.publicarbitration.com—aggregates thousands of people who want to be online judges in an arbitration. (Capturing names shouldn't be difficult; online pollsters already have a database of millions, and this process is more fun—it makes everyone the judge in their own episode of Judge Judy.) Each party makes its case, in writing—then, a master arbiter asks a half hour of questions to each side; the video is streamed live, and archived. The master arbiter also selects the alternatives, e.g., Party A prevails, Party B prevails, they split the difference. The public votes over a period of time—say two weeks (during the voting the tally is not visible, so as not to skew anyone's judgment). It is a very Emersonian idea—and contracts may eventually be written that incorporate binding public arbitration as a provision.

Counter-Naturalism — our knee-jerk response that natural is automatically better will come up against research which makes us stop and reconsider. Counter-naturalism is based on findings like the investigation into rotentone. This "natural" pesticide, which appears in more than 50 products, has been shown—in animal studies—to produce the symptoms of Parkinson's disease. This is the first time the disease—which affects more than a million Americans, mostly over the age of 50, including Michael J. Fox and Janet Reno—has been linked to an environmental agent. What's scary is that rotentone is marketed as an "organic" pesticide and is used by not just home gardeners, but by fishery managers in lakes and streams as well. Driven by findings like this one, counter-naturalism will add a new, more skeptical dimension to the natural vs. synthetic debate.

Data Fast — when you're exhausted from the burden of sorting through your email, instant messages and voice mail, when the stack of magazines in your office is taller than a third-round basketball draft choice, it's time for a data fast. With studies showing that we get an average of more than 200 emails and voice mails a day, the data-deluged will be taking a day, a week or a month to sort out their thinking rather than sort through their messages. "Don't even try to call me today—I'm data-fasting." As the noted writer and philosopher Blaise Pascal said, "I've often said that the sole cause of man's unhappiness is that he does not know how to stay quietly in his own room."

Dare Tactics — as baby boomers reach 60, they will start smoking, either for the first time or as returnees. They figure that cigarettes will take around 20 years to kill them, and somewhere in that time it is likely that science will find a way to make lung cancer a chronic condition. So why not enjoy all those seductive, hedonistic pleasures now?

E-Quaintance — the method by which individuals previously unknown to each other are introduced by a third party on the Internet. From this will spring language such as "Pleased to make your e-quaintance" and "Bridget is an e-quaintance of mine." E-quaintances can be made through email, instant text messaging, and Internet telephony.

Ex-thusiasm — also ex-thusiast. The angry opposite of enthusiasm, the word was coined because no other term exists to describe the vehement rejection of a formerly beloved activity, point-of-view, policy or philosophy. With the cultural rate of change and rapid opinion shifts, we need a way to characterize these sudden flip-flops, e.g., "He argued, wrote and lectured with a passion about the virtues of the free market; now, he's a total ex-thusiast."

15 Minutes of Shame — the downside of Andy Warhol's famous epigram that in the future, everyone will be famous for 15 minutes. What we're saying is that in the future, every-

Nn

one will have a heightened experience of shame or humiliation or embarrassment. Why? Because technology makes our lives totally public and transparent. Because we have more to be embarrassed about. And because the same forces that create the Warholian moment of glory have a dark side.

Guidance Avoidance — with so many people caught up in dozens of self-help movements, it is to be expected that an opposing social phenomenon will emerge, advocating independence from the 12-step and counseling industry.

Guilt Credits — when you want to offset your anti-environment behavior, but don't know how to measure the extent of the sins, you need to know what your guilt credits amount to. As an example, *The New York Times* reported that in a year, an SUV produces roughly 5,600 more pounds of carbon dioxide than a typical car. To earn enough "guilt credits" to offset the damage, you would have to replace all your incandescent bulbs with fluorescents (saving 1,250 pounds of ozone-depleting CO_2), and install new windows with multiple glazing layers (saving 4,300 pounds of CO_2). To simplify matters, we envision a nonprofit setting up a Web site—www.guiltcredits.org— that provides the equivalencies. See also *ecological footprint.*

Infidelity Credits — couples will agree, in advance, to a certain number of extra-marital affairs over the lifetime of their marriage; they can use these credits whenever they want, by notifying each other in advance. It may seem shocking, but no more than our relaxed sexual codes compared to even a few generations ago. Infidelity credits fit cleanly into the trends— they are an example of our "have it both ways" society.

Infophobia — a psychological syndrome marked by the fear of being incompletely informed. And with the amount of available data growing by leaps and bounds, infophobia will be striking more and more victims. For an infophobic, any statement that begins "Do you know . . ." results in accelerated heartbeat and panic symptoms. Some will suffer from infophobia in their narrow fields of specialization; more serious cases will involve generalized fear of data gaps. And the truth is, we will never catch up. Which means that in an era when we can buy and own more and more, we will have to get used to—ironically—knowing less and less.

Informalizing — brings together a number of disparate but related threads in contemporary culture, all of them characterized by a relaxation of authority and a rejection of formality. Manifestations include: casual dress at work, the demise of the corner office and the emergence of alternative corporate working environments; the decline of the dining room and the rise of "great rooms" that combine cooking, family activities and entertaining; the movement toward informal and rustic furniture (Robert Redford's Sundance catalog advocates "a mirror or towel rack with a natural rust patina"); the growing popularity of outsider art which rejects formal training and celebrates a more authentic expression. Further evidence: *The Wall Street Journal* reports that "thousands of homeowners have spent huge sums to rip up their perfectly groomed lawns and go rustic . . . known as naturescaping . . . the concept involves mirroring the natural milieu." While some argue that we will see a reaction to our informalized lives, *DOF* believes that while there could be some momentary and short-lived reversals, the informalizing of society is pretty much unstoppable.

Lobby Life — *DOF* believes that the lobbies of apartment buildings—traditionally under-utilized public spaces—will become vibrant and active centers. This mirrors the way that hotel lobbies have been turned into social magnets as opposed to "pass through" places that discourage lingering. Lobby life in apartments will feature bars (run by hot hoteliers and restaurateurs), small outposts of chic boutiques and other urban attractions. (Banana Republic already sets up temporary on-site boutiques at corporate offices, so the infrastructure exists for moving to residential lobbies.)

Love Testing — entrepreneurial psychologists will aggregate a battery of physiological measurements and introduce a love testing procedure. The tests, which will include galvanic skin

Nn

response, neural functioning, hormonal production and cardiac levels, will purport to determine whether someone is in love, or just swept away by evanescent lust. Part of being in love, of course, is the belief that you actually *are* in love, and in that regard the pioneering work of Dr. Lawrence Farwell might come in handy. Dr. Farwell has patented the process of *brain fingerprinting* (see listing); it uses a battery of electronic sensors, sewn into a headband, to register a person's neurological response to images flashed on a screen. Testing for whether or not you *believe* you are telling the truth when you swear "for better or for worse" could be just down the road.

Me-Quel — a personal sequel, a radical change of life, whether in career or personal relationships. As self-help books convince us that we can transform our lives, and as the entertainment culture convinces us that scene changes can happen on and off the big screen, millions of Americans will begin to see their lives in cinematic terms: cut to next scene in my life.

Next Anxiety — the fear of being yesterday's news—of being caught in a moment of crushing uncoolness by eating at the wrong restaurant, carrying the wrong personal digital assistant, reading the wrong book, using the wrong word (we can help you there). So deep is this anxiety that National Public Radio—the arbiter of sober balance, with an allergy to the trendy—has a new show called, what else, "The Next New Thing."

Outro — in television, you have an intro—which is either the copy or the musical signature that takes you into a segment. An outro, as you might guess, is the opposite. The term will expand in its usage to describe the graceful, or not-so-graceful, exit from a relationship. "I have to go to Omaha for three months to take care of my sick aunt and no, don't take me to the airport."

Phone Zones — want to yak on your cell phone about some meaningless drivel? Public resentment to wanton cellspeak will create dedicated phone zones, like the smoking areas for people who have a different kind of oral fixation. See also *secondhand speech.*

Pre-Civ Collectibles — also called P.C. Collecting, it is the next obsession of those on the front lines of the acquisition army. This collecting zone includes fossils, asteroids, scarabs and other items that were created before man walked the earth (or subdivided it). While there are several fossil auctions on the Internet (*www.extinctions.com* is one) this collecting trend is only at the beginning of its meteoric climb. The fascination is driven by an almost primal need to connect with a tangible part of the past in a world that has grown increasingly virtual and de-materialized. The trend will also be driven by increasing interest in NASA's upcoming space probes and planetary journeys.

Premature Adopters — early adopters are those people who are the first to try new technologies; premature adopters are the earliest of the early triers. They run a high risk of investing in technologies that go nowhere, but for them, that's a small price to pay for the reward of someone pointing to that futuristic device in your hand and asking "what is it and where did you get it?" See also *neophiles.*

Pre-Pre-Nuptial Agreements — men and women will start to draft agreements before they move in together, recognizing that the messiness of splitting stuff up isn't limited to divorce.

Prozac Bounce — also called Pharma Factor. With 6 million Americans on one kind of anti-depressant or another, experts are starting to wonder what kind of unexpected societal effect this pharmacological influence is having. Some are suggesting that everything from the long-term buoyancy of the stock market, to high levels of consumption and consumer confidence, are due to these agents that take the edge off feelings of anxiety, negativity, gloom and doom. So is the only difference between today and the 1929 depression a *prescription* for depression? See also *mindwash.*

Nn

Relationshopping — ready to settle down, feeling a strange urge to browse in Volvo showrooms? That means you're looking to move beyond relationsurfing to relationshopping. Consider that *USA Today* reports that nearly half of adults 25 to 49 are single, and that 55 percent of them don't have a significant other.

Taxicab Tactic — a phrase from the world of trade negotiation. You simply get up from the table, pack your bag—Hermes or otherwise—and say you are getting into a cab for the airport the next morning. We are predicting that this term will gain currency as a descriptor for any gently delivered ultimatum—"I'm going to use the taxicab tactic to finally see if he wants to get married or not."

The people who track this stuff say that by the year 2015, more than half (some argue 80 percent) of us will be working at jobs that don't exist yet. Tom Peters has said that 90 percent of white-collar jobs will be either "destroyed or altered beyond recognition in 10–15 years." While those predictions seem overly dramatic—they project the current rate of change, which is not the way cycles of innovation tend to behave— there is no question that the workplace is shifting rapidly. Jobs that are commonplace today will become museum pieces, along with buggy- whip manufacturers, typewriter repair people, and those who own the money-changing kiosks seen all over Europe that will be rendered obsolete by the Euro, sooner rather than later.

Our new jobs will have implications across the board, influencing where we live and work, educational policy and the environment. What we've done here is collect those jobs that are just beginning to show up on the employment radar, and those that we project based on the trends we are closely watching. In a society that defines who we are by what we do, what could be more important than understanding what we will be doing next? Another way to put it: job descriptions are the subtitles of the culture.

Bioinformationists — a new kind of scientist who works with the enormous quantities of genetic information currently being generated. They are the bridge between the geneticists who are involved in the basic science, and the researchers who develop the drugs, clinical techniques and other applications.

Chief Privacy Officers — an important and emerging corporate position, thanks to the intensive attention that's been paid to online privacy. "There are between 50 to 75 chief privacy officers . . . working inside U.S. companies today," said Alan Westin, publisher of the Hackensack, N.J.–based journal *Privacy and American Business.* CPOs have to work across the entire organization, because their positions integrate legal, marketing and technical concerns—and they'll have to work with regulators and consumer groups as well. It's a key hire: companies who invade privacy are susceptible to swift and damaging consumer backlash, so CPOs will become visible and public figures in their own right. See also *corporate stalkers.*

Cybrarians — a librarian of the Internet. Traditional librarians operated in a world that was basically fixed—with the exception of new books and magazines which appeared on a regular basis. Cybrarians will have to learn new techniques for mapping and monitoring the unruly Internet which is growing at the unfathomable rate of more than a million pages a day.

Disability Enablers — a unique kind of personal assistant who enables severely disabled people to continue to work productively. An example is Wendy Brown, who accompanies Richard Bergeron—president of a computer consulting company and victim of Lou Gehrig's disease—everywhere he goes. Bergeron is completely paralyzed, and Wendy Brown translates his whispered words, gives presentations on his behalf and follows up with clients. Similarly, Heidi Van Arnem, who is president of i.can.com—and is a quadraplegic as a result of a shooting—has a personal assistant who performs comparable functions. *DOF* believes this job category—part nurse, part personal assistant, part administrator—will take off as the disability rights movement encourages those who have even extreme disabilities to enter the workforce.

Disability Managers — a new corporate job title whose function, according to *The Wall Street Journal*, is to "better manage employee absences." Disability managers have been shown to lower absence rates and increase productivity, while keeping employees happy. The number one criterion for the job: the ability to accurately assess the statement "the dog ate my homework." See also *employer of choice, pleading economy*.

Embodied Energy Engineers — a new profession consisting of those who study the emerging field of *embodied energy* (see listing).

Explanation Graphics Designers — as our world becomes more complicated, the media—including magazines—will need new visual approaches for communicating and simplifying the message, hence explanation graphics. Explanation graphics experts combine technological proficiency with the ability to render the complex in compelling visual language.

Extreme Scientists — those who are not interested in the security of the ivory tower. Peter Lane Taylor claims credit for the term, and in his book *Science at the Extreme*, he profiles this new breed, those who "hang from suspension bridges, climb the world's tallest trees, and crawl through narrow shafts into the deepest bowels of the earth. They swim with great white sharks, rappel into active volcanoes, and scuba dive inside creaking glacial caves." Next step: movies and TV shows built around these heroic figures. Extreme science will attract lots more people to careers in science, now that the stakes are raised beyond repetitive motion injury from your calculator.

Food Sociologists — those who study the relationship of food to the society at large. The area is broad, including diet and nutrition, food and its relationship to family structure, acceptance of genetically modified foodstuffs, and how our perspective on these issues varies from culture to culture. Many universities have already started to offer courses in the field, and *DOF* believes that they will be in demand as food marketers and fast food companies discover the discipline.

Gap Year Counselors — a new occupation that will advise students on the best way to optimize the time spent during their *gap year* (see listing).

Geomicrobiologists — the study of the slow but profound process by which microbes have shaped our geological environment, and the investigation of new applications for them. This is one of a number of dynamic new disciplines that are created by the convergence of other, more established fields. Geomicrobiology draws from geology, environmental science and microbiology itself, studying the way that microbes interact with different ecosystems in order to create, as *Wired* magazine writes, "newer microorganisms—with unique metabolic properties useful for making new medicines—or cleaning up toxic waste sites." Geomicrobiologists, like Dianne Newman—one of the field's leaders and an assistant professor at Caltech—also use their skills to better understand the geologic evolution of the earth. Budding geomicrobiologists can check in at www.publish.uwo.ca/~rleveill/GMB/GMBhome.html.

Geriatric Care Managers — a new health care role that combines elements of counseling and social work. Geriatric care managers take an integrative role that includes managing the health care needs of their clients, as well as living arrangements and even legal affairs. If this sounds like the role once filled by families, you're right. But in an era when families are sundered, a void has been created which these new health care providers fill. "The systems are so complex now that even some of us who think we know something about them get confused," offers Raymond T. Coward, a leading gerontologist.

Glycobiologists — these researchers are focused on a relatively new discipline, which involves the investigation of complex sugars and carbohydrate molecules. Over the last few years, this has emerged as a field worthy of study, because critical biological processes, including the regulation of cell growth, are mediated by carbohydrates. Further, carbohydrates on the surface of cells are the entry point for many viruses and bacteria. For these reasons, glycobiological research could yield highly significant breakthroughs with regard to cancer, cardiovascular disease and inflammation. See also *AGE*.

Holistic Nurses — a nursing specialty that integrates traditional care with the values of holistic medicine: tending to the whole patient, creating a healing environment, and a recognition of a patient's spiritual nature—the totality of which enables the nurse to become a therapeutic partner with the patient. Currently, there is a serious shortage of conventional nurses, largely because the profession is perceived as being underpaid, unsatisfying and limited in rewarding opportunities for patient interaction. *DOF* believes that holistic nursing is capable of attracting many more people to the profession—but the medical establishment needs to embrace the discipline and recognize the importance of a healing partnership between nurse and patient.

Hospitalists — a relatively new medical specialty, the hospitalist takes charge of the patient's care from the moment he or she is admitted, until discharge. Hospitalists—and there are now 3,000 of them—are well-versed in the institution's bureaucracy and eccentricities, and can work the system for the patient's benefit. With primary care physicians pulled in a million directions, and with medical residents similarly overburdened, this new kind of physician-ombudsman seems welcome and overdue. Some critics object to the practice, saying that hospitalists are overly focused on the specific condition and not the patient as a whole. That's true, but when you're in the hospital you need someone who's going to make the system work, who cares about the holistic stuff when—like a plane on a runway—you're backed up waiting for an MRI.

Industrial Recruiters — an individual who is hired by a municipality to identify and attract new industry, both domestically and abroad. With profound structural effects in the economy creating serious problems for many small towns, industrial recruiters—part economists, part marketers, part urban planners, part salespeople—will be in increasing demand. See also *cool consultants.*

Interventional Radiologists — traditional radiologists identify and screen, but don't act. New technologies, such as *closure treatment* (see listing), enable radiologists to actually get involved in treatment. Not unexpectedly, this opens up new revenue streams, and we expect to see aggressive marketing of closure treatment by these interventional radiologists, just as we are seeing optometrists hawking laser eye surgery.

Mathematical Epidemiologists — a new discipline that combines epidemiology—the study of how diseases are spread and travel—with the ability of computer-aided mathematics to gain a better understanding of these patterns. Previously, epidemiologists had limited tools at their disposal—hospital reports, death records and so forth. Now, mathematical epidemiologists are studying everything from the spread of AIDS to the way that computer viruses replicate and travel. See also *digital immune system, ecological medicine.*

Outdoor Concierges — *Men's Journal* magazine writes that at Iron Horse Ranch in Montana you can call "one of their 'outdoor concierges,' who lines up the very best local guide available." This is the only reference we've found to an outdoor concierge, but with our interest in outdoor activities growing—both of the extreme and more relaxed varieties—*DOF* believes that resorts will soon start offering this additional service.

Paternity Experts — the ease and low cost of DNA testing has created a surge in paternity testing, which means a new category of paternity experts is emerging to handle the demand. Paternity experts, who are also known as DNA consultants, are part therapists and part scientists, as they help men navigate the treacherous waters that are involved with determining if their children are really their children. The *Financial Times* reports that "after shying away from paternity tests for years, American men are now turning to DNA consultants in record numbers . . . male insecurity about their partner's fidelity is creating a massive new client base." Many of the testing companies are marketing their expertise; Identigene uses outdoor advertising to ask "Who's the father?" (No subtlety there.) And, while most of their work is with suspicious dads, paternity experts also work for the government to investigate those seeking residency by claiming they are related to American citizens. See also *burden of knowledge*.

Personal Career Coaches — also called life coaches, they position themselves as a cross between a psychologist, a mentor and a recruiter who always calls you back. As one Web site puts it, and aptly so, "some people have made consultations with a career coach a normal part of their lives—as normal as having a regular tune-up on your car or an annual physical." With the old job-for-life model dead and buried, and with many of us planning to have two and three career lifetimes, the personal career coach becomes a key part of your extended personal tribe of supporters. For more information check out coachfederation.org.

Rational Choice Scholars — it's a bit heady, but the intellectuals among you might turn your attention to this hot area of political science which uses mathematics to construct a framework to analyze and predict human behavior. For more, see *rational choice theory*.

Reality Prospectors — someone who functions as a bridge between the media and life on the streets, searching for programming concepts, characters and opportunities. An example is Tod Low, who started as the host of a show in New York called *Subway Q&A*, where he approaches strangers and sees what he can get them to do—like going off to feed the sea lions in the Central Park Zoo. *The New York Times* calls Mr. Low "a reality prospector who might fairly be considered an MTV-style Studs Turkel." With reality shows the current and future

Nn

direction of jaded TV audiences, becoming a reality prospector looks like a good career move. See also *scavenger executive.*

Taxonomists — taxonomy is the creation of order and rankings, and taxonomists—who figure out how things stand in relationship to one another—will be in increasing demand as the Internet creates the need for structure and organizational wisdom. Anybody who's ever searched for anything on the Web knows how much irrelevant information pops up; taxonomists have to categorize all those hits, analyze the most common requests and then present the most responsive answer. Taxonomists need to understand something of library science, software, language and behavior. One initiative, Netscape's Open Directory Project, is attempting to organize nearly 1.5 million Web sites, in 58 languages, into 200,000 well-defined categories. There are 20,000 volunteer taxonomists working on the project, reports *Wired* magazine, so if you want to see if you have a future in taxonomy make your move to www.dmoz.org and find out.

Technology Butler — a twenty-first-century luxury hotel service. (*The Wall Street Journal* calls it an "egghead amenity.") When you arrive at Atlanta's Ritz-Carlton hotel, and your computer won't log onto the Internet or your printer won't print, a technology butler pops up to your room. As hotels compete to outdo each other, and 24-hour in-room massage service becomes as commonplace as one of those little sewing kits, they need to find new ways to serve demanding guests. *DOF* predicts that these technology butlers will start showing up elsewhere: in luxury apartment buildings, first-class airport lounges, corporate centers.

Terrorism Analysts — we are in a period where much of the world's violence will come from civil wars, independence movements, regional conflicts and other struggles that trigger terrorism, both globally and at home. Thus, terrorism analysts will grow in importance; in fact, there won't be enough of them since so many of the regions involved have not been hot areas of study. See also *distance terrorists, hyber-nation, terror entrepreneurs.*

Web Gardeners — those who keep Web sites planted, weeded, inviting and perfectly maintained. Web sites, like gardens, are about the balance of consistency and change, an arrangement of elements competing for attention, and pathways that connect different areas. Jakob Nielsen, who is a Web design guru at Sun Microsystems and author of the iconic *Designing Web Usability: The Practice of Simplicity,* tells those in charge of these things to "Hire a Web gardener. Maintenance is a cheap way to enhance the content on your Web site." Art Spiegelman, the writer and cartoonist, descibed Peter Givadi, who develops interactive products, as "the best of the new gardeners landscaping our new virtual jungle." See also *cobweb.*

Whisperers — because customers are angrier than ever, customer service strategies are starting to change. Rather than yelling back, they whisper. (At Amazon, calming furious customers is called "flipping the turtle.") The magazine *Darwin* notes that a "whisperer" is a customer service or tech rep who excels in gentling enraged customers. The term comes from the book and movie *The Horse Whisperer.*

Wildlife Rehabilitators — when wild animals who have been fully or partially domesticated need to be returned to their natural habitat, wildlife rehabilitators are called in. Why the need? One reason is that it's cool—and easier than ever—to own an exotic pet. It is estimated that there are 7,000 pet tigers in the United States—roughly the same number that are living in the wild. (Some are owned by drug dealers as "watch cats.") But when the novelty wears off—and the animals become too much to handle—the trouble begins. Having grown used to human beings—as opposed to fearing them—these thoughtlessly domesticated animals have lost their survival skills, and require wildlife rehabilitators to help them re-learn their natural skills—get in touch with their inner brute, if you will. See also *conservation genetics, extinction savings bank.*

Dictionary of the Future Predicts:

Chauffers-to-Go — a new regional service that will provide drivers by the hour. Retired men and women who are anxious to earn a few extra bucks will make themselves available to wealthy (and not-so-wealthy) individuals who need someone to drive them to work, or home from the theater (or a party with free-flowing alcohol)—in their own cars. Reservations are made on the Internet or by phone. It costs less than a car service and you can listen to your own CDs.

Chief Seed Officer — a new position which will manage and direct a company's investment in start-ups, incubating businesses, and other new opportunities. *DOF* sees this as a position growing in importance because, increasingly, companies are using their profits to invest in these outside businesses. A study by PriceWaterhouseCoopers conducted among more than 400 of the fastest growing U.S. businesses found that 18 percent of them are using surplus capital to invest in businesses outside their own. Chief seed officers, who will need to be part investment banker and part industry expert, will help run these mini-venture capital operations. *DOF* believes that more and more companies will require chief seed officers, that the trend to external investment will continue, and that employees will also be given the opportunity to invest a portion of their 401-K and pension plans into these high growth—but high risk—investments. See also *corportfolios.*

Chief Triage Officer — also affectionately called Chief Death Officer. Rapid changes in the economy, combined with the usual corporate mismanagement, mean that there are hundreds of divisions and subsidiaries that are either under-performing or no longer fit the corporate strategy. The chief triage officer will be a new position, blessed with the responsibility of figuring out what to do with these laggards. It involves making sure that the best people find positions within the parent company, deciding between sale and liquidation, understanding patent and other proprietary assets. The position requires broad-gauge knowledge: marketing, real estate, technology, sales, business strategy, the best place to sell used computers. Here's a hint—if you see him (or her) enter an elevator, wait for the next one.

Collectologists — our species is driven to collect, whether it's butterflies, Old Masters, Pez dispensers, vintage cars, or 1950s lunchboxes. (Just visit eBay and the breadth of our collecting obsession is manifest.) We engage in these hunter/gatherer/hoarder activities for deep-seated psychological and adaptive reasons, and they will become the focus of a new discipline called Collectology. This area has long been ignored; *The New York Times* reports Professor Susan M. Pearce at the University of Leicester as saying "the act received little academic attention . . . because it is on the cusp of several disciplines including psychology, sociology, history, economics and archeology." That's what makes it so interesting: we are what we save.

Complexity Analysts — the growth of the Internet has been extraordinarily rapid, a vast structure that has grown essentially without regulation. By looking at this growth biologically, experts are finding that the Internet can be explained by some of the same principles that govern the laws of nature. These laws apply to the organization of molecules in a cell, species within an ecosystem or people within a social network (see also *social network analysts*). *The New York Times* quotes Dr. Albert-Laszlo Barbasi, a physicist, as saying, "We are getting to understand the architecture of complexity." *DOF* believes that a new generation of complexity analysts, schooled in multiple disciplines, will emerge; one think tank that is driving this movement is the Hybrid Vigor Institute (www.hybridvigor.org) started by Denise Caruso. See also *digital immune system, mathematical biology, mathematical epidemiologists.*

Cool Consultants — a meld between city planners, marketing mavens and architects. They will be hired to help municipalities turn stagnant neighborhoods into hip destinations. See also *consumers of place.*

Corporate Jesters — increasingly, jesters are being studied for both their historical and contemporary ability to speak truth to power, and act in a positive yet subversive fashion. Beatrice Otto, in her book *Fools Are Everywhere*, chronicles the importance of the jester in cultures as diverse as seventeenth-century France and China, as well as the Aztecs and the Maori. *Lingua Franca* writes, "Otto sees the business world, with its talk of 'flattened hierarchies' and its out-of-touch top-down rule, as a likely place for a jester renaissance." *DOF* agrees, and predicts a mini-boom in in-house corporate jesters—if not as a full-time job, then as a "rotating position"—to challenge decisions, skewer formality and put authority in its place.

Email Coaches — businesses are finding that employees who lack the proper writing skills are creating problems by sending harsh, insensitively worded email messages. Thus, a new job title—Email Coach—will be created to help people learn to communicate effectively given the compressed, immediate and risky nature of email. See also *ERR*.

Experimental Therapy Experts — this will be a new specialty that helps connect patients with the appropriate experimental therapy for their particular condition. With hundreds of experimental treatments in a variety of clinical trials, these experts will be a much-needed, and in-demand, addition to the health care system.

Medlationists — the growing diversity of our population, and the resultant explosion in foreign-speaking patients, is creating problems for physicians trained in English. For example—as *American Demographics* magazine has noted—the word for "fever" in Khmer, the language of Cambodia, covers a vast range of symptoms. We believe that a new discipline of medlation—or medical translation—will emerge to bridge this gap. Medlationists, who are fluent in multiple languages and have a basic understanding of medicine (like paralegals) will emerge as a new discipline to help modulate this transition.

Micro-Acoustic Researchers — experts are working on microphones that will go dramatically beyond anything developed before. Using *nanotubes* (see listing) these devices will be structured like the stereocilia, or the microscopic hairs of the inner ears—except they will be far more sensitive. These microphones—or "nanoscale ears" as *Science News* referred to them—will be able to pick up the sounds inside the body, or potentially travel into space and do the same. Because they will detect sounds no one has ever heard before, *DOF* predicts that we will need micro-acoustic researchers to analyze what we're hearing, and its implications. What does a cancer cell sound like?

Online Learning Experts — online learning is already a $2 billion business, and experts predict it will reach $9 billion by 2005. *DOF* believes this will create a new kind of online learning specialist, who will need to combine an understanding of technology, education and production—all required to create the most compelling and effective online learning environments.

Personal Archivists — technology will enable us to preserve virtually our entire lives, in our own hard drives and dedicated Internet storage repositories. Every second of every day can potentially be recorded and relived. To help sort through this tonnage of imagery and information, personal archivists—a kind of life editor—will appear on the scene.

Retirement Consultants — nothing is as simple as it was, and retirement is no exception. More people are entering into it with more money—and more opportunities—than ever before. Thus, a new crop of experts will appear, combining financial and estate planning skills, relocation expertise, knowledge of leisure time activities, and employment counseling to help those in transition create a new, more vital and engaged genus of retirement. See also *phased retirement, returnment.*

Simplicity Experts — many can make technology complicated, but far fewer possess the intuition and brilliance to make it simple. For those reasons, *DOF* believes that we will see the emergence of "Simplicity Experts," whose mission will be to scale back the complexity of software and corporate networks. We're already seeing the beginnings: *Information Week* has hosted a conference called "Radical Simplicity" because, as they put it, "business technology has often become complex and so wide-ranging that customers are going back to their IT vendors and demanding software or new approaches that will bury or at least hide the mounting complexity." David Gelernter, Yale professor and Unabomber target, says that software designers with the gift of simplicity possess "topsight."

Social Network Analysts — if you're fascinated by the concept of six degrees of separation, the career for you might be a social network analyst. This profession will be based on social network theory, which studies the inter-relationships among people, and is a framework for analyzing "epidemiology, discrimination, migration, and business organization," according to *Forbes*. For example, theorists study the real flow of power in a company, not the way it appears on an organization chart. Social network analysts will be in great demand in the future, both academically and corporately, where they can do everything from help businesses improve the flow of knowledge and information internally, to creating intensified word of mouth around products.

NEW STRUCTURES AND STUDIES

While we could have slotted many of these new terms into their respective vertical categories, it seemed to us that it would be intriguing, as well as helpful, to gather them together into their own section. Reading one after the other creates a dramatic sense of how new disciplines and planes of thinking are emerging, often through the collision of multiple disciplines, or the application of one set of principles to another field. The historical hero of this section is John Maynard Keynes: as the *Economist* magazine observed, "he inhabited that frontier area where economic theory met philosophy, the arts, morals, finance and administration to create the modern consciousness."

This intellectual and cultural cross-cutting is, we think, something that is going to intensify in the future. Why? Our deeper understanding of the fundamental ways in which systems work, and the almost miraculous ability of computers to process this data, allows us to make connections in ways undreamed of before. How do the laws of physics help us understand economics? How do mathematics and biology—traditionally distant—come together to create a bold and vibrant new discipline?

The Internet, and its hyperlinked, nonlinear structure could be partly responsible, perhaps providing a brain-liberating ethos for conceptual collaboration. While cultural critics wail about a dumbed-down world of infotainment, we could actually be at the brink of a New Enlightenment.

Behavioral Finance — the study of the way our preconceptions, anxieties, fears and other all-too-human tics influence our investing decisions. This area is suddenly hot, and will get hotter because the stock market matters more than ever. As an example, *Newsday* writes of "prospect theory," which describes the tendency to hold losers too long (because you think they will rebound) and sell winners too soon (because you think they are ready to tank). Understanding the behaviors that work against us, including "overconfidence, predicting events from random patterns and extrapolating long-term results from short-term events" are at the heart of the behavioral finance discipline.

Biomimetics — the application of design and engineering principles found in nature to other problems. Nature, after all, has optimized all of its design components; man has not. Velcro and the Eiffel Tower were built this way; Velcro was created by a Belgian who got the idea from the way burdocks stuck to his dog; the designer of the Eiffel Tower drew inspiration from a plant stem. Today, biologists, designers and engineers—disciplines usually walled off from one another—are working closely together. Think of an apple as a package that is 97 percent water but never leaks, and you can understand why a package designer might want to have lunch with a plant biologist.

Chaordic Theory — an intriguing theory of management that balances elements of discipline and liberation. Practitioners cite flexibility, innovation, adaptability and inclusiveness as hallmarks. If you want to find out more, head on to www. chaordic.org/chaordic/whatwedo.html. We believe that institutions of all kinds, including nonprofits, can benefit from chaordic principles.

Conservation Genetics — an emerging field that identifies and maps DNA to protect and preserve endangered and threatened species. Species are threatened not only by hunters and by changes in natural habitats, but also when their gene pools shrink to the point where they lack genetic diversity. Conservation geneticists address this problem by doing DNA matchmaking—mating animals that are genetically diverse in order to keep the gene pool of the species from narrowing.

But the most controversial area for conservation geneticists is reviving extinct species through their preserved DNA; for example, in Sydney, Australia, they are attempting to clone the Tasmanian tiger from the DNA of a cub that has been kept in a jar since the nineteenth century. Half of this miracle has already been performed: a cow in Iowa gave birth to a gaur, which is an endangered species, an example of cross-species surrogate motherhood, or nuclear exchange. A company called Advanced Cell Technology removed cellular material from the last living burcardo—a mountain goat—after it had the misfortune of standing under a falling tree. Cloning is planned.

While the possibilities are endless, some, like Malcolm Tait, editor of *The Ecologist*, are opposed, believing that cloning endangered and extinct species is "lazy science" that gives us an excuse not to protect ecosystems and recognize the long-term commitment that conservation and environmental management demand. See also *wildlife rehabilitators*.

Cradle-to-Cradle — an economic model which proposes that rather than selling consumer goods, they should be leased or rented—thus converting a consumer economy to a service economy. Paul Hawken, in his book *Natural Capitalism*, writes "manufacturers [will] cease thinking of themselves as sellers of products and become, instead, deliverers of services." You lease a washing machine much as a business leases a copier—the manufacturer maintains it and, when you're finished, takes it back and remanufactures it or uses the parts for something else: hence, cradle-to-cradle. This is just starting to emerge; as Hawken points out, the Carrier Corporation is starting to market "coolth" (as opposed to warmth); they retain ownership of the air conditioner, and the customer pays for the benefit. A company named Interface is also starting to lease carpeting. See also *natural capital, solenium, subscription appliances*.

Nn

Ecological Medicine — a movement that seeks to understand (and advance) the relationship between the health of the planet and the health of any one individual. As the *Utne Reader* puts it: "Its central idea is that industrial civilization has made a basic error in acting as if humans are *apart from* rather than a *part of* nature" and that "a mounting number of our health problems can only be understood as part of a larger pattern." They go on to point out that "Ecological medicine could well emerge as a force for dramatic cultural change." Advocates of ecological medicine ask: Why is it that when you visit the doctor you get asked about your family history, but not about the health history of your neighbors and the people in your community? See also *bioneers*.

Econophysics — we have been attempting to explain the vagaries of the financial markets since the first caveman traded a slingshot for a rock. Now, experts are turning to the principles of mathematical physics to figure it all out and are discovering that the world economy behaves like a collection of electrons or a group of water molecules that interact with each other. How useful is this abstract notion? Very. By crunching one year's worth of the world's financial markets—about 24 CD-ROMs' worth of data—experts might be able to find underlying patterns beneath what seems to be random market movement. Creating logic out of wild volatility could have significant investment implications—one day we may be getting the econophysics report along with the Dow Jones and the NASDAQ.

Embodied Energy — a new field that investigates the total amount of energy expended in all the activities of the production process—whether for a car, a jar of pickles or an office building. It also factors in the recyclability of the finished product. This method allows us to quickly understand how these products rank on the scale of energy hog to poster child of sustainability. Once the debates over the calculations are resolved—and an impartial third party is given the responsibility for the rankings—we anticipate that embodied energy metrics will become one of the universal guideposts of everyday life, like calories, fat content, and miles per gallon. Consumers will seek out products with low embodied energy ratings; the federal government and local municipalities will give tax breaks to those who build and occupy buildings with eco-friendly embodied energy ratings. See also *ecological footprint, guilt credits, solenium.*

Family Firm Studies — the most common, and under-investigated kind of business in the world is the family firm. It is estimated that 80 percent of the world's businesses are run by families, but according to the French business school Insead (www.insead.fr)—which has received funding to dedicate a chair to this study—they have received little attention. *DOF* predicts this will be a growing area that combines consulting, economics, psychology (they are *family* firms, after all) and sociology.

Fault Study — Michael Dertouzos, in his book *What Will Be*, has identified some basic faults that plague our tech-happy world. The study of these faults will emerge as a full-scale discipline; just as we study what makes us sick (it's called medicine), we will examine what makes society ill. Below, some of the faults that Michael has led us to see:

- The additive fault—when we add technology to a task, but people continue to do what they did before. Witness the airport check-in, which takes as long as ever, despite computer advances.
- The rachet fault—where we add one layer of complexity onto another, rather than redesigning the system from scratch.
- The excessive learning fault—Dertouzos writes that the total length of his computer manuals and handbooks is greater than the *Encyclopedia Britannica*. Who needs it all? See also *just-in-time education.*
- The machine-in-charge fault—when you need to send an email ASAP, but your ISP decides at that moment to force you to download the system upgrades.

Nn

Geographic Information Systems — the use of maps to help us weigh options and make decisions. For example, if you're assessing the implications of 500 new houses on a neighborhood—including traffic, air quality, education—a geographic information system would combine all those elements in a graphic form, using computer modeling, spatial analysis and database technologies. As *The New York Times* put it, "People that have a hard time relating to statistics can instantly grasp the impact of a map."

Laughter Studies — the study of laughter, from a physiological, biological and cultural standpoint. It involves looking into the way primates react; the study of jokes and humor; laughter and power; laughter and truth-telling; the analysis of the way different societies use laughter; and the use of MRIs to investigate the brains of those who either tickle themselves or are tickled robotically (yes, this was done at University College, London). Robert Provine, whose book is called *Laughter: A Scientific Investigation*, is a leader in the field. He has collected 1,200 "laugh episodes" that allowed him to analyze the nature of laughter as a social signal. See also *laughing clubs*.

Mathematical Biology — the mapping of the human genome—and the emergence of techniques that require the monitoring of thousands of cellular components at the same time—bring mathematics and biology together in a new discipline called mathematical biology. While mathematicians and biologists used to sit at opposite sides of the university dining hall, mathematical biologists will "apply mathematical models to the manipulation of biological systems," writes the journal *Nature*. One team of scientists used differential equations to create a circuit that is actually composed of genes, and gets turned on and off based on external chemical signals, what *Nature* calls a "genetic toggle switch." They also point out that the "surest sign of the growing importance of mathematical biology is the . . . crop of new projects and even entire institutes. The eminent biologists Leroy Hood and Sydney Brenner, for example, have founded the Institute for Systems Biology in Seattle."

Natural Capital — coined by Paul Hawken, one of the founders of Smith & Hawken. Hawken believes that to create a sustainable world, business must be respectful of our natural capital, which includes the resources we all know: water, minerals, trees, fish, coral reefs and far beyond. In the future, Hawken argues, limits to growth and prosperity will not come from shortcomings in "industrial prowess" but in natural capital. He maintains that a new kind of natural capitalism must be developed, which recognizes "the critical interdependency between the production and use of human-made capital and the maintenance and supply of natural capital." He concedes that our current industrial capitalism is financially profitable but believes it to be an "aberration" that is nonsustainable and is inherently flawed in that it "does not fully conform to its own accounting principles." Meaning that we are going to bankrupt our own environment if we keep going the way we're headed. See also *biomimetics, cradle-to-cradle, green accounting.*

Nuclear Financial Economics — a concept developed by Nobel Prize winner William Sharpe. The theory goes like this: just as we understand the physical world by breaking things down to their smallest, nuclear particles, so too can we understand complex financial structures. This framework can result in the analysis of risk in simple yet powerful ways; Sharpe argues that nuclear financial economics can result in breakthroughs in insurance and investments. There's a lot to understand—after all, it was developed by a Nobel Prize winner—so interested parties should head for the Web site and learn more: www.gsb.stanford.edu/community/bmag/newsreleases/sbsm623/sbsm62308a.htm

Rational Choice Theory — a controversial political science theory which argues that when you boil it down, all decisions can be reduced to a mathematical formula. The formula is based on variables that are related to our self-interest. In other words, we don't act out of pure emotion or reflex. As *The New Republic* puts it, "Rational choice scholars seek to identify universal explanations for political behavior . . . by treating it the way physicists treat atoms and subatomic particles. They make

Nn

assumptions about motives, derive mathematical models representing a predictive theory about how those motivations will cause people to behave . . . and then determine whether the predictions hold true by plugging in data." Advocates say it is the only way to make political science a true science. Others, according to *The New Republic*, resist a model that "reduces all human behavior to a set of preferences independent of things such as values, culture or history." As this theory evolves, it could change the way history is viewed and public policy is developed and advocated. See also *behavioral finance*.

Swarm Intelligence — describes the behavior of ants and how their collaboration yields problem-solving strategies that can be systemized to improve many human tasks. Assessing the way ants collectively figure out the shortest path to a food source, or move a heavy object, gives researchers valuable information. As *Science News* puts it, "This sort of self-organizing behavior . . . has become the envy of engineers and computer scientists as they work to solve tough path-finding, scheduling and control problems." A computer model of ant colony optimization, for example, is helping truckers in Switzerland. Further, "Unilever is considering . . . a version of the algorithm to schedule production at a large chemical plant," notes *Science News*. Similarly, ant colony routing can help telecom companies efficiently transmit multiple packets of information across a number of networks, using "antlike agents" to patrol a network and report delays.

Swarm intelligence is also being studied for creating robots, controlling crowds and designing office buildings. In a world of *ubiquitous computing* (see listing), where multiple computers need to communicate, "more applications of swarm intelligence will continue to emerge," said Eric Bonabeau, a leader in the field. See also *biomimetics*.

Telegeography — a new way of looking at geography that was started by a Washington, D.C., research group that believes that the old geography of countries and borders "is giving way to a new geography marked by telephone codes, satellite 'footprints' and Internet addresses." Their publication, *TeleGeography*, which costs $985, includes traffic data for more than 100 countries, such as statistics on submarine cables, satellite capacity and infrastructure details. *Business 2.0* magazine writes that "Seeing these numbers and connections in stark detail is a reminder of the true global potential of the Internet." *DOF* wonders how long it will be before "Jeopardy" has a "Telegeography" category?

Translational Medicine — a new field of medicine that fills the void between what happens in the research laboratory and its translation to clinical medicine. A paper by two physicans at Massachusetts General Hospital, David A. Shaywitz and Dennis A. Ausiello, puts it well: "To date, we have really not trained anyone to navigate the nebulous region between the lab and the clinic—mostly because we have been so distracted by the excitement of contemporary science, and so preoccupied by the demands of modern medicine. Consequently, we are just now beginning to recognize that the region between biology and medicine is not a simple extension of either; rather, it represents a discrete intellectual space, a nascent academic discipline—translational medicine."

Unconventional Innovation Program — an effort underway within the National Cancer Institute to use novel technologies to seek "quantum improvements and entirely novel approaches" in the battle, according to the *MIT Technology Review*. The program is modeled on DARPA, the division of the Defense Department that was the initial sponsor of the Internet. A member of NCI's Board of Scientific Advisors, Franklin Prendergast—who is also the director of cancer research at the Mayo Clinic—reminds us that "the bizarre and the weird can sometimes have the greatest impact." Grants will be in multi-disciplinary areas like microfabrication, photonics and chemical engineering. Corporate America should pay heed: every Fortune 500 company should have an unconventional innovation program of its very own.

Nn

Dictionary of the Future Predicts

Alphaday — a tongue-in-cheek movement for a proposed eighth day of the week. It will be created by those who believe that the demands of contemporary life call for a re-evaluation of our biblical seven-day week. The Alphaday Project would shorten each of our current days to 21 hours, so that we could cram in an extra day (Alphaday) and the work week could move from five to six days. Think about the productivity gains! The sales and marketing opportunities! The extra homework!

Audience Studies — a new branch of sociology will emerge to investigate the effect of group dynamics on our "consumption" of entertainment, and to analyze how we react when we are watching something as a member of the audience, as opposed to being alone. How does our interaction with the movie change when we are together versus alone? Julie Taymor, who directed *The Lion King*, writes that "the communal sense of anticipation and the space itself all add to the story of entertainment." Another area for study is the "shopping audience"— how does consumer behavior differ when we are shopping in a communal environment, with feedback from other individuals, versus when we are shopping alone, on the Internet?

Consolidation Studies — a new, integrated discipline which will focus its research on an analysis of the profound effects of industry-wide consolidations. From the media to airlines to chicken growers to supermarkets, fewer and fewer companies are wielding more and more power. This concentration influences the economy in ways that have never been studied in their totality. Consolidation shapes everything from the supply chain—large companies prefer to buy from large vendors, thus making life difficult (if not impossible) for innovative small producers—to architecture, since the increasing sameness of our shopping environment, from Milan to Milwaukee, is due to multi-national retailers enforcing a visual branding consistency. Consolidation studies will sit at the intersection of economics, architecture, agriculture, cultural history and media studies.

Nn

Fusionomics — the study of cultural fusion as it relates to food, music, literature, dance, even religion; the magazine *U.S. News & World Report* notes that the ketubah, the 2,000-year-old Jewish wedding document, is crossing over to Christian newlyweds.

Knowledge Membranes — as theoreticians study business structures and analyze the ways that they parallel biological structures, they will identify the issue of "knowledge membranes." Just as cell membranes keep material from traveling too far, knowledge membranes keep information close to the source, for organizational, political, emotional and territorial reasons. And no amount of technology, or sophisticated intranets, can liberate it. Breaking down the barriers of the knowledge membrane will enable organizations to share learning and become the equivalent of integrated cellular organisms. See also *knowledge blockage*.

Semi-Profit Corporations — the explosion of joint ventures between public and private partnerships will encourage the creation of a new kind of corporation whose mission is to return a percentage, say 50 percent of its profits to charity. In return, this new legal structure will be taxed at a rate between the two current extremes of tax-exempt and fully taxable.

Technology Impact Studies — it's hard to imagine, but there was a time before Environmental Studies existed as a discipline. *DOF* believes that Technology Impact Studies—which hasn't yet emerged as an academic field—will have a similar trajectory. This multi-disciplinary area will examine the impact of technology on our lives and our culture—both positive and negative (the latter will be given the moniker "wrecknowledgy"). Technology Impact Studies will include the social—the effect of computers on family life; the physiological—what are the effects on our brain function of data streaming at us constantly; and the economic—the influence of technology on productivity and innovation. Universities will soon be establishing Technology Impact Studies departments, journals will appear and the area will become a full-fledged discipline.

Nn

PERSONAL FINANCE

The message here is that if personal finance seems complicated now, just wait. You'll have to deal with "black information" that besmirches your credit rating, with "non-actuarial risk" that threatens to raise the insurance premiums of the genetically unlucky, with "PERM," a new way to value stocks—just when you've mastered the p/e ratio—plus the risks/reward of "SAM," the shared appreciation mortgage.

In the nineties, personal finance was our consuming passion. We read about it, watched endless hours of cable TV that followed every lurch and hiccup of the market. While the 2001 correction is dimming our passion temporarily, our language continues to erupt with new terms that reflect the cultural centrality of all aspects of creating and enhancing wealth—as well as the consequences of this irrational exuberance. In other words: Have you been "401-K'd" yet?

Affluenza — the disease of incessant focus on the accumulation of wealth. Like every disease, it has its convenient list of symptoms, which can be diagnosed, according to the Affluenza Institute, by asking: Do you find yourself working late to meet a standard others have set? Are you drifting away from family and friends in pursuit of financial success? Have you lost touch with who you really are?

Black Information — an English term used to describe all the negative stuff a bank or a credit-reporting agency might have in your file. It will gain increasing frequency in the United States as the Internet makes it dangerously easy for this kind of personal credit data to be circulated. Pay one bill a few days late and it will stick with you all your days.

Death Futures — a colloquial expression for the technical term, "viatical settlements." The idea is simple: an investor pays less than the face value of an insurance policy belonging to an old or sick policyholder. The policyholder gets the chance to derive some value from the asset while still alive; the investor can realize a substantial return, but only if the policyholder doesn't live too long (the investor keeps paying the premium). It's controversial. Some say the idea is humanitarian because it can make a huge lifestyle difference for the policyholder, while others say there is something fundamentally unethical about betting someone will die quickly. Despite some previous glitches and scams, *DOF* anticipates that death futures will be reborn as a mutual fund–type investment where there will be a pooling of risk.

Indicating Ahead — when brokers get together before the trading starts on the NASDAQ—the "pre-opening"—to work out prices so that the market can open smoothly. The theory is that a smooth market benefits all investors in general, even though some customers must sacrifice, by getting a lower price. Consumer activists are starting to believe, however, that this practice is wrong, that too many investors are hurt and that only the brokers truly benefit. They also maintain that brokers should have a higher level of duty to their customers than the abstract notion of "what's best" for the market. *DOF* believes that the little known practice of indicating ahead—little known outside of the financial industry, that is—will hit the headlines and come under intense scrutiny as another example of how small investors get hurt by the system.

Investorism — an emerging term that describes a new kind of investor consumerism, a movement that keeps us aware of scams and lets investors share their experiences and collective strength. For more, see www.investorism.com.

Loss Aversion Behavior — a psychological phenomenon that explains why housing prices don't fall immediately after a stock market or other economic decline. Studies show that after a bust, sales volume falls—often by as much as 50 percent—long before prices do. That's because sellers will do whatever they can to avoid lowering prices, even if it means keeping their properties on the market longer. A study on this subject, conducted for the National Bureau of Economic Research, can be found at www.papers.nber.org/papers/W8143. Loss aversion behavior will be increasingly observed to gain insight into why widely held stocks rise or fall; if someone could mathematically model this, it would be an interesting way to play the stock market. See also *behavioral finance.*

Manic-Depressive Markets — being used on Wall Street to describe a stock market that is alternatively euphoric and suicidal.

Microinvesting — an innovative way to turn those tiny Internet rebates and other online savings into something more meaningful. Innovative companies like SaveDaily.com allow consumers to aggregate their rebates and, in turn, invest them in mutual funds. Another approach comes from UPromise, which links savings on Internet purchases from leading merchants to a college funding program.

Non-Actuarial Risk — an insurance company euphemism for a highly controversial process: pricing insurance based on an individual's genetic profile, as opposed to generalized actuarial risk. Of course, there is still a debate over how definitive our biological make-up is—tests with 45,000 identical twins have shown that lifestyle is as important as fate—but insurance companies would still love to get their hands on that information. This could go in any number of directions: federal legislation, high-risk pooling (like in the auto industry), outright banning of the practice.

Already, as the *New Scientist* reports, "The British government has sanctioned insurance companies' requests for the results of genetic tests. This makes Britain the first country to give official approval to insurers' use of human genetic information to refuse coverage or increase premiums." See also *genetic underclass*.

Pay-As-You-Go Insurance — Progressive, the country's fifth largest insurer, has been testing a system that lets drivers pay based on a simple principle: your rate is based on how much you drive, and the kind of roads you use. For generations, the insurance industry has been structured by general risk factors; no individualized pricing has ever existed. Progressive tracks drivers via a satellite—a transmitter called the Autograph gets installed in each car—and they are charged by how much they drive and where. Thus far, drivers in Houston have saved an average of 25 percent on their premiums. Of course, there are privacy issues: is it worth the savings for an insurance company to know your whereabouts every time you get behind the wheel? These concerns aside, *DOF* predicts that pay-as-you-go will become a widely accepted concept. It's another example of how technology creates more accurate and efficient transactional structures; see also *transparent pricing, road-pricing*.

PERM — a new way to value companies, which challenges (or at least supplements) the old P/E (price/earnings) model. PERM stands for price divided by the total of earnings plus research plus marketing. It's a way to compare companies by valuing their investment in R&D and marketing, which, in theory, are critical parts of a company's prospects that the traditional P/E model doesn't account for. See also *shock accounting*.

Pump and Dump — the technique, basically illegal, of buying a stock, using the Internet to drive the price up and then getting out of it. What you do is go into chat rooms, send phony email messages and generally mislead the markets using the power and speed of the Internet. A 15 year old used pump and dump tactics to make more than $250,000 in the stock market; the humorless SEC tracked him down and made him give it back.

SAM — short for "shared appreciation mortgage." Though introduced with a whimper two decades ago, *DOF* notes that they are re-appearing, and we believe they will become an important part of home-buying due to a number of reasons. SAMs, unlike traditional mortgages, let the borrower and the lender "share" any appreciation. And in return for its participation in future profits, the lender—usually a bank—accepts a lower down payment (as little as 20 percent) and charges a lower interest rate (up to 3 percent less).

Conditions are ripe for SAMs. Housing prices are still high. The demand for second homes is increasing. And cash-rich banks are looking for places to invest. *DOF* expects that SAMs will become one of the most widely adopted new mortgage options since the ARM decades ago, and that they will enter the commercial real estate market as well.

Single-Stock Futures — for years, investors were not permitted to trade futures in single stocks. You could buy a stock on margin—and pay a minimum of 50 percent in cash—but you couldn't trade futures, because it was seen as too dangerous. The Commodity Futures Modernization Act of 2000 has changed that, to the dismay of many. As Frank Partnoy, professor at the University of San Diego Law School, writes, "the new single-stock futures could be dangerous—for the market as well as for individual investors . . . you can buy stock futures with very little cash up front. For $1000 you might buy $10,000 worth of stock futures, or even more." Partnoy believes that savvy financial services companies will aggressively market single stock futures, creating futures-based products that mask the risk. Investors, who don't always act rationally (see *behav-*

ioral finance), will over-commit, and if they bet wrong, says Partnoy, they "will simultaneously dump their portfolios to pay their debts to brokers, causing stocks to crash." *DOF* predicts that single-stock futures will enter our investment vocabulary, and that, after some well-publicized disasters, Congress will limit or ban them once again.

TIPS — short for "Treasury Inflation-Protection Securities," this investment provides safety (TIPS are guaranteed by the U.S. government) while providing inflation protection (TIPS are indexed against the cost of living), thus making them an important portfolio asset. Though they have been around for a number of years, not many investors know about them because of our focus on the NASDAQ in the nineties. *DOF* expects to see TIPS gain in popularity in the years to come.

Uncle Visa — a name that has been bestowed, rather lovingly, upon the Visa card by those who have started entrepreneurial businesses—or shot their first film—by obtaining multiple Visa cards and maxxing out the credit limits on each. *DOF* wonders why Visa hasn't seized upon this as a marketing opportunity. What could be more appealing than demonstrating how your product makes the entrepreneurial dreams and artistic visions of Americans a reality? We can imagine Web site testimonials, a documentary film, a book of success stories.

Warm Currency — a term that describes private, local currencies that are the transaction exchange mechanism of the barter economy. Here's how this works in Calgary, Canada: "At Kensington's Sunnyside Market, a bag of carrots can be bought for babysitting time. At Trend clothing store . . . snow shoveling can purchase a pair of pants. Soon, home-grown vegetables may be used to pay for city utility bills. What started out as an idea four years ago in Calgary has steadily grown into a formidable economic force." We believe that an explosion of these warm currencies will surprise just about everyone; expect major marketers and retailers to join the warm currency movement. See also *barter credits*.

Entrepreneurs Channel — a cable channel devoted to entrepreneurs who are trying to raise start-up capital. The audience will be potential investors as well as those watching for the sheer fun and entertainment of seeing the pitch. Business opportunities will range from technology to retail to, we're sure, Ralph Kramden–like schemes. (Of course, there will be a Web site where you can read the full business plan.) While there are some Internet sites that offer this, there's no substitute for watching the entrepreneurs themselves pitch their ideas, so investors can ask themselves: Is that the gleam of a billion-dollar business in his eye, or is he just plain crazy?

401-K'd — if you're expecting your retirement plan to keep you living in the style to which you have become accustomed— be prepared to be 401-K'd. The decline in the value of our 401-K plans, along with the cost of retirement—particularly with our extended lifespans and the hidden costs of life without a paycheck—will result in millions of rude awakenings. *DOF* believes that as a result, retirements will either be postponed, or alternatively, sunset careers will be launched. See also *BABOONS, transitional retirement.*

Fund of Funds — mutual funds offer one level of diversification; this fund of funds offers still another. Rather than investing, say $10,000, in a single fund, investors would invest ten grand in the fund of funds—which, in turn, allocates the money across a number of funds in different fund families. These are selected based on various computer algorithms as having the best potential for future growth.

Indoor Information — hey, anyone can get inside information today—who doesn't know someone who knows someone else who just heard something really big? That's why the next step in tipsterland will be indoor information—the ultra-insider stuff.

Socially Irresponsible Investing — socially responsible funds are mutual funds that operate with screens and filters that eliminate companies that sell tobacco, that pollute, that do businesses in countries with repressive governments and so forth. Committed investors, and many pension funds, own these funds. As a reaction to these politically correct funds, *DOF* predicts that at least one socially *irresponsible* fund will emerge. Its holdings: companies cited for pollution, companies in the casino business, companies that make sub-par loans to consumers at exorbitant interest rates and other unabashedly capitalist organizations. Now here's an ethical question: Who does more for society, an investor who puts his money into a socially responsible fund, and keeps all the profits—or one who invests in a socially irresponsible fund, and gives all the profits away to charity? Let us know by email what you think at www.dictionaryofthefuture.com.

Specurators — those who speculate on interest rates and the vagaries of the Federal Reserve Bank; will grow in number as an increasing number of new financial products will be linked to interest rate movement. (Contributed by Frank Thomas.)

TEST — tax-exempt savings treatment. Concerned by our extremely low national savings rate, the government will introduce a trial plan to see if it can encourage increased savings. Consumers will be able to open special TEST accounts, and depending upon your income, a certain percentage of interest will be tax-free if it remains in the account for a fixed amount of time.

PHILANTHROPY AND NONPROFITS

What is called the "third sector" had been in a time warp for generations. The nonprofit world, though profoundly well-intentioned, often lacked accountability, rejected sophisticated marketing and communications strategies, and saw no reason for cooperation or partnering with the private sector—other than raising money from it.

That was then. The third sector has exploded into change, driven in large part by two trends: the shifting nature of wealth, creating younger philanthropists who are applying the business principles that helped them achieve their fortunes through the concept of "venture philanthropy," and changes in American business—bursty entrepreneurship, squashed hierarchies, a distaste for business as usual.

This section throbs with the new vitality of the world of philanthropy, including the use of technology to solve social problems, as reflected in the work of the Sustainable Science Institute, and the development of innovations such as "self-adjusting eyeglasses." Because of this ferment, there are many *DOF* predictions in this section, including an "Adopt-a-Building" concept, and the notion of "corporate-backed bonds" as a mechanism to help nonprofits access additional capital for their worthy goals. At this pace, the for-profit world will be borrowing the techniques of its nonprofit sibling, rather than the other way around.

Conversion Foundations — little known but important vehicles in the nonprofit world. When a tax exempt asset is sold—for example a nonprofit hospital—federal law requires that the money from the sale continues to serve the community. Conversion foundations were created to manage that transition; there are currently nearly 150 of them, and one report—published by Grantmakers in Health—estimates their combined assets at nearly $16 billion. This is a stunning amount of money which can significantly change the philanthropic picture in a community. However, some argue that all too often, the foundations have adopted far too broad a definition of their mission, and as a result their funds are actually used to support for-profit heath institutions, never finding their way down to those who need it most. A good overview of the complexities of the issue can be found at: www.thenation.com/doc.mhtml?i=20001218&c=5&s=fuentes.

eBus — former Oakland and Seattle city buses have been converted into teaching "vehicles" in Los Angeles (shades of the old bookmobile). It's an innovative effort that is the brainchild of the nonprofit Community College Foundation and Wells Fargo Bank. The eBus travels to community centers and other locations to teach residents of low income communities how to go online, and use the Internet for health information, educational support and for addressing family problems. Each eBus will have 20 PCs and one or two instructors. What a great use for buses that are headed for the scrap heap, and for all those millions of PCs that companies get rid of each year in the constant march to upgrading. *DOF* envisions more of them will hit the road, including some eBuses which blend nonprofit and for-profit activities; for example, Dell or Compaq could fund the buses, and sell hardware at the same time.

GAVI — the Global Alliance for Vaccines and Immunizations, a nonprofit group started in 1999 with a donation of $750 million from the Bill and Melinda Gates Foundation. GAVI's goal: to vaccinate the millions of children—25 percent of all the kids in the world—who are not protected against scourges such as polio, diphtheria and TB. It is estimated that every 10 seconds, a child dies from a preventable disease, which is why we will be seeing a world focus on this tragedy, and why GAVI—with the Gates fortune behind it—will soon be as well-known as UNICEF and CARE. Vaccinating children in poor countries is more complex than it might seem; for example, many vaccines need to be refrigerated, and maintaining the "cool chain" in hot areas with no electricity poses a real problem. (One solution, reports the *Economist*, is to "hitch a ride on Coca-Cola trucks, which reach places not even marked on maps.") *DOF* expects to see GAVI's name—and mission—gain currency through cause-marketing programs and the support of the entertainment community. See also *Sustainable Science Institute.*

MBA Enterprise Corps — also dubbed the Business Peace Corps. A volunteer program which sends MBA graduates to various emerging economies for one year to help local businesses. *DOF* expects this program to grow dramatically in the years to come, as wealthy MBA holders seek to find innovative, personal expressions of philanthropy. We also expect corporations to start giving one-year leaves of absence as they encourage their senior management to participate in the program.

Nondirected Donation — if there is a better display of altruism, we haven't heard it yet. Nondirected donation is when you decide to give up an organ, without specifying the beneficiary. There are more than 70,000 people awaiting organs, and each year thousands on the list die while waiting. Joyce Roush, who deserves mention here, is a Baltimore nurse who decided to donate a kidney to a stranger; it ended up saving the life of a 13-year-old boy. *DOF* predicts that nondirected donations will increase over the years, as procedure becomes less risky and the need to make a difference, in the most powerful of all ways, becomes more central.

Self-Adjusting Eyeglasses — there are one billion people in the world—including 10 percent of all schoolchildren—who need glasses but have no access to them. A company called Adaptive Eyecare, in England, is working to change that. They have developed a prototype of a self-correcting lens that can normalize the vision of 90 percent of us. The lenses are filled with a liquid and are adjusted by a pump by the user; the entire unit costs just $10. This could have enormous public health benefits—no trained optometrist, no inventory of lenses required. What a perfect opportunity for some innovative corporate philanthropy.

Sustainable Science Institute — a nonprofit started by MacArthur Genius Award winner Eva Harris. Her group identifies ways for third world countries to diagnose and treat disease using what Harris calls "appropriate technology." In places like Nicargua, where there is not even reliable access to electricity and water, she has innovated new and improvisational ways to identify DNA. Go to www.ssilink.org and learn more about what this remarkable and visionary group is doing.

Venture Philanthropy — a new approach which finds wealthy benefactors taking a more active role in their nonprofit work, as opposed to just passively contributing. (This new generation of philathropists is also called "social entrepreneurs.") They set goals, are involved operationally and demand performance. Sometimes, benefactors employ the principles of venture capital to create their own projects, setting objectives, strategies and benchmarks for success. Venture philanthropy, which is inspired by the aggressiveness and performance drive of today's new benefactors, will shake up the traditional world of philanthropy where accountability is not generally part of the culture.

Dictionary of the Future Predicts

Adopt-a-Building — a logical and long overdue extension of the successful "Adopt a Highway" campaign. Major U.S. corporations will adopt apartment buildings in inner-city neighborhoods—usually in their own communities—supplying funds for renovation, Internet access and improved security, and also providing an opportunity for employees to volunteer for tutoring and job training. And of course, they gain the bragging rights to signage that says, "455 Elm Street has been adopted by Alcoa."

Advocacy Products — we expect the larger nonprofits, e.g., the Audubon Society, the Sierra Club, AMFAR and so forth, to begin to market their own branded products that reflect their core mission and values, either directly or through license arrangements. These will allow you to show your support of a nonprofit by direct purchase of products you'd buy anyway, e.g., environmentally safe disposable diapers with the Sierra Club brand, organic apple juice from Friends of the Earth. It's taking the successful Girl Scout cookie model to a broader and higher level. Considering that the first Girl Scout cookies were baked in 1917, it's quite remarkable that no one has innovated in this area since then.

Babyanthropy — a new genre of philanthropy that targets the young and the wealthy, given the need nonprofits have to cultivate new sources of revenue. Some institutions have started the process of creating new categories to attract baby philanthropists—but the work has just begun. The Metropolitan Museum of Art of New York, for example, has an Apollo Program targeted to those affluent youngies who are 21 to 39; Lincoln Center has a Young Patron's Program for those in their twenties and thirties who have contributed between $250 and $1,000. *DOF* avers that it won't be long before every alert nonprofit has a babyanthropy initiative of its own.

Contextual Fund-Raising — there you are, buying a book from Amazon.com, and a pop-up window appears that asks you to donate money to a nonprofit that buys books for poor children. Or you're on a Web site doing research on diabetes and a message appears asking you to contribute to the Juvenile Diabetes Association. You can imagine the possibilities. That will be the new art—and science—of contextual fund-raising, motivating you to give on an immediate, visceral level by catching you at the right time, and linking your behavior (or concerns) to a specific cause.

Corporate-Backed Bonds — nonprofits will raise money in the public markets by issuing bonds that are backed by large corporations. For example, the American Cancer Society will raise $10 million for a public awareness campaign and Ford will stand behind payment of the debt. That will allow the ACS to borrow money at a low interest rate; Ford performs a philanthropic service that will cost it no money, as long as the ACS makes good on the debt. This is a win-win innovation that we believe can provide nonprofits with access to capital they have never had before.

Give-Backing — a form of philanthropy in which a benefactor buys and returns an object to its rightful owner. Example: Peter Norton buys the Joyce Maynard letters at the Sotheby sale and returns them to Salinger, to protect his privacy. We expect this trend to grow, with wealthy individuals buying everything from Native American burial artifacts to African tribal masks, and returning them to where they came from originally, and where they belong.

Hip-Help — stung by criticism that they take money out of the inner city without putting anything back, the rap community will launch a philanthropic effort called Hip-Help.

Immersion Philanthropy — nonprofits, in their search for new ways to capture the public's attention, will create dramatic three-dimensional worlds. An early example of this: a walk-through refugee camp created by the group Doctors Without Borders. The replica of the camp was constructed in New York's Central Park, as well as other cities across the country. *Time Out New York* described it as having "shelter tents, nutrition areas and health clinics"; visitors will be led by guides, either refugees themselves or volunteers from Doctors Without Borders. While critics will decry the theme-park nature of it, immersion philanthropy will be a valuable tool for waking people up. What Kafka wrote about literature applies here: it should be an icepick to break the frozen sea within us.

Language Extinction — the globalization of the planet, and the rise of the Internet, where English is the primary language, conspire to threaten many local languages and dialects. *DOF* predicts that language extinction will capture our attention and we will see fund-raising concerts, cause-marketing programs and other activities normally associated with endangered species, for endangered languages.

Nonprofit Savings Bonds — these will take the successful marketing formula of U.S. Savings bonds, and apply it to the nonprofit world. Here's an example of how *DOF* sees it working: the World Wildlife Fund, partnering with a bank, offers Wildlife Savings Bonds at denominations of $50, $100 and beyond; they are priced at a discount to face value, just like savings bonds are, and have varying maturities. It's a win-win: the gift giver gets a chance to support a worthwhile cause, while giving a gift that is less impersonal than cash, while the nonprofit has a vehicle to raise millions for its cause.

Non-Profiteering — a *DOF* coinage to describe what happens when wealthy nonprofit organizations decide to sell their vast holdings of land. As *The New York Times* reports, soaring land values have encouraged many nonprofits to cash in. That includes the MacArthur Foundation (bestowers of the famous Genius awards) which sold 15,000 acres in Florida, and Rockefeller University, which sold their holdings in a suburb north of New York City to Donald Trump, who intends to build a golf course. Environmentalists, and local property owners, are outraged. But aren't nonprofits supposed to make the most of their assets? It's a real moral dilemma, and one that won't go away.

PRIVACY

In 1890, in their famous essay "The Right to Privacy," Supreme Court Justices Louis Brandeis and Samuel Warren warned against invasions of our privacy from "modern enterprise and invention."

They couldn't have been more accurate. More than 100 years later, in his novel *Ravelstein*, Saul Bellow picks up where they left off: "The crooks learn to get ahead of high technology like inventive bacteria that outwit the pharmaceuticals, while the brainy researchers in the labs figure out how to stay ahead. Little campus geniuses, outsmarting the Pentagon."

For all these reasons, if we were drafting the Bill of Rights today, it is likely that the right of privacy would join the other exalted protections that we have. Consider the threats to it—from privacy invaders like "Packet Sniffing" technologies and "Project Echelon"—both of which push us to the limit of what *DOF* calls our "Intrusion Threshold." And it's not just the Internet that poses the dangers, although it certainly enriches them; microprocessors in our cars and eventually our clothing will make our whereabouts known just about every minute of the day.

Driven by these invasions, privacy protection promises to be a multibillion- dollar industry, with innovations like "Omniva's" disappearing email and Zero-Knowledge's "nyms" hoping to grab their share. Of course, privacy is an issue not just for individuals but businesses as well. It will be one of the most passionate and far-reaching struggles of this century, as privacy-invading technology battles privacy-enabling technology in a bloodless but high-stakes war.

Address Munging — a way of modifying one's email address to prevent spamming; the address changes in such a way that computers can't read it, but humans can. It's a kind of Internet judo, because it transfers power to the person being attacked. For info, check out: www.members.aol.com/emailfaq/mungfag.html.

Carnivore — the original name for the FBI tracking system that can follow each and every email to its source. They claim it's for criminal and national security issues only, but privacy advocates are up in arms about its potential to invade our personal space. Even though the government has changed the name to the more benign-sounding DCS 1000, what hasn't changed is the intensity of the debate.

The E-911 Bill — Congress has passed a bill which establishes 911 as a universal emergency number for cell phones. It sounds like an apple pie and motherhood idea—which is why the Senate approved it unanimously. But there is a dark side to this. In order for the network to work, emergency service personnel need to have access to the precise location you are calling from. This information is enormously valuable to marketers who want to send you email messages about Burger King as you're approaching the vicinity (see also *geo-targeting*). Distressingly, they could gain access to that personal information through this same legislation, since the FCC has ruled that wireless carriers can sell location information to third parties *without your approval.* It's the law of unintended consequences: the emergency number system creates its very own privacy emergency.

Hundredth Window — an Internet privacy metaphor, which became the title of a book about the subject by Charles Jennings and Lori Fener. The idea is that no matter how careful you are, no matter how many security devices you have on your windows, it is likely that you will leave just one of them unprotected; in which case, you're done. Everyone can—and will—know everything about you. And there will truly be nowhere left to hide.

Identity Theft — when a criminal gains access to your vital information—name, social security number, credit card data—and begins to buy products, sign leases or even enter into other kinds of contracts posing as you. It's the largest kind of white-collar crime, and it happens to half a million people every year. In fact, the incidence is growing because of the amount of personal information available over the Internet; there are dozens of Web sites, where, for a small fee, you can get anyone's social security number, which begins the process. Many people don't realize it until they do a credit search for one reason or another. The cost of unraveling the mess—which often involves hiring a lawyer—can be significant. That's why Travelers offers identity fraud insurance—because today it doesn't take an alien to enter your body and take it over, just a smart criminal.

Iris Code — a fraud-protection device based on the unique pattern found in the iris of each individual eye. A computer scans your eye—from as far as three feet away—digitizes the results and then matches it to a stored pattern. If you're successfully identified you get to withdraw cash from an ATM, open your car door or get on a plane. (This technology was actually foreshadowed in Ian Fleming's James Bond novel *Never Say Die*.) Supposedly it works if you're wearing contacts or even sunglasses. But will criminals try to outwit the system with counterfeit iris pattern contact lenses? See also *biometrics*.

Nyms — "untraceable pseudonymous digital identities," according to the *Atlantic Monthly*, which enable you to travel the Internet, or send email, without anyone tracking you. Nyms are available through the Freedom Network, which is offered by privacy innovators Zero-Knowledge (www.zero-knowledge. com) out of Montreal. Their mission is to develop pervasive technology that gets installed in PCs and other devices so consumers will ask, "Is it privacy-enabled?"

Omniva — both a company (www.omniva.com) and a technology that enable the user to have total control over email messages. With Omniva you can specify how long you want your emails to remain readable, whether they were sent or forwarded. The current alternative: your emails will remain in your computer's hardware, where they can be viewed by your employer, or by anyone else in the event of litigation. As privacy concerns elevate, we see this and related technologies moving to the front burner. The next trick—letting you hit a key that makes those really impetuous ones disappear before they arrive in the first place. See also *ERR.*

Packet-Sniffing — the monitoring of data traveling over a network. Packets, which are digital chunks of data, can be analyzed for key words or phrases—by the government, for example, or potentially by private investigators or employers. Packet-sniffing could mean that any and all of your emails are vulnerable; it's one of the many aspects of the Internet that's got privacy watchdogs sniffing around themselves. See also *Carnivore, Project Echelon.*

PII — personally identifiable information. All those little digital breadcrumbs we leave: a credit card number on a Web site, a transaction at a cash machine, an insurance form submitted to an HMO, an extended warranty. More than 200 categories of PII can be tracked and stored—and with the growth of wireless communication, even more are coming. Beyond increasing the risk of *identity theft* (see listing), many believe that some of the fundamental underpinnings of a free society are being threatened. Expect a powerful anti-tracking, anti-PII movement to erupt, cutting across political lines. Also expect anti-PII training programs.

Project Echelon — a massive spy network that is coordinated by the U.S. National Security Agency, in partnership with the U.K., Australia, New Zealand and Canada. Reportedly, it's capable of monitoring just about every telephone call, fax, email or other electronic transmission. Echelon is not designed for military spying, but to monitor governments, individuals and companies—as well as terrorists. Highly classified for a long time, details are now emerging. "A grid of listening posts linked to supercomputers" is how the *Economist*

describes it. As you would expect, privacy advocates are up in arms; if you are, too, check out: www.echelonwatch.org. Here's a question for our friends at the NSA: If you're going to read our emails, can you please fix any typos you find at the same time?

TRUSTe — a nonprofit group that awards a privacy seal to those Web sites that do not share consumers' buying history or track Web visitation. Currently, the seal is hidden away in a corner of most Web sites, but we believe that as the privacy wars rage on, we will be seeing a bigger and bolder use of the TRUSTe symbol. We also see an opportunity for TRUSTe to move off the Internet to bricks and mortar retailers, as well as catalogs—since both of those merchant classes are busy making a profit off our name and buying habits through their mailing lists and databases.

Dictionary of the Future Predicts

Corporate Stalkers — companies who aggressively track consumer behavior, both online and offline, and then market it. See also *chief privacy officer*.

Intrusion Threshold — we all accept a certain amount of privacy compromise, but we also have our intrusion threshold, a limit to how far the government or corporations can go as they track us. This limit will be expressed by boycotts, political activism and demands for privacy protection. While some consumers don't mind a cookie in their hard drive, others will avoid observation at almost any cost. See also *no tracers*.

No Tracers — describes those who aggressively avoid behavior that lets the government, corporations and other institutions learn about their individual behavior. Viewed as paranoid by some, no tracers pay cash, avoid ATMs, use pay phones not cell phones, would never consider any of the electronic toll payment systems and spend hundreds on computer security software that blocks E-vesdropping.

Outcognito — the opposite of incognito, it's the trend of celebrities seeking visibility at restaurants, sporting events and industry gatherings. Magazines like *People, Talk, Vanity Fair* and *InStyle* prove that celebrities, given the proper flattery, are more interested in going outcognito than incognito.

Privacy Guards — an intelligent agent that will travel with you, from Web site to Web site, automatically disabling any tracking mechanism. (It outsmarts the cookies.) Web surfers will contract with privacy guards on a per day, per month or annual basis. (Who will offer them? Start-up entrepreneurs of course, but *DOF* also sees an opportunity for companies already in the security business like Pinkerton and Brinks.) Currently all the privacy mechanisms on the Internet are passive—in other words, you have to rely on the representations of a Web site or search engine. Privacy guards will be proactive, giving an individual the ability to disable the observers and trackers rather than relying on someone else's questionable promises.

RELIGION AND SPIRITUALITY

If there is any institution in our lives that we expect to be fixed, not variable, it's religion. But America makes everything its own, which is why this section contains so many examples of change in an area that has traditionally been one of the slowest to react to the new.

These shifts are the result, in part, of forces outside religion itself. Environmentalism—which is expanding from the fight for specific causes to the development of a new approach to living on the planet—is responsible for the "eco-Kosher" movement. The sheer amount of time we spend at work, combined with a gnawing doubt about our winner-take-all-society, is responsible for "corporate spirituality." (As for the amount of time we spend in our cars, it is the basis for a *DOF* prediction: "Auto Services," religious services delivered to a congregation over satellite radio.)

New Age values have helped to shape and direct the growing Home Funeral Movement, which is also a way to take control of this most intensely private movement from the "grief industry." Major social problems—like the cost of prescription drugs—are energizing traditional faiths to use their moral high ground, what *DOF* is calling the "God Lobby." Technology, never a stranger to religion—the first printed book, remember, was a bible—brings us the phenomena of "share prayer" and "distance healing." The search for "spiritual intelligence" claims to have identified a physical "God spot" in the brain.

We continue to search for ways to reconcile our need for faith with the unrelenting demands and pressures in our lives. These reconciliations, adjustments and permutations require a new secular liturgy.

Rr

Church Planting — the practice by which evangelical congregations establish multiple small groups of core worshippers who then "grow" into full-fledged churches.

Corporate Spirituality — policies, formal or informal, that provide workplace time for employee meditation or prayer, and for talks and/or employee discussion on spirituality. These are often initiated by the human resources department in the effort to keep valuable employees happy (deeply happy, in fact) by meeting the full range of human needs. It is also seen as a means for accelerating employee creativity. Corporate spirituality is also indicative of the blurring of home and work; as the influence of traditional spiritual groups wanes, some people look to the workplace to pick up the slack. And if you have a really bad fourth quarter, and need some group prayer, the team will be prepared to help.

Distance Healing — a New Age practice which permits the healer to solve spiritual and physical problems from a remote location. For those so inclined, there are thousands of Internet sites on the subject, including one that can address the needs of your pet—www.the-dhn.net/pets.htm. See also *share prayer*.

Eco-Kosher — a trend that has some observant Jews combining the Biblical imperatives of keeping kosher with principles of environmentalism. For example, these Jews are extending their principles to include rejection of genetically modified foods, to the use of only recycled materials in their homes and so forth. They find support for this not just in their personal ethics, but in the Bible, citing a number of references including this "green" injunction from Deuteronomy: "When in your war against a city you have besieged it a long time in order to capture it, you must not destroy its trees, wielding the ax against them. You may eat of them but you must not cut them down."

Home Funeral Movement — a national trend that rejects funeral homes and encourages individuals to make their own arrangements, either for burial or cremation. An outgrowth of the hospice movement, it was inspired by Lisa Carlson who wrote *Caring for Your Own Dead* based on her own experience. Now, organizations such as the Natural Death Care Project in California advise families on the legal steps they must take for a home funeral. It's the ultimate stage in cocooning, and the ultimate rejection of the formulaic, routinized, depersonalized nature of death in America.

Intelligent Design Theory — the latest alternative to Darwinian evolutionary biology. Rather than arguing that the Bible is literal fact—as creationism does—intelligent design theorists concede that the earth is billions of years old, but posit an "intelligent designer" rather than evolution to explain how we got where we are. (It reminds us of Einstein's statement, "The mathematical precision of the universe reveals the mathematical mind of God.") They argue that certain complex cellular structures could never have been arrived at through an evolutionary process. Many intelligent design supporters were persuaded by Dr. Michael J. Behe's book *Darwin's Black Box: The Biochemical Challenges to Evolution.*

In Michigan, nine legislators introduced a bill to amend educational practice and put intelligent design on the same level as evolution; in Pennsylvania, as *The New York Times* writes, "officials are close to adopting educational standards that would allow the teaching of theories on the origin and development of life other than evolution." As this theory gains momentum, is there another Scopes trial in the offing?

Share Prayer — the power and reach of the Internet is put to work on behalf of those who believe in the efficacy of prayer—individually and collectively—see www.theprayersite.com. See also *distance healing.*

Spiritual Intelligence — advocated by Danah Zohar and Ian Marshall—(their book is called *SQ: The Ultimate Intelligence*)—spiritual intelligence is something that all of us possess, to varying degrees. The argument is not just philosophical; they point to 40-Hz oscillations across the brain, which, they argue, bind perceptual and cognitive events into an integrated whole.

Rr

A key part of spiritual intelligence: a "God Spot" located in the temporal lobes. We see this intriguing hypothesis catching fire, as it aligns with so many trends, and anticipate that it will create an entire growth industry: books, tapes, seminars. Politicians and religious leaders will grab onto spiritual intelligence as well.

Taize — a method of Christian prayer that is increasingly attracting young men and women; it involves readings from the Bible, chanting and meditation. Named after a village in France where Brother Roger, a Swiss monk who developed the movement, hid refugees from Nazi Germany. "Many U.S. churches in mainstream Catholic and Protestant denominations are adding Taize to their menu of services, not least because of its popularity with young people," writes *The Wall Street Journal.*

Tumo — a Tibetan meditation technique used most often during times of illness or extreme stress. You concentrate on an image of fire within your body, which purifies body and spirit, while purging the demons. Expect to see a growing audience for tumo techniques, as the search for natural healing and stress-reduction measures continues.

Dictionary of the Future Predicts

Auto Services — the ability of *satellite radio* (see listing) to deliver narrowly targeted content, combined with the increasing time we're spending in our cars, will lead houses of worship to create morning and evening "Auto Services." A minister, priest or rabbi addresses his or her individual congregation on the way to or from work.

Bible SAT Classes — *DOF* believes that our college preparation focus (see *madmission*) will combine with religious education to create Bible SAT classes. All the SAT questions, from analogies to vocabulary to critical reading, will be posed through biblical subjects and themes.

Faith-Based Business — *DOF* predicts that the intersection of business and religion will become a more active phenomenon. We define faith-based businesses as those that are focused both on their greater responsibility to the community, as well as incorporating religious principles into their everyday activities. Kao, the large Japanese consumer goods company (they own Jergens, among other brands) embodies the principles of Zen Buddhism in its management approach. This includes the principle of *kangyo ichijo*, which—as the *Financial Times* reported—is about finding many paths to the truth, or "investigating business ideas until something is learned, often without the manager realizing it." Faith-based businesses won't be doing missionary work, but will be applying the values and philosophical intensity of religion to the challenges of running a contemporary corporation: balancing profit and responsibility, creating loyalty, motivating employees, making "work" a part of something larger, rather than an all-consuming focus.

God Lobby — it isn't just politicians and consumer groups who are beating up the drug companies—religion is now getting into the fight. The Interfaith Council on Corporate Responsibility is coordinating efforts by a number of religious groups that are intended to put pressure on them to do something about drug costs. Using their position as shareholders, they have put resolutions in front of 10 large pharmaceutical manufacturers. *DOF* believes that the drug companies will have to make some serious concessions in the very near future—there is too much concerted pressure. Ralph Nader is one thing—ministers, priests and rabbis are something else. We also believe the God Lobby, as we're calling it, will move beyond drugs and take a more active role as moral and ethical advocates in the consumer marketplace. See also *bureauclout.*

Imagination Therapists — a new kind of therapeutic counselor who will assist individuals who want to regain their capacity for dreaming, for stretching their imagination and creative reach. Why is this necessary? Because the dominance of computers and the Internet structure breeds linear thinking—we

Rr

click from site to site, toggle from program to program. Thus, we get progressively narrower and narrower—following a single thread—which destroys our natural gift of wonder. Imagination therapy frees us from these restrictive patterns—it's a psychic emancipation. These therapists will combine elements of yoga, Jungian therapy and other mind-freeing techniques to put us back in touch with a childhood connection to the logic of the impossible. See also *lucid dreaming*.

Jerusalem Syndrome — when an individual believes he or she is actually a Biblical prophet of one kind or another. The condition was identified as long ago as 1982 by Dr. Yair Bar-El, who runs Jerusalem's municipal psychiatric hospital, where they've treated King David, Samson, Jesus and the Virgin Mary, among others. The twist, as we see it, is that this richly evocative term will start to be used to describe anyone who believes he or she is the savior—of a company for example, but also of a sports team, a university, any organization or institution. We've all seen the new hire with the Jerusalem Syndrome—and we've all seen what usually happens when the worship stops. See also *saviorize*.

Does outer space matter? Probably not since the days of the *Apollo* program, when America was gripped by man-on-the-moon fever, has space been as relevant, either emotionally or practically.

We care about "space weather" because it affects our cell phones and other telecommunications. We will care about "BLAST" and "UWB" because they have the potential to deliver vast quantities of data, through space, over wireless systems. We might care about "space bugs"—because of their infectious potential—and about the "Kuiper Belt," where asteroids with Earth-destroying potential are orbiting.

Our ancestors looked up at the heavens, saw how insignificant they themselves were, and invented a language of gods and myths to explain it. We gaze upward and see the potential for profit, for terror (*DOF* predicts a new kind of satellite terrorism), and for boundless travel—the Cassini Mission is scheduled to reach Saturn around July 1, 2004—and invent new language for the outer reaches of what we can know.

Aerobots — in their simplest terms, space balloons. As NASA puts it, "These are unmanned scientific exploration vehicles designed to float like balloons for up to several months in the atmospheres of planets . . . equipped to conduct sophisticated observational programs from their unique vantage points." Aerobots are able to come much closer to the surface than satellites and thus are extraordinarily useful for investigative purposes.

Astrotel — a hotel designed for space tourists, perhaps even making its way between the Earth, the Moon and Mars. So far it's just one of those drawing-board doodles at NASA, but predictions suggest it will be in existence by 2040. Remember to take the thirtieth edition of *DOF*— brain-implanted version of course—along for the trip.

BLAST — short for Bell Labs Layered Space-Time, BLAST has the potential to be a revolutionary new way to coax more bandwidth from existing frequencies. Simply put, BLAST sends multiple signals over a single frequency, which are captured and "unscrambled" by 16 antennae at the receiving end of the transmission. If tests continue to be promising, and the system can be commercialized, BLAST might be able to deliver far more quantities of data over wireless systems than ever before.

Cassini Mission — a spacecraft that is right now, as you read this, hurtling toward Saturn. It is expected to land around July 1, 2004, and to start sending back all sorts of valuable information immediately thereafter. What's important about Saturn is that its rings contain matter which enable us to "observe processes that were ongoing in the very early life of our solar system," according to Dr. Carolyn Porco, who is the leader of the team. In other words, Saturn will help us understand earth because it's a living portrait of the way we were. See also *geomicrobiology*.

Free-Space Optics — can also be described by the shorthand "wireless fiber." In the search of ever-increasing bandwidth, why be limited by fiber-optics? Free-space optics is a technology that sends photons—particles of light—through the air. These photons, boosted by lasers and optical amplifiers, send voice, video and data straight to the desktop thanks to a series of transceivers and telescopes that transport the digital information. (Unlike radio frequencies, no licenses are required.) Since it is estimated that only 5 percent of office buildings are equipped with fiber, free-space optics is an amazing growth area. Investors take note: Avanex and LanOptics are two companies involved in this industry.

Interplanetary Protocol — Vinton Cerf, who was the co-developer of the TCP/IP transmission technology that allowed the Internet to step into the world-sculpting role it has assumed, is working with NASA and DARPA (the division of the Defense Department that helped launch the Internet itself) on a system that will enable communication between the planets, say email between earth and those living (or vacationing) on Mars. Plans are for it to be working by 2008. *DOF* philosophical question: Does an email make a noise if it arrives and nobody hears it?

The Kuiper Belt — if you're worried about asteroids creating a catastrophic event here on earth, direct your attention to the Kuiper Belt, a danger zone in the vicinity of Neptune that is the unfortunate landlord of around 100,000 ice-balls, each of which is more than 50 miles in diameter. If one of those breaks free and makes it all the way to our planet, then all those hours you've spent in the gym won't mean a thing. (Remember that 99 percent of all species that ever lived are now extinct.) See also *asteroid anxiety.*

LIDAR — stands for light-based radar, which measures air conditions by tracking the dispersal of light by small airborne particles. LIDAR, which is in its early stages of development, has a number of possible applications; one of the most important is airline safety, specifically as it relates to clear air turbulence (CAT), which is one of the most threatening conditions a pilot faces. CAT is relatively common—storms are actually responsible for only 40 percent of all turbulence problems—and pilots currently have no way to detect it in advance. Early tests of LIDAR showed it effective and *DOF* expects public pressure (any passenger who's ever felt the impact of violent turbulence knows what we mean) to accelerate its implementation.

Lightcraft — a new kind of laser propulsion system, initially for satellites. Infrared lasers are focused on the Lightcraft, which in turn concentrates them for propulsion purposes. As the Air Force Research Laboratory describes it, "this focused laser light is so intense that it rips the air molecules apart and tears the electrons from the resulting atoms of oxygen and nitrogen, thus forming a high temperature plasma . . . that literally explodes out the back end." The technology could allow satellites to be launched far more economically than now, and imagine what else this laser propulsion could be used for: aircraft, missiles, high-speed ships.

Liquid Mirror Telescopes — a new technology (albeit with roots that go back to Sir Isaac Newton) that replaces a rigid mirror with a liquid—a small amount of mercury—that is placed into a container and then rotated. The spinning spreads the mercury into a thin layer that, according to the *Economist*, "is a liquid mirror as accurately shaped as a conventional rigid one—but at about 1 percent of the cost." They go on to write that low-cost telescopes could revolutionize the nature of astronomy: "individual research groups could have their own telescopes, instead of having to book time on shared instruments months in advance . . . having sole use of a dedicated telescope would make new kinds of research possible, too." It's the equivalent of the move from mainframes to a PC on every desk.

Roton — right now, launching a satellite is hugely expensive. But what if it could be done far more economically—with a reusable vehicle? Roton—a cylindrically shaped vehicle with a rotor on top (beanie-like)—is attempting to lead that revolution. The private company is funded by novelist Tom Clancy and others; as their Web site (www.rotaryrocket.com) puts it: "management has opted for an innovative . . . business strategy to break into an industry characterized by dependence on government grants and contracts, large work forces, ponderous bureaucracies, entrenched corporate interests, and low profitability." If it works, the applications "include satellite solar power generation and relay, satellite in-orbit servicing, zero-gravity manufacturing, space tourism, ultra high-speed package delivery, hazardous waste disposal and space resource exploration." Sounds as improbable as a Tom Clancy novel, doesn't it?

Seascan — probably the most advanced unmanned aerial vehicle (UAV) ever built. It's the result of a collaboration between an aeronautics firm called the Insitu Group (www.insitugroup.com) and the University of Washington. This soaring robot, which has a wingspan of less than ten feet, and weighs only 33 pounds, is being readied (as *DOF* goes to press) for a 5,000-mile flight across the Pacific. Its developers believe that there are a multitude of commercial applications for their UAV, including weather reporting, environmental monitoring, even rescue missions. The tiny plane is estimated to cost $50,000 and can be "launched from either a moving car or a pneumatic catapult, and be brought to the ground with a tether," says *Wired*. There are clearly military applications as well; UAVs have long been a fixation of the armed services, and some were reportedly used during the Balkan conflicts. See also *unmanned vehicles*.

Solar Sailing — a spacecraft that uses sunlight as its fuel; Cosmos I, the first solar sail vehicle—the product of a Russian and American consortium—was launched in April 2001. Cosmos, which loosely resembles a sail, is launched by an ICBM. Once it reaches an altitude of roughly 300 miles, it sprouts mylar wings which capture the light energy of the sun and convert it to power. The energy behind the experiment comes from Ann Druyan, the widow of Carl Sagan, who runs the Planetary Society, a think tank Sagan started. Believing that the principle will work, NASA is investigating 17 future missions; solar sailing could revolutionize interstellar travel, and provide a techno-logical twist on the Icarus myth; here, amazing things can hap-pen from traveling too close to the sun.

Space Bugs — living organisms, including potentially highly contagious bacteria and viruses, that could inadvertently be brought back from space through NASA explorations. Panic about space bugs—for which we have no immune defense and no known treatment—will gain increased attention as un-manned spacecraft reach further in the next decade, includ-ing not just Mars, but comets and asteroids. The federal government is coordinating a joint effort of the Agriculture Department, Interior Department, the National Institute of Health and the Centers for Disease Control to map out strate-gies to prevent space bugs from being released.

Space Imaging — we are at the beginning of a transition which will put high-resolution satellite images, once available only to governments, into the hands of everyone. This "one-meter imaging" has a wide range of commercial applica-tions—oil companies can map out routes for pipelines, municipalities can track sprawl, fishermen can spot shoals of fish, real estate agents can provide unparalleled vistas, farmers can monitor crop health. Space imaging could just as easily have gone into the "Privacy" chapter, because while some-thing called "shutter control" seeks to limit satellite imaging for national defense purposes, according to the *Economist*, "Before long it will be impossible to stop anybody from obtain-ing an image of any part of the world, no matter how sensitive, from one source or another." To see what's available now, go to www.spaceimaging.com. They call themselves "a new global earth information industry."

Space Weather — climatic conditions, including meteor showers beyond the earth's atmosphere, will be increasingly important as global telecommunications become dependent on satellite transmission. This will create a whole new business for weather map makers, and a good argument for TV weath-ermen to expand their segments.

UWB — short for "ultrawide band," UWB is method of transmitting data on multiple frequencies at the same time in an attempt to squeeze more room out of our limited—and valuable—radio spectrum. The technology is being pioneered by a company called Time-Domain (www.time-domain.com), and it works by sending data in a sequence of pulses; the intervals change—by the nanosecond—creating a digital pattern that is interpreted by the receiver. In theory, UWB transmission can be as fast as 10 million bits per second, which would be an improvement of major proportions. *Telephony* magazine has called it "An entirely new technology that could have a tremendous effect in the wireless world." UWB could have additional benefits—for example, it could be at the heart of a "super radar" that could see through walls; Time-Domain calls it "RadarVision." The technology is still in its relative infancy, although UWB believers are encouraged by a partnership between Time-Domain and GE to develop a host of new applications.

Weather Manufacturing — in a study conducted by NASA and presented at the American Association for the Advancement of Science, it was found that urban areas actually create their own weather. Sensing equipment tucked on research aircraft found that high density regions become heat islands, creating atmospheric instability and even localized thunderstorms. *DOF* believes that as urban sprawl continues (see *smart growth, sprawl brawl*), we will spend more time investigating the way in which we don't just report on—but create and influence—the weather. Which means that rather than a weather map just showing the movement of cold fronts and warm fronts, it might also show the sources of local pollution and greenhouse gas production.

Dictionary of the Future Predicts

Asteroid Anxiety — over the next two decades we believe there will be periods of intense fear over the threatened collision of a large asteroid, meteor or comet with the earth. No

Ss

one knows for sure how many PHAs (potentially hazardous asteroids) and NEOs (near-earth objects) there are whizzing over our heads. *Time* has noted that we have identified 500 to 1000 asteroids that are six-tenths of a mile or larger—sufficient to cause a "light's out on earth" event—and that an equal number remain undetected. Even more scary are "long-period" comets that can have twice the velocity of an asteroid, and are usually not detected until they begin to die near the planet Jupiter, which is just a few months away from our orbit. Not a lot of time, especially if you've got a large wine cellar. The government is "unprepared" to "deal with this kind of low-probability, high-consequence risk," says Lawrence Roberts, director of the Archimedes Institute, an aerospace policy think tank. See also *climbdown*.

Astro-Environmentalism — the growth of space travel, and the Webcasts of earth from satellites, will create a new generation of astro-environmentalists who have seen with their own eyes how small, fragile and threatened our planet is. *DOF* expects that these astro-environmentalists will be vocal members in the fight against global warming and the burning of fossil fuels.

De-Orbit — when satellites are put out of commision, they are de-orbited. Also used to describe any failed entity, personal or business, e.g., "David is rapidly de-orbiting."

EST — short for "experimental space therapy." By 2006, when six full-time laboratories on the space station will be operational, researchers will be treating certain diseases in space—cancer and certain auto-immune diseases, for example—where the lack of gravity changes cellular absorption and other body functioning, thus allowing for superior delivery of medicine and other treatments. (NASA has already signed agreements with two dozen companies for biological and cellular research while in orbit.) The cost will be significant, however, and only the wealthy will be able to afford it.

Plutonics — the increasing fascination we will have with the outer planets, from Saturn to Pluto, as our probes reach further and further into space and bring back more and more exciting information and material that add greatly to our understanding of the creation of the universe.

Satellite Terrorism — we foresee a risk to the hundreds of orbiting satellites from a variety of terrorists, including rogue states and individuals who are acting from political and even environmental motivations. Once you hack into the system that controls the satellite's orbit, it's easy to reprogram the software to bring the satellite out of orbit, causing it to fall to earth and burn up in the atmosphere. *DOF* also contemplates these same terrorists holding companies (and governments, for that matter) ransom. See also *distance terrorism.*

Space Funds — investment vehicles focused entirely on space and space exploration. They will include public companies—such as SpaceHab—and privately held firms that focus on areas such as RLVs (reusable launch vehicles), space tourism, biochemical research and the like.

SPORTS, LEISURE AND RECREATION

Americans work longer hours and take far fewer vacations than our industrialized-world counterparts; *DOF* calls this "vacation starvation." Perhaps the preciousness of our spare time is responsible for the innovation (as well as the not-uncommon extremism) that characterizes the way we use the few hours and days that we have.

Indeed, we seem to have a bipolar way of handling our time away from work. On one hand, we have "hard-adventure vacations," "gonzo golf," "black-water rafting," and "free-diving"—with none of them representing a relaxing week away. On the other hand, we are exploring new kinds of hedonism with "massage menus" and "watsu." And then there is "full-time vacationing," a phenomenon that finds retirees chucking their permanent residences for a permanent, post-Kerouac life on the road.

We also believe that the hunt for unexpected vacation destinations, another kind of "testing," will continue, bringing us to places off Fodor's radar, from "Ayia Napa" to the "Zemalek district" of Cairo.

What we do with our unprogrammed time reveals much about where we are and where we are going. And our seemingly contradictory need for pushing ourselves and de-stressing ourselves, we think, is a reaction to the same realities of American life—a high-pressure existence that drives us to create temporary diversions, either through forms of ultimate testing or ultimate relaxation.

Ayia Napa — a virtually unknown part of Cyprus that was "discovered" by young British clubbers who turned to this beach after they abandoned Ibiza for being too old, too been there, done that. *DOF* predicts that once these same clubbers move on, as they inevitably do, Ayia Napa will become the next chic, luxury vacation spot for wealthy world travelers who want high cool, plus high amenities.

Aviation Archeologists — a group of amateurs who comb the deserts of the West in search of planes that have crashed, some as long as 50 years ago. Motivated by a search for treasure, including "rumored caches of jewelry and cash" according to *The Wall Street Journal,* or by a love of history and adventure (some are hobbyists seeking to re-create vintage planes), these dedicated souls have much to target: there are around 1,500 wrecked planes on mountainsides in California alone.

Black-Water Rafting — an extreme sport—also called cave tubing—that comes to us courtesy of New Zealand. This relaxing vacation takes you to underground complexes of streams and caves, in the dark of course. Glowworms provide the only light. There's no raft, you just navigate the stream in a wet suit and with an inner tube. (What else can you expect from the people who brought the world bungee jumping?)

Canyoneering — an adventure sport that combines elements of hiking, swimming, boulder hopping, rock climbing and rappelling. The American Canyoneering Association—www.canyoneering.net—makes some fine distinctions, sternly warning us that the ACA "differentiates between Canyon Paddling, Canyon Hiking and Canyoneering." Define them as you will, the growth of this adventure sport is part of a broad extreme-sports arena, and as we spend more time safely in front of our computers, the need to test ourselves will continue to capture our imaginations.

Free-Diving — fast-growing activity that involves diving without oxygen and air tanks. In other words, scuba without a net. Free-diving allows you to get closer to marine life and experience the environment more totally; many divers get to reach depths of 30 or 40 feet and remain for up to two minutes or more. And there's no chance of a mechanical glitch—you just have to remember what it feels like to not be able to breathe anymore. See also *hard adventure vacations.*

Full-Time Vacationing — a growing phenomenon, which finds retirees traveling constantly, from cruises to sailing to RV travel. While many are wealthy, this nomadic existence isn't limited to the rich; *USA Today* quotes Stephanie Bernhagen, author of *Take Back Your Life,* as saying it's "an affordable lifestyle," and notes that "Nobody knows how many people have turned their lives into endless vacations. But everyone—from travel agents to cruise line executives to hotel managers—says the number is on the rise." Unlike those *aging in place* (see listing), many of these people literally have nowhere to live—they've sold everything so that, Zen-like, they can enjoy the freedom of intellectual and experiential wanderers. *DOF* anticipates that this trend will blossom, with many of the 10,000 baby boomers who turn 50 every day deciding to take their pensions, their IRAs, and the money they've inherited from their parents and sprinkle it around the world. We also expect to see hotels, airlines, rent-a-car agencies and others create special affinity and loyalty programs for this audience.

Gonzo Golf — a form of extreme golf played on mountain ranges and deserts, for those who need more of an eco-challenge than traditional greens.

Hard Adventure Vacations — it's not exactly sitting on the beach with a pina colada in one hand and a John Grisham novel in the other. These trips are non-traditional, physically demanding vacations involving such aggressive activities as mountain climbing, heli-skiing, *canyoneering* and *free-diving* (see listings) and that ultimate vacation thrill: throwing yourself off a bridge. The phrase was coined by the Travel Industry Association of America to cover the more than 30 million Americans who have taken one of these vacations in the last five years. And if you needed any further reason to question the value of a college education, 82 percent of these adventurers have attended college. We expect even more growth, as young people search for adventures beyond the manufactured world of Internet virtuality, and baby boomers refuse to admit they are no longer cut out for this kind of abuse.

Kitesurfing — hook up a kite to a windsurfer and you have kitesurfing, an activity that *Men's Journal* reports is surging in popularity. The magazine writes that experts believe "the heat surrounding the sport [is equal to] that around windsurfing in its early days, two decades ago." Kitesurfers begin on land, holding a bar which is attached to the kite, and wait for it to take off. When the kite is grabbed by the air currents, they walk into the water—putting their feet into the straps of their boards—and let the power of water and wind take them away.

Massage Menus — the days of hotels and resorts offering a single kind of massage are long gone. Pampering continues to be one of our most consistent growth industries, and to make sure that there are as many massages available as there are flavored vodkas, massage menus have arrived. They offer alternatives that include: traditional Swedish massage, ayurvedic (long, firm strokes); Thai (uses a mixture of oils), and Balinese (deep tissue). With all these choices, it's likely we'll need a massage just from the stress of choosing the right one. Perhaps a new kind of massage consultant is next.

Pororoca — in the language of Brazil's Tupi-Guarani Indians it means "crashing sound," and it is their word for an enormous tidal wave that occurs twice a day, every day, on the Amazon river and its tributaries. Surfers seeking greater challenges are taking on the pororoca, which—at its most dangerous (and hence alluring)—can reach heights of 15 feet and 35 miles an hour. Already, there are pororoca surfing contests, and *DOF* foresees the word crashing into the American vernacular, since it has the combined appeal of all things Brazilian and all things extreme. Beyond television coverage of pororoca championships, we anticipate a full complement of pororoca merchandise: not just surfboards themselves, but clothing, pool accessories, even food and beverages.

Rogaining — this isn't the sport of hair re-growth. It is a rapidly growing outdoor activity related to orienteering that has worldwide enthusiasts. Here's the definition, straight from a Rogaining Web site: "Rogaining is the sport of long distance cross-country navigation . . . teams of two to five members visit as many checkpoints as possible in twenty-four hours. Teams travel entirely on foot, navigating by map and compass . . . a central base camp provides hot meals throughout the event and teams may return at any time to eat, rest or sleep. Teams travel at their own pace and anyone from children to grandparents can experience the personal satisfaction." At some point, marketers may decide to sponsor a family, the way they sponsor cars in NASCAR.

Trimulcast — the simultaneous presentation of a concert, sports or other event on TV, the radio and the Internet.

Watsu — a water therapy that is a kind of aquatic shiatsu massage with a spiritual overlay. The watsu spa phenomenon is experiencing a tidal wave of enthusiasm for its ability to deliver theraputic and meditative benefits. The watsu practitioner helps you stretch, relax and enter into a calming state while pressure is removed from your joints, and your body is suspended in 94-degree water. Watsu is so popular that Canyon Ranch is building a new center with three watsu pools, and physical therapy centers are experimenting with watsu as a way to increase mobility and relieve pain in those with chronic conditions.

Dictionary of the Future Predicts

End of the Home Team — baseball teams were created in a period when local loyalty was a real phenomenon. You grew up in the same town your parents did, and your roots went deep. Today, with mobility and globalization, populations are fluid and the tug is far less meaningful. (*American Demographics* magazine reports that of Americans aged 15 to 19, just about half expected to live in the *country* of their birth, and only slightly more than 25 percent expected to live in their hometowns.) *DOF* predicts that sports teams will suffer the fate of diminishing local fanhood. We're already seeing it with sports merchandising: most logo'd items are bought by people who live elsewhere.

Hostel Takeover — tongue-in-cheek description of hotels and other lodging facilities that are being converted from old military installations. Such an example is the Canopy Tower (www.canopytower.com/) in Panama that is now an eco-lodge, but was built in 1965 to house an enormous radar system. As U.S. défense needs change—and as we're looking for more experiential vacations—we expect the creative use of these old facilities to expand. Imagine, guided yoga exercises where there used to be guided missiles.

Insparation — spa + inspiration; we are heading for spas and retreats like never before, the autobody shops of the mind, body and spirit. Spa visits—many of them in search of daily or weekend insparation—racked up $5.3 billion in 1999, up from $2.1 billion in 1997, and it's growing. That's much more than the $3.1 billion spent at ski resorts (better *me* than *ski*, apparently) and is approaching the $6.3 billion spent on movies.

Plastic Surgery Cruises — travel entrepreneurs will outfit cruise ships with state-of-the-art surgical facilities for aging boomers who want to combine some R&R with some nip-and-tuck. By the time you come back, the black and blue marks will be gone, and people will just think you're really, really, really rested.

Vacation Starvation — Americans get the least amount of time off of any workers in the industrialized world. Consider that employees of small businesses—that's most of us—get an average of eight days off a year; our European and Australian counterparts still get four to six weeks of paid leave. Add the days together, and we work two months longer each year than the Germans and two weeks longer than the allegedly industrious Japanese. The "burn-out prevention unit" at Ernst & Young estimates that it costs 150 percent of an annual salary to replace a departing, stressed-out employee. Joe Robinson, editor of an adventure-travel magazine, has been hitting the talk show circuit to pitch a law guaranteeing three weeks vacation to anyone who's been at the job a year, with four weeks after three years. Not a bad idea—but Congress would have to come back from vacation to work on it. See also *vacation deficit disorder.*

Wind Tunnel Running — a new kind of cardiovascular exercise that *DOF* believes will be the next health club craze. Treadmills will get set up in wind tunnels, and the incoming wind velocity is adjusted based on the desired intensity of the workout. The constant resistance raises your level of cardiovascular conditioning—at the same time, you get a full-body workout, including legs and arms, without the risk of orthopedic injury. It's like upright swimming.

Zamalek District — an Art Deco section of Cairo that *DOF* believes will become one of the chic and cool tourist destinations once Mideast peace is achieved—which will be in the next two years. Restaurants and bars like La Bodega, Flux (in the adjacent Mohandiseen district) and Tabasco will attract the buzz-moths from all over the world.

Technology once happened at a pace that was close to manageable. Look at how long it took for the country to be wired for electricity, for flight to be commercialized, for there to be an automobile in every driveway. Look how long it took for the room-filling mainframe to move through successive generations and be reborn as the PC.

This sequencing did two things—it gave people a chance to get comfortable with technological changes, and it gave us the ability to have our finger, reasonably, on the pulse of change. Neither are possible today. Technology is simply moving ahead too quickly, in too many categories, for even an astute generalist to keep up. This is the challenge we faced in writing this section of the *Dictionary of the Future*. Too many initiatives, not enough room.

Our approach was to range over the wide scope of technology research and applications. This led us to "aerogels," an extraordinary substance that is one of the lightest solids in existence and could be a breakthrough insulation; "nanotubes," one of the many outgrowths of the spectacularly exciting nanotechnology boom; "fuel cells" and "micropower," because they can change our national approach to electricity; and "tele-immersion," because it can (and will) change the nature of place and time.

The intrusiveness of technology is such that there are two analogies we keep falling back on: just as it is impossible to talk about the nature of human existence without talking about the brain, and just as it was once inconceivable—and still is, for many—to think about the universe without considering God, so too is it impossible to discuss the structure of twenty-first-century life without coming back, again and inevitably, to technology.

Aerogels — these remarkable substances—first created in the 1930s and then abandoned—could be an environmental salvation. Sometimes called frozen smoke, they are super-advanced gels—96 percent air and 4 percent silicon—and are one of the lightest solids in existence, yet a one pound block supports half a ton. These properties make aerogels amazingly effective insulators—one thin sheet is a better insulator than yards of the pink stuff. Eventually, aerogels could replace insulating foam, which is blown in by a process that spills CFCs—chlorofluorocarbons—into the ozone layer. Since refrigerators alone use 300 million square feet of insulation, aerogels could have substantial environmental and economic benefits. The next step: create a consumer brand around aerogel technology. Owens-Corning did it with fiberglass insulation, so imagine a commercial where you heat one side of this thin material with a blowtorch, and put your hand on the other side without getting burned. Now that's a product demo.

Blue Lasers — short-wave lasers with concentration in the blue and violet part of the spectrum, as opposed to the red portion. Blue lasers have wide commercial applications—they can create high-definition DVDs that deliver HDTV quality reproduction; a single disc could contain more than 12 hours of music per side. Blue lasers can also make possible digital tape recorders that are comparable to today's VCRs, but can store high-definition images. The first blue laser with commercial possibilities was developed in January 1999 by Shuji Nakamura, a Japanese inventor.

Cobot — a unique kind of robot, designed to work directly with a human being within "a shared workspace" according to its inventors, Professors Edward Colgate and Michael Peshkin of the Laboratory for Intelligent Mechanical Systems at Northwestern University. Rather than threatening to put humans out of work, friendly cobots are collaborative. For example, when a cobot and a UAW member work together to install a large truck instrument panel, the human being does the lifting (see how smart the machines really are) while the cobot provides guidance and direction. CoMoCo, Inc. (www. comoco-inc.com) is the commercial vehicle that develops, manufactures and licenses cobotic technology. The acid test: when you can put down your tools and go have a beer with your cobot friend.

Fuel Cells — finally, the long-awaited alternatives to traditional electric power are coming fully into their own. These devices produce electricity by chemical reactions, combining oxygen from the air with hydrogen from natural gas to create three by-products: water, heat and electric current. Ford has a fuel-cell powered vehicle in the works, and others are working on technologies that will allow affordable and reliable home generators so that consumers can go "off the grid." By contrast, tiny fuel cells are being developed to operate laptops and cell phones. The transformative changes that will leap out of this revolution are economy and culture-shaping.

Gallium Nitride — a semi-conductor material that emits blue light, as opposed to the red light which is produced by its cousin gallium arsenide—and which has been traditionally used in LEDs. Gallium nitride has become the techno-rage because it is extraordinarily reliable and consumes very little power. One of the first applications of gallium nitride is the traffic light; while conventional ones are replaced once every six months—for safety reasons—traffic lights with gallium nitride LEDs could last for about 100,000 hours, or 11 years. Next steps for gallium nitride: it can increase the storage capacity of optical discs by four times, and could add efficiency to microwave radio transmissions for cell phones and other devices.

Gastrobots — the term was coined by Dr. Stuart Wilkinson, and he defines it as "an intelligent machine that derives all its energy requirements from the digestion of real food." Thus far, gastrobots have been created that can run on sugar, and work is being done on other self-sustaining gastrobots, including a "living battery" (a microbial fuel cell) that runs on food, water and air. Gastrobot technology could also provide power to larger robots; check out www.gastrobots.com to digest additional information.

Graetzel Cell — named after inventor Michael Graetzel, who developed it in the early 1990s, it is a photovoltaic cell that turns sunlight into power. While a breakthrough, its commercial applications were limited because of certain impractical aspects of the technology. Now, an improvement on the Graetzel cell, pioneered by Toshiba, could revolutionize solar energy. The new solar panel is transparent, inexpensive to manufacture and has a high conversion efficiency—7.3 percent for those of you who understand those things. *The MIT Technology Review* writes that further work is being done, and "improved Graetzel cells . . . may ultimately grace cellular phones, laptop computers, and windows in energy-efficient homes."

Ionic Liquids — first invented in the 1940s, they are only now being studied as a medium for performing chemical reactions. Because they have a chemical structure similar to table salt—but resemble and have the properties of water—ionic liquids could, eventually, replace some of the toxic solvents used in the manufacture of everything from paint to pharmaceuticals. But it's "brand new chemistry," said one of the scientists working on them, and it will take a number of years for the full benefits to be realized.

Holographic Storage — a technology which will, eventually, radically expand the amount of data storage currently available, and the speed of access. Images of data are stored on holographic crystals; more than a million bits of data can be stored on a single hologram, and thousands of holograms can fit on a square that is just a single centimeter. This kind of storage, which can accommodate massive amounts of text, graphics and video, relies on no moving parts. Experts predict holographic storage will emerge as a commercially available technology by the middle of the decade, and will change the economics and extent of data storage. See also *storage Alzheimer's.*

Micropower — signaling a profound change in our reliance on large power plants sending electricity through a grid system, micropower will shift the production of electricity closer to each individual home—possibly to the home itself. Many technologies are fighting over this profound transition. One alternative is *fuel cells* (see listing) and there are several warring approaches in that camp. Another alternative is the microturbine, and a third is solar, which has moved well beyond the problems that plagued it when it first emerged as an alternative in the 1970s. They need not be mutually exclusive, though. As the *Economist* observes, "Add a bit of information technology to a microgenerator and it will be able . . . to talk to other plants on the grid." Visionaries see a future in which dozens, even hundreds, of disparate micropower units are linked together in so-called microgrids. All this becomes a reality as the cost of micropower drops, which also opens the way for electricity to be brought to the three billion people in the world who don't have access to power at all.

Nanotubes — microscopic carbon threads, just a few molecules in size, that were identified in the early 1990s but are just beginning to find their first applications. Nanotubes have, as *Scientific American* reports, "extraordinary properties . . . among them, superlative resilience, tensile strength and thermal stability." Nanotubes also have a wide variety of potential applications, including the replacement of silicon-based microchip circuitry, thus allowing electronic devices to be made even smaller. Nanotube probes have already been used to identify the individual variants of a specific gene with a strand of DNA; they are also capable of concentrating the transmission of electronics at a lower voltage than existing alternatives, which could lead to an entirely new generation of bright, thin, efficient television screens and monitors. Down the road: nanotubes "might store hydrogen in their hollow centers and release it gradually in efficient and inexpensive fuel cells," reports *Scientific American*. Further down the road: as part of a composite material, nanotubes are theoretically capable of creating car bodies that bounce back after a crash

Tt

or anti-earthquake buildings with built-in flex. Expect to see a lot of nanotube news.

Personal Scanners — individual bar code scanning devices that mark the migration of this omnipresent language of stripes from a retail device for pricing and inventory control into a communication link between products and consumers. Right now, personal scanners such as the CueCat, the Gamut and the CS 2000 (made by bar code granddaddy Symbol Technology) allow you to link directly from an ad in a magazine to a Web site. Gamut's scanner reads bar codes off a TV screen— letting you watch a commercial, scan in a code and download an electronic coupon for later redemption. Sooner than later, we'll all have personal scanners— whether they're independent devices or built into our cell phones and PDAs; every piece of our lives will be digitally inventoried.

Rear-Window Captioning — new technology that enables the hearing and visually impaired to enjoy movies at their local theaters. The system, which was developed by the National Center for Accessible Media, uses a "smoked Plexiglas panel [that's] attached to a gooseneck arm that fits into the cupholder," *The Wall Street Journal* reports. For the hearing-impaired, red-lettered subtitles are displayed, which are projected from the back of the theater. Those with vision problems are given a special headset which supplements the dialogue with a quick narrative description as well— a technique called DVS Theatrical—that "sneaks into the movie's natural pauses," according to the *Journal*. Right now, more than a dozen cities have theaters that are equipped with rear-window captioning, but there's a long way to go, considering there are 34 million people who could benefit from it.

Smart Packages — a joint venture between International Paper and Motorola. The packages contain tiny silicon chips that send out signals which can be picked up by a wireless device. What makes it all work is Motorola's new radio frequency identification technology—called BiStatix—that merges silicon with printed ink (*DOF* predicts this will be called "slink technology"). It's the next step beyond bar codes and scanners to improve inventory control and productivity; these smart packages (or smart labels) can be tracked all the way from the factory to the warehouse to the checkout counter. They can also reduce theft and counterfeiting. Expect to see this show up in other places—slink technology in your kids' notebooks (so you can make sure they're not cutting class). Or for your reading glasses, umbrellas or anything else that inevitably gets lost.

Smart Tires — utilizing electronic sensors and other devices, this new generation "would warn in real time if a tire was accelerating, spinning, losing traction . . . smart tires can become an entirely new vehicle automotive system . . . the management point to run electronic, braking, traction control, electronic stability programs, adaptive cruise control and/or antilock brakes." So states *Automotive News*, and we believe them.

Spintronics — the study of the spin of the electron in pursuit of new ways to manipulate and harness it. Research could accelerate the development of computers that use atomic particles instead of chips (see *quantum computing*). Spintronics is also behind the M-RAM chip—short for magneto-resistive memory. The M-RAM chip will be able to keep data alive even when the power is off, which could lead to instant-on, boot-up free computing.

Surfers and Serfs — describes a two-tier economy of technologically forward consumers and low-wage earners, the serfs of the service economy as union leader Bruce Raynor put it in *The New York Times*. Another way to look at the digital divide.

Tele-Immersion — the next generation of video conferencing, which will solve the problem of stilted conversation with no eye contact. Tele-immersion creates the powerful illusion that everyone has gathered together in the same room. At this point, in order to simulate a shared environment you need to wear goggles and a head-tracker, but the thing works. (Ultimate implementation will require *Internet2*—see listing.) As

Tt

Jaron Lanier, chief scientist for the project (and inventor of virtual reality) said: "It's a significant accomplishment . . . we demonstrated viewpoint-independent real-time sensing and reconstruction." When asked what the killer-app will be, Lanier responded, "It's not so much a matter of particular applications. It will just become part of life."

Viseme — a visual phoneme. When we speak, our mouths move in such a way as to create a distinctive facial characteristic. By reading a few sentences into a camera, computers can capture these visemes and create a visual library, which can later be digitally synched up to any pre-recorded soundtrack. In other words, a simulation of you or me or Geraldo Rivera saying just about anything on camera can be achieved.

Wearable Office — miniaturization of computers, personal digital assistants, Internet devices and MP3 players to a point where they can be worn as part of clothing or backpacks. As for the water cooler—Evian has already done that. Charmed (charmed.com) is one of the companies leading this charge into the future. See also *Batbelt*.

Dictionary of the Future Predicts

Belief Detectors — brain wave monitors will move one step beyond undependable lie detectors, enabling the measurement of not just whether you're telling the truth, but how deeply you believe it. Will be adopted by political pollsters, market researchers and employers who will ask: "How much do you really want to work here?" The ultimate devotees will be the soon-to-be-married. "Do you really love me, or are you just glad to see my stock options?" See also *brain fingerprinting*.

Crush Tech – advances are leading to the introduction of bendable computer screens, thanks to roll-to-roll manufacturing, which involves putting film electronics on a flexible substrate (much of this work is being done by Rolltronics—

www.rolltronics.com). This will create a new generation of foldable, bendable computers and cell phones, which will not just be more convenient, but will create a new tactile and personal relationship with technology.

Inkists — a group of those who reject technology and insist on writing and signing all documents in ink. See also *wet signature*.

Portable Factories — automated manufacturing will advance to the point where factories that produce reasonably small parts or items can be disassembled, transported to another location, and reassembled on a cost-effective basis. This will have serious economic impacts—companies can switch their manufacturing to where labor costs are cheaper, the exchange rate is better, or taxation more favorable (adding a new twist to Ricardo's famous "Law of Comparative Advantage"). Perhaps the *cargo lifter* (see listing) could be utilized as a transportation solution.

Reality Re-Entry — the psychological problems that confront individuals as they undergo continual shifts from a virtual reality environment to the real world. Characterized by depression, relational problems, delusional states. An entire school of psychology, as well as new psychotropic drugs and treatment, will grow out of this new problem.

Storage Alzheimer's — we think that all the data captured in the technology age will be preserved forever. Think again. There are huge issues dealing with crashing hard drives, compatible technology and disintegrating storage media. (Zip drives, for example, are warranted for only five years, and floppies can start to deteriorate after a mere 18 months.) No wonder the director of the Smithsonian's division of Information Technology said that "Even though we have the best technology to store information, we may be living in a period less rich for permanent information than the nineteenth century." That's why we're calling the problem storage Alzheimer's, and that's why you'll be hearing a lot more about the loss of our collective memory.

Techno-Prisoners — despite the technological power we have in our homes—with more computer technology at our disposal than NASA had when it launched the Apollo mission to the moon—we are prisoners. Let one computer glitch erupt, and your smart microwave won't be able to read the bar code on the pizza, your smart countertop won't be able to weigh the ingredients, and your smart trash won't be able to recognize what you're tossing out so it can alert the supermarket to send you more. In our homes, offices and cars, technology has made us the most powerful prisoners the world has ever seen. See also *independent products, ubiquitous computing.*

Twentieth-Century Clearance Sale — when a business (or the government), or consumers (through a tag or garage sale) tosses out old last-century technology, manufacturing equipment or machinery, and replaces it with something new (and probably cheaper, more reliable and more efficient than what came before).

Wake-Up Mail — alarm clocks that wake users by reading their email. Can be programmed to be read by different voices, e.g., your wife, your husband or celebrities. Users will also be able to choose their own background music, and will also be able to screen out undesired mail, and decide which messages to hear first.

Suddenly, in the last five years, telecommunications have moved from occupying a part of our life to playing a stage-hogging role. After decades of incremental innovation—with the replacement of the rotary phone by the touch-tone representing a magnificent leap forward—the microprocessor revolution has turned the field (if you can call it that) on its ear. New language about these multiple and intersecting communication revolutions—the Internet, wireless, email, the works— seems only natural. We like to talk about the way we talk—and communicate. The territory is also blessed (or cursed, depending on your perspective) with acres of technical terminology; fortunately, the Internet is loaded with glossaries of jargon that are yours for the clicking. We are, by contrast, drawn urgently to language that gets at how we use, relate to and struggle with these innovations and revelations.

3G — the next generation wireless network that will allow the superfast transmission of vast quantities of information. Over $120 billion has been spent globally to buy the licenses, but some argue that consumers are reasonably happy with their current wireless performance, and don't really need to move money from checking into savings while scuba diving. *DOF* believes that it may take some time to find the killer-apps, but that our need for speed is insatiable and high-speed wireless will become part of our daily entertainment and info-fix.

Celliquette — emerging rules for cell phone use; some restaurants are banning them completely, some public places are instituting three-minute limits (but who's going to time you, a new job-description of cell watchers?). The phrase also extends to pagers and other personal communicators—what could be ruder than someone checking their email in the middle of a conversation with you? Expect to see "Please Observe Proper Celliquette" signs wherever we go. See also *continuous partial attention, second hand speech, submeetings, two-tasking.*

Dirt-Road Connection — a slow route to the Internet, and the subject of never-ending complaint. As a quote from a message board put it: "The average user with the average rig on the average dirt road connection will not be amused that the average page will require 10–15 minutes or more to download." Till broadband's penetration expands, these dirt-road connections will slow the adoption rate of video streaming.

Earcon — an auditory version of the icon, a short, memorable burst of sound—less than two seconds long—that is musical but not music. Earcons will be used by telephone companies and wireless providers as tiny branding signatures. Cynthia Sikora and Linda Roberts of Bell Labs are working furiously on earcons; in a research paper they talk about "steer[ing] the emotional reaction of the listener in support of the desired image." Expect to be inundated by a symphony of earcons, emanating from phones, Internet enabled PDAs, wearable electronics, computers, refrigerators, medicine chests. A completely hummable world, what higher level of aesthetic perfection could we possibly demand? See also *digital autograph, programmable horns.*

F-Secure — an innovative company out of Espoo, Finland—Scandinavia's Silicon Valley. F-Secure is ahead of the pack in securing your wireless transmissions; since wireless devices are "always on," they are sitting ducks for hackers and viruses. F-Secure has a new approach, as reported in *The Standard.* A program they call a "management agent" gets installed in your phone or your PDA. From that point on, the software is in constant contact with F-Secure's server, receiving antivirus updates and other key messages all the time. Wherever you go, your shield of protection travels with you. F-Secure charges by the month—but we think your wireless carrier will pick up the cost as a way of keeping you loyal. See also *wireless viruses.*

iMode — the enormously popular Japanese instant messaging system developed and marketed by DoCoMo—a joint venture with Nippon Telephone. Millions of Japanese are communicating via short messages; the platform is expanding to include services like stocks, weather and shopping—and, of course, advertising. iMode, which has a deal with AOL, is heading to the U.S. market, and it should have the same contagious influence in America, particularly with young people.

Last Mile — so close and yet so far; in the Internet access business, the key to profitability (and harsh economic reality) is what's called the last mile, the distance between the final node in the system, and your house. The race to solve the last mile problem involves all sorts of technologies, including fiber-optic cable and a light-transmission approach favored by TeraBeam. But the term is also being used to describe the final journey that any business has to travel to reach your front door. Describing an upcoming joint venture between FedEx and the post office, *Time* magazine writes that the deal would "hand FedEx the Postal Service's crown jewel: the exclusive, government-mandated right to the mailbox at the end of every American driveway, known . . . as 'the last mile.' "

Conventional wisdom is that whoever owns the last mile gets the last word, suggesting an untapped business opportunity for any organization with a widely dispersed truck network: Deer Park, Roto-Rooter, Lawn Doctor?

Optoelectronics — the use of optical fibers to carry Internet traffic. Improvements in optoelectronics are happening at blazing speed. A single strand of optical fiber can now carry the entire traffic that the public telephone network handled just three years ago.

Personalized Rings — another example of how technology, which many believe to be a dehumanizing force, is having the opposite effect. From pagers to phones to PDAs, consumers are customizing their rings. *Wired* magazine has noted that most hip hop tunes have a "companion pager alert" which is a version of the song that is translated to beep speak. A site called www.yourmobile.com describes itself as "the world's most popular free ringtone site." What's more, many users are creating their own rings, and trading them. *DOF* expects that this will spread beyond the young people who started it—why couldn't the cell phones that companies like Nabisco and NBC give their employees ring with their corporate signature? See also *earcon, digital autograph, programmable horns*.

Ping — the process of reaching someone electronically, either as an instant message (IM) or an email. "I'll ping him" will be as common as "I'll call him." Derived from submarine-speak, the sound of a returning sonar message.

SAR — stands for "specific absorption rate," a measurement of the emissions of radiation from cell phones and other devices. While the most current research suggests the risks are low, the future will see shifting opinions, so SAR obsession will grow. (To check out the radiation of any phone go to www.sardata. com/sardata.htm.)

Telenomics — bandwidth economics, referring to the buying and selling of bandwidth as a commodity on one or more of many exchanges that are appearing. While businesses are the first to purchase bandwidth in this way, *DOF* imagines that consumers will be next, and software will be developed to let you switch providers from a cable company, to a phone company, to a satellite provider—whoever is cheaper at the moment.

Texting — cell phone communication that uses the limited text message space available. The United States is well behind the rest of the world in "bursty" SMS (short message service) technology, because our communications platforms don't talk to each other.

Eventually, texting will arive in the United States, and—like cell phones—it will create new social patterns and habits, as well as new language and lingo, as we struggle to compress our communication to fit into the 26-character limit. This will inspire new linguistic creativity and a private cryptography, the technology equivalent of baby talk. See also *iMode, thumb-typing.*

Throttling — when you're wondering why your supposedly high-speed broadband access seems pokey, blame throttling. It's when your ISP provider—whether it's your telephone or cable supplier—cuts down the speed of your Internet access because they need to conserve the bandwidth of their network. *DOF* suggests that someone set up www.throttling.com to let you know when someone has their hands around your digital throat.

Thumb-Typing — it's what we do on our BlackBerrys and other small wireless devices. Millions of years from now, when most *Homo sapiens* have curiously small fingertips, this will be the evolutionary reason.

Voice-Jail — you know those voice mail systems that trap you and won't let you out—that's voice-jail. And once you're stuck, there's no parole, that's for sure. We're waiting for some smart marketers to recognize how much consumers hate voice-jail, and start offering real people again, not disembodied com-

T̄t

puter voices on their customer service lines. Here's a relevant comment that was made before Congress, by a patient who had a horrendous HMO experience: "voice jail is being held on the phone for 30 minutes while you wait for prior authorization, while you're waiting to be connected . . . you then only get authorization for an evaluation. I think it's a new word we should put in the vocabulary." See also *consumer serf.*

Dictionary of the Future Predicts

Band Brands — *DOF* believes that the way bandwidth is now marketed will undergo some dramatic changes. Currently, your bandwidth provider is the same as your bandwidth "product," e.g. your cable company is both Internet service provider and your connectivity brand. But in the future, a menu of new bandwidth options (see *UWB* and *BLAST*) will separate the provider from the product. With this new model, an Internet service provider will offer a number of "Band Brands," services will differ based on speed, price and performance. We think that both existing and new companies will brand their bandwidth in this manner; Cisco, for example, could easily jump from "powering" the Internet to being a bandwidth product.

Designer Telephone Booths — driven by our love of retro and our search for privacy, *DOF* predicts that we will be seeing high-end telephone booths appearing in cities across the country. These small luxury spaces, street furniture of a higher order, will be created by our best architects—who enter and win local design competitions—and will feature ergonomic seating, Internet connectivity, plus heat in the winter and air-conditioning in the summer.

Employomers — telecommunication providers will hire their own customers to perform telemarketing and other services (employees + customers = employomers). Employomers will work from home, making cold calls to sell people on phone company services. They won't be paid in cash, but in credits on their bills. For the employomer it's a way to earn some extra money; for the company it's convenient and cost-efficient access to labor, since they are "paying" in phone bill credits, which is for them a low-cost currency.

Personal Jammers — a consumer electronics product which will enable users to jam any radio-transmitters—including those in their phones, cars or even implanted in their bodies—thus blocking the ability of marketers and others to track them. See also *no tracers*.

TeleStorage — *DOF* anticipates that phone companies will be linking their customers to massive hard drive storage facilities that will use voice recognition technology to store conversations, digitally and permanently, for review and replay any time.

Uni-Minutes — telecommunications companies will create "universal billing minutes" that are bought in advance, and can be used for landlines or wireless calls. This will give them the ability to capture all of a customer's telecom business with a simple cost and billing structure.

TRANSPORTATION

With so much attention being paid to the movement of the insubstantial—data and "content" trafficking through the Internet, intranets and broadband networks—it's easy to lose sight of the dramatic changes in the transportation of the physical.

No such distraction, however, prevails in this section. Here, we look at "car sharing"—a new concept of automobile utilization that started in Europe but is gaining traction here. We introduce you to new modes of air travel that are in mid-stage development, including a personal aircraft (complete with whole-plane parachute) called Cirrus. We bring you Talgo, which many view as the best hope that train travel has to recapture the imagination of Americans. And we investigate in-the-works changes to our automobile culture, from the way cars are built and powered to new ways of looking at the economics of it all: Are you prepared for private highways and road-pricing?

Transportation, of course, isn't just about getting there. It is an equation in motion whose inputs are urban development, family structures, environmental issues, the range of contemporary concerns. We hope that this section helps you think about the subject in this integrative fashion, and that the language—like the Th!nk electric bicycle—takes you quietly but surely into the future.

A3XX-100 — the new super-size, super-luxury plane designed by Airbus and scheduled to be operational by 2006. It is an aircraft "that allows airlines to completely redefine the airline experience," says Jean-Louis Mourisot, an analyst at Goldman-Sachs. Carrying 555 passengers, the plane will have cruise ship amenities, including bars, restaurants and even a casino. Yet Airbus claims that it will fly more passengers over longer distances, for less cost. But spectacular aircraft alone can't solve the problem of insufficient runway supplies, soul-crushing delays and otherwise unfriendly skies.

AIVs — short for aluminum-intensive vehicles: cars made out of aluminum instead of steel. The advantages are dramatic. AIVs weigh about half as much as traditional cars, which means that fuel economy is improved by 40 percent. The hang-up has always been that aluminum is tough to work with, and that it cost three times as much as steel. Now, breakthroughs like ASF (aluminum space frame) technology— using metal skeletons similar to aircraft construction—make manufacturing easier. (Aluminum cars may also spark a new generation of start-ups; Panoz Auto Development Company, out of Hoschton, Georgia, has launched its own limited production AIV roadster.) The *Economist* writes that "Aluminum cars, if they sell, would change the economics of motor manufacturing, as well as being cheaper to run and greener."

Automated Parking — sooner than later, the parking attendant will become a victim of technology. With automated parking, the garage parks the car for you. The first one in the United States was built in Hoboken, a tightly packed New Jersey town a stone's throw from Manhattan. Built at the cost of $6 million, the process is simple: you drive in and leave your car on a pallet, where it is lifted up to an empty space on a rack. When you return, the same system retrieves your vehicle. Timing: about a minute for each transaction. The Hoboken garage packs 324 cars into half the space that would be required for an old-fashioned system of ramps and levels. Equally impressive is the fact that a garage can be designed to harmonize with its neighbors; says JoAnn Seranno, director of the Hoboken Parking Authority, "the façade will blend in with the architecture of the neighborhood . . . so it will look like rowhouses."

Biodiesel — a natural substitute for diesel fuel that is produced from sources as humble as vegetable oils, animal fats and recycled cooking oils. It can be used in diesel engines and is non-toxic and biodegradable. While efforts are being made to develop cars that run on solar power and fuel cells, we can't forget that biodiesel fuel also reduces our dependence on OPEC.

CargoLifter — a bold attempt to create a twenty-first century airship; the vision of Carl-Heinrich von Gablenz. Scheduled for launch sometime in 2002 (although skeptics wonder) CargoLifter would be the biggest airborne vessel in history, 850 feet long, 21 stories high. Designed to transport immense cargo, the airship would be able to pick up and drop off items as large as 160 tons—including huge turbines and construction items—anywhere. If it works, it would revolutionize shipping, and could even transport modular relief hospitals to disaster areas. Von Gablenz has also tantalized investors (the company is public on the Frankfurt Stock Exchange) with romantic visions of the walls of the CargoLifter carrying advertising messages during the day, and showing movies to crowds below in the evening. Whether it will be filled with helium or just hot air remains to be seen. See also *portable factories*.

Car Sharing Services — a growing trend that enables city dwellers who don't need to own a car to share the use of one, thus eliminating insurance and parking problems. "Car Sharing, an idea born in Europe, gains some ground in the U.S.," reported *The Wall Street Journal*. Zipcar in Cambridge, Massachusetts, is one such service, others can be found in Seattle, San Francisco, Washington, D.C., and Portland, Oregon, where car sharing is expected to grow by 50 percent. In Switzerland, a company called Mobility Car Sharing has 1,300 cars at 800 different locations. This is one of those revolutionary ideas— dare we say paradigm shifts—that can plod along and then suddenly catch fire (as Malcolm Gladwell described in his wonderful *The Tipping Factor*). See also *natural capital.*

Charging Sites — the locations at which electric vehicles get juiced. The key question: Will they be run by the power companies, the oil companies (who have the real estate), the car companies or entrepreneurs we haven't even heard from yet?

Cirrus Design — a revolutionary aerospace company (www. cirrusdesign.com) that is in the process of bringing to market an affordable, easy-to-fly personal aircraft (that will come equipped with a whole-plane parachute.) The company is prominently featured in James Fallows' well-regarded book on a new age of travel called *Free Flight.* See also *Eclipse Aviation.*

Eclipse Aviation — an innovative company that is working to build a low-cost jet that can become the backbone of an entirely new concept in transportation: an air-taxi fleet that, as the *Atlantic Monthly* puts it "could enable travelers to summon a small 'air taxi' on short notice and fly directly from the nearest small airport to the desired destination without breaking the bank." The company's Web site (www.eclipseaviation.com) states that they are "applying revolutionary propulsion, manufacturing, and electronics systems to produce aircraft that cost less than a third of today's small jet aircraft, will be significantly safer and easier to operate than those of today, and have the lowest cost of ownership ever achieved in a jet aircraft." See also *Cirrus Design.*

Eyetickets — using biometric technologies like iris code (see listing) airlines are moving ahead with tickets that identify you by the unique pattern of your eyes. (Question at the check-in counter: "Are those your own eyes, or did you borrow someone else's?")

Gaze Trackers — a new automotive safety concept that will eventually become standard equipment, since so many drivers are literally being driven to distraction by all their whizzy onboard accessories. (*USA Today* describes a phenomenon of

"Road Theater," which includes 3 million customized vans.)
Gaze Trackers let drivers know when their eyes have moved off
the road with an audio reminder—a beep, or a voice remind-
ing you to "Keep your eyes on the road." A number of companies are pursuing Gaze Trackers; Seeing Machines is one of
the furthest along. Their device, called faceLAB, uses two
video cameras and specially designed processing software to
analyze the position of the driver's head. Further steps could
include linking systems like faceLAB to your car's complete
information ecosystem; as *The New York Times* notes "When the
traffic around a driver becomes heavy . . . the system might
hold phone calls and email." Gaze Trackers could replace ad
hoc local legislation against cell phone use—so we suspect
that cell phone manufacturers will get behind it—as they
become the seat belts of the information age.

Gulp & Go — a start-up operation that intends to be the first
company to sell beverages at toll booths across the country.
Here's the logic: toll plazas are becoming increasingly automated; drivers seek speed and convenience; toll road opera-
tors are more aggressively seeking new revenue streams;
beverage companies are looking for new channels of distribution. The company claims to have developed proprietary technology that has minimal impact on traffic flow. That's the
right idea: Who wants to get stuck behind the guy who orders
a half regular half-decaf latte with skim milk and half of a
Sweet 'n Low? See also *road-pricing*.

Hybrid Cars — vehicles that run on a combination of battery
power and gasoline. Several varieties are in development: full
hybrids run on battery power alone at low speeds; mini-hybrids
and mild hybrids use electrical power only to run smaller systems like water pumps and power steering. Some technologies
use the brake as a recharging mechanism; the gasoline engine
turns off when the foot touches the brakes, and goes on when
the foot hits the accelerator. Depending upon the technology
and the weight of the vehicle, there can be a fuel savings of
10 percent, all the way to 60 percent. Over the next decade we
will see a phase-in of these electrically assisted engines. Inter-

estingly, the shift is not driven by legislation—federal standards have been the same since the late 1980s. The industry, responding to public pressure and more enlightened management, is coming around on its own. See also *fuel cells*.

Life Breath — a new, super-powerful automotive purification material designed by Mazda, which should become an industry standard as we spend more and more time in our *carcoons* (see listing). When ordinary air filters are enhanced with Life Breath they are able to remove aldehydes (pungent chemicals) from the air and turn them into "stable and harmless byproducts." Mazda expects Life Breath will also be applicable to improving the air purification systems in homes and office buildings as aldehydes are believed to be one of the culprits in "sick building syndrome," causing headaches, dizziness and eye irritation.

Night Vision — developed by Raytheon for the military (see also *multitary*), night vision uses an infrared camera mounted on the front of the car to capture images of people and animals that the driver would not otherwise see at night. These thermal images are projected onto a 3-by-7-inch portion of the windshield, creating a heads-up display that gives the driver a primitive kind of X-ray vision. The technology is currently available as an option, but as the cost comes down it could become standard equipment in luxury cars. An additional benefit: when you come home at night, it acts as a security system, able to identify someone hiding in the bushes.

Paradigm — low-cost plastic car based on a simple 11-piece chassis. Designed for China, the third-world and emerging countries by Automotive Designs and Composites. Technically speaking, it is a thermoformed vehicle, as is the Baja, another car made by the same company. Check out www.plastics-car com/spotlight/spotlight.html for the future of your garage. See also *fash*.

Pneumatic Cars — vehicles that can run on compressed air, a power source which is free and non-polluting. While some say such a vehicle is technically impossible—and while some environmentalists believe that work on pneumatic cars deflects attention from the more realistic development of fuel cell and hybrid vehicles—one company persists. Its name is Zero Pollution (www.zeropollution.com), and they are developing a line of vehicles under the M.D.I. brand. They are designed to be urban vehicles, including a minivan-style taxi, a small pickup truck and a delivery van. Prices are projected to be around $15,000. Compressed, or just a lot of hot air? We'll soon see.

Private Highways — traffic is the one thing that even the wealthy have to put up with—until the advent of private highways. Started in Europe as part of their great privatization movement, private lanes on public highways are coming to America—the first one is I-91 in California. Electronic tolls like EZ-Pass make payments instantaneous. Developers see huge opportunities for revenue that will come not just from tolls, but from retail stores that can be opened along these private lanes, and even from radio stations that broadcast exclusively to them. See also *satellite radio.*

Road-Pricing — a radically different way to look at the way roads are used, and how we pay for them. The basic theory is that public policy should be used to encourage drivers to use highways when there is less traffic (also called congestion pricing); that they should be rewarded for driving fuel efficient cars, and that those who use the roads more should pay more. Until recently, this subject has kept economists busy, but had little practical value because there was no way to implement the solutions, whether heroic or hare-brained. But now, computerized tolls and smart roads make it possible to track your movement, making these road-pricing innovations very real. The debates will be loud; the special interest groups are scattered, like land mines, all over the place; and the stakes are high. To probe the complexity of the subject, log on to: www.drivers.com/Top_Traffic_Road_Pricing_Tolls.html. See also *pay-as-you-go insurance.*

Roodrunner — a vehicle that is currently being used for mail delivery, designed by the innovative Dutch company Springtime (www.springtime.nl). It's part bicycle, part delivery van and powered by both pedal power and a non-polluting electric motor, and is a far better choice than a heavy postal bag or a polluting truck. The head of Springtime describes the Roodrunner as a "synergy between the simplicity and transparency of the bicycle and the comfort and performance of the car." *DOF* believes that the Roodrunner will find its way to America, and be adopted not just by the Post Office, but for all sorts of urban delivery needs. Check out the Springtime Web site for other intriguing products of the future that, in their words, fill "missing links in the mobility chain." They don't have any U.S. distribution partners, but it's an opportunity that won't go unnoticed for long.

Skycar — just what it sounds like. The brand name of the personal aircraft marketed by Paul Moller, who is trying to commercialize an idea that was originally conceived in the 1950s. Moller is attempting to create skyways that parallel highways. Skeptical? NASA's already developed a "General Aviation Road Map" to govern their use. Currently two percent of travel is done via personal aircraft, but the number is expected to rise to more than 50 percent by 2025.

Superpave — a paving method that uses new technology to create the right mix of asphalt and aggregate for a road based on geographic and other conditions. Believe it or not, the old method was costly, but basically intuitive; pretty remarkable considering the amount we spend on road maintenance. It's no wonder ruts and potholes occur just weeks after a road was resurfaced. Superpaved roads are supposed to last 15 years, which should save highway departments half a billion dollars a year, not counting the taxpayers' $2 billion lost to traffic delays and car repairs.

Talgo — a revolutionary passenger train that could be a catalyst for the serious return of rail travel in America. Currently, there is a Talgo (www.talgo.com) operated by Amtrak in the Pacific Northwest, and other regions—including California, for the Los Angeles–San Francisco run—are seriously considering it. Talgo, which was designed in Spain and is built in Washington, uses very short, light and low center-of-gravity cars with a unique wheel arrangement that enables the cars to piggyback on each other. Together with the patented suspension system, Talgos are able to smoothly negotiate curves at high speeds, reducing bumpiness. Amenities include a bistro car, and sleepers and showers for overnight trips. As car and plane travel become increasingly frustrating, we expect more and more communities to invest in Talgo.

Telematics — an emerging industry that includes the totality of wireless communication between your car and the larger world. Telematics includes services like OnStar from General Motors, which combines safety and security features: accident assistance, stolen vehicle identification, directions—with a live operator available. On-board email, traffic updates, Internet access, remote diagnostics and speech synthesis from a computerized voice (safer than looking at a stock market screen at 60 mph, but equally depressing) are also part of telematics. The industry is just beginning to blossom; sooner than later, your dealer will not just be able to detect a problem—say one of the computer chips that regulates the firing of your engine—but repair it, and charge your credit card, from hundreds of miles away.

Th!nk — a division of Ford that was created to manufacture zero-emission, battery-powered cars and bicycles. Th!nk is already selling Th!nk City, a battery-run two-seater in Norway, and a Th!nk bicycle which was introduced in Vietnam is now available in America. On the drawing board is Th!nk Neighbor, a low-speed vehicle for private communities, resorts and industrial sites. Th!nk Technologies is also charged with leading the fuel cell research project for Ford. William Clay Ford Jr., chairman of Ford, is clear that these are not intended to be niche vehicles. "To make a significant impact on the environment, we have to sell millions of vehicles with clean technology," he maintains. To learn more—or place your order—go to www.thinkmobility.com. See also *fuel cells.*

Traffic Temperature — a new way to monitor traffic congestion, developed by Dr. John Leonard of the Georgia Institute of Technology. Traffic would be expressed by degrees, so for example, a temperature of 80 degrees could translate to a 20-minute delay on any given road. News reports and Web sites would report traffic temperature, based upon roadside cameras and in-road sensors. We can hear the excuses now: "Sorry I'm late, but the temperature on Route 80 was over 120."

Dictionary of the Future Predicts

Airportal — the ultimate airport security device; will function as a combined metal and drug detector, passport check, ticket reader and health monitor to assure against the spread of contagious diseases. Will also be able to scan all the products you have with you and be able to sell that tracking data, if privacy issues can be dealt with. So marketers will not only know where you're going, but what you're taking with you.

Autotasking — as Americans spend more and more time in their cars, and as their cars become technically enabled, a new species of work will be done in automobiles. This includes "drive work" activities that require less thought and attention, such as ordering groceries, making appointments, responding to basic email. See also *gaze trackers.*

Carcoon — with commuting times increasing, and with automobiles offering everything from Internet access to microwave ovens, our cars are becoming cocoons of their own. These carcoons, our beloved moving sanctuaries, will make it more difficult than ever for urban planners to pry us out of our vehicles and into mass transit. (Carcoons are a direct descendant of the "Wandering Cocoon" predicted in 1991 in *The*

Popcorn Report.) Next for our carcoons: changing interior design, by taste, by season. Cup holders by Ikea, carpeting by Pottery Barn, and in-vehicle plants by Martha Stewart (to purify the area and lift our spirits when we're stuck in 10 mile back-ups). VW already offers a little bud vase, as a New Age amenity.

CEV — short for craft electric vehicle. As electric vehicles gain increasing market share, entrepreneurs will move to create their own boutique cars; electronic technology makes it easier to manufacture these vehicles as opposed to the capital investment involved with the traditional internal combustion engine. CEVs will bypass the conventional dealer structure and will be sold on the Internet, as well as through retailers such as Wal*Mart and Home Depot.

SHUV — An accident caused by a SUV (Sport Utility Vehicle). Reduced visibility and a sense of road entitlement create an epidemic of SHUVs, causing insurance companies to raise their rates for these behemoths (only to get worse, with planned introductions of behemoths like GM's Hummer). Better keep your seat belt on, because you'll never know when push will come to SHUV.